HAND TO MOUTH

Paul Auster was born in New Jersey in 1947. After attending Columbia University he lived in France for four years. Since 1974 he has published poems, essays, novels, translations and screenplays. He lives in Brooklyn, New York.

by the same author

THE NEW YORK TRILOGY:
CITY OF GLASS, GHOSTS, THE LOCKED ROOM

IN THE COUNTRY OF LAST THINGS

THE INVENTION OF SOLITUDE

MOON PALACE

GROUND WORK:
SELECTED POEMS AND ESSAYS 1970–1979

THE MUSIC OF CHANCE

LEVIATHAN

MR VERTIGO

THE RED NOTEBOOK

screenplay

SMOKE & BLUE IN THE FACE

Paul Auster

HAND TO MOUTH

A Chronicle of Early Failure

faber and faber

First published in the United States of America in 1997
by Henry Holt and Company, Inc., New York
First published in Great Britain in 1997
by Faber and Faber Ltd
3 Queen Square London WC1N 3AU
Open market paperback edition first published in 1998
This paperback edition first published in 1998

Printed and bound in Great Britain by Mackays of Chatham plc, Chatham, Kent

A CIP record for this book is available
from the British Library

ISBN 0–571–19597–0

2 4 6 8 10 9 7 5 3 1

Contents

HAND TO MOUTH

IN MY LATE TWENTIES and early thirties, I went through a period of several years when everything I touched turned to failure. My marriage ended in divorce, my work as a writer foundered, and I was overwhelmed by money problems. I'm not just talking about an occasional shortfall or some periodic belt tightenings—but a constant, grinding, almost suffocating lack of money that poisoned my soul and kept me in a state of never-ending panic.

There was no one to blame but myself. My relationship to money had always been flawed, enigmatic, full of contradictory impulses, and now I was paying the price for refusing to take a clear-cut stand on the matter. All along, my only ambition had been to write. I had known that as early as sixteen or seventeen years old, and I had never deluded myself into thinking I could make a living at it. Becoming a writer is not a "career decision" like becoming a doctor or a policeman. You don't choose it so much as get chosen, and once you accept the fact that you're not fit for anything else, you have to be prepared to walk a long, hard road for the rest of your days. Unless you turn out to be a favorite of the gods (and woe to the man who banks on that), your work will never bring in enough to support you, and if you mean to have a roof over your head and not starve to death, you must resign yourself to doing other work to pay the bills. I understood all that, I was prepared for it, I had no complaints. In that respect, I was immensely lucky. I didn't particularly want anything in the way of material goods, and the prospect of being poor didn't frighten me. All I wanted was a chance to do the work I felt I had it in me to do.

Most writers lead double lives. They earn good money at legitimate professions and carve out time for their writing as best they can: early in the morning, late at night, weekends, vacations. William Carlos Williams and Louis-Ferdinand Céline were doctors. Wallace Stevens worked for an insurance company. T. S. Eliot was a banker, then a publisher. Among my own acquaintances, the French poet Jacques Dupin is codirector of an art gallery in Paris. William Bronk, the American poet, managed his family's coal and lumber business in upstate New York for over forty years. Don DeLillo, Peter Carey, Salman Rushdie, and Elmore Leonard all worked for long stretches in advertising. Other writers teach. That is probably the most common solution today, and with every major university and Podunk college offering so-called creative writing courses, novelists and poets are continually scratching and scrambling to land themselves a spot. Who can blame them? The salaries might not be big, but the work is steady and the hours are good.

My problem was that I had no interest in leading a double life. It's not that I wasn't willing to work, but the idea of punching a clock at some nine-to-five job left me cold, utterly devoid of enthusiasm. I was in my early twenties, and I felt too young to settle down, too full of other plans to waste my time earning more money than I either wanted or needed. As far as finances went, I just wanted to get by. Life was cheap in those days, and with no responsibility for anyone but myself, I figured I could scrape along on an annual income of roughly three thousand dollars.

I tried graduate school for a year, but that was only because Columbia offered me a tuition-free fellowship with a two-thousand-dollar stipend—which meant that I was actually paid to study. Even under those ideal conditions, I quickly understood that I wanted no part of it. I had had enough of school, and the prospect of spending another five or six years as a student struck me as a fate worse than death. I didn't want to talk about books anymore, I wanted to write them. Just on principle, it felt wrong to me for a writer to hide out in a university, to surround himself with too many like-minded people, to get too comfortable. The risk was complacency, and once that happens to a writer, he's as good as lost.

I'm not going to defend the choices I made. If they weren't practical, the truth was that I didn't want to be practical. What I wanted were new experiences. I wanted to go out into the world and test myself, to move from this to that, to explore as much as I could. As long as I kept my eyes open, I figured that whatever happened to me would be useful, would teach me things I had never known before. If this sounds like a rather old-fashioned approach, perhaps it was. Young writer bids farewell to family and friends and sets out for points unknown to discover what he's made of. For better or worse,

I doubt that any other approach would have suited me. I had energy, a head crammed full of ideas, and itchy feet. Given how big the world was, the last thing I wanted was to play it safe.

It's not difficult for me to describe these things and to remember how I felt about them. The trouble begins only when I question why I did them and why I felt what I felt. All the other young poets and writers in my class were making sensible decisions about their futures. We weren't rich kids who could depend on handouts from our parents, and once we left college, we would be out on our own for good. We were all facing the same situation, we all knew the score, and yet they acted in one way and I acted in another. That's what I'm still at a loss to explain. Why did my friends act so prudently, and why was I so reckless?

I came from a middle-class family. My childhood was comfortable, and I never suffered from any of the wants and deprivations that plague most of the human beings who live on this earth. I never went hungry, I never was cold, I never felt in danger of losing any of the things I had. Security was a given, and yet for all the ease and good fortune in the household, money was a subject of continual conversation and worry. Both of my parents had lived through the Depression, and neither one had fully recovered from those hard times. Each had been marked by the experience of not having enough, and each bore the wound in a different way.

My father was tight; my mother was extravagant. She spent; he didn't. The memory of poverty had not loosened its hold on his spirit, and even though his circumstances had changed, he could never quite bring himself to believe it. She, on the other hand, took great pleasure in those altered circumstances. She enjoyed the rituals of consumerism, and like so many Americans before her and since, she cultivated shopping as a means of self-expression, at times raising it to the level of an art form. To enter a store was to engage in an alchemical process that imbued the cash register with magical, transformative properties. Inexpressible desires, intangible needs, and unarticulated longings all passed through the money box and came out as real things, palpable objects you could hold in your hand. My mother never tired of reenacting this miracle, and the bills that resulted became a bone of contention between her and my father. She felt that we could afford them; he didn't. Two styles, two worldviews, two moral philosophies were in eternal conflict with each other, and in the end it broke their marriage apart. Money was the fault line, and it became the single, overpowering source of dispute between them. The tragedy was that they were both good people—attentive, honest, hardworking—and aside from that one ferocious battleground, they seemed to get along rather well. For the life of me I could never understand how such a relatively unimportant issue could cause so much trouble between them. But money, of course, is never just money. It's always something else, and it's always something more, and it always has the last word.

As a small boy, I was caught in the middle of this ideological war. My mother would take me shopping for clothes, sweeping me up in the whirlwind of her enthusiasm and generosity, and again and again I would allow myself to be talked into wanting the things she offered me—always more than I was expecting, always more than I thought I needed. It was impossible to resist, impossible not to enjoy how the clerks doted on her and hopped to her commands, impossible not to be carried away by the power of her performance. My happiness was always mixed with a large dose of anxiety, however, since I knew exactly what my father was going to say when he got the bill. And the fact was that he always said it. The inevitable outburst would come, and almost inevitably the matter would be resolved with my father declaring that the next time I needed something, he was the one who would take me shopping. So the moment would roll around to buy me a new winter jacket, say, or a new pair of shoes, and one night after dinner my father and I would drive off to a discount store located on a highway somewhere in the New Jersey darkness. I remember the glare of fluorescent lights in those places, the cinder-block walls, the endless racks of cheap men's clothing. As the jingle on the radio put it: "Robert Hall this season / Will tell you the reason— / Low overhead / Bum, bum, bum / Low overhead!" When all is said and done, that song is as much a part of my childhood as the Pledge of Allegiance or the Lord's Prayer.

The truth was that I enjoyed this bargain hunting with my father as much as I enjoyed the buying sprees orchestrated by my mother. My loyalties were equally divided between my two parents, and there was never any question of pitching my tent in one camp or the other. My mother's approach was more appealing, perhaps, at least in terms of the fun and excitement it generated, but there was something about my father's stubbornness that gripped me as well, a sense of hard-won experience and knowledge at the core of his beliefs, an integrity of purpose that made him someone who never backed down, not even at the risk of looking bad in the eyes of the world. I found that admirable, and much as I adored my beautiful, endlessly charming mother for dazzling the world as she did, I also adored my father for resisting that same world. It could be maddening to watch him in action—a man who never seemed to care what others thought of him—but it was also instructive, and in the long run I think I paid more attention to those lessons than I ever realized.

As a young boy I fell into the mold of your classic go-getter. At the first sign of snow, I would run out with my shovel and start ringing doorbells, asking people if they would hire me to clear their driveways and front walks. When the leaves fell in October, I would be out there with my rake, ringing those same doorbells and asking about the lawns. At other times, when there was nothing to remove from the ground, I would inquire about "odd jobs." Straightening up the garage, cleaning out the cellar, pruning the hedges—whatever needed to be done, I was the man to do it. In the summer, I sold lemonade for ten cents a glass on the sidewalk in front of my house. I gathered up empty bottles from the kitchen pantry, loaded them in my little red wagon, and lugged them to the store to turn in for cash. Two cents for the small ones; five cents for the big. I mostly used my earnings to buy baseball cards, sports magazines, and comic books, and whatever was left over I would diligently put in my piggy bank, which was built in the shape of a cash register. I was truly the child of my parents, and I never questioned the principles that animated their world. Money talked, and to the degree that you listened to it and followed its arguments, you would learn to speak the language of life.

Once, I remember, I was in possession of a fifty-cent piece. I can't recall how I came to have that coin—which was just as rare then as it is now—but whether it had been given to me or whether I had earned it myself, I have a keen sense of how much it meant to me and what a large sum it represented. For fifty cents in those days you could buy ten packs of baseball cards, five comic books, ten candy bars, fifty jawbreakers—or, if you preferred, various combinations of all of them. I put the half-dollar in my back pocket and marched off to the store, feverishly calculating how I was going to spend my little fortune. Somewhere along the way, however, for reasons that still confound me, the coin disappeared. I reached into my back pocket to check on it—knowing it was there, just wanting to make sure—and the money was gone. Was there a hole in my pocket? Had I accidentally slid the coin out of my pants the last time I'd touched it? I have no idea. I was six or seven years old, and I still remember how wretched I felt. I had tried to be so careful, and yet for all my precautions, I had wound up losing the money. How could I have allowed such a thing to happen? For want of any logical explanation, I decided that God had punished me. I didn't know why, but I was certain that the All-Powerful One had reached into my pocket and plucked out the coin Himself.

Little by little, I started turning my back on my parents. It's not that I began to love them less, but the world they came from no longer struck me as such an inviting place to live. I was ten, eleven, twelve years old, and already I was becoming an internal émigré, an exile in my own house. Many of these changes can be attributed to adolescence, to the simple fact that I was growing up and beginning to think for myself—but not all of them. Other forces were at work on me at the same time, and each one had a hand in pushing me onto the road I later followed. It wasn't just the pain of having to witness my parents' crumbling marriage, and it wasn't just the frustration of being trapped in a small suburban town, and it wasn't just the American climate of the late 1950s—but put them all together, and suddenly you had a powerful case against materialism, an indictment of the orthodox view that money was a good to be valued above all others. My parents valued money, and where had it gotten them? They had struggled so hard for it, had invested so much belief in it, and yet for every problem it had solved, another one had taken its place. American capitalism had created one of the most prosperous moments in human history. It had produced untold numbers of cars, frozen vegetables, and miracle shampoos, and yet Eisenhower was President, and the entire country had been turned into a gigantic television commercial, an incessant harangue to buy more, make more, spend more, to dance around the dollar-tree until you dropped dead from the sheer frenzy of trying to keep up with everyone else.

It wasn't long before I discovered that I wasn't the only person who felt this way. At ten, I stumbled across an issue of *Mad* magazine in a candy store in Irvington, New Jersey, and I remember the intense, almost stupefying pleasure I felt at reading those pages. They taught me that I had kindred spirits in this world, that others had already unlocked the doors I was trying to open myself. Fire hoses were being turned on black people in the American South, the Russians had launched the first Sputnik, and I was starting to pay attention. No, you didn't have to swallow the dogma they were trying to sell you. You could resist them, poke fun at them, call their bluff. The wholesomeness and dreary rectitude of American life were no more than a sham, a halfhearted publicity stunt. The moment you began to study the facts, contradictions bubbled to the surface, rampant hypocrisies were exposed, a whole new way of looking at things suddenly became possible. We had been taught to believe in "liberty and justice for all," but the fact was that liberty and justice were often at odds with one another. The pursuit of money had nothing to do with fairness; its driving engine was the social principle of "every man for himself." As if to prove the essential inhumanity of the marketplace, nearly all of its metaphors had been taken from the animal kingdom: dog eat dog, bulls and bears, the rat race, survival of the fittest. Money divided the world into winners and losers, haves and have-nots. That was an excellent arrangement for the winners, but what about the people who lost? Based on the evidence available to me, I gathered that they were to be cast aside and forgotten. Too bad, of course, but those were the breaks. If you construct a world so primitive as to make Darwin your leading philosopher and Aesop your leading poet, what else can you expect? It's a jungle out there, isn't it? Just look at that Dreyfus lion strolling down the middle of Wall Street. Could the message be any clearer? Either eat or be eaten. That's the law of the jungle, my friend, and if you don't have the stomach for it, then get out while you still can.

I was out before I was ever in. By the time I entered my teens, I had already concluded that the world of business would have to get along without me. I was probably at my worst then, my most insufferable, my most confused. I burned with the ardor of a newfound idealism, and the stringencies of the perfection I sought for myself turned me into a pint-sized puritan-in-training. I was repulsed by the outward trappings of wealth, and every sign of ostentation my parents brought into the house I treated with scorn. Life was unfair. I had finally figured this out, and because it was my own discovery, it hit me with all the force of a revelation. As the months went by, I found it increasingly difficult to reconcile my good luck with the bad luck of so many others. What had I done to deserve the comforts and advantages that had been showered on me? My father could afford them—that was all—and whether or not he and my mother fought over money was a small point in comparison to the fact that they had money to fight over in the first place. I squirmed every time I had to get into the family car—so bright and new and expensive, so clearly an invitation to the world to admire how well off we were. All my sympathies were for the downtrodden, the dispossessed, the underdogs of the social order, and a car like that filled me with shame—not just for myself, but for living in a world that allowed such things to be in it.

MY FIRST JOBS don't count. My parents were still supporting me, and I was under no obligation to fend for myself or contribute to the family budget. The pressure was therefore off, and without any pressure, nothing important can ever be at stake. I was glad to have the money I earned, but I never had to use it on nuts-and-bolts necessities, I never had to worry about putting food on the table or not falling behind with the rent. Those problems would come later. For now I was just a high school kid looking for a pair of wings to carry me away from where I was.

At sixteen, I spent two months working as a waiter at a summer camp in upstate New York. The next summer, I worked at my uncle Moe's appliance store in Westfield, New Jersey. The jobs were similar in that most of the tasks were physical and didn't require much thought. If carrying trays and scraping dishes was somewhat less interesting than installing air conditioners and unloading refrigerators from forty-foot trailer trucks, I wouldn't want to make too big a point of it. This isn't a question of apples and oranges—but of two kinds of apples, both the same shade of green. Dull as the work might have been, however, I found both jobs immensely satisfying. There were too many colorful characters around, too many surprises, too many new thoughts to absorb for me to resent the drudgery, and I never felt that I was wasting my time just to earn a paycheck. The money was an important part of it, but the work wasn't just about money. It was about learning who I was and how I fit into the world.

Even at the camp, where my coworkers were all sixteen- and seventeen-year-old high school boys, the kitchen help came from a starkly different universe. Down-and-outs, Bowery bums, men with dubious histories, they had been rounded up from the New York streets by the owner of the camp and talked into accepting their low-paying jobs—which included two months of fresh air and free room and board. Most of them didn't last long. One day they would just disappear, wandering back to the city without bothering to say good-bye. A day or two later, the missing man would be replaced by a similar lost soul, who rarely lasted very long himself. One of the dishwashers, I remember, was named Frank, a grim, surly guy with a serious drinking problem. Somehow or other, we managed to become friends, and in the evening after work was done we would sometimes sit on the steps behind the kitchen and talk. Frank turned out to be a highly intelligent, well-read man. He had worked as an insurance agent in Springfield, Massachusetts, and until the bottle got the better of him, he had lived the life of a productive, tax-paying citizen. I distinctly remember not daring to ask him what had happened, but one evening he told me anyway, turning what must have been a complicated story into a short, dry account of the events that had done him in. In the space of sixteen months, he said, every person who had ever meant anything to him died. He sounded philosophical about it, almost as if he were talking about someone else, and yet there was an undertow of bitterness in his voice. First his parents, he said, then his wife, and then his two children. Diseases, accidents, and burials, and by the time they were all gone, it was as if his insides had shattered. "I just gave up," he said. "I didn't care what happened to me anymore, so I became a bum."

The following year, in Westfield, I made the acquaintance of several more indelible figures. Carmen, for example, the voluminously padded, wisecracking bookkeeper, who to this day is still the only woman I've known with a beard (she actually had to shave), and Joe Mansfield, the assistant repairman with two hernias and a ravaged Chrysler that had wiped out the odometer three times and was now up to 360,000 miles. Joe was sending two daughters through college, and in addition to his day job at the appliance store, he worked eight hours every night as a foreman in a commercial bakery, reading comic books beside the huge vats of dough so as not to fall asleep. He was the single most exhausted man I have ever met—and also one of the most energetic. He kept himself going by smoking menthol cigarettes and downing twelve to sixteen bottles of orange soda a day, but not once did I ever see him put a morsel of food in his mouth. If he ate lunch, he said, it would make him too tired and he would collapse. The hernias had come a few years earlier, when he and two other men were carrying a jumbo refrigerator up a narrow flight of stairs. The other men had lost their grip, leaving Joe to bear the entire weight of the thing himself, and it was exactly then, as he struggled not to be crushed by the several hundred pounds he was holding, that his testicles had shot up out of his scrotum. First one ball, he said, and then the other. Pop . . . pop. He wasn't supposed to lift heavy objects anymore, but every time there was an especially large appliance to deliver, he would come along and help us—just to make sure we didn't kill ourselves.

The *us* included a nineteen-year-old redhead named Mike, a

tense, wiry shrimp with a missing index finger and one of the fastest tongues I had yet encountered. Mike and I were the air conditioner installation team, and we spent a lot of time together in the store van, driving to and from jobs. I never tired of listening to the onslaught of loopy, unexpected metaphors and outrageous opinions that came pouring out of him whenever he opened his mouth. If he found one of the customers too snotty, for example, he wouldn't say "that person's an asshole" (as most would) or "that person's stuck-up" (as some would), but "that person acts as if his shit doesn't smell." Young Mike had a special gift, and on several occasions that summer I was able to see how well it served him. Again and again we would enter a house to install an air conditioner, and again and again, just as we were in the middle of the job (screwing in the screws, measuring strips of caulking to seal up the window), a girl would walk into the room. It never seemed to fail. She was always seventeen, always pretty, always bored, always "just hanging around the house." The instant she appeared, Mike would turn on the charm. It was as if he knew she was going to come in, as if he had already rehearsed his lines and was fully prepared. I, on the other hand, was always caught with my guard down, and as Mike launched into his song and dance (a combination of bullshit, razzle-dazzle, and raw nerve), I would dumbly plod on with the work. Mike would talk, and the girl would smile. Mike would talk a little more, and the girl would laugh. Within two minutes they were old friends, and by the time I'd put the finishing touches on the job, they were swapping phone numbers and arranging where to meet on Saturday night. It was preposterous; it was sublime; it made my jaw drop. If it had happened only once or twice, I would have dismissed it as a fluke, but this scene was played out repeatedly, no less than five or six times over the course of the summer. In the end, I grudgingly had to admit that Mike was more than just lucky. He was someone who created his own luck.

IN SEPTEMBER, I started my senior year of high school. It was the last year I spent at home, and it was also the last year of my parents' marriage. Their breakup had been so long in coming that when the news was announced to me at the end of Christmas vacation, I wasn't upset so much as relieved.

It had been a mismatch from the start. If they hung in together as long as they did, it was more for "the children's sake" than for their own. I don't presume to have any answers, but I suspect that a decisive moment occurred two or three years before the end, when my father took over the grocery-shopping duties for the household. That was the last great money battle my parents fought, and it stands in my mind as the symbolic last straw, the thing that finally knocked the stuffing out of both of them. It was true that my mother enjoyed filling her cart at the local Shop-Rite until it was almost too heavy to push; it was true that she took pleasure in providing the treats my sister and I asked her for; it was true that we ate well at home and that the pantry was abundantly stocked. But it was also true that we could afford these things and that the family finances were in no way threatened by the sums my mother forked over at the checkout counter. In my father's eyes, however, her spending was out of control. When he finally put his foot down, it landed in the wrong place, and he wound up doing what no man should ever do to his wife. In effect, he relieved her of her job. From then on, he was the one who took responsibility for bringing food into the house. Once, twice, even three times a week, he would stop off somewhere on the way home from work (as if he didn't have enough to do already) and load up the back of his station wagon with groceries. The choice cuts of meat my mother had brought home were replaced by chuck and shoulder. Name-brand products became generic products. After-school snacks vanished. I don't remember hearing my mother complain, but it must have been a colossal defeat for her. She was no longer in charge of her own house, and the fact that she didn't protest, that she didn't fight back, must have meant that she had already given up on the marriage. When the end came, there were no dramas, no noisy showdowns, no last-minute regrets. The family quietly dispersed. My mother moved to an apartment in the Weequahic section of Newark (taking my sister and me along with her), and my father stayed on alone in the big house, living there until the day he died.

In some perverse way, these events made me extremely happy. I was glad that the truth was finally out in the open, and I welcomed the upheavals and changes that followed as a consequence of that truth. There was something liberating about it, an exhilaration in knowing that the slate had been wiped clean. An entire period of my life had ended, and even as my body continued to go through the motions of finishing up high school and helping my mother move to her new place, my mind had already decamped. Not only was I about to leave home, but home itself had disappeared. There was nothing to return to anymore, nowhere to go but out and away.

I didn't even bother to attend my high school graduation. I offer that as proof, evidence of how little it meant to me. By the time my classmates were donning their caps and gowns and receiving their diplomas, I was already on the other side of the Atlantic. The school had granted me a special dispensation to leave early, and I had booked passage on a student boat that sailed out of New York at the beginning of June. All my savings went into that trip. Birthday money, graduation money, bar mitzvah money, the little bits I'd hoarded from summer jobs—fifteen hundred dollars or so, I can't remember the exact amount. That was the era of Europe on Five Dollars a Day, and if you watched your funds carefully, it was actually possible to do it. I spent over a month in Paris, living in a hotel that cost seven francs a night ($1.40); I traveled to Italy, to Spain, to Ireland. In two and a half months, I lost more than twenty pounds. Everywhere I went, I worked on the novel I had started writing that spring. Mercifully, the manuscript has disappeared, but the story I carried around in my head that summer was no less real to me than the places I went to and the people I crossed paths with. I had some extraordinary encounters, especially in Paris, but more often than not I was alone, at times excessively alone, alone to the point of hearing voices in my head. God knows what to make of that eighteen-year-old boy now. I see myself as a conundrum, the site of inexplicable turmoils, a weightless, wild-eyed sort of creature, slightly touched, perhaps, prone to desperate inner surges, sudden about-faces, swoons, soaring thoughts. If someone approached me in the right way, I could be open, charming, positively gregarious. Otherwise, I was walled off and taciturn, barely present. I believed in myself and yet had no confidence in myself. I was bold and timid, light-footed and clumsy, single-minded and impulsive—a walking, breathing monument to the spirit of contradiction. My life had only just begun, and already I was moving in two directions at once. I didn't know it yet, but in order for me to get anywhere, I was going to have to work twice as hard as anyone else.

The last two weeks of the trip were the strangest. For reasons that had everything to do with James Joyce and *Ulysses,*

I went to Dublin. I had no plans. My only purpose in going was to be there, and I figured the rest would take care of itself. The tourist office steered me to a bed-and-breakfast in Donnybrook, a fifteen-minute bus ride from the center of town. Besides the elderly couple who ran the place and two or three of the guests, I scarcely talked to anyone in all that time. I never even found the courage to set foot in a pub. Somewhere during the course of my travels, I had developed an ingrown toenail, and while it sounds like a comical condition, it wasn't the least bit funny to me. It felt as if the tip of a knife had been lodged in my big toe. Walking was turned into a trial, and yet from early in the morning to late in the afternoon, I did little else but walk, hobbling around Dublin in my too-tight, disintegrating shoes. I could live with the pain, I found, but the effort it called for seemed to drive me ever further into myself, to erase me as a social being. There was a crotchety American geezer in full-time residence at the boardinghouse—a seventy-year-old retiree from Illinois or Indiana—and once he got wind of my condition, he started filling my head with stories about how his mother had left an ingrown toenail untended for years, treating it with patchwork home remedies—dabs of disinfectant, little balls of cotton—but never *taking the bull by the horns,* and wouldn't you know it, she came down with *cancer of the toe,* which worked its way into her foot, and then into her leg, and then spread through her whole body and eventually did her in. He loved elaborating on the small, gruesome details of his mother's demise (for my own good, of course), and seeing how susceptible I was to what he told me, he never tired of telling the story again. I'm not going to deny that I was affected. A cumbersome annoyance had been turned into a life-threatening scourge, and the longer I delayed taking action, the more dismal my prospects would become. Every time I rode past the Hospital for Incurables on my way into town, I turned my eyes away. I couldn't get the old man's words out of my head. Doom was stalking me, and signs of impending death were everywhere.

Once or twice, I was accompanied on my rambles by a twenty-six-year-old nurse from Toronto. Her name was Pat Gray, and she had checked into the bed-and-breakfast the same evening I had. I fell desperately in love with her, but it was a hopeless infatuation, a lost cause from the start. Not only was I too young for her, and not only was I too shy to declare my feelings, but she was in love with someone else—an Irishman, of course, which explained why she'd come to Dublin in the first place. One night, I recall, she came home from a date with her beloved at around half-past twelve. I was still up at that hour, scribbling away at my novel, and when she saw light coming through the crack under my door, she knocked and asked to come in. I was already in bed, working with a notebook propped against my knees, and she burst in laughing, her cheeks flushed with drink, bubbling over with excitement. Before I could say anything, she threw her arms around my neck and kissed me, and I thought: Miracle of miracles, my dream has come true. But alas, it was only a false alarm. I didn't even have a chance to kiss her back before she was drawing away from me and explaining that her Irishman had proposed to her that night and that she was the happiest girl in the world. It was impossible not to feel glad for her. This straightforward, pretty young woman, with her short hair and innocent eyes and earnest Canadian voice, had chosen me as the person to share the news with. I did my best to congratulate her, to hide my disappointment after that brief, wholly implausible rush of expectation, but the kiss had undone me, had absolutely melted my bones, and it was all I could do not to commit a serious blunder. If I managed to control myself, it was only by turning myself into a block of wood. No doubt a block of wood has good manners, but it's hardly a fitting companion for a celebration.

Everything else was solitude, silence, walking. I read books in Phoenix Park, journeyed out to Joyce's Martello Tower along the strand, crossed and recrossed the Liffey more times than I could count. The Watts riots took place then, and I remember reading the headlines at a kiosk on O'Connell Street, but I also remember a small girl singing with a Salvation Army band early one evening as people shuffled home from work—some sad, plaintive song about human misery and the wonders of God—and that voice is still inside me, a voice so crystalline as to make the toughest person fall down and weep, and the remarkable thing about it was that no one paid the slightest attention to her. The rush-hour crowd rushed past her, and she just stood on the corner singing her song in the eerie, dusky, northern light, as oblivious of them as they were of her, a tiny bird in tattered clothes chanting her psalm to the broken heart.

Dublin is not a big city, and it didn't take me long to learn my way around. There was something compulsive about the walks I took, an insatiable urge to prowl, to drift like a ghost among strangers, and after two weeks the streets were transformed into something wholly personal for me, a map of my inner terrain. For years afterward, every time I closed my eyes before going to sleep, I was back in Dublin. As wakefulness dribbled out of me and I descended into semiconsciousness, I would find myself there again, walking through those same streets. I have no explanation for it. Something important had happened to me there, but I have never been able to pinpoint exactly what it was. Something terrible, I think, some mesmerizing encounter with my own depths, as if in the loneliness of those days I had looked into the darkness and seen myself for the first time.

I STARTED Columbia College in September, and for the next four years the last thing on my mind was money. I worked intermittently at various jobs, but those years were not about making plans, not about preparing for my financial future. They were about books, the war in Vietnam, the struggle to figure out how to do the thing I was proposing to do. If I thought about earning a living at all, it was only in a fitful, haphazard sort of way. At most I imagined some kind of marginal existence for myself—scrounging for crumbs at the far edges of the workaday world, the life of a starving poet.

The jobs I had as an undergraduate were nevertheless instructive. If nothing else, they taught me that my preference for blue-collar work over white-collar work was well founded. At one point in my sophomore year, for example, I was hired by the subdivision of a publishing company to write material for educational filmstrips. I had been subjected to a barrage of "audiovisual aids" during my childhood, and I remembered the intense boredom they invariably produced in me and my friends. It was always a pleasure to leave the classroom and sit in the dark for twenty or thirty minutes (just like going to the movies!), but the clunky images on screen, the monotone voice of the narrator, and the intermittent *ping* that told the teacher when to push the button and move on to the next picture soon took their toll on us. Before long, the room was abuzz with whispered conversations and frantic, half-suppressed giggles. A minute or two later, the spitballs would begin to fly.

I was reluctant to impose this tedium on another generation of kids, but I figured I'd do my best and see if I couldn't put some spark into it. My first day on the job, the supervisor told me to take a look at some of the company's past filmstrips and acquaint myself with the form. I picked out one at random. It was called "Government" or "Introduction to Government," something like that. He set up the spool on a machine and then left me alone to watch the film. About two or three frames into it, I came across a statement that alarmed me. The ancient Greeks had invented the idea of democracy, the text said, accompanied by a painting of bearded men standing around in togas. That was fine, but then it went on to say (*ping:* cut to a painting of the Capitol) that America was a democracy. I turned off the machine, walked down the hall, and knocked on the door of the supervisor's office. "There's a mistake in the filmstrip," I said. "America isn't a democracy. It's a republic. There's a big difference."

He looked at me as if I had just informed him that I was Stalin's grandson. "It's for little children," he said, "not college students. There's no room to go into detail."

"It's not a detail," I answered, "it's an important distinction. In a pure democracy, everyone votes on every issue. We elect representatives to do that for us. I'm not saying that's bad. Pure democracy can be dangerous. The rights of minorities need to be protected, and that's what a republic does for us. It's all spelled out in *The Federalist Papers.* The government has to guard against the tyranny of the majority. Kids should know that."

The conversation became quite heated. I was determined to make my point, to prove that the statement in the filmstrip was wrong, but he refused to swallow it. He pegged me as a troublemaker the instant I opened my mouth, and that was that. Twenty minutes after starting the job, I was given the boot.

Much better was the job I had in the summer after my freshman year—as groundskeeper at the Commodore Hotel in the Catskills. I was hired through the New York State Employment Agency in midtown Manhattan, a vast government office that found work for the unskilled and the unfortunate, the bottom dogs of society. Humble and badly paid as the position was, at least it offered a chance to get out of the city and escape the heat. My friend Bob Perelman and I signed on together, and the next morning we were dispatched to Monticello, New York, via the Short Line Bus Company. It was the same setup I'd seen three years before, and our fellow passengers were the same bums and down-and-outs I'd rubbed shoulders with during my stint as a summer camp waiter. The only difference was that now I was one of them. The bus fare was deducted from the first paycheck, as was the employment agency's fee, and unless you hung in with the job for some little time, you weren't going to make any money. There were those who didn't like the work and quit after a couple of days. They wound up with nothing—dead broke and a hundred miles from home, feeling they'd been had.

The Commodore was a small, down-at-the-heels Borscht Belt establishment. It was no match for the local competition, the Concord and Grossinger's, and a certain wistfulness and nostalgia hung about the place, a memory of rosier days. Bob and I arrived several weeks in advance of the summer season, and we were responsible for getting the grounds into shape to welcome an influx of visitors in July and August. We mowed lawns, clipped bushes, collected trash, painted walls, repaired screen doors. They gave us a little hut to live in, a ramshackle box with less square footage than a beach cabana, and bit by bit we covered the walls of our room with poems—crazy doggerel, filthy limericks, flowery quatrains—laughing our heads off as we downed endless bottles of Budweiser chug-a-lug beer. We drank the beer because there was nothing better to do, but given the food we had to eat, the hops became a necessary component of our diet as well. There were only a dozen or so workers on the premises at the time, and they gave us the low-budget treatment where culinary matters were concerned. The menu for every lunch and dinner was the same: Chun King chicken chow mein, straight out of the can. Thirty years have gone by since then, and I would still rather go hungry than put another morsel of that stuff in my mouth.

None of this would be worth mentioning if not for Casey and Teddy, the two indoor maintenance men I worked with that summer. Casey and Teddy had been palling around together for more than ten years, and by now they were a pair, an indissoluble team, a dialectical unit. Everything they did, they did in tandem, traveling from place to place and job to job as if they were one. They were chums for life, two peas in a pod, buddies. Not gay, not the least bit interested in each other sexually—but buddies. Casey and Teddy were classic American drifters, latter-day hoboes who seemed to have stepped forth from the pages of a Steinbeck novel, and yet they were so funny together, so full of wisecracks and drunkenness and good cheer, that their company was irresistible. At times they made me think of some forgotten comedy duo, a couple of clowns from the days of vaudeville and silent films. The spirit of Laurel and Hardy had survived in them, but these two weren't bound by the constraints of show business. They were part of the real world, and they performed their act on the stage of life.

Casey was the straight man, Teddy was the card. Casey was

thin, Teddy was round. Casey was white, Teddy was black. On their days off they would tramp into town together, drink themselves silly, and then return for their chow mein dinner sporting identical haircuts or dressed in identical shirts. The idea was always to spend all their money in one big binge—and to spend it in exactly the same way, even-steven, penny for penny. The shirts stand out in my mind as a particularly raucous event. They couldn't stop laughing when they showed up in those twin outfits, holding their sides and pointing at each other as if they'd just played an enormous joke on the world. They were the loudest, ugliest shirts imaginable, a double insult to good taste, and Casey and Teddy were positively seized with mirth as they modeled them for me and Bob. Teddy then shuffled off to the empty ballroom on the ground floor of the main building, sat down at the piano, and launched into what he called his Port Wine Concerto. For the next hour and a half, he clanged forth tuneless improvisations, filling the hall with a tempest of inebriation and noise. Teddy was a man of many gifts, but music was not one of them. Yet there he sat, happy as a clam in the fading light, a Dada maestro at peace with himself and the world.

Teddy had been born in Jamaica, he told me, and had joined the British Navy during World War II. Somewhere along the line, his ship was torpedoed. I don't know how much time elapsed before he was rescued (minutes? hours? days?), but whenever he was found, it was an American ship that found him. From then on he was in the American Navy, he said, and by the end of the war he was an American citizen. It sounded a little fishy to me, but that's the story he told, and who was I to doubt him? In the past twenty years, he seemed to have done everything a man can possibly do, to have run the entire gamut of occupations. Salesman, sidewalk artist in Greenwich Village, bartender, skid row drunk. None of it mattered to him. A great, rumbling basso laugh accompanied every story he told, and that laugh was like an unending bow to his own ridiculousness, a sign that his only purpose in talking was to poke fun at himself. He made scenes in public places, misbehaved like a willful child, was forever calling people's bluff. It could be exhausting to be with him, but there was also something admirable about the way he caused trouble. It had an almost scientific quality to it, as if he were conducting an experiment, shaking things up for the pure pleasure of seeing where they would land once the dust had settled. Teddy was an anarchist, and because he was also without ambition, because he didn't want the things that other people wanted, he never had to play by anybody's rules but his own.

I have no idea how or where he met Casey. His sidekick was a less flamboyant character than he was, and what I remember best about him was that he had no sense of taste or smell. Casey had been in a barroom fight some years back, had received a knock on the head, and had thenceforth lost all of his olfactory functions. As a result, everything tasted like cardboard to him. Cover his eyes, and he couldn't tell you what he was eating. Chow mein or caviar, potatoes or pudding—there was no difference. Aside from this affliction, Casey was in excellent trim, a feisty welterweight with a New York Irish voice that made him sound like a Dead End Kid. His job was to laugh at Teddy's jokes and make sure his friend didn't take things too far and get himself hauled off to jail. Teddy got close to it one night that summer—standing up in a Monticello restaurant and waving around the menu as he shouted, "I ain't gonna eat this Japanese dog food!"—but Casey calmed him down, and we all managed to finish our meal. I don't suppose it's necessary to add that we weren't in a Japanese restaurant.

By any objective standard, Casey and Teddy were nobodies, a pair of eccentric fools, but they made an unforgettable impression on me, and I have never run across their likes since. That was the reason for going off to work at places like the Commodore Hotel, I think. It's not that I wanted to make a career of it, but those little excursions into the backwaters and shit holes of the world never failed to produce an interesting discovery, to further my education in ways I hadn't expected. Casey and Teddy are a perfect example. I was nineteen years old when I met them, and the things they did that summer are still feeding my imagination today.

IN 1967, I signed up for Columbia's Junior Year Abroad Program in Paris. The weeks I'd spent there after finishing high school had whetted my appetite for the place, and I jumped at the chance to go back.

Paris was still Paris, but I was no longer the same person I'd been during my first visit. I had spent the past two years living in a delirium of books, and whole new worlds had been poured into my head, life-altering transfusions had reconstituted my blood. Nearly everything that is still important to me in the way of literature and philosophy I first encountered during those two years. Looking back on that time now, I find it almost impossible to absorb how many books I read. I drank them up in staggering numbers, consumed entire countries and continents of books, could never even begin to get enough of them. Elizabethan playwrights, pre-Socratic philosophers, Russian novelists, Surrealist poets. I read books as if my brain had caught fire, as if my very survival were at stake. One work led to another work, one thought led to another thought, and from one month to the next, I changed my ideas about everything.

The program turned out to be a bitter disappointment. I went to Paris with all sorts of grandiose plans, assuming I would be able to attend any lectures and courses I wanted to (Roland Barthes at the Collège de France, for example), but when I sat down to discuss these possibilities with the director of the program, he flat out told me to forget them. Out of the question, he said. You're required to study French language and grammar, to pass certain tests, to earn so many credits and half-credits, to put in so many class hours here and so many hours there. I found it absurd, a curriculum designed for babies. I'm past all that, I told him. I already know how to speak French. Why go backward? Because, he said, those are the rules, and that's the way it is.

He was so unbending, so contemptuous of me, so ready to interpret my enthusiasm as arrogance and to think I was out to insult him, that we immediately locked horns. I had nothing against the man personally, but he seemed bent on turning our disagreement into a personal conflict. He wanted to belittle me, to crush me with his power, and the longer the conversation went on, the more I felt myself resisting him. At last, a moment came when I'd had enough. All right, I said, if that's the way it is, then I quit. I quit the program, I quit the college, I quit the whole damn thing. And then I got up from my chair, shook his hand, and walked out of the office.

It was a crazy thing to do. The prospect of not getting a B.A. didn't worry me, but turning my back on college meant that I would automatically lose my student deferment. With the troop buildup in Vietnam growing at an alarming rate, I had suddenly put myself in a good position to be drafted into the army. That would have been fine if I supported the war, but I didn't. I was against it, and nothing was ever going to make me fight in it. If they tried to induct me into the army, I would refuse to serve. If they arrested me, I would go to jail. That was a categorical decision—an absolute, unbudgeable stance. I wasn't going to take part in the war, even if it meant ruining my life.

Still, I went ahead and quit college. I was utterly fearless about it, felt not the slightest tremor of hesitation or doubt, and took the plunge with my eyes wide open. I was expecting to fall hard, but I didn't. Instead, I found myself floating through the air like a feather, and for the next few months I felt as free and happy as I had ever been.

I lived in a small hotel on the rue Clément, directly across from the Marché Saint-Germain, an enclosed market that has long since been torn down. It was an inexpensive but tidy place, several notches up from the fleabag I'd stayed in two years before, and the young couple who ran it were exceedingly kind to me. The man's name was Gaston (stout, small mustache, white shirt, ever-present black apron), and he spent the bulk of his time serving customers in the café on the ground floor, a minuscule hole-in-the-wall that doubled as neighborhood hangout and hotel reception desk. That's where I drank my coffee in the morning, read the newspaper, and became addicted to pinball. I walked a lot during those months, just as I had in Dublin, but I also spent countless hours upstairs in my room, reading and writing. Most of the work I did then has been lost, but I remember writing poems and translating poems, as well as composing a long, exhaustingly complex screenplay for a silent film (part Buster Keaton movie, part philosophical tap dance). On top of all the reading I'd done in the past two years, I had also been going to the movies, primarily at the Thalia and New Yorker theaters, which were no more than a short walk down Broadway from Morningside Heights. The Thalia ran a different double feature every day, and with the price of admission just fifty cents for students, I wound up spending as much time there as I did in the Columbia classrooms. Paris turned out to be an even better town for movies than New York. I became a regular at the Cinémathèque and the Left Bank revival houses, and after a while I got so caught up in this passion that I started toying with the idea of becoming a director. I even went so far as to make some inquiries about attending IDHEC, the Paris film institute, but the application forms proved to be so massive and daunting that I never bothered to fill them out.

When I wasn't in my room or sitting in a movie theater, I was browsing in bookstores, eating in cheap restaurants, getting to know various people, catching a dose of the clap (very painful), and generally exulting in the choice I had made. It would be hard to exaggerate how good I felt during those months. I was at once stimulated and at peace with myself, and though I knew my little paradise would have to end, I did everything I could to prolong it, to put off the hour of reckoning until the last possible moment.

I managed to hold out until mid-November. By the time I returned to New York, the fall semester at Columbia was half over. I assumed there was no chance of being reinstated as a student, but I had promised my family to come back and discuss the matter with the university. They were worried about me, after all, and I figured I owed them that much. Once I had taken care of that chore, I intended to go back to Paris and start looking for a job. Let the draft be damned, I said to myself. If I wound up as a "fugitive from justice," so be it.

None of it worked out as I thought it would. I made an appointment to see one of the deans at Columbia, and this man turned out to be so sympathetic, so fully on my side, that he broke down my defenses within a matter of minutes. No, he said, he didn't think I was being foolish. He understood what I was doing, and he admired the spirit of the enterprise. On the other hand, there was the question of the war, he said. Columbia didn't want to see me go into the army if I didn't want to go, much less wind up in jail for refusing to serve in the army. If I wanted to come back to college, the door was open. I could start attending classes tomorrow, and officially it would be as if I had never missed a day.

How to argue with a man like that? He wasn't some functionary who was just doing his job. He spoke too calmly for that and listened too carefully to what I said, and before long I understood that the only thing in it for him was an honest desire to prevent a twenty-year-old kid from making a mistake, to talk someone out of fucking up his life when he didn't have to. There would be time for that later, n'est-ce pas? He wasn't very old himself—thirty, thirty-five, perhaps—and I still remember his name, even though I never saw him again. Dean Platt. When the university shut down that spring because of the student strike, he quit his job in protest over the administration's handling of the affair. The next thing I heard, he had gone to work for the UN.

THE TROUBLES AT Columbia lasted from early 1968 until my class graduated the following June. Normal activity all but stopped during that time. The campus became a war zone of demonstrations, sit-ins, and moratoriums. There were riots, police raids, slugfests, and factional splits. Rhetorical excesses abounded, ideological lines were drawn, passions flowed from all sides. Whenever there was a lull, another issue would come up, and the outbursts would begin all over again. In the long run, nothing of any great importance was accomplished. The proposed site for a university gymnasium was changed, a number of academic requirements were dropped, the president resigned and was replaced by another president. That was all. In spite of the efforts of thousands, the ivory tower did not collapse. But still, it tottered for a time, and more than a few of its stones crumbled and fell to the ground.

I took part in some things and kept my distance from others. I helped occupy one of the campus buildings, was roughed up by the cops and spent a night in jail, but mostly I was a bystander, a sympathetic fellow traveler. Much as I would have liked to join in, I found myself temperamentally unfit for group activities. My loner instincts were far too ingrained, and I could never quite bring myself to climb aboard the great ship *Solidarity.* For better or worse, I went on paddling my little canoe—a bit more desperately, perhaps, a bit less sure of where I was going now, but much too stubborn to get out. There probably wouldn't have been time for that anyway. I was steering through rapids, and it took every ounce of my strength just to hold on to the paddle. If I had flinched, there's a good chance I would have drowned.

Some did. Some became casualties of their own righteousness and noble intentions, and the human loss was catastrophic. Ted Gold, one class ahead of me, blew himself to smithereens in a West Village brownstone when the bomb he was building accidentally went off. Mark Rudd, a childhood friend and Columbia dorm neighbor, joined the Weather Underground and lived in hiding for more than a decade. Dave Gilbert, an SDS spokesman whose speeches had impressed me as models of insight and intelligence, is now serving a seventy-five-year prison sentence for his involvement in the Brinks robbery. In the summer of 1969, I walked into a post office in western Massachusetts with a friend who had to mail a letter. As she waited in line, I studied the posters of the FBI's ten most wanted men pinned to the wall. It turned out that I knew seven of them.

That was the climate of my last two years of college. In spite of the distractions and constant turmoil, I managed to do a fair amount of writing, but none of my efforts ever added up to much. I started two novels and abandoned them, wrote several plays I didn't like, worked on poem after poem with largely disappointing results. My ambitions were much greater than my abilities at that point, and I often felt frustrated, dogged by a sense of failure. The only accomplishment I felt proud of was the French poetry I had translated, but that was a secondary pursuit and not even close to what I had in mind. Still, I must not have been totally discouraged. I kept on writing, after all, and when I began publishing articles on books and films in the *Columbia Daily Spectator,* I actually got to see my work in print fairly often. You have to start somewhere, I suppose. I might not have been moving as fast as I wanted to, but at least I was moving. I was up on my feet and walking forward, step by wobbly step, but I still didn't know how to run.

When I look back on those days now, I see myself in fragments. Numerous battles were being fought at the same time, and parts of myself were scattered over a broad field, each one wrestling with a different angel, a different impulse, a different idea of who I was. It sometimes led me to act in ways that were fundamentally out of character. I would turn myself into someone I was not, try wearing another skin for a while, imagine I had reinvented myself. The morose and contemplative stuffed shirt would dematerialize into a fast-talking cynic. The bookish, overly zealous intellectual would suddenly turn around and embrace Harpo Marx as his spiritual father. I can think of several examples of this antic bumbling, but the one that best captures the spirit of the time was a little piece of jabberwocky I contributed to the *Columbia Review,* the undergraduate literary magazine. For reasons that utterly escape me now, I took it upon myself to launch the First Annual Christopher Smart Award. I was a senior then, and the contest rules were published on the last page of the fall issue. I pluck these sentences from the text at random: "The purpose of the award is to give recognition to the great anti-men of our time . . . men of talent who have renounced all worldly ambition, who have turned their backs on the banquet tables of the rich. . . . We have taken Christopher Smart as our model . . . the eighteenth-century Englishman who spurned the easy glory that awaited him as an inventor of rhymed couplets . . . for a life of drunkenness, insanity, religious fanaticism, and prophetic writings. In excess he found his true path, in rejecting the early promise he showed to the academic poets of England, he realized his true greatness. Defamed and ridiculed over the past two centuries, his reputation run through the mud . . . Christopher Smart has been relegated to the sphere of the unknowns. We attempt now, in an age without heroes, to resurrect his name."

The object of the competition was to reward failure. Not common, everyday setbacks and stumbles, but monumental falls, gargantuan acts of self-sabotage. In other words, I wanted to single out the person who had done the least with the most, who had begun with every advantage, every talent, every expectation of worldly success, and had come to nothing. Contestants were asked to write an essay of fifty words or more describing their failure or the failure of someone they knew. The winner would receive a two-volume boxed set of Christopher Smart's *Collected Works.* To no one's surprise but my own, not one entry was submitted.

It was a joke, of course, an exercise in literary leg pulling, but underneath my humorous intentions there was something disturbing, something that was not funny at all. Why the compulsion to sanctify failure? Why the mocking, arrogant tone, the know-it-all posturing? I could be wrong, but it strikes me now that they were an expression of fear—dread of the uncertain future I had prepared for myself—and that my true motive in setting up the contest was to declare myself the winner. The cockeyed, Bedlamite rules were a way of hedging my bets, of ducking the blows that life had in store for me. To lose was to win, to win was to lose, and therefore even if the worst came to pass, I would be able to claim a moral victory. Small comfort, perhaps, but no doubt I was already clutching at straws. Rather than bring my fear out into the open, I buried it under an avalanche of wisecracks and sarcasm. None of it was conscious. I was trying to come to terms with anticipated defeats, hardening myself for the struggles that lay ahead. For the next several years, my favorite sentence in the English language was from the Elizabethan poet Fulke Greville: "I write for those on whom the black ox hath trod."

As it happened, I wound up meeting Christopher Smart. Not the real Christopher Smart, perhaps, but one of his reincarnations, a living example of failed promise and blighted literary fortune. It was the spring of my senior year, just weeks before I was supposed to graduate. Out of nowhere, a man turned up on the Columbia campus and started causing a stir. At first I was only dimly aware of his presence, but little fragments of the stories circulating about him occasionally fell within my earshot. I'd heard that he called himself "Doc," for example, and that for obscure reasons that had something to do with the American economic system and the future of mankind, he was handing out money to strangers, no strings attached. With so many oddball doings in the air back then, I didn't pay much attention.

One night, a couple of my friends talked me into going down to Times Square with them to see the latest Sergio Leone spaghetti western. After the movie let out, we decided to cap off the evening with a little lark and repaired to the Metropole Café at Broadway and Forty-eighth Street. The Metropole had once been a quality jazz club, but now it was a topless go-go bar, complete with wall-to-wall mirrors, strobe lights, and half a dozen girls in glittering G-strings dancing on an elevated platform. We took a table in one of the back corners and started drinking our drinks. Once our eyes had adjusted to the darkness, one of my friends spotted "Doc" sitting alone in the opposite corner of the room. My friend went over and asked him to join us, and when the bearded, somewhat disheveled mystery man sat down beside me, mumbling something about Gene Krupa and what the hell had happened to this place, I turned my eyes away from the dancers for a moment and shook hands with the legendary, forgotten novelist, H. L. Humes.

He had been one of the founders of the *Paris Review* back in the fifties, had published two successful early books (*The Underground City* and *Men Die*), and then, just as he was beginning to make a name for himself, had vanished from sight. He just dropped off the literary map and was never heard from again.

I don't know the full story, but the bits and pieces I heard from him suggested that he'd had a rough time of it, had endured a long run of reversals and miseries. Shock treatments were mentioned, a ruined marriage, several stays in mental hospitals. By his own account, he'd been forced to stop writing for physical reasons—not by choice. The electroshock therapy had damaged his system, he said, and every time he picked up a pen, his legs would start to swell up, causing him unbearable pain. With the written word no longer available to him, he now had to rely on talk to get his "message" across to the world. That night, he gave a full-scale demonstration of how thoroughly he had mastered this new medium. First in the topless bar, and then on a nearly seventy-block walk up Broadway to Morningside Heights, the man talked a blue streak, rattling and rambling and chewing our ears off with a monologue that resembled nothing I had ever heard before. It was the rant of a hipster-visionary-neoprophet, a relentless, impassioned outflow of paranoia and brilliance, a careening mental journey that bounced from fact to metaphor to speculation with such speed and unpredictability that one was left dumbfounded, unable to say a word. He had come to New York on a mission, he told us. There were fifteen thousand dollars in his pocket, and if his theories about finance and the structures of capitalism were correct, he would be able to use that money to bring down the American government.

It was all quite simple, really. His father had just died, leaving Doc the aforementioned sum as an inheritance, and rather than squander the money on himself, our friend was proposing to give it away. Not in a lump, and not to any particular charity or person, but to everyone, to the whole world all at once. To that end he had gone to the bank, cashed the check, and converted it into a stack of fifty-dollar bills. With those three hundred portraits of Ulysses S. Grant as his calling cards, he was going to introduce himself to his coconspirators and unleash the greatest economic revolution in history. Money is a fiction, after all, worthless paper that acquires value only because large numbers of people choose to give it value. The system runs on faith. Not truth or reality, but collective belief. And what would happen if that faith were undermined, if large numbers of people suddenly began to doubt the system? Theoretically, the system would collapse. That, in a nutshell, was the object of Doc's experiment. The fifty-dollar bills he handed out to strangers weren't just gifts; they were weapons in the fight to make a better world. He wanted to set an example with his profligacy, to prove that one could disenchant oneself and break the spell that money held over our minds. Each time he disbursed another chunk of cash, he would instruct the recipient to spend it as fast as he could. Spend it, give it away, get it circulating, he would say, and tell the next person to do the same. Overnight, a chain reaction would be set in motion, and before you knew it, so many fifties would be flying through the air that the system would start to go haywire. Waves would be emitted, neutron charges from thousands, even millions of different sources would bounce around the room like little rubber balls. Once they built up enough speed and momentum, they would take on the strength of bullets, and the walls would begin to crack.

I can't say to what degree he actually believed this. Deranged as he might have been, a man of his intelligence surely would have known a stupid idea when he heard it. He never came out and said so, but deep down I think he understood what drivel it was. That didn't stop him from enjoying it, of course, and from spouting off about his plan at every opportunity, but it was more in the spirit of a wacko performance piece than a genuine political act. H. L. Humes wasn't some crackpot schizo taking orders from Martian command center. He was a ravaged, burnt-out writer who had run aground on the shoals of his own consciousness, and rather than give up and renounce life altogether, he had manufactured this little farce to boost his morale. The money gave him an audience again, and as long as people were watching, he was inspired, manic, the original one-man band. He pranced about like a buffoon, turning cartwheels and jumping through flames and shooting himself out of cannons, and from all I could gather, he loved every minute of it.

As he marched up Broadway that night with me and my friends, he put on a spectacular show. Between the cascading words and the barks of laughter and the jags of cosmological music, he would wheel around and start addressing strangers, breaking off in midsentence to slap another fifty-dollar bill in someone's hand and urge him to spend it like there was no tomorrow. Rambunctiousness took control of the street that night, and Doc was the prime attraction, the pied piper of mayhem. It was impossible not to get caught up in it, and I must admit that I found his performance highly entertaining. However, just as we neared the end of our journey and I was about to go home, I made a serious blunder. It must have been one or two in the morning by then. Somewhere off to my right, I heard Doc muttering to himself. "Any of you cats got a place to crash?" he said, and because he sounded so cool and nonchalant, so profoundly indifferent to the matters of this world, I didn't think twice about it. "Sure," I said, "you can sleep on my couch if you want to." Needless to say, he accepted my invitation. Needless to say, I had no idea what I had gotten myself into.

It's not that I didn't like him, and it's not that we didn't get along. For the first couple of days, in fact, things went rather smoothly. Doc planted himself on the couch and rarely stirred, rarely even brought the soles of his feet into contact with the floor. Aside from an occasional trip to the bathroom, he did nothing but sit, eat pizza, smoke marijuana, and talk. I bought the pizza for him (with his money), and after telling him five or six times that I wasn't interested in dope, he finally got the message and stopped offering it to me. The talk was incessant, however, the same repertoire of addled riffs he'd unfurled on the first night, but his arguments were more ample now, more fleshed out, more focused. Hours would go by, and his mouth never stopped moving. Even when I got up and left the room, he would go on talking, delivering his ideas to the wall, the ceiling, the light fixtures, and scarcely even notice that I was gone.

There wouldn't have been a problem if the place had been a little larger. The apartment had just two rooms and a kitchen, and since my bedroom was too small to hold anything but a bed, my work table was set up in the living room—which also happened to be where the couch was. With Doc permanently installed on the couch, it was all but impossible for me to get any work done. The spring semester was drawing to a close, and I had a number of term papers to write in order to complete my courses and graduate, but for the first two days I didn't even bother to try. I figured that I had a little margin and therefore didn't panic. Doc would be leaving soon, and once I had my desk back, I would be able to get down to work. By the morning of the third day, however, I realized that my houseguest had no intention of leaving. It wasn't that he was overstaying his welcome on purpose; the thought of leaving simply hadn't entered his head. What was I supposed to do? I didn't have the heart to kick him out. I already felt too sorry for him, and I couldn't find the courage to take such a drastic step.

The next few days were exceedingly difficult. I did what I could to cope, to see if some minor adjustments could improve the situation. In the end, things might have panned out—I don't know—but three or four days after I put Doc in the bedroom and took over the living room for myself, disaster struck. It happened on one of the most beautiful Sundays I can remember, and it was no one's fault but my own. A friend called to invite me to play in an outdoor basketball game, and rather than leave Doc alone in the apartment, I took him along with me. Everything went well. I played in the game and he sat by the side of the court, listening to the radio and yakking to himself or my friends, depending on whether anyone was within range. As we were returning home that evening, however, someone spotted us on the street. "Aha," this person said to me, "so that's where he's been hiding." I had never particularly liked this person, and when I told him to keep Doc's whereabouts under his hat, I realized that I might just as well have been talking to a lamppost. Sure enough, the buzzer of my apartment started ringing early the next morning. The campus celebrity had been found, and after his mysterious weeklong absence, H. L. Humes was more than happy to indulge his followers. All day long, groups of nineteen- and twenty-year-olds tramped into my apartment to sit on the floor and listen to Doc impart his skewed wisdom to them. He was the philosopher king, the metaphysical pasha, the bohemian holy man who saw through the lies their professors had taught them, and they couldn't get enough of it.

I was deeply pissed off. My apartment had been turned into a twenty-four-hour meeting hall, and much as I would have liked to hold Doc responsible for it, I knew that he wasn't to blame. His acolytes had come of their own accord, without invitations or appointments, and once the crowds began to gather, I could no more ask him to turn them away than I could ask the sun to stop shining. Talk was what he lived for. It was his final barrier against oblivion, and because those kids were there with him now, because they sat at his feet and hung on his every word, he could temporarily delude himself into thinking that all was not lost for him. I had no problem with that. For all I cared, he could go on talking until the next century. I just didn't want him doing it in my apartment.

Torn between compassion and disgust, I came up with a coward's compromise. It happened during one of the rare lulls of that period, at a moment when no unannounced visitors were in the apartment. I told Doc that he could stay—and that I would clear out instead. I had piles of work to do, I explained, and rather than dump him on the street before he'd found another place to live, I would go to my mother's apartment in Newark and write my school papers. In exactly one week I would return, and when I came back I expected him to be gone. Doc listened carefully as I outlined this plan to him. When I had finished, I asked him if he understood. "I dig, man," he said, speaking in his calmest, most gravelly jazzman's voice, "it's cool," and that was all there was to it. We went on to talk about other things, and somewhere in the course of our conversation that night he mentioned that many years back, as a young man in Paris, he had occasionally played chess with Tristan Tzara. This is one of the few concrete facts that has stayed with me. Over time, nearly everything else I heard from the mouth of H. L. Humes has disappeared. I can remember what his voice sounded like, but very little of what he said. All those great verbal marathons, those forced marches to the hinterlands of reason, those countless hours of listening to him unravel his plots and conspiracies and secret correspondences—all that has been reduced to a blur. The words are no more than a buzzing in my brain now, an unintelligible swarm of nothingness.

The next morning, as I was packing my bag and getting ready to leave, he tried to give me money. I turned him down, but he kept insisting, peeling off fifties from his wad like some racetrack gambler, telling me to take it, that I was a good kid, that we had to "share the wealth," and in the end I caved in to the pressure and accepted three hundred dollars from him. I felt terrible about it then and still feel terrible about it now. I had wanted to stay above that business, to resist taking part in the pathetic game he was playing, and yet when my principles were finally put on the line, I succumbed to temptation and allowed greed to get the better of me. Three hundred dollars was a large sum in 1969, and the lure of that money turned out to be stronger than I was. I put the bills in my pocket, shook Doc's hand good-bye, and hurried out of the apartment. When I returned a week later, the place was neat as a pin, and there was no sign of him anywhere. Doc had left, just as he had promised he would.

I saw him only once more after that. It was about a year later, and I was riding uptown on the number 4 bus. Just as we made the turn onto 110th Street, I spotted him through the window—standing on the corner of Fifth Avenue and the northern edge of Central Park. He appeared to be in bad shape. His clothes were rumpled, he looked dirty, and his eyes had a lost, vacant expression that had not been there before. He's slipped into hard drugs, I said to myself. Then the bus moved on, and I lost sight of him. Over the next days and weeks, I kept expecting to see him again, but I never did. Twenty-five years went by, and then, just five or six months ago, I opened *The New York Times* and stumbled across a small article on the obituary page announcing that he was dead.

LITTLE BY LITTLE, I learned how to improvise, trained myself to roll with the punches. During my last two years at Columbia, I took any number of odd freelance jobs, gradually developing a taste for the kind of literary hackwork that would keep me going until I was thirty—and which ultimately led to my downfall. There was a certain romance in it, I suppose, a need to affirm myself as an outsider and prove that I could make it on my own without kowtowing to anyone else's idea of what constituted the good life. My life would be good if and only if I stuck to my guns and refused to give in. Art was holy, and to follow its call meant making any sacrifice that was demanded of you, maintaining your purity of purpose to the bitter end.

Knowing French helped. It was hardly a rarefied skill, but I was good enough at it to have some translation jobs tossed my way. Art writings, for example, and an exceptionally tedious document from the French Embassy about the reorganization of its staff that droned on for more than a hundred pages. I also tutored a high school girl one spring, traveling across town every Saturday morning to talk to her about poetry, and another time I was collared by a friend (for no pay) to stand on an outdoor podium with Jean Genet and translate his speech in defense of the Black Panthers. Genet walked around with a red flower tucked behind his ear and rarely stopped smiling the whole time he was on the Columbia campus. New York seemed to make him happy, and he handled the attention he received that day with great poise. One night not long after that, I bumped into an acquaintance in the West End, the old student watering hole at Broadway and 114th Street. He told me that he had just started working for a pornography publisher, and if I wanted to try my hand at writing a dirty book, the price was fifteen hundred dollars per novel. I was more than willing to have a go at it, but my inspiration petered out after twenty or thirty pages. There were just so many ways to describe that one thing, I discovered, and my stock of synonyms soon dried up. I started writing book reviews instead—for a shoddily put together publication aimed at students. Sensing that the magazine wasn't going to add up to much, I signed my articles with a pseudonym, just to keep things interesting. Quinn was the name I chose for myself, Paul Quinn. The pay, I remember, was twenty-five dollars per review.

When the results of the draft lottery were announced at the end of 1969, I lucked out with number 297. A blind draw of the cards saved my skin, and the nightmare I had been girding myself against for several years suddenly evaporated. Who to thank for that unexpected mercy? I had been spared immense amounts of pain and trouble, had literally been given back control of my life, and the sense of relief was incalculable. Jail was no longer in the picture for me. The horizon was clear on all sides, and I was free to walk off in any direction I chose. As long as I traveled light, there was nothing to stop me from going as far as my legs would take me.

That I wound up working on an oil tanker for several months was largely a matter of chance. You can't work on a ship without a Merchant Seaman's card, and you can't obtain a Merchant Seaman's card without a job on a ship. Unless you know someone who can break through the circle for you, it's impossible to get in. The someone who did it for me was my mother's second husband, Norman Schiff. My mother had remarried about a year after her divorce from my father, and by 1970 my stepfather and I had been fast friends for nearly five years. An excellent man with a generous heart, he had consistently stood behind me and supported my vague, impractical ambitions. His early death in 1982 (at age fifty-five) remains one of the great sorrows of my life, but back then as I was finishing up my year of graduate work and preparing to leave school, his health was still reasonably good. He practiced law, mostly as a labor negotiator, and among his many clients at the time was the Esso Seaman's Union, for which he worked as legal counsel. That was how the idea got planted in my head. I asked him if he could swing me a job on one of the Esso tankers, and he said he would handle it. And without further ado, that was precisely what he did.

There was a lot of paperwork to take care of, trips to the union hall in Belleville, New Jersey, physical exams in Manhattan, and then an indefinite period of waiting until a slot opened up on one of the ships coming into the New York area. In the meantime, I took a temporary job with the United States Census Bureau, collecting data for the 1970 census in Harlem. The work consisted of climbing up and down staircases in dimly lit tenement buildings, knocking on apartment doors, and helping people fill out the government forms. Not everyone wanted to be helped, of course, and more than a few were suspicious of the white college boy prowling around their hallways, but enough people welcomed me in to make me feel that I wasn't completely wasting my time. I stayed with it for approximately a month, and then—sooner than I was expecting—the ship called.

I happened to be sitting in a dentist's chair at that moment, about to have a wisdom tooth pulled. Every morning since my name had gone on the list, I had checked in with my stepfather to let him know where I could be reached that day, and he was the one who tracked me down at the dentist's office. The timing couldn't have been more comical. The Novocain had already been injected into my gums, and the dentist had just picked up the pliers and was about to attack my rotten tooth when the receptionist walked in and announced that I was wanted on the phone. Extremely urgent. I climbed out of the chair with the bib still tied around my neck, and the next thing I knew, Norman was telling me that I had three hours to pack and get myself aboard the S.S. *Esso Florence* in Elizabeth,

New Jersey. I stammered my apologies to the dentist and hightailed it out of there.

The tooth stayed in my mouth for another week. When it finally came out, I was in Baytown, Texas.

THE *Esso Florence* was one of the oldest tankers in the fleet, a pip-squeak relic from a bygone age. Put a two-door Chevy next to a stretch limousine, and you'll have some idea of how it compared to the supertankers they build today. Already in service during World War II, my ship had logged untold thousands of watery miles by the time I set foot on it. There were enough beds on board to accommodate a hundred men, but only thirty-three of us were needed to take care of the work that had to be done. That meant that each person had his own room—an enormous benefit when you considered how much time we had to spend together. With other jobs you get to go home at night, but we were boxed in with each other twenty-four hours a day. Every time you looked up, the same faces were there. We worked together, lived together, and ate together, and without the chance for some genuine privacy, the routine would have been intolerable.

We shuttled between the Atlantic coast and the Gulf of Mexico, loading and unloading airplane fuel at various refineries along the way: Charleston, South Carolina; Tampa, Florida; Galveston, Texas. My initial responsibilities were mopping floors and making beds, first for the crew and then for the officers. The technical term for the position was "utilityman," but in plain language the job was a combination of janitor, garbage collector, and chambermaid. I can't say that I was thrilled to be scrubbing toilets and picking up dirty socks, but once I got the hang of it, the work turned out to be incredibly easy. In less than a week, I had polished my custodial skills to such a point that it took me only two or two and a half hours to finish my chores for the day. That left me with abundant quantities of free time, most of which I spent alone in my room. I read books, I wrote, I did everything I had done before—but more productively, somehow, with better powers of concentration now that there was so little to distract me. In many ways, it felt like an almost ideal existence, a perfect life.

Then, after a month or two of this blissful regimen, I was "bumped." The ship rarely traveled more than five days between ports, and nearly everywhere we docked some crew members would get off and others would get on. The jobs for the fresh arrivals were doled out according to seniority. It was a strict pecking order, and the longer you had worked for the company, the more say you had in what you were given. As low man on the totem pole, I had no say at all. If an old-timer wanted my job, he had only to ask for it, and it was his. After my long run of good luck, the boom finally fell on me somewhere in Texas. My replacement was a man named Elmer, a bovine Fundamentalist bachelor who happened to be the longest-serving, most famous utilityman of them all. What I had been able to do in two hours, Elmer now did in six. He was the slowest of the slow, a smug and untalkative mental lightweight who waddled about the ship in a world of his own, utterly ignored by the other crew members, and in all my experience I have never met a person who ate as much as he did. Elmer could pack away mountains of food—two, three, and four helpings at every meal—but what made it fascinating to watch him was not so much the scope of his appetite as the way he went about satisfying it: daintily, fastidiously, with a compulsive sense of decorum. The best part was the cleanup operation at the end. Once Elmer had eaten his fill, he would spread his napkin on the table before him and begin patting and smoothing the flimsy paper with his hands, slowly transforming it into a flat square. Then he would fold the napkin into precise longitudinal sections, methodically halving the area until it had been divided into eighths. In the end, the square would be turned into a long, rectilinear strip with all four edges exactly aligned. At that point, Elmer would carefully take hold of the edges, raise the napkin to his lips, and begin to rub. The action was all in the head: a slow back-and-forth swiveling that went on for twenty or thirty seconds. From start to finish, Elmer's hands never stirred. They would be fixed in the air as his large head turned left, right, and left again, and through it all his eyes never betrayed the slightest thought or emotion. The Cleaning of the Lips was a dogged, mechanical procedure, an act of ritual purification. Cleanliness is next to godliness, Elmer once told me. To see him with that napkin, you understood that he was doing God's work.

I was able to observe Elmer's eating habits at such close range because I had been bumped into the galley. The job of messman quadrupled my hours and made my life altogether more eventful. My responsibilities now included serving three meals a day to the crew (about twenty men), washing dishes by hand, cleaning the mess hall, and writing out the menus for the steward, who was generally too drunk to bother with them himself. My breaks were short—no more than an hour or two between meals—and yet in spite of having to work much harder than before, my income actually shrank. On the old job, there had been plenty of time for me to put in an extra hour or two in the evenings, scraping and painting in the boiler room, for example, or refurbishing rusty spots on deck, and those volunteer jobs had padded my paycheck quite nicely. Still, in spite of the disadvantages, I found working in the mess hall more of a challenge than mopping floors had been. It was a public job, so to speak, and in addition to all the hustling around that was now required of me, I had to stay on my toes as far as the men were concerned. That, finally, was my most important task: to learn how to handle the griping and rough-tempered complaints, to fend off insults, to give as good as I got.

Elmer aside, the crew was a fairly grimy, ill-mannered bunch. Most of the men lived in Texas and Louisiana, and apart from a handful of Chicanos, one or two blacks, and the odd foreigner who cropped up now and then, the dominant tone on board was white, redneck, and blue collar. A jocular atmosphere prevailed, replete with funny stories and dirty jokes and much talk about guns and cars, but there were deep, smoldering currents of racism in many of those men, and I made a point of choosing my friends carefully. To hear one of your coworkers defend South African apartheid as you sat with him over a cup of coffee ("they know how to treat niggers down there") doesn't bring much joy to the soul, and if I found myself hanging out mostly with the dark-skinned and Spanish-speaking men around me, there was a good reason for it. As a New York Jew with a college degree, I was an entirely alien specimen on that ship, a man from Mars. It would have been easy to make up stories about myself, but I had no interest in doing that. If someone asked me what my religion was or where I came from, I told him. If he didn't like it, I figured that was his problem. I wasn't going to hide who I was or pretend to be someone else just to avoid trouble. As it happened, I had only one awkward run-in the whole time I was there. One of the men started calling me Sammy whenever I walked by. He seemed to think it was funny, but as I failed to see any humor in the epithet, I told him to stop it. He did it again the next day, and once again I told him to stop it. When he did it again the day after that, I understood that polite words were not going to be enough. I grabbed hold of his shirt, slammed him against the wall, and very calmly told him that if he ever called me that again, I would kill him. It shocked me to hear myself talk like that. I was not someone who trafficked in violence, and I had never made that kind of threat to anyone, but for that one brief instant, a demon took possession of my soul. Luckily, my willingness to fight was enough to defuse the fight before it began. My tormentor threw up his hands in a gesture of peace. "It was just a joke," he said, "just a joke," and that was the end of it. As time went on, we actually became friends.

I loved being out on the water, surrounded by nothing but sky and light, the immensity of the vacant air. Seagulls accompanied us wherever we went, circling overhead as they waited for buckets of garbage to be dumped overboard. Hour after hour, they would hover patiently just above the ship, scarcely beating their wings until the scraps went flying, at which point they would plunge frantically into the foam, calling out to each other like drunks at a football game. Few pleasures can match the spectacle of that foam, of sitting at the stern of a large ship and staring into the white, churning tumult of the wake below. There is something hypnotic about it, and on still days the sense of well-being that washes through you can be overpowering. On the other hand, rough weather also holds its charms. As summer melted away and we headed into autumn, the inclemencies multiplied, bringing down some wild winds and pelting rains, and at those moments the ship felt no more safe or solid than a child's paper boat. Tankers have been known to crack in half, and all it takes is one wrong wave to do the job. The worst stretch, I remember, occurred when we were off Cape Hatteras in late September or early October, a twelve- or fifteen-hour period of flipping and flopping through a tropical storm. The captain stayed at the wheel all night, and even after the worst of it was over and the steward instructed me to carry the captain his breakfast the next morning, I was nearly blown overboard when I stepped onto the bridge with my tray. The rain might have stopped, but the wind speed was still at gale force.

For all that, working on the *Esso Florence* had little to do with high-seas adventure. The tanker was essentially a floating factory, and rather than introduce me to some exotic, swashbuckling life, it taught me to think of myself as an industrial laborer. I was one of millions now, an insect toiling beside countless other insects, and every task I performed was part of the great, grinding enterprise of American capitalism. Petroleum was the primary source of wealth, the raw material that fueled the profit machine and kept it running, and I was glad to be where I was, grateful to have landed in the belly of the beast. The refineries where we loaded and unloaded our cargo were enormous, hellish structures, labyrinthine networks of hissing pipes and towers of flame, and to walk through one of them at night was to feel that you were living in your own worst dream. Most of all, I will never forget the fish, the hundreds of dead, iridescent fish floating on the rank, oil-saturated water around the refinery docks. That was the standard welcoming committee, the sight that greeted us every time the tugboats pulled us into another port. The ugliness was so universal, so deeply connected to the business of making money and the power that money bestowed on the ones who made it—even to the point of disfiguring the landscape, of turning the natural world inside out—that I began to develop a grudging respect for it. Get to the bottom of things, I told myself, and this was how the world looked. Whatever you might think of it, this ugliness was the truth.

Whenever we docked somewhere, I made it my business to leave the ship and spend some time ashore. I had never been south of the Mason-Dixon line, and those brief jaunts onto solid ground took me to places that felt a lot less familiar or understandable than anything I'd met up with in Paris or Dublin. The South was a different country, a separate American universe from the one I'd known in the North. Most of the time, I tagged along with one or two of my shipmates, going the rounds with them as they visited their customary haunts. If Baytown, Texas, stands out with particular clarity, that is because we spent more time there than anywhere else. I found it a sad, crumbling little place. Along the main drag, a row of once elegant movie theaters had been turned into Baptist churches, and instead of announcing the titles of the latest Hollywood films, the marquees now sported fiery quotations from the Bible. More often than not, we wound up in sailors' bars on the back streets of broken-down neighborhoods. All of them were essentially the same: squalid, low-life joints; dim drinking holes; dank corners of oblivion. Everything was always bare inside. Not a single picture on the walls, not one touch of publican warmth. At most there was a quarter-a-rack pool table, a jukebox stuffed with country-and-western songs, and a drink menu that consisted of just one drink: beer.

Once, when the ship was in a Houston dry dock for some minor repairs, I spent the afternoon in a skid row bar with a Danish oiler named Freddy, a wild man who laughed at the slightest provocation and spoke English with an accent so thick that I scarcely understood a word he said. Walking down the street in the blinding Texas sun, we crossed paths with a drunken couple. It was still early in the day, but this man and woman were already so soused, so entrenched in their inebriation, they must have been going at the booze since dawn. They wobbled along the sidewalk with their arms around each other, listing this way and that, their heads lolling, their knees buckling, and yet both with enough energy left to be engaged in a nasty, foul-mouthed quarrel. From the sound of their voices, I gathered they'd been at it for years—a pair of bickering stumblebums in search of their next drink, forever repeating the same lines to each other, forever shuffling through the same old song and dance. As it turned out, they wound up in the same bar where Freddy and I chose to while away the afternoon, and because I was not more than ten feet away from them, I was in a perfect position to observe the following little drama:

The man leaned forward and barked out at the woman across the table. "Darlene," he said, in a drawling, besotted voice, "get me another beer."

Darlene had been nodding off just then, and it took her a good long moment to open her eyes and bring the man into focus. Another long moment ticked by, and then she finally said, "What?"

"Get me a beer," the man repeated. "On the double."

Darlene was waking up now, and a lovely, fuck-you sassiness suddenly brightened her face. She was clearly in no mood to be pushed around. "Get it yourself, Charlie," she snapped back at him. "I ain't your slave, you know."

"Damn it, woman," Charlie said. "You're my wife, ain't you? What the hell did I marry you for? Get me the goddamn beer!"

Darlene let out a loud, histrionic sigh. You could tell she was up to something, but her intentions were still obscure. "Okay, darling," she said, putting on the voice of a meek, simpering wife, "I'll get it for you," and then stood up from the table and staggered over to the bar.

Charlie sat there with a grin on his face, gloating over his small, manly victory. He was the boss, all right, and no one was going to tell him different. If you wanted to know who wore the pants in that family, just talk to him.

A minute later, Darlene returned to the table with a fresh bottle of Bud. "Here's your beer, Charlie," she said, and then, with one quick flick of the wrist, proceeded to dump the contents of the bottle onto her husband's head. Bubbles foamed up in his hair and eyebrows; rivulets of amber liquid streamed down his face. Charlie made a lunge for her, but he was too drunk to get very close. Darlene threw her head back and burst out laughing. "How do you like your beer, Charlie?" she said. "How do you like your fucking beer?"

Of all the scenes I witnessed in those bars, nothing quite matched the bleak comedy of Charlie's baptism, but for overall oddness, a plunge into the deepest heart of the grotesque, I would have to single out Big Mary's Place in Tampa, Florida. This was a large, brightly lit emporium that catered to the whims of dockhands and sailors, and it had been in business for many years. Among its features were half a dozen pool tables, a long mahogany bar, inordinately high ceilings, and live entertainment in the form of quasi-naked go-go dancers. These girls were the cornerstone of the operation, the element that set Big Mary's Place apart from other establishments of its kind—and one look told you that they weren't hired for their beauty, nor for their ability to dance. The sole criterion was size. The bigger the better was how Big Mary put it, and the bigger you got, the more money you were paid. The effect was quite disturbing. It was a freak show of flesh, a cavalcade of bouncing white blubber, and with four girls dancing on the platform behind the bar at once, the act resembled a casting call for the lead role in *Moby-Dick.* Each girl was a continent unto herself, a mass of quivering lard decked out in a string bikini, and as one shift replaced another, the assault on the eyes was unrelenting. I have no memory of how I got there, but I distinctly recall that my companions that night were two of the gentler souls from the ship (Martinez, a family man from Texas, and Donnie, a seventeen-year-old boy from Baton Rouge) and that they were both just as flummoxed as I was. I can still see them sitting across from me with their mouths hanging open, doing everything they could not to laugh from embarrassment. At one point, Big Mary herself came over and sat down with us at our table. A splendid dirigible of a woman dressed in an orange pants suit and wearing a ring on every finger, she wanted to know if we were having a good time. When we assured her that we were, she waved to one of the girls at the bar. "Barbara," she yelled, belting out the word in a brassy, three-pack-a-day voice, "get your fat butt over here!" Barbara came, all smiles and good humor, laughing as Big Mary poked her in the stomach and pinched the ample rolls bulging from her hips. "She was a scrawny one at first," Mary explained, "but I've fattened her up pretty good. Ain't that so, Barbara?" she said, cackling like some mad scientist who's just pulled off a successful experiment, and Barbara couldn't have agreed with her more. As I listened to them talk, it suddenly occurred to me that I had it all wrong. I hadn't gone to sea. I'd run off and joined the circus.

Another friend was Jeffrey, the second cook (a.k.a. breakfast chef), from Bogalusa, Louisiana. We happened to have been born on the same day, and apart from the near-infant Donnie, we were the youngest members of the crew. It was the first time out for both of us, and since we worked together in the galley, we got to know each other reasonably well. Jeffrey was one of life's winners—a bright, handsome, fun-loving ladies' man with a taste for flashy clothes—and yet very practical and ambitious, a down-to-earth schemer who was quite consciously using his job on the ship to learn the ins and outs of cooking. He had no intention of making a career out of oil tankers, no desire to turn himself into an old salt. His dream was to become a chef in a high-class restaurant, maybe even to own that restaurant himself, and if nothing unexpected rose up to stop him, I don't doubt that that's exactly what he's doing today. We couldn't have been more unlike, Jeffrey and I, but we got along comfortably with each other. It was only natural that we should sometimes go ashore together when the ship was in port, but because Jeffrey was black, and because he had spent his whole life in the South, he knew that many of the places I went to with white crew members were off-limits to him. He made that perfectly clear to me the first time we planned an outing. "If you want me to go with you," he said, "you'll have to go where I can go." I tried to convince him that he could go anywhere he pleased, but Jeffrey wasn't buying the argument. "Maybe up North," he said. "Down here it's different." I didn't force the issue. When I went out for beers with Jeffrey, we drank them in black bars instead of white bars. Except for the skin color of the clientele, the atmosphere was the same.

One night in Houston, Jeffrey talked me into going to a dance club with him. I never danced and never went to clubs, but the thought of spending a few hours in a place that wasn't a low-rent dive tempted me, and I decided to take my chances. The club turned out to be a splashy disco hall thronged with hundreds of young people, the hottest black nightspot in town. There was a live band onstage, psychedelic strobe lights bouncing off the walls, hard liquor available at the bar. Everything pulsed with sex and chaos and loud music. It was Saturday night fever, Texas style.

Jeffrey was dressed to the teeth, and within four minutes he struck up a conversation with one of the many stunning girls floating around the bar, and four minutes after that they were out on the dance floor together, lost in an ocean of bodies. I sat down at a table and sipped my drink, the only white person in the building. No one gave me any trouble, but I got some odd, penetrating looks from a number of people, and by the time I finished my bourbon, I understood that I should be shoving off. I phoned for a cab and then went outside to wait in the parking lot. When the driver showed up a few minutes later, he started cursing. "Goddammit," he said. "Goddammit to hell. If I'd known you were calling from here, I wouldn't have come." "Why not?" I said. "Because this is the worst fucking place in Houston," he said. "They've had six murders here in the past month. Every damn weekend, somebody else gets shot."

In the end, the months I spent on that ship felt like years. Time passes in a different way when you're out on the water, and given that the bulk of what I experienced was utterly new to me, and given that I was constantly on my guard because of that, I managed to crowd an astonishing number of impressions and memories into a relatively small sliver of my life. Even now, I don't fully understand what I was hoping to prove by shipping out like that. To keep myself off balance, I suppose. Or, very simply, just to see if I could do it, to see if I could hold my own in a world I didn't belong to. In that respect, I don't think I failed. I can't say what I accomplished during those months, but at the same time I'm certain I didn't fail.

I received my discharge papers in Charleston. The company

provided airfare home, but you could pocket the money if you wanted to and make your own travel arrangements. I chose to keep the money. The trip by milk train took twenty-four hours, and I rode back with a fellow crew member from New York, Juan Castillo. Juan was in his late forties or early fifties, a squat, lumpy man with a big head and a face that looked like something pieced together with the skins and pulps of nineteen mashed potatoes. He had just walked off an oil tanker for the last time, and in appreciation of his twenty-five years of service to the company, Esso had given him a gold watch. I don't know how many times Juan pulled that watch out of his pocket and looked at it during the long ride home, but every time he did, he would shake his head for a few seconds and then burst out laughing. At one point, the ticket collector stopped to talk to us during one of his strolls down the aisle of the car. He looked very natty in his uniform, I remember, a black Southern gentleman of the old school. In a haughty, somewhat condescending manner, he opened the conversation by asking: "You boys going up North to work in the steel mills?"

We must have been a curious pair, Juan and I. I recall that I was wearing a beat-up leather jacket at the time, but other than that I can't see myself, have no sense of what I looked like or what other people saw when they looked at me. The ticket collector's question is the only clue I have. Juan had taken pictures of his shipmates to put in the family album at home, and I remember standing on the deck and looking into the camera for him as he clicked the shutter. He promised to send me a copy of the photo, but he never did.

I TOYED WITH THE idea of going out for another run on an Esso tanker, but in the end I decided against it. My salary was still being sent to me through the mail (for every two days I'd been on the ship, I received one day's pay on land), and my bank account was beginning to look fairly robust. For the past few months, I had been slowly coming to the conclusion that my next step should be to leave the country and live abroad for a while. I was willing to ship out again if necessary, but I wondered if I hadn't built up a large enough stake already. The three or four thousand dollars I'd earned from the tanker struck me as a sufficient sum to get started with, and so rather than continue in the merchant marine, I abruptly shifted course and began plotting a move to Paris.

France was a logical choice, but I don't think I went there for logical reasons. That I spoke French, that I had been translating French poetry, that I knew and cared about a number of people who lived in France—surely those things entered into my decision, but they were not determining factors. What made me want to go, I think, was the memory of what had happened to me in Paris three years earlier. I still hadn't gotten it out of my system, and because that visit had been cut short, because I had left on the assumption that I would soon be returning, I had walked around with a feeling of unfinished business, of not having had my fill. The only thing I wanted just then was to hunker down and write. By recapturing the inwardness and freedom of that earlier time, I felt that I would be putting myself in the best possible position to do that. I had no intention of becoming an expatriate. Giving up America was not part of the plan, and at no time did I think I wouldn't return. I just needed a little breathing room, a chance to figure out, once and for all, if I was truly the person I thought I was.

What comes back to me most vividly from my last weeks in New York is the farewell conversation I had with Joe Reilly, a homeless man who used to hang around the lobby of my apartment building on West 107th Street. The building was a run-down, nine-story affair, and like most places on the Upper West Side, it housed a motley collection of people. With no effort at all, I can summon forth a fair number of them, even after a quarter of a century. The Puerto Rican mailman, for example, and the Chinese waiter, and the fat blonde opera singer with the Lhasa apso. Not to mention the black homosexual fashion designer with his black fur coat and the quarreling clarinetists whose vicious spats would seep through the walls of my apartment and poison my nights. On the ground floor of this gray brick building, one of the apartments had been divided down the middle, and each half was occupied by a man confined to a wheelchair. One of them worked at the news kiosk on the corner of Broadway and 110th Street; the other was a retired rabbi. The rabbi was a particularly charming fellow, with a pointy artist's goatee and an ever-present black beret, which he wore at a rakish, debonair angle. On most days, he would wheel himself out of his apartment and spend some time in the lobby, chatting with Arthur, the superintendent, or with various tenants getting in and out of the elevator. Once, as I entered the building, I caught sight of him through the glass door in his usual spot, talking to a bum in a long, dark overcoat. It struck me as an odd conjunction, but from the way the bum stood there and from the tilt of the rabbi's head, it was clear that they knew each other well. The bum was an authentic down-and-outer, a scab-faced wino with filthy clothes and cuts dotting his half-bald scalp, a scrofulous wreck of a man who appeared to have just crawled out of a storm drain. Then, as I pushed open the door and stepped into the lobby, I heard him speak. Accompanied by wild, theatrical gestures—a sweep of the left arm, a finger darting from his right hand and pointing to the sky—a sentence came booming out of him, a string of words so unlikely and unexpected that at first I didn't believe my ears. "It was no mere fly-by-night acquaintance!" he said, rolling each syllable of that florid, literary phrase off his tongue with such relish, such blowhard bravura, such magnificent pomposity, that he sounded like some tragic ham delivering a line from a Victorian melodrama. It was pure W. C. Fields—but several octaves lower, with the voice more firmly in control of the effects it was striving to create. W. C. Fields mixed with Ralph Richardson, perhaps, with a touch of barroom bombast thrown in for good measure. However you wanted to define it, I had never heard a voice do what that voice did.

When I walked over to say hello to the rabbi, he introduced me to his friend, and that was how I learned the name of that singular gentleman, that mightiest of fallen characters, the one and only Joe Reilly.

According to the rabbi, who filled me in on the story later, Joe had started out in life as the privileged son of a wealthy New York family, and in his prime he had owned an art gallery on Madison Avenue. That was when the rabbi had met him—back in the old days, before Joe's disintegration and collapse. The rabbi had already left the pulpit by then and was running a music publishing company. Joe's male lover was a composer, and as the rabbi happened to publish that man's work, in the natural course of things he and Joe crossed paths. Then, very suddenly, the lover died. Joe had always had a drinking problem, the rabbi said, but now he hit the bottle in earnest, and his life began to fall apart. He lost his gallery; his family turned its back on him; his friends walked away. Little by little, he sank into the gutter, the last hole at the bottom of the world, and in the rabbi's opinion he would never climb out again. As far as he was concerned, Joe was a hopeless case.

Whenever Joe came around after that, I would dig into my pocket and hand him a few coins. What moved me about these encounters was that he never let his mask drop. Blustering forth his thanks in the highly embroidered, Dickensian language that came so effortlessly to him, he would assure me that I would be paid back promptly, just as soon as circumstances allowed. "I am most grateful to you for this bounty, young man," he would say, "most grateful indeed. It's just a loan, of course, so you needn't fret about being reimbursed. As you might or might not know, I've suffered some small setbacks lately, and this generosity of yours will go a long way towards helping me back to my feet." The sums in question were never more than a pittance—forty cents here, twenty-five cents there, whatever I happened to be carrying around with me—but Joe never flagged in his enthusiasm, never once let on that he realized what an abject figure he was. There he stood, dressed in a circus clown's rags, his unwashed body emitting the foulest of stinks, and still he persisted in keeping up his pose as a man of the world, a dandy temporarily down on his luck. The pride and self-deception that went into this act were both comical and heartbreaking, and every time I went through the ritual of giving him another handout, I had trouble keeping my balance. I never knew whether to laugh or cry, whether to admire him or shower him with pity. "Let me see, young man," he would continue, studying the coins I had just put in his palm. "I have, let's see, I have here in my hand, hmmm, fifty-five cents. Add that to the eighty cents you gave me that last time, and then add that, hmmm, add that to the forty cents you gave me the time before that, and it turns out that I owe you a grand total of, hmmm, let's see, a grand total of . . . one dollar and fifteen cents." Such was Joe's arithmetic. He just plucked figures out of thin air and hoped they sounded good. "No problem, Joe," I would say. "A dollar and fifteen cents. You'll give it to me the next time."

When I came back to New York from the Esso ship, he seemed to be floundering, to have lost some ground. He looked more bruised to me, and the old panache had given way to a new heaviness of spirit, a whining, tearful sort of despair. One afternoon, he broke down in front of me as he recounted how he had been beaten up in some alleyway the night before. "They stole my books," he said. "Can you imagine that? The animals stole my books!" Another time, in the middle of a snowstorm, as I left my ninth-floor apartment and walked to the elevator down the hall, I found him sitting alone on the staircase, his head buried in his hands.

"Joe," I said, "are you all right?"

He lifted his head. His eyes were infused with sorrow, misery, and defeat. "No, young man," he said. "I'm not all right, not the least bit all right."

"Is there anything I can do for you?" I asked. "You look terrible, just terrible."

"Yes," he said, "now that you mention it, there is one thing you can do for me," and at that point he suddenly reached out and took hold of my hand. Then, looking me straight in the eye, he gathered up his strength and said, in a voice trembling with emotion, "You can take me back into your apartment, lie down on the bed, and let me make love to you."

The bluntness of his request took me completely by surprise. I had been thinking more along the lines of a cup of coffee or a bowl of soup. "I can't do that," I said. "I like women, Joe, not men. Sorry, but I don't do that kind of thing."

What he said next lingers in my mind as one of the best and most pungent statements I have ever heard. Without wasting a second, and without the slightest trace of disappointment or regret, he dismissed my answer with a shrug of the shoulders and said, in a buoyant, ringing tone of voice, "Well, you asked me—and I told you."

I left for Paris some time in the middle of February 1971. After that encounter on the staircase, I didn't see Joe again for several weeks. Then, just days before my departure, I bumped into him on Broadway. He was looking much better, and the hangdog look had disappeared from his face. When I told him I was about to move to Paris, he was off and running again, as effusive and full of himself as ever. "It's odd that you should mention Paris," he said. "Indeed, it's a most timely coincidence. Not two or three days ago, I happened to be walking down Fifth Avenue, and who should I bump into but my old friend Antoine, director of the Cunard Lines. 'Joe,' he said to me, 'Joe, you're not looking too well,' and I said, 'No, Antoine, it's true, I haven't been at my best lately,' and Antoine said that he wanted to do something for me, lend a helping hand, so to speak, and put me back on track. What he proposed, right there on Fifth Avenue the other day, was to sail me over to Paris on one of his ships and put me up at the Hôtel Georges V. All expenses paid, of course, with a new wardrobe thrown into the bargain. He said I could stay there as long as I liked. Two weeks, two months, even two years if I wanted. If I decide to go, which I think I will, I'll be leaving before the end of the month. Which means, young man, that we'll be in Paris at the same time. A pleasant prospect, no? Expect to see me there. We'll have tea, dinner. Just leave a message for me at the hotel. On the Champs-Elysées. That's where we'll meet next, my friend. In Paris, on the Champs-Elysées." And then, bidding me farewell, he shook my hand and wished me a safe and happy voyage.

I never saw Joe Reilly again. Even before we said good-bye

that day, I knew that I was talking to him for the last time, and when he finally disappeared into the crowd a few minutes later, it was as if he had already turned into a ghost. All during the years I lived in Paris, I thought of him every time I set foot on the Champs-Elysées. Even now, whenever I go back there, I still do.

MY MONEY DIDN'T last as long as I thought it would. I found an apartment within a week of my arrival, and once I had shelled out for the agency commission, the security deposit, the gas and electric service, the first month's rent, the last month's rent, and the state-mandated insurance policy, I didn't have much left. Right from the start, therefore, I had to scramble to keep my head above water. In the three and a half years I lived in France, I had any number of jobs, bounced from one part-time gig to another, freelanced until I was blue in the face. When I didn't have work, I was looking for work. When I had work, I was thinking about how to find more. Even at the best of times, I rarely earned enough to feel secure, and yet in spite of one or two close calls, I managed to avoid total ruin. It was, as they say, a hand-to-mouth existence. Through it all, I wrote steadily, and if much of what I wrote was discarded (mostly prose), a fair chunk of it (mostly poems and translations) was not. For better or worse, by the time I returned to New York in July 1974, the idea of not writing was inconceivable to me.

Most of the work I landed came through friends or the friends of friends or the friends of friends of friends. Living in a foreign country restricts your opportunities, and unless you know some people who are willing to help you, it is next to impossible to get started. Not only will doors not open when you knock on them, but you won't even know where to look for those doors in the first place. I was lucky enough to have some allies, and at one time or another they all moved small mountains on my behalf. Jacques Dupin, for example, a poet whose work I had been translating for several years, turned out to be director of publications at the Galerie Maeght, one of the leading art galleries in Europe. Among the painters and sculptors shown there were Miró, Giacometti, Chagall, and Calder, to mention just a few. Through Jacques's intervention, I was hired to translate several art books and catalogues, and by my second year in Paris, when my funds were perilously close to bottoming out, he saved the situation by giving me a room to live in—free of charge. These acts of kindness were essential, and I can't imagine how I would have survived without them.

At one point, I was steered to the Paris bureau of *The New York Times.* I can't remember who was responsible for the connection, but an editor named Josette Lazar began throwing translations my way whenever she could: articles for the Sunday *Book Review,* op-ed pieces by Sartre and Foucault, this and that. One summer, when my money was at low ebb again, she finagled a position for me as the nighttime switchboard operator at the *Times* office. The phone didn't ring very often, and mostly I just sat at a desk, working on poems or reading books. One night, however, there was a frantic call from a reporter stationed somewhere in Europe. "Sinyavsky's defected," she said. "What should I do?" I had no idea what she should do, but since none of the editors was around at that hour, I figured I had to tell her something. "Follow the story," I said. "Go where you have to go, do what you have to do, but stick with the story, come hell or high water." She thanked me profusely for the advice and then hung up.

Some jobs started out as one thing and ended up as another,

like a botched stew you can't stop tinkering with. Just stir in some additional ingredients and see if it doesn't taste better. A good example would be my little adventure among the North Vietnamese in Paris, which began with an innocent phone call from Mary McCarthy to my friend André du Bouchet. She asked him if he knew of anyone who could translate poetry from French into English, and when he gave her my name, she called and invited me to her apartment to discuss the project. It was early 1973, and the war in Vietnam was still dragging on. Mary McCarthy had been writing about the war for several years, and I had read most of her articles, which I found to be among the best pieces of journalism published at the time. In the course of her work, she had come in contact with many Vietnamese from both the northern and southern halves of the country. One of them, a professor of literature, was putting together an anthology of Vietnamese poetry, and she had offered to help arrange for an English-language version to be published in America. The poems had already been translated into French, and the idea was to translate those translations into English. That was how my name had come up, and that was why she wanted to talk to me.

In her private life, Mary McCarthy was Mrs. West. Her husband was a well-to-do American businessman, and their Paris apartment was a large, richly appointed place filled with art objects, antiques, and fine furniture. Lunch was served to us by a maid in a black and white uniform. A china bell sat on the table next to my hostess's right hand, and every time she picked it up and gave it a little shake, the maid would return to the dining room to receive further instructions. There was an impressive, *grande dame* quality to the way Mary McCarthy handled these domestic protocols, but the truth was that she turned out to be everything I had hoped she would be: sharp-witted, friendly, unpretentious. We talked about many things that afternoon, and by the time I left her apartment several hours later, I was loaded down with six or seven books of Vietnamese poetry. The first step was for me to familiarize myself with their contents. After that, the professor and I would meet and get down to work on the anthology.

I read the books and enjoyed them, particularly *The Book of Kieu,* the national epic poem. The details escape me now, but I remember becoming interested in some of the formal problems presented by traditional Vietnamese verse structures, which have no equivalents in Western poetry. I was happy to have been offered the job. Not only was I going to be paid well, but it looked as if I might learn something into the bargain. A week or so after our lunch, however, Mary McCarthy called to tell me that there had been an emergency, and her professor friend had gone back to Hanoi. She wasn't sure when he would be returning to Paris, but for the time being at least, the project had been put on hold.

Such were the breaks. I pushed the books aside and hoped the job wasn't dead, even though I knew it was. Several days went by, and then, out of the blue, I received a telephone call from a Vietnamese woman living in Paris. "Professor So-and-so gave us your name," she said. "He told us you can translate into English. Is that true?" "Yes," I said, "it's true." "Good," she said. "We have a job for you."

The job turned out to be a translation of the new North Vietnamese constitution. I had no qualms about doing the work, but I found it strange that they should have come to me. You would think that a document of that sort would be translated by someone in the government—directly from Vietnamese into English, and not from French, and if from French, not by an enemy American living in Paris. I didn't ask any questions, however. I still had my fingers crossed about the anthology and didn't want to ruin my chances, so I accepted the job. The following evening, the woman came to my apartment to drop off the manuscript. She was a biologist in her mid-thirties—thin, unadorned, exceptionally reserved in her manner. She didn't say anything about a fee for the work, and from her silence I gathered that there wasn't going to be one. Given the tangled political nuances of the situation (the war between our two countries, my feelings about that war, and so on), I was hardly disposed to press her about money. Instead, I began asking her questions about the Vietnamese poems I had been reading. At one point, I got her to sit down at my desk with me and draw a diagram that explained the traditional verse forms that had piqued my curiosity. Her sketch proved to be very helpful, but when I asked her if I could keep it for future reference, she shook her head, crumpled up the paper, and put it in her pocket. I was so startled, I didn't say a word. In that one small gesture, an entire world had been revealed to me, an underground universe of fear and betrayal in which even a scrap of paper was suspect. Trust no one; cover your tracks; destroy the evidence. It wasn't that she was afraid of what I might do with the diagram. She was simply acting out of habit, and I couldn't help feeling sorry for her, sorry for both of us. It meant that the war was everywhere, that the war had tainted everything.

The constitution was eight or ten pages long, and apart from some standard Marxist-Leninist phrases ("running dogs of imperialism," "bourgeois lackeys"), it was pretty dry stuff. I did the translation the next day, and when I called my biologist friend to tell her that the work was finished, she sounded inordinately pleased and grateful. It was only then that she told me about my payment: an invitation to dinner. "By way of thanks," as she put it. The restaurant happened to be in the Fifth Arrondissement, not far from where I lived, and I had eaten there several times before. It was the simplest and cheapest Vietnamese restaurant in Paris, but also the best. The only ornament in the place was a black-and-white photograph of Ho Chi Minh hanging on the wall.

Other jobs were entirely straightforward, the essence of simplicity: tutoring a high school boy in English, serving as simultaneous translator at a small international conference of Jewish scholars (dinner included), translating material by and about Giacometti for the art critic David Sylvester. Few of these jobs paid well, but they all brought in something, and if I didn't always have great stocks of food in my refrigerator, I was rarely without a pack of cigarettes in my pocket. Still, I couldn't have sustained myself on odds and ends alone. They helped to keep me going, but add them all together, and they wouldn't have been enough to live on for more than a few weeks, a few months at most. I needed another source of income to pay the bills, and as luck would have it, I found one. To put it more accurately, it found me. For the first two years I spent in Paris, it was the difference between eating and not eating.

The story goes back to 1967. During my earlier stay as a student, an American friend had introduced me to a woman I will call Madame X. Her husband, Monsieur X, was a well-known film producer of the old style (epics, extravaganzas, a maker of deals), and it was through her that I started working for him. The first opportunity arose just a few months after I arrived. There was no telephone in the apartment I had rented, which was still the case with many Paris apartments in 1971, and there were only two ways of contacting me: by *pneumatique,* a rapid intracity telegram sent through the post office, or by coming to the apartment and knocking on the door. One morning, not long after I had woken up, Madame X knocked on the door. "How would you like to earn a hundred dollars today?" she said. The job seemed simple enough: read a movie script, then write out a six- or seven-page summary. The only constraint was time. A potential backer of the film was waiting on a yacht somewhere in the Mediterranean, and the outline had to be delivered to him within forty-eight hours.

Madame X was a flamboyant, stormy character, the first larger-than-life woman I had ever met. Mexican by birth, married since the age of eighteen or nineteen, the mother of a boy just a few years younger than I was, she lived her own independent life, drifting in and out of her husband's orbit in ways I was still too unsophisticated to understand. Artistic by temperament, she dabbled by turns at painting and writing, showing talent in both fields but with too little discipline or concentration to take those talents very far. Her true gift was encouraging others, and she surrounded herself with artists and would-be artists of all ages, hobnobbing with the known and the unknown as both a colleague and a patroness. Wherever she went, she was the center of attention, the gorgeous, soulful woman with the long black hair and the hooded cloaks and the clattering Mexican jewelry—moody, generous, loyal, her head full of dreams. Somehow or other, I had made it onto her list, and because I was young and just starting out, she counted me among those friends who needed looking after, the poor and struggling ones who required an occasional helping hand.

There were others too, of course, and a couple of them were invited along with me that morning to earn the same round figure that I had been promised. A hundred dollars sounds like pocket change today, but back then it represented more than half a month's rent, and I was in no position to turn down a sum of that magnitude. The work was to be done at the X's' apartment, an immense, palatial establishment in the Sixteenth Arrondissement with untold numbers of high-ceilinged rooms. The starting time was set for eleven o'clock, and I showed up with half an hour to spare.

I had met each of my coworkers before. One of them was an American in his mid-twenties, a fey unemployed pianist who walked around in women's high heels and had recently spent time in a hospital with a collapsed lung. The other was a Frenchman with decades of film experience, mostly as a second-unit director. Among his credits were the chariot scenes in *Ben-Hur* and the desert scenes in *Lawrence of Arabia,* but since those days of wealth and success, he had fallen on hard times: nervous breakdowns, periods of confinement in mental wards, no work. He and the pianist were major reclamation projects for Madame X, and throwing me together with them was just one example of how she operated. No matter how good her intentions were, they were invariably undermined by complex, impractical schemes, a desire to kill too many birds with a single stone. Rescuing one person is hard enough, but to think you can save the whole world at once is to ask for disappointment.

So there we were, the most mismatched trio ever assembled, gathered around the gigantic table in the dining room of the X's' gigantic apartment. The script in question was also gigantic. A work of nearly three hundred pages (three times the length of the normal script), it looked like the telephone book of a large city. Because the Frenchman was the only one with any professional knowledge of the movies, the pianist and I deferred to him and allowed him to take charge of the discussion. The first thing he did was pull out a sheet of blank paper and begin jotting down the names of actors. Frank Sinatra, Dean Martin, Sammy Davis, Jr., followed by six or seven others. When he was finished, he slapped his hands on the table with great satisfaction. "You see this piece of paper?" he asked. The pianist and I nodded our heads. "Believe it or not, this little piece of paper is worth ten million dollars." He patted the list once or twice and then pushed it aside. "Ten, maybe twelve million dollars." He spoke with the utmost conviction, betraying not the slightest hint of humor or irony. After a brief pause, he opened the manuscript to the first page. "Well," he said, "are we ready to begin?"

Almost immediately, he became excited. On the second or third line of the first page, he noticed that the name of one of the characters began with the letter Z. "Aha!" he said. "Z. This is very important. Pay close attention, my friends. This is going to be a political film. Mark my words."

Z was the title of a film by Costa-Gavras, a popular hit two years earlier. That film had most assuredly been about politics, but the screenplay we had been asked to summarize was not. It was an action thriller about smuggling. Largely set in the Sahara Desert, it featured trucks, motorcycles, several gangs of warring bad guys, and a number of spectacular explosions. The only thing that set it apart from a thousand other movies was its length.

We had been at work for approximately a minute and a half, and already the pianist had lost interest. He stared down at the table and snickered to himself as the Frenchman rambled on, lurching from one bit of nonsense to another. Suddenly, without any transition or preamble, the poor man started talking about David Lean, recalling several philosophical discussions he'd had with the director fifteen years earlier. Then, just as abruptly, he broke off from his reminiscences, stood up from the table, and walked around the room, straightening the pictures on the walls. When he was finished with that task, he announced that he was going to the kitchen to look for a cup of coffee. The pianist shrugged. "I think I'll go play the piano," he said, and just like that, he was gone as well.

As I waited for them to return, I started reading the script. I couldn't think of anything else to do, and by the time it dawned on me that neither one of them would be coming back, I had worked my way through most of it. Eventually, one of Monsieur X's associates drifted into the room. He was a youngish, good-natured American who also happened to be Madame X's special friend (the complexities of the household were fathomless), and he instructed me to finish the job on my own, guaranteeing that if I managed to produce an acceptable piece of work by seven o'clock, all three of the hundred-dollar payments would be mine. I told him I would do my best. Before I hustled out of there and went home to my typewriter, he gave me an excellent bit of advice. "Just remember," he said. "This is the movies, not Shakespeare. Make it as vulgar as you can."

I wound up writing the synopsis in the extravagant, overheated language of Hollywood coming attractions. If they wanted vulgar, I would give them vulgar. I had sat through enough movie trailers to know what they sounded like, and by dredging up every hackneyed phrase I could think of, by piling one excess on top of another, I boiled the story down to seven pages of frantic, nonstop action, a bloodbath wrought in pulsing, Technicolor prose. I finished typing at six-thirty. An hour later, a chauffeur-driven car arrived downstairs to take me and my girlfriend to the restaurant where Madame and Monsieur X had invited us for dinner. The moment we got there, I was supposed to deliver the pages to him in person.

Monsieur X was a small, enigmatic man in his mid to late fifties. Of Russian-Jewish origin, he spoke several languages with equal fluency, often shifting from French to English to Spanish in the course of a single conversation, but always with the same cumbersome accent, as if in the end he didn't feel at home in any of them. He had been producing movies for over thirty years, and in a career of countless ups and downs, he had backed good films and bad films, big films and small films, art films and trash films. Some had made piles of money for him, others had put him miserably in debt. I had crossed paths with him only a few times before that night, but he had always struck me as a lugubrious person, a man who played things close to the vest—shrewd, hidden, unknowable. Even as he talked to you, you sensed that he was thinking about something else, working out some mysterious calculations that might or might not have had anything to do with what he was saying. It's not that they didn't, but at the same time it would have been wrong to assume that they did.

That night in the restaurant, he was noticeably edgy when I arrived. A potentially lucrative deal hinged on the work of one of his wife's arty friends, and he was anything but optimistic. I had barely settled into my seat when he asked to see the pages I had written. As the rest of us made small talk around the table, Monsieur X sat hunched in silence, reading through my florid, slam-bang paragraphs. Little by little, a smile began to form on his lips. He started nodding to himself as he turned the pages, and once or twice he was even heard to mutter the word "good" under his breath. He didn't look up, however. Not until he'd come to the last sentence did he finally raise his head and give me the verdict.

"Excellent," he said. "This is just what I wanted." The relief in his voice was almost palpable.

Madame X said something about how she'd told him so, and he confessed that he'd had his doubts. "I thought it would be too literary," he said. "But this is good. This is just right."

He became very effusive after that. We were in a large, gaudy restaurant in Montmartre, and he immediately started snapping his fingers for the flower girl. She came scurrying over to our table, and Monsieur X bought a dozen roses, which he handed to my girlfriend as an impromptu gift. Then he reached into his breast pocket, pulled out his checkbook, and wrote me a check for three hundred dollars. It was the first check I had ever seen from a Swiss bank.

I was glad to have delivered the goods under pressure, glad to have earned my three hundred bucks, glad to have been roped into the absurd events of that day, but once we left the restaurant and I returned to my apartment on the rue Jacques Mawas, I assumed that the story was over. It never once crossed my mind that Monsieur X might have further plans for me. One afternoon the following week, however, as I sat at my table working on a poem, I was interrupted by a loud knock on the door. It was one of Monsieur X's gofers, an elderly gentleman I'd seen lurking about the house on my visits there but had never had the pleasure of talking to. He wasted no time in getting to the point. Are you Paul Auster? he asked. When I told him I was, he informed me that Monsieur X wanted to see me. When? I asked. Right now, he said. There's a taxi waiting downstairs.

It was a little like being arrested by the secret police. I suppose I could have refused the invitation, but the cloak-and-dagger atmosphere made me curious, and I decided to go along to see what was up. In the cab, I asked my chaperon why I had been summoned like this, but the old man merely shrugged. Monsieur X had told him to bring me back to the house, and that was what he was doing. His job was to follow orders, not ask questions. I therefore remained in the dark, and as I mulled over the question myself, the only answer I could think of was that Monsieur X was no longer satisfied with the work I had done for him. By the time I walked into his apartment, I was fully expecting him to ask me for the money back.

He was dressed in a paisley smoking jacket with satin lapels, and as he entered the room where I'd been told to wait for him, I noticed that he was rubbing his hands together. I had no idea what that gesture meant.

"Last week," he said, "you do good works for me. Now I want to make package deal."

That explained the hands. It was the gesture of a man ready to do business, and all of a sudden, on the strength of that dashed-off, tongue-in-cheek manuscript I'd concocted for him the other day, it looked as though I was about to be in business with Monsieur X. He had at least two jobs for me right away, and if all went well with those, the implication was that others would follow. I needed the money and accepted, but not without a certain wariness. I was stepping into a realm I didn't understand, and unless I kept my wits about me, I realized that strange things could be in store for me. I don't know how or why I knew that, but I did. When Monsieur X started talking about giving me a role in one of his upcoming movies, a swashbuckling adventure story for which I would need fencing and riding lessons, I held my ground. "We'll see," I said. "The fact is, I'm not much interested in acting."

Apparently, the man on the yacht had liked my synopsis just as much as Monsieur X had. Now he wanted to take things to the next level and was commissioning a translation of the screenplay from French into English. That was the first job. The second job was somewhat less cut-and-dried. Madame

X was at work on a play, Monsieur X told me, and he had agreed to finance a production at the Round House Theatre in London next season. The piece was about Quetzalcoatl, the mythical plumed serpent, and since much of it was written in verse, and since much of that verse was written in Spanish, he wanted me to turn it into English and make sure that the drama was in playable shape. Fine, I said, and that was how we left it. I did both jobs, everyone was satisfied, and two or three months later, Madame X's play was performed in London. It was a vanity production, of course, but the reviews were good, and all in all the play was quite well received. A British publisher happened to attend one of the performances, and he was so impressed by what he'd seen that he proposed to Madame X that she turn the play into a prose narrative, which he would then publish as a book.

That was where things started getting sticky between me and Monsieur X. Madame X didn't have it in her to write the book on her own, and he believed that I was the one person on earth capable of helping her. I might have accepted the job under different circumstances, but since he also wanted me to go to Mexico to do the work, I told him I wasn't interested. Why the book had to be written in Mexico was never made clear to me. Research, local color, something along those lines, I'm not sure. I was fond of Madame X, but being thrown together with her for an unspecified length of time struck me as less than a good idea. I didn't even have to think about Monsieur X's offer. I turned him down on the spot, figuring that would close the matter once and for all. Events proved me wrong. True indifference has power, I learned, and my refusal to take the job irritated Monsieur X and got under his skin. He wasn't in the habit of having people say no to him, and he became hell-bent on changing my mind. Over the next several months, he launched an all-out campaign to wear down my resistance, besieging me with letters, telegrams, and promises of ever greater sums of money. In the end, I reluctantly gave in. As with every other bad decision I've made in my life, I acted against my better judgment, allowing secondary considerations to interfere with the clarity of my instincts. In this case, what tipped the balance was money. I was having a hard time of it just then, desperately falling behind in my struggle to remain solvent, and Monsieur X's offer had grown so large, would eliminate so many of my problems at once, that I talked myself into accepting the wisdom of compromise. I thought I was being clever. Once I had climbed down from my high horse, I laid out my conditions in the toughest terms I could think of. I would go to Mexico for exactly one month, I told him—no more, no less—and I wanted full payment in cash before I left Paris. It was the first time I had ever negotiated for anything, but I was determined to protect myself, and I refused to yield on any of these points. Monsieur X was less than thrilled with my intractability, but he understood that I'd gone as far as I would go and gave in to my demands. The same day I left for Mexico, I deposited twenty-five one-hundred-dollar bills in my bank account. Whatever happened in the next month, at least I wouldn't be broke when I returned.

I was expecting things to go wrong, but not quite to the degree that they did. Without rehashing the whole complicated business (the man who threatened to kill me, the schizophrenic girl who thought I was a Hindu god, the drunken, suicidal misery that permeated every household I entered), the thirty days I spent in Mexico were among the grimmest, most unsettling days of my life. Madame X had already been there for a couple of weeks when I arrived, and I quickly learned that she was in no shape to work on the book. Her boyfriend had just left her, and this love drama had plunged her into the throes of an acute despair. It's not that I blamed her for her feelings, but she was so distraught, so distracted by her suffering, that the book was the last thing she wanted to think about. What was I supposed to do? I tried to get her started, tried to make her sit down with me and discuss the project, but she simply wasn't interested. Every time we took a stab at it, the conversation would quickly veer off onto other subjects. Again and again, she broke down and cried. Again and again, we got nowhere. After several of these attempts, I understood that the only reason she was bothering to make an effort was because of me. She knew that I was being paid to help her, and she didn't want to let me down, didn't want to admit that I had come all this way for nothing.

That was the essential flaw in the arrangement. To assume that a book can be written by a person who is not a writer is already a murky proposition, but granting that such a thing is possible, and granting that the person who wants to write the book has someone else to help with the writing of it, perhaps the two of them, with much hard work and dedication, can arrive at an acceptable result. On the other hand, if the person who is not a writer does not want to write a book, of what use is the someone else? Such was the quandary I found myself in. I was willing to help Madame X write her book, but I couldn't help her unless she wanted to write it, and if she didn't want to, there was nothing I could do but sit around and wait until she did.

So there I sat, biding my time in the little village of Tepotzolán, hoping that Madame X would wake up one morning and discover that she had a new outlook on life. I was staying with Madame X's brother (whose unhappy marriage to an

American woman was on its last legs), and I filled my days with aimless walks around the dusty town, stepping over mangy dogs, batting flies out of my face, and accepting invitations to drink beers with the local drunks. My room was in a stucco outbuilding on the brother's property, and I slept under muslin netting to guard against the tarantulas and mosquitoes. The crazy girl kept showing up with one of her friends, a Central American Hare Krishna with a shaved head and orange robes, and boredom ate away at me like some tropical disease. I wrote one or two short poems, but otherwise I languished, unable to think, bogged down by a persistent, nameless anxiety. Even the news from the outside world was bad. An earthquake killed thousands of people in Nicaragua, and my favorite baseball player, Roberto Clemente, the most elegant and electrifying performer of his generation, went down in a small plane that was trying to deliver emergency relief to the victims. If anything pleasant stands out from the miasma and stupor of that month, it would be the hours I spent in Cuernavaca, the radiant little city that Malcolm Lowry wrote about in *Under the Volcano.* There, quite by chance, I was introduced to a man who was described to me as the last living descendant of Montezuma. A tall, stately gent of around sixty, he had impeccable manners and wore a silk ascot around his neck.

When I finally returned to Paris, Monsieur X arranged to meet me in the lobby of a hotel on the Champs-Elysées. Not the Hôtel Georges V, but another one directly across the street. I can't remember why he chose that place, but I think it had something to do with an appointment he'd scheduled there before mine, strictly a matter of convenience. In any case, we didn't talk in the hotel. The instant I showed up, he led me outside again and pointed to his car, which was waiting for us just in front of the entrance. It was a tan Jaguar with leather upholstery, and the man behind the wheel was dressed in a white shirt. "We'll talk in there," Monsieur X said. "It's more private." We climbed into the back seat, the driver started up the engine, and the car pulled away from the curb. "Just drive around," Monsieur X said to the chauffeur. I suddenly felt as if I had landed in a gangster movie.

Most of the story was known by then, but he wanted me to give him a full report, an autopsy of the failure. I did my best to describe what had happened, expressing more than once how sorry I was that things hadn't worked out, but with Madame X's heart no longer in the book, I said, there wasn't much I could do to motivate her. Monsieur X seemed to accept all this with great calm. As far as I could tell, he wasn't angry, not even especially disappointed. Just when I thought the interview was about to end, however, he brought up the subject of my payment. Since nothing had been accomplished, he said, it seemed only right that I should give him back the money, didn't it? No, I said, it didn't seem right at all. A deal is a deal, and I had gone to Mexico in good faith and had kept up my end of the bargain. No one had ever suggested that I write the book *for* Madame X. I was supposed to write it *with* her, and if she didn't want to do the work, it wasn't my job to force her to do it. That was precisely why I'd asked for the money in advance. I was afraid that something like this would happen, and I needed to know that I would be paid for my time—no matter how things turned out.

He saw the logic of my argument, but that didn't mean he was willing to back down. All right, he said, keep the money, but if you want to go on working for me, you'll have to do some more jobs to square the account. In other words, instead of asking me to return the money in cash, he wanted me to give it back in labor. I told him that was unacceptable. Our account was square, I said, I wasn't in debt to him, and if he wanted to hire me for other jobs, he would have to pay me what those jobs were worth. Needless to say, that was unacceptable to him. I thought you wanted a part in the movie, he said. I never said that, I answered. Because if you do, he continued, we'll have to clear up this business first. Once again, I told him there was nothing to clear up. All right, he said, if that's how you feel about it, then we have nothing to say to each other anymore. And with that remark he turned away from me and told the driver to stop the car.

We had been riding around for about half an hour by then, slowly drifting toward the outer fringes of Paris, and the neighborhood where the car had stopped was unfamiliar to me. It was a cold January night, and I had no idea where I was, but the conversation was over, and there was nothing for me to do but say good-bye to him and get out of the car. If I remember correctly, we didn't even shake hands. I stepped out onto the sidewalk, shut the door, and the car drove off. And that was the end of my career in the movies.

I STAYED ON in France for another eighteen months—half of them in Paris and half of them in Provence, where my girlfriend and I worked as caretakers of a farmhouse in the northern Var. By the time I returned to New York, I had under ten dollars in my pocket and not a single concrete plan for the future. I was twenty-seven years old, and with nothing to show for myself but a book of poems and a handful of obscure literary essays, I was no closer to having solved the problem of money than I'd been before I left America. To further complicate the situation, my girlfriend and I decided to get married. It was an impulsive move, but with so many things about to change, we figured why not go ahead and change everything at once?

I immediately began casting about for work. I made telephone calls, followed up on leads, went in for interviews, explored as many possibilities as I could. I was trying to act sensibly, and after all the ups and downs I'd been through, all the tight corners and desperate squeezes that had trapped me over the years, I was determined not to repeat my old mistakes. I had learned my lesson, I told myself, and this time I was going to take care of business.

But I hadn't, and I didn't. For all my high-minded intentions, it turned out that I was incorrigible. It's not that I didn't find a job, but rather than accept the full-time position I had been offered (as junior editor in a large publishing house), I opted for a half-time job at half the pay. I had vowed to swallow my medicine, but just when the spoon was coming toward me, I shut my mouth. Until it happened, I had no idea that I was going to balk like that, no idea how stubbornly I was going to resist. Against all the odds, it seemed that I still hadn't given up the vain and stupid hope of surviving on my own terms. A part-time job looked like a good solution, but not even that was enough. I wanted total independence, and when some freelance translation work finally came my way, I quit the job and went off on my own again. From start to finish, the experiment lasted just seven months. Short as that time might have been, it was the only period of my adult life when I earned a regular paycheck.

By every standard, the job I had found was an excellent one. My boss was Arthur Cohen, a man of many interests, much money, and a first-rate mind. A writer of both novels and essays, a former publishing executive, and a passionate collector of art, he had recently set up a little business as an outlet for his excess energies. Part hobbyhorse, part serious commercial venture, Ex Libris was a rare-book concern that specialized in publications connected with twentieth-century art. Not books *about* art, but manifestations of the art itself. Magazines from the Dada movement, for example, or books designed by members of the Bauhaus, or photographs by Stieglitz, or an edition of Ovid's *Metamorphoses* illustrated by Picasso. As the back cover of each Ex Libris catalogue announced: "Books and Periodicals in Original Editions for the Documentation of the Art of the 20th Century: Futurism, Cubism, Dada, Bauhaus and Constructivism, De Stijl, Surrealism, Expressionism, Post War Art, as well as Architecture, Typography, Photography and Design."

Arthur was just getting the operation off the ground when he hired me as his sole employee. My chief task was to help him write the Ex Libris catalogues, which were issued twice a year and ran to a little over a hundred pages. Other duties included writing letters, preparing the catalogues for bulk mailings, fulfilling orders, and making tuna fish sandwiches for lunch. Mornings I spent at home, working for myself, and at twelve o'clock I would go downstairs to Riverside Drive and take the number 4 bus to the office. An apartment had been rented in a brownstone building on East Sixty-ninth Street to store Ex Libris's holdings, and the two rooms were crammed with thousands of books, magazines, and prints. Stacked on tables, wedged onto shelves, piled high in closets, these precious objects had overwhelmed the entire space. I spent four or five hours there every afternoon, and it was a bit like working in a museum, a small shrine to the avant-garde.

Arthur worked in one room and I worked in the other, each of us planted at a desk as we combed through the items for sale and prepared our meticulous catalogue entries on five-by-seven index cards. Anything having to do with French and English was given to me; Arthur handled the German and Russian materials. Typography, design, and architecture were his domain; I was in charge of all things literary. There was a certain fusty precision to the work (measuring the books, examining them for imperfections, detailing provenances when necessary), but many of the items were quite thrilling to hold, and Arthur gave me free rein to express my opinions about them, even to inject an occasional dose of humor if I felt like it. A few examples from the second catalogue will give some idea of what the job entailed:

233. DUCHAMP, M. & HALBERSTADT, V. L'Opposition et les cases conjuguées sont réconciliées par M. Duchamp et V. Halberstadt. Editions de L'Echiquier. St. Germain-en-Laye and Brussels, 1932. Parallel text in German and English on left-hand pages. 112 double-numbered pp., with 2-color illustrations. 9 5/8 × 11″. Printed paper covers.

The famous book on chess written and designed by Duchamp. (Schwarz, p. 589). Although it is a serious text, devoted to a real chess problem, it is nevertheless so obscure as to be virtually worthless. Schwarz quotes Duchamp as having said: "The endgames on which this fact turns are of no interest to any chess player; and that's the funniest thing about it. Only three or four people in the world are interested in it, and they're the ones who've tried the same lines of research as Halberstadt and myself, since we wrote the book together. Chess champions never read this book, because the problem it poses never really turns up more than once in a lifetime. These are possible endgame problems, but they're so rare that they're almost utopian." (p. 63). $1000.00

394. (STEIN, GERTRUDE). Testimony: Against Gertrude Stein. Texts by Georges Braque, Eugene Jolas, Maria Jolas, Henri Matisse, André Salmon, Tristan Tzara. Servire Press. The Hague, February, 1935. (Transition Pamphlet no. 1; supplement to Transition 1934–1935; no. 23). 16 pp. 5 11/16 × 8 7/8″. Printed paper covers. Stapled.

In light of the great Stein revival of the Seventies, the continuing value of this pamphlet cannot be denied. It serves as an antidote to literary self-serving and, in its own right, is an important document of literary and artistic history. Occasioned by the inaccuracies and distortions of fact in The Autobiography of Alice B. Toklas, Transition produced this forum in order to allow some of the figures treated in Miss Stein's book to rebut her portrayal of them. The verdict seems to be unanimous. Matisse: "In short, it is more like a harlequin's costume the different pieces of which, having been more or less invented by herself, have been sewn together without taste and without relation to reality." Eugene Jolas: "The Autobiography of Alice B. Toklas, in its hollow, tinsel bohemianism and egocentric deformations, may very well become one day the symbol of the decadence that hovers over contemporary literature." Braque: "Miss Stein understood nothing of what went on around her." Tzara: "Underneath the 'baby' style, which is pleasant enough when it is a question of simpering at the interstices of envy, it is easy to discern such a really coarse spirit, accustomed to the artifices of the lowest literary prostitution, that I cannot believe it necessary for me to insist on the presence of a clinical case of megalomania." Salmon: "And what confusion! What incomprehension of an epoch! Fortunately there are others who have described it better." Finally, the piece by Maria Jolas is particularly noteworthy for its detailed description of the early days of Transition. This pamphlet was originally not for sale separately. $95.00

437. GAUGUIN, PAUL. Noa Noa. Voyage de Tahiti. Les Editions G. Crès & Cie. Paris, 1924. 154 pp., illustrated with 22 woodcuts after Paul Gauguin by Daniel de Monfreid. 5 3/4 × 7 15/16". Illustrated paper wrappers over paper.

This is the first definitive edition, including introductory material and poems by Charles Morice. The record of Gauguin's first two years in Tahiti, remarkable not only for its significant biographical revelations, but for its insightful anthropological approach to a strange culture. Gauguin follows Baudelaire's persuasive dictum: "Dites, qu'avez-vous vu?" and the result is this miracle of vision: a Frenchman, at the height of European colonialism, travelling to an "underdeveloped country" neither to conquer nor convert, but to learn. This experience is the central event of Gauguin's life, both as an artist and as a man. Also: Noa Noa, translated into English by O.F. Theis. Nicholas L. Brown. New York, 1920. (Fifth printing; first printing in 1919). 148 pp. + 10 Gauguin reproductions. 5 5/16 × 7 13/16". Paper and cloth over boards. (Some minor foxing in French edition; slight fraying of spine in both French and English editions.) $65.00

509. RAY, MAN. Mr. and Mrs. Woodman. Edition Unida. No place, 1970. Pages unnumbered; with

> 27 original photographs and 1 signed and numbered engraving by Man Ray. 10 1/2 × 11 7/8″. Leather bound, gilt-edged cardboard pages; leather and marbleized fitted box.
>
> One of the very strangest of Man Ray's many strange works. Mr. and Mrs. Woodman are two puppet-like wood figures constructed by Man Ray in Hollywood in 1947, and the book, composed in 1970, is a series of mounted photographs of these witty, amazingly life-like characters in some of the most contorted erotic postures imaginable. In some sense, this book can best be described as a wood-people's guide to sex. Of an edition of only 50 copies, this is number 31, signed by Man Ray. All photographs are originals of the artist and carry his mark. Inserted is an original, numbered and signed engraving, specially made by Man Ray for this edition. $2100.00

Arthur and I got along well, with no strain or conflict, and we worked together in a friendly, unruffled atmosphere. Had I been a somewhat different person, I might have held on to that job for years, but seeing that I wasn't, I began to grow bored and restless after a few months. I enjoyed looking through the material I had to write about, but I didn't have the mind of a collector, and I could never bring myself to feel the proper awe or reverence for the things we sold. When you sit down to write about the catalogue that Marcel Duchamp designed for the 1947 Surrealist exhibition in Paris, for example—the one with the rubber breast on the cover, the celebrated bare falsie that came with the admonition *"Prière de Toucher"* ("Please Touch")—and you find that catalogue protected by several layers of bubble wrap, which in turn have been swathed in thick brown paper, which in turn has been slipped into a plastic bag, you can't help but pause for a moment and wonder if you aren't wasting your time. *Prière de toucher.* Duchamp's imperative is an obvious play on the signs you see posted all over France: *Prière de ne pas toucher* (Do Not Touch). He turns the warning on its head and asks us to fondle the thing he has made. And what better thing than this spongy, perfectly formed breast? Don't venerate it, he says, don't take it seriously, don't worship this frivolous activity we call art. Twenty-seven years later, the warning is turned upside down again. The naked breast has been covered. The thing to be touched has been made untouchable. The joke has been turned into a deadly serious transaction, and once again money has the last word.

This is not to criticize Arthur. No one loved these things more than he did, and if the catalogues we mailed out to potential customers were vehicles of commerce, they were also works of scholarship, rigorous documents in their own right. The difference between us was not that I understood the issues any better than he did (if anything, it was just the opposite), but that he was a businessman and I wasn't, which explained why he was the boss and I made just a few measly dollars per hour. Arthur took pleasure in turning a profit, enjoyed the push and pull of running the enterprise and making it succeed, and while he was also a man of great sophistication and refinement, a genuine intellectual who lived in and for the world of ideas, there was no getting around the fact that he was a crafty entrepreneur. Apparently, a life of the mind was not incompatible with the pursuit of money. I understood myself well enough to know that such a thing wasn't possible for me, but I saw now that it was possible for others. Some people didn't have to choose. They didn't have to divide the world into two separate camps. They could actually live in both places at the same time.

A few weeks after I started working for him, Arthur recommended me to a friend who was looking to hire someone for a short-term job. Arthur knew that I could use the extra money, and I mention this small favor as an example of how well he treated me. That the friend turned out to be Jerzy Kosinski, and that the job involved me in editing the manuscript of Kosinski's latest book, makes the episode worth talking about a little more. Intense controversy has surrounded Kosinski in recent years, and since a large share of it emanated from the novel I worked on (*Cockpit*), I feel that I should add my testimony to the record. As Arthur explained it to me, the job was a simple matter of looking through the manuscript and making sure that the English was in good order. Since English wasn't Kosinski's first language, it seemed perfectly reasonable to me that he should want to have the prose checked before he handed the book to his publisher. What I didn't know was that other people had worked on the manuscript before me—three or four others, depending on which account you read. Kosinski never mentioned this earlier help to me, but whatever problems the book still had were not because the English didn't sound like English. The flaws were more fundamental than that, more about the book itself than how the story was told. I corrected a few sentences here, changed a few words there, but the novel was essentially finished by the time the manuscript was given to me. If left to my own devices, I could have completed the work in one or two days, but because Kosinski wouldn't let the manuscript out of his house, I had to go to his apartment on West Fifty-seventh Street to do the work, and because he hovered around me constantly, interrupting me every twenty minutes with stories, anecdotes, and nervous chatter, the job dragged on for seven days. I don't know why, but Kosinski seemed terribly eager to impress me, and the truth was that he did. He was so thoroughly high-strung, so odd and manic in his behavior, that I couldn't help but be impressed. What made these interruptions doubly odd and intriguing was that nearly every story he told me also appeared in the book he had written—the very novel spread out before me when he came into the room to talk. How he had masterminded his escape from Poland, for example. Or how he would prowl around Times Square at two in the morning disguised as a Puerto Rican undercover cop. Or how, occasionally, he would turn up at expensive restaurants dressed in a sham military uniform (made for him by his tailor and representing no identifiable rank, country, or branch of service), but because that uniform looked good, and because it was covered with countless medals and stars, he would be given the best table in the house by the awestruck maître d'—without a reservation, without a tip, without so much as a glance. The book was supposedly a work of fiction, but when Kosinski told me these stories, he presented them as facts, real events from his life. Did he know the difference? I can't be sure, can't even begin to guess, but if I had to give an answer, I would say that he did. He struck me as too clever, too cunningly aware of himself and his effect on others not to enjoy the confusion he created. The common theme in the stories was deception, after all, playing people for fools, and from the way he laughed when he told them—as if gloating, as if reveling in his own cynicism—I felt that perhaps he was only toying with me, buttering me up with compliments in order to test the limits of my credulity. Perhaps. And then again, perhaps not. The only thing I know for certain is that Kosinski was a man of labyrinthine complexity. When the rumors started circulating about him in the mid-eighties and magazine articles began to appear with accusations of plagiarism and the use of ghost writers and false claims concerning his past, I wasn't surprised. Years later, when he took his own life by suffocating himself with a plastic bag, I was. He died in the same apartment where I had worked for him in 1974, in the same bathroom where I had washed my hands and used the toilet. I have only to think about it for a moment, and I can see it all.

Otherwise, my months at Ex Libris passed quietly. Nothing much happened, and since most of the business was conducted through the mail, it was a rare day when anyone came to the apartment and disturbed us at our work. Late one afternoon, however, when Arthur was out on an errand, John Lennon knocked on the door, wanting to look at Man Ray photographs.

"Hi," he said, thrusting out his hand at me, "I'm John."

"Hi," I said, taking hold of the hand and giving it a good shake, "I'm Paul."

As I searched for the photographs in one of the closets, Lennon stopped in front of the Robert Motherwell canvas that hung on the wall beside Arthur's desk. There wasn't much to the painting—a pair of straight black lines against a broad orange background—and after studying it for a few moments, he turned to me and said, "Looks like that one took a lot of work, huh?" With all the pieties floating around the art world, I found it refreshing to hear him say that.

Arthur and I parted on good terms, with no hard feelings on either side. I made it my business to find a replacement for myself before I quit, and that made my departure relatively simple and painless. We stayed in touch for a little while, occasionally calling each other to catch up on the news, but eventually we lost contact, and when Arthur died of leukemia several years ago, I couldn't even remember the last time I had talked to him. Then came Kosinski's suicide. Add that to John

Lennon's murder more than a decade earlier, and nearly everyone associated with the months I spent in that office has disappeared. Even Arthur's friend Robert Motherwell, the good artist responsible for the bad painting that provoked Lennon's comment, is no longer with us. Reach a certain moment in your life, and you discover that your days are spent as much with the dead as they are with the living.

THE NEXT TWO YEARS were an intensely busy time. Between March 1975, when I stopped working for Ex Libris, and June 1977, when my son was born, I came out with two more books of poetry, wrote several one-act plays, published fifteen or twenty critical pieces, and translated half a dozen books with my wife, Lydia Davis. These translations were our primary source of income, and we worked together as a team, earning so many dollars per thousand words and taking whatever jobs we were offered. Except for one book by Sartre (*Life/Situations,* a collection of essays and interviews), the books the publishers gave us were dull, undistinguished works that ranged in quality from not very good to downright bad. The money was bad as well, and even though our rate kept increasing from book to book, if you broke down what we did on an hourly basis, we were scarcely a penny or two ahead of the minimum wage. The key was to work fast, to crank out the translations as quickly as we could and never stop for breath. There are surely more inspiring ways to make a living, but Lydia and I tackled these jobs with great discipline. A publisher would hand us a book, we would split the work in two (literally tearing the book in half if we had only one copy), and set a daily quota for ourselves. Nothing was allowed to interfere with that number. So many pages had to be done every day, and every day, whether we felt in the mood or not, we sat down and did them. Flipping hamburgers would have been just as lucrative, but at least we were free, or at least we thought we were free, and I never felt any regrets about having left my job. For better or worse, this was how I had chosen to live. Between translating for money and writing for myself, there was rarely a moment during those years when I wasn't sitting at my desk, putting words on a piece of paper.

I didn't write criticism for money, but I was paid for most of the articles I published, and that helped pad my income to a certain degree. Still, getting by was a struggle, and from month to month we were no more than a short dry spell away from real poverty. Then, in the fall of 1975, just half a year into this tightrope walk *à deux,* my luck turned. I was given a five-thousand-dollar grant from the Ingram Merrill Foundation, and for the next little while the worst of the pressure was off. The money was so unexpected, so enormous in its ramifications, that I felt as if an angel had dropped down from the sky and kissed me on the forehead.

The man most responsible for this stroke of good fortune was John Bernard Myers. John didn't give me the money out of his own pocket, but he was the person who told me about the foundation and encouraged me to apply for the grant. The real benefactor, of course, was the poet James Merrill. In the quietest, most discreet manner possible, he had been sharing his family's wealth with other writers and artists for many years, hiding behind his middle name so as not to call attention to his astounding generosity. A committee met every six months to consider new applications and to dole out the awards. John was secretary of the committee, and although he didn't take part in choosing the recipients, he sat in on the meetings and knew how the members thought. Nothing was sure, he said, but he suspected that they would be inclined to support my work. So I put together a sampling of my poems and sent them in. At the next semiannual meeting, John's hunch proved to be correct.

I don't think I've ever known a funnier or more effusive person than John. When I first met him, in late 1974, he had been an integral part of the New York scene for the past thirty years, most famously as director of the Tibor de Nagy Gallery in the fifties, but also as cofounder of the Artists Theatre, editor of various short-lived literary magazines, and all-around champion and impresario of young talent. John was the first to give major shows to such artists as Red Grooms, Larry Rivers, Helen Frankenthaler, and Fairfield Porter, and he published the first books of Frank O'Hara, John Ashbery, and other poets of the New York School. The plays he produced were collaborations between many of these same poets and painters—O'Hara and Rivers, for example, or James Schuyler and Elaine de Kooning, the one writing the words and the other designing the sets. The Artists Theatre didn't bring in much at the box office, but John and his partner kept it running for years, and at a time when Off Broadway had yet to come into being, it was about the only experimental theater available in New York. What set John apart from all the other dealers, publishers, and producers I've known is that he wasn't in it for the money. Truth be told, he probably wasn't much of a businessman, but he had a genuine passion for art in all its forms, rigorous standards, openness of spirit, and an immense hunger for work that was different, challenging, new. A large man of six three or six four, he often made me think of John Wayne in his physical appearance. This John, however, in that he was proudly and flagrantly homosexual, in that he gleefully mocked himself with all manner of mincing gestures and extravagant poses, in that he took delight in silly jokes and ridiculous songs and a whole repertoire of childish humor, had nothing to do with that other John. No tough guy stuff for him. This John was all enthusiasm and goodwill, a man who had dedicated his life to beautiful things, and he wore his heart on his sleeve.*

When I met him, he was just starting up a new magazine—"of words and pictures"—called *Parenthèse.* I can't remember who suggested that I send him my work, but I did, and from then on John made a point of putting something of mine in nearly every issue. Later, when he discontinued the magazine and began publishing books instead, the first title on the list was a collection of my poems. John's belief in my work was absolute, and he backed me at a time when few people even knew that I was alive. In the endnotes to *Parenthèse* 4, for example, buried among the dry accounts of contributors' past achievements, he took it upon himself to declare that "Paul Auster has created a stir in the literary world by his brilliant analysis of the work of Laura Riding Jackson, by his essays on French paintings, and his poetry." It didn't matter that this statement wasn't true, that John was the only one paying attention. *Someone* was behind me, and in those early days of struggle and uncertainty, of not stirring up much of anything, that encouragement made all the difference. John was the first person who took a stand for me, and I have never stopped feeling grateful to him for that.

When the grant money came, Lydia and I hit the road again. We sublet our apartment and went to the Laurentian Mountains in Quebec, holing up in the house of a painter

---

*For a vivid account of his adventures, see John's *Tracking the Marvelous: A Life in the New York Art World,* published by Random House in 1983.

friend for a couple of months while he was away, then returned to New York for a week or two, and then promptly packed our bags again and took a cross-country train to San Francisco. We eventually settled in Berkeley, renting a small efficiency apartment not far from the university, and lived there for six months. We weren't flush enough to stop translating, but the pace was less frantic now, and that allowed me to spend more time with my own work. I went on writing poems, but new impulses and ideas started coming as well, and before long I found myself writing a play. That led to another play, which in turn led to another play, and when I returned to New York in the fall, I showed them to John. I didn't know what to make of what I had written. The pieces had surged up unexpectedly, and the results were quite different from anything I had done before. When John told me he liked them, I felt that perhaps I had taken a step in the right direction. The farthest thing from my mind was to do anything with them in a practical sense. I had given no thought to having them performed, no thought to publishing them. As far as I was concerned, they were hardly more than spare, minimalist exercises, an initial stab at something that might or might not turn out to be real. When John said that he wanted to take the longest of the plays and mount a production of it, I was caught totally by surprise.

No one was to blame for what happened. John jumped in with his customary excitement and energy, but things kept going wrong, and after a while it began to seem that we weren't putting on a play so much as trying to prove the indestructible power of Murphy's Law. A director and three actors were found, and shortly after that a reading was scheduled to drum up financial support for the production. That was the plan, in any case. It didn't help that the actors were young and inexperienced, not up to the task of delivering their lines with conviction or true feeling, but even worse was the audience who came to hear them deliver those lines. John had invited a dozen of his richest art collector friends, and not one of these potential backers was under sixty or had the slightest interest in the theater. He was counting on the play to seduce them, to overwhelm their hearts and minds with such stunning finality that they would feel no choice but to reach into their pockets and start pulling out their checkbooks. The event was held at a posh Upper East Side apartment, and my job was to charm these wealthy patrons, to smile and chat and reassure them that they were putting their money on the right horse. The problem was that I had no talent for smiling and chatting. I arrived in a state of extreme tension, nervous to the point of being ill, and quickly downed two bourbons to undo the knot in my stomach. The alcohol had precisely the opposite effect, and by the time the reading started, I had come down with a massive headache, a blistering, brain-bending assault that grew ever more unbearable as the evening wore on. The play thudded forward, and from start to finish the rich people sat in silence, utterly unmoved. Lines that I had imagined were funny did not produce the faintest titter. They were bored by the gags, indifferent to the pathos, perplexed by the whole thing. At the end, after some grim, perfunctory applause, I could only think about how to get out of there and hide. My head was cracking with pain. I felt stabbed and humiliated, unable to speak, but I couldn't abandon John, and so for the next half hour I listened to him talk about the play to his befuddled friends, doing everything I could not to pass out on the carpet. John put up a brave front, but every time he turned to me for help, I could do no more than stare down at my shoes and mumble a brief, unintelligible comment.

Finally, apropos of nothing, I blurted out some lame excuse and left.

A lesser man would have given up after such a defeat, but John was undaunted. Not a penny of aid emerged from that gruesome evening, but he went ahead and started improvising a new plan, scuttling his dream of theatrical glory for a more modest, workable approach. If we couldn't afford a real theater, he said, we would make do with something else. The play was the only thing that mattered, and even if the run was limited to just a single, invitation-only performance, there was going to be a production of my play. If not for me, he said, and if not for him, then at least for his friend Herbert Machiz, who had died that summer. Herbert had directed the plays at the old Artists Theatre, and because he had been John's companion for twenty-five years, John was determined to revive the Theatre in Herbert's memory—if only for just one night.

A man who owned a restoration studio on East Sixty-ninth Street offered John the use of his space. It happened to be just down the block from the Ex Libris office—an interesting, if minor, coincidence—but more to the point was that in its previous incarnation the carriage house where John's friend now worked had been the studio of Mark Rothko. Rothko had killed himself there in 1970, and now, less than seven years later, my play was going to be presented in that same room. I don't want to sound overly superstitious about it, but given how things turned out, it feels that we were cursed, that no matter what any of us did or didn't do, the project was bound to fail.

Preparations began. The director and the three actors worked hard, and little by little the performances improved. I wouldn't go so far as to call them good, but at least they were no longer an embarrassment. One of the actors stood out from the others, and as the rehearsals went on, I began to pin my hopes on him, praying that his inventiveness and daring might pull the production up to a reasonably competent level. A date in early March was chosen for the performance, invitations were sent out, and arrangements were made for a hundred and fifty folding chairs to be delivered to the carriage house. I should have known better, but I actually began to feel optimistic. Then, just days before the big night, the good actor came down with pneumonia, and because there were no understudies (how could there have been?), it looked as if the performance would have to be canceled. The actor, however, who had put weeks of time and effort into the rehearsals, was not about to give up. In spite of a high temperature, in spite of the fact that he was coughing up blood just hours before the play was supposed to start, he crawled out of bed, pumped his system full of antibiotics, and staggered on at the appointed time. It was the noblest of noble gestures, the gutsy act of a born trouper, and I was impressed by his courage—no, more than impressed: filled with admiration—but the sad truth was that he was in no shape to do what he did. Everything that had sparkled in the rehearsals suddenly lost its shine. The performance was flat, the timing was off, scene after scene was blown. I stood at the back of the room and watched, powerless to do a thing. I saw my little play die in front of a hundred and fifty people, and I couldn't lift a finger to stop it.

Before putting the whole miserable experience behind me, I sat down and reworked the play. The performances had been only part of the problem, and I wasn't about to palm off responsibility for what had happened on the director or the actors. The play was too long, I realized, too rambling and diffuse, and radical surgery was needed to mend it. I began chopping and trimming, hacking away at everything that felt weak or superfluous, and by the time I was finished, half of the play was gone, one of the characters had been eliminated, and the title had been changed. I typed up this new version, now called *Laurel and Hardy Go to Heaven,* put it in a folder along with the other two plays I had written (*Blackouts* and *Hide and Seek*), and stuck the folder in a drawer of my desk. My plan was to keep it there and never look inside the drawer again.*

THREE MONTHS AFTER the flop of the play, my son was born. Watching Daniel come into the world was a moment of supreme happiness for me, an event of such magnitude that even as I broke down and wept at the sight of his small body and held him in my arms for the first time, I understood that the world had changed, that I had passed from one state of being into another. Fatherhood was the dividing line, the great wall that stood between youth and adulthood, and I was on the other side now forever.

I was glad to be there. Emotionally, spiritually, and even physically, there was nowhere else I wanted to be, and I was fully prepared to take on the demands of living in this new place. Financially, however, I wasn't the least bit prepared for anything. You pay a toll when you climb over that wall, and by the time I landed on the other side, my pockets were nearly empty. Lydia and I had left New York by then, moving to a house about two hours up the Hudson, and it was there that the hard times finally hit. The storm lasted for eighteen months, and when the wind died down enough for me to crawl out of my hole and inspect the damage, I saw that everything was gone. The entire landscape had been leveled.

---

*See Appendix 1.

Moving out of the city was the first step in a long series of miscalculations. We figured we could live on less money in the country, but the plain fact was that we couldn't. Car expenses, heating expenses, house repairs, and pediatrician's bills ate up whatever advantage we thought we had gained, and before long we were working so hard just to make ends meet that there was no time left for anything else. In the past, I had always managed to keep a few hours to myself every day, to push on with my poems and writing projects after spending the first part of the day working for money. Now, as our need for money rose, there was less time available to me for my own work. I started missing a day, then two days, then a week, and after a while I lost my rhythm as a writer. When I did manage to find some time for myself, I was too tense to write very well. Months went by, and every piece of paper I touched with my pen wound up in the garbage.

By the end of 1977, I was feeling trapped, desperate to find a solution. I had spent my whole life avoiding the subject of money, and now, suddenly, I could think of nothing else. I dreamed of miraculous reversals, lottery millions falling down from the sky, outrageous get-rich-quick schemes. Even the ads on matchbook covers began to hold a certain fascination. "Make Money Growing Worms in Your Basement." Now that I lived in a house with a basement, don't think I wasn't tempted. My old way of doing things had led to disaster, and I was ripe for new ideas, a new way of tackling the dilemma that had dogged me from the start: how to reconcile the needs of the body with the needs of the soul. The terms of the equation were still the same: time on the one hand, money on the other. I had gambled on being able to manage both, but after years of trying to feed first one mouth, then two mouths, and then three mouths, I had finally lost. It wasn't difficult to understand why. I had put too much of myself into working for time and not enough into working for money, and the result was that now I didn't have either one.

In early December, a friend came up from the city to visit for a few days. We had known each other since college, and he, too, had turned into a struggling writer—yet one more Columbia graduate without a pot to piss in. If anything, he was having an even rougher time of it than I was. Most of his work was unpublished, and he supported himself by bouncing from one pathetic temporary job to another, aimlessly traveling around the country in search of strange, down-and-out adventures. He had recently landed in New York again and was working in a toy store somewhere in Manhattan, part of the brigade of surplus help who stand behind the counters during the Christmas shopping season. I picked him up at the train station, and during the half-hour ride back to the house, we talked mostly about toys and games, the things he sold in the store. For reasons that still mystify me, this conversation dislodged a small pebble that had been stuck somewhere in my unconscious, an obstruction that had been sitting over a tiny pinprick hole of memory, and now that I was able to look down that hole again, I found something that had been lost for nearly twenty years. Back when I was ten or twelve, I had invented a game. Using an ordinary deck of fifty-two playing cards, I had sat down on my bed one afternoon and figured out a way to play baseball with them. Now, as I went on talking to my friend in the car, the game came rushing back to me. I remembered everything about it: the basic principles, the rules, the whole setup down to the last detail.

Under normal circumstances, I probably would have forgotten all about it again. But I was a desperate man, a man with my back against the wall, and I knew that if I didn't think of something fast, the firing squad was about to fill my body with bullets. A windfall was the only way out of my predicament. If I could rustle up a nice large chunk of cash, the nightmare would suddenly stop. I could bribe off the soldiers, walk out of the prison yard, and go home to become a writer again. If translating books and writing magazine articles could no longer do the job, then I owed it to myself and my family to try something else. Well, people bought games, didn't they? What if I worked up my old baseball game into something good, something really good, and managed to sell it? Maybe I'd get lucky and find my bag of gold, after all.

It almost sounds like a joke now, but I was in dead earnest. I knew that my chances were next to nil, but once the idea grabbed hold of me, I couldn't shake free of it. Nuttier things had happened, I told myself, and if I wasn't willing to put a little time and effort into having a go at it, then what kind of spineless shit was I?

The game from my childhood had been organized around a few simple operations. The pitcher turned over cards: each red card from ace to 10 was a strike; each black card from ace to 10 was a ball. If a face card was turned over, that meant the batter swung. The batter then turned over a card. Anything from ace to 9 was an out, with each out corresponding to the position numbers of the defensive players: Pitcher = ace (1); Catcher = 2; First Baseman = 3; Second Baseman = 4; Third Baseman = 5; Shortstop = 6; Left Fielder = 7; Center Fielder = 8; Right Fielder = 9. If the batter turned over a 5, for example, that meant the out was made by the Third Baseman. A black 5 indicated a ground ball; a red 5 indicated a ball hit in the air (diamond = pop-up; heart = line drive). On balls hit to the outfield (7, 8, 9), black indicated a shallow fly ball, red a deep fly ball. Turn over a 10, and you had yourself a single. A jack was a double, a queen was a triple, and a king was a home run.

It was crude but reasonably effective, and while the distribution of hits was mathematically off (there should have been more singles than doubles, more doubles than home runs, and more home runs than triples), the games were often close and exciting. More important, the final scores looked like the scores of real baseball games—3 to 2, 7 to 4, 8 to 0—and not football or basketball games. The fundamental principles were sound. All I had to do was get rid of the standard deck and design a new set of cards. That would allow me to make the game statistically accurate, add new elements of strategy and decision making (bunts, stolen bases, sacrifice flies), and lift the whole thing to a higher level of subtlety and sophistication. The work was largely a matter of getting the numbers right and fiddling with the math, but I was well versed in the intricacies of baseball, and it didn't take me long to arrive at the correct formulas. I played out game after game after game, and at the end of a couple of weeks there were no more adjustments to be made. Then came the tedious part. Once I had designed the cards (two decks of ninety-six cards each), I had to sit down with four fine-tipped pens (one red, one green, one black, one blue) and draw the cards by hand. I can't remember how many days it took me to complete this task, but by the time I came to the end, I felt as if I had never done anything else. The design was nothing to brag about, but since I had no experience or talent as a designer, that was to be expected. I was striving for a clear, serviceable presentation, something that could be read at a glance and not confuse anyone, and given that so much information had to be crammed onto every card, I think I accomplished at least that. Beauty and elegance could come later. If anyone showed enough interest to want to manufacture the game, the problem could be turned over to a professional designer. For the time being, after much dithering back and forth, I dubbed my little brainchild Action Baseball.*

Once again, my stepfather came to the rescue. He happened to have a friend who worked for one of the largest, most successful American toy companies, and when I showed the game to this man, he was impressed by it, thought it had a real chance of appealing to someone. I was still working on the cards at that point, but he encouraged me to get the game in order as quickly as I could and take it to the New York Toy Fair, which was just five or six weeks down the road. I had never heard of it, but by all accounts it was the most important annual event in the business. Every February, companies from around the world gathered at the Toy Center at Twenty-third Street and Fifth Avenue to display their products for the upcoming season, take note of what the competition was up to, and make plans for the future. What the Frankfurt Book Fair is for books and the Cannes Film Festival is for films, the New York Toy Fair is for toys. My stepfather's friend took charge of everything for me. He arranged to have my name put on the list of "inventors," which qualified me for a badge and an open pass to the fair, and then, as if that weren't enough, set up an appointment for me to meet with the president of his company—at nine o'clock in the morning on the first day of the fair.

I was grateful for the help, but at the same time I felt like someone who had just been booked on a flight to an unknown planet. I had no idea what to expect, no map of the terrain, no guidebook to help me understand the habits and customs of the creatures I would be talking to. The only solution I could

---

*See Appendix 2.

think of was to wear a jacket and tie. The tie was the only one I owned, and it hung in my closet for emergency use at weddings and funerals. Now business meetings could be added to the list. I must have cut a ridiculous figure as I strode into the Toy Center that morning to collect my badge. I was carrying a briefcase, but the only thing inside it was the game, which was stowed inside a cigar box. That was all I had: the game itself, along with several Xeroxed copies of the rules. I was about to go in and talk to the president of a multimillion-dollar business, and I didn't even have a business card.

Even at that early hour, the place was swarming with people. Everywhere you turned, there were endless rows of corporate stands, display booths decked out with dolls and puppets and fire engines and dinosaurs and extraterrestrials. Every kiddie amusement and gadget ever dreamed of was packed into that hall, and there wasn't one of them that didn't whistle or clang or toot or beep or roar. As I made my way through the din, it occurred to me that the briefcase under my arm was the only silent object in the building. Computer games were all the rage that year, the biggest thing to hit the toy world since the invention of the wind-up jack-in-the-box, and I was hoping to strike it rich with an old-fashioned deck of cards. Maybe I would, but until I walked into that noisy fun house, I hadn't realized how likely it was that I wouldn't.

My talk with the company president turned out to be one of the shortest meetings in the annals of American business. It didn't bother me that the man rejected my game (I was prepared for that, was fully expecting bad news), but he did it in such a chilling way, with so little regard for human decency, that it still causes me pain to think about it. He wasn't much older than I was, this corporate executive, and with his sleek, superbly tailored suit, his blue eyes and blond hair and hard, expressionless face, he looked and acted like the leader of a Nazi spy ring. He barely shook my hand, barely said hello, barely acknowledged that I was in the room. No small talk, no pleasantries, no questions. "Let's see what you have," he said curtly, and so I reached into my briefcase and pulled out the cigar box. Contempt flickered in his eyes. It was as if I had just handed him a dog turd and asked him to smell it. I opened the box and took out the cards. By then, I could see that all hope was gone, that he had already lost interest, but there was nothing to do but forge ahead and start playing the game. I shuffled the decks, said something about how to read the three levels of information on the cards, and then got down to it. One or two batters into the top half of the first inning, he stood up from his chair and extended his hand to me. Since he hadn't spoken a word, I had no idea why he wanted to shake my hand. I continued to turn over cards, describing the action as it unfolded: ball, strike, swing. "Thank you," the Nazi said, finally taking hold of my hand. I still couldn't figure out what was going on. "Are you saying you don't want to see any more?" I said. "I haven't even had a chance to show you how it works." "Thank you," he said again. "You can leave now." Without another word, he turned and left me with my cards, which were still spread out on the table. It took me a minute or two to put everything back in the cigar box, and it was precisely then, during those sixty or ninety seconds, that I hit bottom, that I reached what I still consider to be the low point of my life.

Somehow or other, I managed to regroup. I went out for breakfast, pulled myself together, and returned to the fair for the rest of the day. One by one, I visited every game company I could find, shook hands, smiled, knocked on doors, demonstrated the wonders of Action Baseball to anyone willing to spare me ten or fifteen minutes. The results were uniformly discouraging. Most of the big companies had stopped working with independent inventors (too many lawsuits), and the small ones either wanted pocket-sized computer games (beep-beep) or else refused to look at anything connected with sports (low sales). At least these people were polite. After the sadistic treatment I'd been given that morning, I found some consolation in that.

Some time in the late afternoon, exhausted from hours of fruitless effort, I stumbled onto a company that specialized in card games. They had produced only one game so far, but that one had been wildly successful, and now they were in the market for a second. It was a small, low-budget operation run by two guys from Joliet, Illinois, a back-porch business with none of the corporate trappings and slick promotional methods of the other companies at the fair. That was a promising sign, but best of all, both partners admitted to being avid baseball fans. They weren't doing much at that hour, just sitting around their little booth and chewing the fat, and when I told them about my game, they seemed more than happy to have a look at it. Not just a peek, but a thorough viewing—to sit down and play a full nine-inning contest to the end.

If I had rigged the cards, the results of the game I played with them could not have been more exciting, more true to life. It was nip and tuck the whole way, tension riding on every pitch, and after eight and a half innings of threats, rallies, and two-out strikeouts with the bases loaded, the score stood at two to one. The Joliet boys were the home team, and when they came up for their last turn at bat, they needed a run to tie and two to win. The first two batters did nothing, and quickly they were down to their last out, with no runners on base. The following batter singled, however, to keep them alive. Then, to everyone's astonishment, with the count at two balls and two strikes, the next batter hit a home run to win the game. I couldn't have asked for more than that. A two-out, two-run homer in the bottom of the ninth inning to steal a victory on the last pitch. It was a classic baseball thriller, and when the man from Joliet turned over that final card, his face lit up with an expression of pure, undisguisable joy.

They wanted to think about it, they said, to mull it over for a while before giving me an answer. They would need a deck to study on their own, of course, and I told them I would send a color Xerox copy to Joliet as soon as possible. That was how we left it: shaking hands and exchanging addresses, promising each other to be in touch. After all the dismal, demoralizing events of that day, there was suddenly cause for hope, and I walked out of the Toy Fair thinking that I might actually get somewhere with my crazy scheme.

Color Xeroxing was a new process then, and it cost me a small fortune to have the copies made. I can't remember the exact amount, but it was more than a hundred dollars, I think, perhaps even two hundred. I shipped the package off to them and prayed they would write back soon. Weeks passed, and as I struggled to concentrate on the other work I had to do, it gradually dawned on me that I was in for a disappointment. Enthusiasm meant speed, indecision meant delay, and the longer they delayed, the worse the odds would be. It took almost two months for them to answer, and by then I didn't even have to read the letter to know what was in it. What surprised me was its brevity, its utter lack of personal warmth. I had spent close to an hour with them, had felt I'd entertained them and aroused their interest, but their rejection consisted of just one dry, clumsily written paragraph. Half the words were misspelled, and nearly every sentence had a grammatical error in it. It was an embarrassing document, a letter written by dunces, and once my hurt began to wear off a little, I felt ashamed of myself for having misjudged them so thoroughly. Put your faith in fools, and you end up fooling only yourself.

Still, I wasn't quite ready to give up. I had gone too far to allow one setback to throw me off course, and so I put my head down and plunged ahead. Until I had exhausted all the possibilities, I felt duty bound to continue, to see the whole misbegotten business through to the end. My in-laws put me in touch with a man who worked for Ruder and Finn, a prominent New York public relations firm. He loved the game, seemed genuinely enthused when I showed it to him, and made an all-out effort to help. That was part of the problem. Everyone liked Action Baseball, enough people at any rate to keep me from abandoning it, and with a kind, friendly, well-connected man like this one pushing on my behalf, it wouldn't have made sense to give up. My new ally's name was George, and he happened to be in charge of the General Foods account, one of Ruder and Finn's most important clients. His plan, which struck me as ingenious, was to get General Foods to put Action Baseball on the Wheaties box as a special coupon offer. ("Hey, kids! Just mail in two Wheaties box tops and a check or money order for $3.98, and this incredible game can be yours!") George proposed it to them, and for a time it looked as if it might happen. Wheaties was considering ideas for a new promotional campaign, and he thought this one might just do the trick. It didn't. They went with the Olympic decathlon champion instead, and for the next umpteen years, every box of Wheaties was adorned with a picture of Bruce Jenner's smiling face. You can't really fault them. It was the Breakfast of Champions, after all, and they had a certain tradition to uphold. I never found out how close George came to getting his idea through, but I must confess (somewhat reluctantly) that I still find it hard to look at a box of Wheaties without feeling a little twinge.

George was almost as disappointed as I was, but now that he'd caught the bug, he wasn't about to quit trying. He knew someone in Indianapolis who was involved with the Babe Ruth League (in what capacity I forget) and thought something good might happen if he put me in contact with this man. The game was duly shipped to the Midwest again, and then followed another inordinately long silence. As the man hastened to explain to me when he finally wrote, he wasn't entirely responsible for the delay: "I am sorry to be so late in acknowledging receipt of your June 22 letter and your game, Action Baseball. They were late reaching me because of a tornado that wiped out our offices. I've been working at home since and did not get my mail until ten days or so ago." My bad luck was taking on an almost biblical dimension, and when the man wrote again several weeks later to tell me that he was passing on my game (sadly, with much regret, in the most courtly terms possible), I barely even flinched. "There is no question that your game is unique, innovative and interesting. There may well be a market for it since it is the only table-top baseball game without a lot of trappings, which makes it faster-moving, but the consensus here is that without big league players and their statistics, the established competition is insurmountable." I called George to give him the news and thank him for his help, but enough was enough, I said, and he shouldn't waste any more time on me.

Things stalled for a couple of months after that, but then another lead materialized, and I picked up my lance and sallied forth again. As long as there was a windmill somewhere in sight, I was prepared to do battle with it. I had not the least shred of hope anymore, but I couldn't quite let go of the stupid thing I had started. My stepfather's younger brother knew a man who had invented a game, and since that game had earned him a pile of money, it seemed reasonable for me to contact him and ask for advice. We met in the lobby of the Roosevelt Hotel, not far from Grand Central Station. He was a fast-talking wheeler-dealer of around forty, a wholly antipathetical man with every kind of bluff and angle up his sleeve, but I must admit that his patter had some verve to it.

"Mail order," he said, "that's the ticket. Approach a major-league star, get him to endorse the game for a share of the profits, and then take out ads in all the baseball magazines. If enough orders come in, use the money to produce the game. If not, send the money back and call it quits."

"How much would a thing like that cost?" I asked.

"Twenty, twenty-five thousand dollars. Minimum."

"I couldn't come up with that much," I said. "Not even if my life depended on it."

"Then you can't do it, can you?"

"No, I can't do it. I just want to sell the game to a company. That's all I've ever had in mind—to make some royalties from the copies they sold. I wouldn't be capable of going into business for myself."

"In other words," the man said, finally realizing what a numskull he was talking to, "you've taken a shit, and now you want someone to flush the toilet for you."

That wasn't quite how I would have expressed it myself, but I didn't argue with him. He clearly knew more than I did, and when he went on to recommend that I find a "game broker" to talk to the companies for me, I didn't doubt that he was pointing me in the right direction. Until then, I hadn't even known of the existence of such people. He gave me the name of someone who was supposed to be particularly good, and I called her the next day. That turned out to be my last move, the final chapter of the whole muddled saga. She talked a mile a minute to me, outlining terms, conditions, and percentages, what to do and what not to do, what to expect and what to avoid. It sounded like her standard spiel, a furious condensation of years of hard knocks and cutthroat maneuvers, and for the first several minutes I couldn't get a word in edgewise. Then, finally, she paused to catch her breath, and that was when she asked me about my game.

"It's called Action Baseball," I said.

"Did you say *baseball?*" she said.

"Yes, baseball. You turn over cards. It's very realistic, and you can get through a full nine-inning game in about fifteen minutes."

"Sorry," she said. "No sports games."

"What do you mean?"

"They're losers. They don't sell, and nobody wants them. I wouldn't touch your game with a ten-foot pole."

That did it for me. With the woman's blunt pronouncement still ringing in my ears, I hung up the phone, put the cards away, and stopped thinking about them forever.

LITTLE BY LITTLE, I was coming to the end of my rope. After the grim, garbled letter from Joliet, I understood that Action Baseball was no more than a long shot. To count on it as a source of money would have been an act of pure self-deception, a ludicrous error. I plugged away at it for several more months, but those final efforts took up only a small fraction of my time. Deep down, I had already accepted defeat—not just of the game, not just of my half-assed foray into the business world, but of all my principles, my lifelong stand toward work, money, and the pursuit of time. Time didn't count anymore. I had needed it in order to write, but now that I was an ex-writer, a writer who wrote only for the satisfaction of crumpling up paper and throwing it in the garbage, I was ready to abandon the struggle and live like everyone else. Nine years of freelance penury had burned me out. I had tried to rescue myself by inventing the game, but no one had wanted the game, and now I was right back where I had been—only worse, only more burned out than ever. At least the game had represented an idea, a temporary surge of hope, but now I had run out of ideas as well. The truth was that I had dug myself into a deep, dark hole, and the only way to crawl out of it was to find a job.

I made calls, wrote letters, traveled down to the city for interviews. Teaching jobs, journalism jobs, editorial jobs—it didn't matter what it was. As long as the job came with a weekly paycheck, I was interested. Two or three things almost panned out, but in the end they didn't. I won't go into the depressing details now, but several months went by without any tangible results. I sank further into confusion, my mind almost paralyzed with worry. I had made a total surrender, had capitulated on every point I had defended over the years, and still I was getting nowhere, was losing ground with every step I took. Then, out of the blue, a grant of thirty-five hundred dollars came in from the New York State Council on the Arts, and I was given an unexpected breather. It wouldn't last long, but it was something—enough to ward off the hour of doom for another minute or two.

One night not long after that, as I lay in bed battling against insomnia, a new idea occurred to me. Not an idea, perhaps, but a thought, a little notion. I had been reading a lot of detective novels that year, mostly of the hard-boiled American school, and beyond finding them to be good medicine, a balm against stress and chronic anxiety, I had developed an admiration for some of the practitioners of the genre. The best ones were humble, no-nonsense writers who not only had more to say about American life than most so-called serious writers, but often seemed to write smarter, crisper sentences as well. One of the conventional plot gimmicks of these stories was the apparent suicide that turns out to have been a murder. Again and again, a character would ostensibly die by his or her own hand, and by the end of the story, after all the tangled strands of the intrigue had finally been unraveled, it would be discovered that the villain was in fact responsible for the character's death. I thought: why not reverse the trick and stand it on its head? Why not have a story in which an apparent murder turns out to be a suicide? As far as I could tell, no one had ever done it.

It was no more than idle speculation, a two-in-the-morning brain wave, but I couldn't fall asleep, and with my heart beginning to race and flutter in my chest, I pursued the thought a little further, trying to calm myself by cooking up a story to go with my curveball premise. I had no stake in the results, was simply groping for a sedative to tranquilize my nerves, but one piece of the puzzle kept fitting beside another, and by the time I drifted off to sleep, I had worked out the bare-bones plot of a mystery novel.

The next morning, it occurred to me that it might not be such a bad idea to sit down and write the damn thing. It wasn't that I had anything better to do. I hadn't written a decent syllable in months, I couldn't find a job, and my bank account was down to almost nothing. If I could crank out a reasonably good detective novel, then surely there would be a few dollars in it. I wasn't dreaming of bags of gold anymore. Just an honest wage for an honest day's work, a chance to survive.

I started in early June, and by the end of August I had completed a manuscript of just over three hundred pages.* The book was an exercise in pure imitation, a conscious attempt to write a book that sounded like other books, but just because I wrote it for money doesn't mean that I didn't enjoy myself. As an example of the genre, it seemed no worse than many others I had read, much better than some. It was good enough to be published, in any case, and that was all I was after. My sole ambition for the novel was to turn it into cash and pay off as many bills as I could.

Once again, I ran straight into problems. I was doing everything in my power to prostitute myself, offering up my wares for rock-bottom prices, and still no one would have me. In this case, the problem wasn't so much what I was trying to sell (as with the game), but my own astonishing ineptitude as a salesman. The only editors I knew were the ones who hired me to translate books, and they were ill qualified to pass judgment on popular fiction. They had no experience with it, had never read or published books like mine, and were scarcely even aware that such a thing as mystery novels existed, let alone the assorted subgenres within the field: private-eye novels, police procedurals, and so on. I sent off my manuscript to one of these editors, and when he finally got around to reading it, his response was surprisingly enthusiastic. "It's good," he said, "very good. Just get rid of the detective stuff, and you'll have yourself an excellent psychological thriller."

"But that's the whole point," I said. "It's a detective novel."

"Maybe so," he said, "but we don't publish detective novels. Rework it, though, and I guarantee that we'll be interested."

---

*See Appendix 3.

Altering the book might have interested him, but it didn't interest me. I had written it in a specific way for a specific purpose, and to begin dismantling it now would have been absurd. I realized that I needed an agent, someone to shop the novel around for me while I took care of more pressing matters. The rub was that I didn't have the first idea how to find one. Poets don't have agents, after all. Translators don't have agents. Book reviewers who make two or three hundred dollars per article don't have agents. I had lived my life in the remote provinces of the literary world, far removed from the commercial center where books and money have something to say to each other, and the only people I knew were young poets whose work appeared in little magazines, publishers of small, not-for-profit presses, and various other cranks, misfits, and exiles. There was no one to turn to for help, not one scrap of knowledge or information available to me. If there was, I was too dumb to know where to find it. Quite by chance, an old high school friend mentioned that his ex-wife happened to run a literary agency, and when I told him about my manuscript, he urged me to send it to her. I did, and after waiting nearly a month for an answer, I was turned down. There wasn't enough money in this kind of thing, she said, and it wasn't worth her trouble. No one read private-eye novels anymore. They were passé, old hat, a losing proposition all around. Word for word, it was identical to the speech the game broker had given me not ten days before.

EVENTUALLY, the book was published, but that didn't happen until four years later. In the meantime, all sorts of catastrophes occurred, one upheaval followed another, and the last thing on my mind was the fate of my pseudonymous potboiler. My marriage broke up in November 1978, and the typescript of the money novel was shoved into a plastic bag, all but lost and forgotten through several changes of address. My father died just two months after that—suddenly, unexpectedly, without ever having been sick a day in his life—and for many weeks the bulk of my time was spent taking care of estate business, settling his affairs, tying up loose ends. His death hit me hard, caused immense sorrow inside me, and whatever energy I had for writing I used to write about him. The terrible irony was that he had left me something in his will. It wasn't a great amount as far as inheritances go, but it was more money than I had ever had before, and it helped see me through the transition from one life into another. I moved back to New York and kept on writing. Eventually, I fell in love and married again. In the course of those four years, everything changed for me.

Sometime in the middle of that period, in late 1980 or early 1981, I received a call from a man I had met once before. He was the friend of a friend, and since the meeting had taken place a good eight or nine years earlier, I could scarcely remember who he was. He announced that he was planning to start a publishing company and wondered if I happened to have a manuscript he could look at. It wasn't going to be just another small press, he explained, but a real business, a *commercial operation.* Hmmm, I said, remembering the plastic bag at the bottom of my bedroom closet, if that's the case, then I just might have something for you. I told him about the detective novel, and when he said that he would be interested in reading it, I made a copy and sent it to him that week. Unexpectedly, he liked it. Even more unexpectedly, he said that he wanted to go ahead and publish it.

I was happy, of course—happy and amused, but also a trifle apprehensive. It seemed almost too good to be true. Publishing books wasn't supposed to be so easy, and I wondered if there wasn't a catch to it somewhere. He was running the company out of his Upper West Side apartment, I noticed, but the contract I received in the mail was a real contract, and after looking it over and deciding that the terms were acceptable, I couldn't think of a reason not to sign it. There was no advance, of course, no money up front, but royalties would begin with the first copy sold. I figured that was normal for a new publisher just getting off the ground, and since he had no investors or serious financial support, he couldn't very well cough up money he didn't have. Needless to say, his business didn't quite qualify as a *commercial operation,* but he was hoping it would become one, and who was I to throw a wet blanket on his hopes?

He managed to bring out one book nine months later (a paperback reprint), but production of my novel dragged on for close to two years. By the time it was printed, he had lost his distributor, had no money left, and to all intents and purposes was dead as a publisher. A few copies made it into a couple of New York bookstores, hand-delivered by the publisher himself, but the rest of the edition remained in cardboard boxes, gathering dust on the floor of a warehouse somewhere in Brooklyn. For all I know, the books are still there.

Having gone that far with the business, I felt I should make one last effort and see if I couldn't conclude it once and for all. Since the novel had been "published," a hardcover edition was no longer possible, but there were still the paperback houses to consider, and I didn't want to walk away from the book until they'd had a chance to turn it down. I started looking for an agent again, and this time I found the right one. She sent the novel to an editor at Avon Books, and three days later it was accepted. Just like that, in no time at all. They offered an advance of two thousand dollars, and I agreed to it. No haggling, no counteroffer, no tricky negotiations. I felt vindicated, and I didn't care about the details anymore. After splitting the advance with the original publisher (as per contract), I was left with a thousand dollars. Deduct the ten percent agent's commission, and I wound up making a grand total of nine hundred dollars.

So much for writing books to make money. So much for selling out.

(1996)

Appendix 1
THREE PLAYS

Laurel and Hardy Go to Heaven

Characters

Stan Laurel, a builder of walls
Oliver Hardy, a builder of walls

Bare stage. A heap of stones, rear right. There are eighteen stones in all, each measuring 30 inches by 30 inches by 30 inches.

Dimness, evolving toward light. The light grows in intensity during the first half of the play, reaching a noon of brilliance at the midpoint, and then diminishes gradually into darkness by the end.

Laurel enters right. Slowly, cautiously, as if in a daze. He is wearing denim overalls and work boots and carries a satchel over his shoulder. A bowler hat sits on his head. He stops, turns, and stares back in the direction he has just come from.

Hardy enters left. Same clothing, same satchel, same bowler hat. He moves purposefully, crossing the stage with great strides. In the dimness, he crashes into Laurel from behind. They both fall down, groaning.

HARDY: *(Recovering. Touching Laurel's face.)* Is it you?

LAUREL: Yes, yes. *(Pause.)* I think so. *(Doubtful, touching his face.)* Is it me?

HARDY: Yes. Of course it's you.

LAUREL: And you? Are you you?

HARDY: Yes. Of course I'm me. *(Pause.)* I'm me, and you're you.

LAUREL: It looks like we're both here, then, doesn't it?

HARDY: *(Standing up, stretching. Enthusiastically.)* And so . . . another day begins.

LAUREL: You don't have to be so happy about it.

HARDY: *(Stops. Seriously.)* You shouldn't talk like that. You know I'm not happy.

LAUREL: You certainly look happy. You certainly sound happy.

HARDY: That's what we call "putting up a good front." It's a way of tricking myself into being something other than what I really am. *(Pause. Brightly.)* I pretend. *(Begins walking toward the heap of stones.)*

LAUREL: Do you know what time it is?

HARDY: It's late. *(Stops, consults watch.)* It's getting later. *(Continues walking toward heap.)*

LAUREL: Where are you going?

HARDY: To see what they've given us today.

LAUREL: As if you didn't know already.

HARDY: Anything is possible. There are nuances . . . variations . . . wheels within wheels.

LAUREL: Wheels?

HARDY: Wheels within wheels. A figure of speech.

LAUREL: *(More vehemently.)* Wheels?

HARDY: Wheels. Wheels within wheels.

LAUREL: *(Shouting.)* Wheels! You think there are wheels! If there were wheels, we wouldn't be here. Wheels! There are no wheels! No wheels within wheels!

(The tirade stops suddenly. Silence.)

HARDY: Are you ready to begin?

LAUREL: And if I weren't?

HARDY: It wouldn't make any difference.

LAUREL: That's what I thought. *(Pause. Thinks.)* I'm ready.

HARDY: I'll get the orders. *(Goes to pick up his satchel.)*

LAUREL: Do you remember what day it is?

HARDY: *(Removing a large black book from his satchel.)* No. But it's all here in the book. We don't have to worry about remembering. *(Starts flipping through the pages of the book.)*

LAUREL: Well?

HARDY: *(Still turning pages.)* Well what?

LAUREL: Have you found it?

HARDY: *(Still turning pages. Impatiently.)* Found what?

LAUREL: The day. Have you found the day?

HARDY: I'd find it a lot faster if you stopped interrupting me. *(Turns pages, muttering to himself.)* One thousand . . . nine hundred . . . October . . . November . . . December . . . *(Stops.)* Ah. Here we are. *(Reads actual date:)* ——— —, 19—.

LAUREL: *(Happily.)* Good. *(Holds out hand.)* Now give me the book.

HARDY: *(Shocked.)* Give *you* the book?

LAUREL: It's my turn to read the orders.

HARDY: *(Belligerent.)* *Your* turn?

LAUREL: We agreed to it. Don't you remember? You said I would be the next one to read the orders. It's my turn, not yours.

HARDY: *(Pause. With conviction.)* But you read them last.

LAUREL: Me?

HARDY: Don't you remember?

LAUREL: *(Exasperated.)* How can I remember something that never happened?

HARDY: But it did happen. *(Forcefully.)* You read the orders last.

LAUREL: I did not.

HARDY: You did.

LAUREL: *(Louder.)* I did not.

HARDY: *(Louder.)* You did.

LAUREL: *(Louder still.)* I did not!

HARDY: *(Louder still.)* You did!

(They turn their backs on each other, fold their arms, and pout. After a moment:)

HARDY: Stan?

(Silence.)

HARDY: Stanley?

(Silence.)

LAUREL: *(At last.)* Yes?

HARDY: It doesn't matter.

LAUREL: Nothing matters.

HARDY: I mean, *it* doesn't matter.

LAUREL: What doesn't matter?

HARDY: The orders.

LAUREL: *(Feigning ignorance.)* The orders? What orders?

HARDY: The orders. It doesn't matter who reads the orders.

(Laurel sighs. They turn around and face each other.)

LAUREL: I suppose you should get on with it, then.

HARDY: *(Holding out the book.)* No, it's your turn today. You read them.

LAUREL: No dice.

HARDY: But I insist.

LAUREL: Out of the question.

HARDY: But I want you to read them.

LAUREL: But it doesn't matter. You said yourself: "It doesn't matter who reads the orders."

HARDY: Nevertheless, I'm asking you to do it. As a favor to me. *(Extends the book to Laurel, but Laurel does not take it. The book falls to the ground between them.)* Well? Aren't you going to pick it up?

LAUREL: *(Shrugs.)* No.

HARDY: *(Consulting his watch.)* It's late, you know. There could be trouble if we don't start soon.

(They both reflect, look down at the book, reflect again. Gradually, each comes to a decision. They simultaneously bend down to pick up the book—and butt heads. Laurel falls to the ground. Hardy grabs his head and staggers around the stage, emitting loud, astonished noises. Laurel sits on the ground, quietly rubbing his head. Eventually, Hardy returns to the book and picks it up.)

HARDY: *(Loudly.)* Damn the orders! Let's get on with it! *(Laurel stands up. Hardy, shaking with anger and frustration, finds the proper page in the book. Clears his throat. Reads in a booming voice.)* "These are the orders of the day!" *(Clears his throat. In a softer voice.)* "These are the orders of the day." *(Pause. Briskly.)* "Preliminary remarks." *(Pause. Laurel is scratching himself frantically, as if bitten by a flea.)* Are you ready?

LAUREL: *(Coming to attention.)* Ready! *(Scratches himself on the sly.)*

HARDY: *(Briskly.)* "Physical exercises for the day."

LAUREL: *(Rubbing his hands together.)* Excellent.

HARDY: Excellent? I haven't even read anything yet.

LAUREL: But it's a start. A good start. Get right down to basics. Very clever.

HARDY: *(Clears his throat.)* "Physical exercises for the day." *(Pause.)* "Take a deep breath, hold the air in your lungs, and then exhale." *(They do this.)* "Lift your hands above your head and then bend down and touch your toes." *(They do this.)* "Jump up and down five times, saying 'ah' each time your feet touch the ground." *(They do this.)* "Put your hands on your hips and then touch your knees with your head." *(They try, but neither one can do it. Several times, grunting.)*

LAUREL: *(Giving up.)* I can't do it.

HARDY: I don't think anyone can do it.

(They straighten up and look at each other.)

LAUREL: *(Apprehensively.)* But we're supposed to do everything it says.

HARDY: *(Angrily.)* No one can do *that.* It's impossible.

LAUREL: Do you think there's been a mistake?

HARDY: There's never been a mistake.

LAUREL: Then what are we supposed to do? We can't just give up.

HARDY: Maybe we're supposed to give up. After all, we did our best, didn't we?

LAUREL: But maybe our best isn't good enough.

HARDY: There's nothing better than best. *(Thinking.)* When they say do something, what they really mean is do your best.

LAUREL: *(Heatedly.)* That's not what it means at all. When they say do something, they mean do it!

HARDY: You can't do something you can't do. That wouldn't make any sense.

LAUREL: *(With loud despair.)* Do you think it's supposed to make sense?

(Silence.)

HARDY: I think we should go on to the next one.

LAUREL: We can't just let it go.

HARDY: But if we don't let it go, we'll never get finished.

LAUREL: Why bother to finish if we can't get past the beginning? Is there anything that says it's better to fail than to do nothing at all?

HARDY: We haven't failed. We're just doing what we have to do. Has it ever occurred to you that maybe we're *supposed* to fail? We might be succeeding just because we're failing. *(Pause.)* It's all a test. They want to see what we're made of.

LAUREL: As if they didn't know already.

HARDY: *(Seriously.)* I think we should go on to the next one.

LAUREL: Whatever you say. It makes no difference. *(Shouts.)* It makes no difference!

HARDY: *(Pause.)* Are you ready?

LAUREL: Yes, I'm ready. What's the next one?

HARDY: *(Consulting the book. After a moment.)* There is no next one.

LAUREL: *(Incredulous.)* There is no next one?

HARDY: No more physical exercises. That's the end of the physical exercises.

LAUREL: Is there anything after that?

HARDY: *(Consulting the book.)* Spiritual exercises.

LAUREL: And what, pray tell, are spiritual exercises?

HARDY: *(Calmly.)* They're a way to get our minds ready, to prepare our spirits for the work to be done.

LAUREL: *(Sarcastically.)* How nice. Just think: our minds would do the work, and we could sit here and watch. *(Exclaiming.)* Mind over matter! Long live the spirit!

HARDY: Are you finished?

LAUREL: And if I weren't?

HARDY: It wouldn't make any difference.

LAUREL: That's what I thought. *(Pause.)* Fire away.

HARDY: *(Consults book. Briskly.)* "Spiritual exercises." *(Pause.)* "Stop. Look. Listen." *(They stop, look, listen.)* "Close your eyes. Think of all the things you have just seen and heard." *(They close their eyes and think. Pause. They open their eyes.)* "Tell yourself: This is where I am. This is who I am. This is what I am."

LAUREL: *(In ringing tones.)* This is where I am. This is who I am. This is what I am.

HARDY: *(With feeling.)* This is where I am. This is who I am. This is what I am.

(Silence.)

LAUREL: Is that all?

HARDY: That's the end of the spiritual exercises.

(Silence. They think.)

LAUREL: What's next?

HARDY: The instructions.

LAUREL: Ah, good. I love to hear you read them. You always do it with such . . . vigor.

HARDY: *(Touched.)* Do you think so?

LAUREL: I really do find it . . . how shall I say? . . . inspiring.

HARDY: *(Very touched.)* Ah, you're too kind. Too kind.

LAUREL: *(Qualifying.)* Not every time, you understand. But much of the time. Perhaps nine out of *(pause)* fifteen times. Yes. Nine out of fifteen *(pause)* or twenty times, I find it truly inspiring.

HARDY: All right, then, listen carefully. *(Clears throat. Briskly.)* "Instructions." *(Pause.)* "Today you have been given eighteen stones to work with. Before going any further, count the stones and make sure there are no mistakes." *(Pause.)* Stan, go count the stones.

(Laurel goes to the heap and begins counting.)

LAUREL: *(Hesitantly.)*
One . . . two . . . three . . . four . . . five . . . six . . . seven . . . eight . . . nine . . . ten . . . eleven . . . twelve . . . thirteen . . . fourteen . . . fifteen . . . sixteen . . . seventeen. *(Pause. Removes hat and scratches head. Turning to Hardy.)* I count seventeen.

HARDY: Seventeen? *(Furious.)* Seventeen! How can there be seventeen? There are eighteen!

LAUREL: *(Abashed.)* What do you want me to do about it? I count seventeen. Am I supposed to lie to you?

HARDY: But you *are* lying!

LAUREL: *(Angrily.)* And you don't think they could have made a mistake?

HARDY: There are no mistakes in this work.

LAUREL: Then take a look for yourself, Mr. Smarty Pants. But don't say I didn't tell you.

HARDY: That's exactly what I'll do. *(Goes to the heap. Pushes Laurel aside.)* Out of my way! *(Begins counting in a loud, decisive voice.)* One. Two. Three. Four. Five. Six. Seven. Eight. Nine. Ten. Eleven. Twelve. Thirteen. Fourteen. Fifteen. Sixteen. Seventeen. Eighteen. *(Pause. Triumphantly.)* Eighteen! Can't you see there are eighteen? Do I have to do everything for you?

LAUREL: *(Embarrassed.)* You don't have to shout.

HARDY: *(Loudly.)* I'll shout if I want to shout! Do you hear me? *(Very loudly.)* I'll shout if I want to shout!

(Silence. They return to center stage.)

HARDY: All right, pay attention. *(Briskly.)* "Instructions." *(Pause.)* "Today you have been given *eighteen* stones to work with." *(Glares contemptuously at Laurel. Resumes reading.)* "Before going any further, count the stones and make sure there are no mistakes." *(Pause.)* "The stones are to be carried to their designated positions along the wall line. The wall line is the furrowed strip of ground you will see at your feet. Before going any further, make sure you have located the wall line." *(Pause. Pointing to the ground at his feet.)* Do you see it?

LAUREL: *(Defensively.)* Of course I see it. Do you think I'm blind?

HARDY: *(Brief pause. Briskly.)* "Today's section of the wall will consist of three rows of six stones each. The stones will be placed in their positions in the following order. Bottom row: stones one and two side by side, equidistant from the two ends of the wall line." *(Pause. They concentrate.)* "Stone three beside stone one. Stone four beside stone two. Stone five beside stone three. Stone six beside stone four." *(Pause. They concentrate.)* Have you got that?

LAUREL: *(Still concentrating. Pause. Then, with confidence.)* No problem. No problem.

HARDY: *(Resumes reading. Briskly.)* "Middle row: Stone seven will be placed on top of stone five." *(Pause. They concentrate.)* "Stone eight on top of stone six. Stone nine on top of stone three. Stone ten on top of stone four. Stone eleven on top of stone one. Stone twelve on top of stone two." *(Pause.)* Have you got that?

LAUREL: *(Still concentrating. Pause. Then with confidence.)* No problem. No problem.

HARDY: *(Resumes reading. Briskly.)* "Top row." *(Pause.)* "Stone thirteen will be placed on top of stone seven." *(Pause. They concentrate.)* "Stone fourteen on top of stone eight. Stone fifteen on top of stone nine. Stone sixteen on top of stone ten . . . *(With increasing enthusiasm.)* Stone seventeen on top of stone eleven. Stone eighteen on top of stone twelve!"

LAUREL: *(Nodding with certainty during the last few instructions.)* I've got it. No problem. It's all tucked away right here. *(Points to his head.)* Is there anything else?

HARDY: *(Consulting the book.)* Final remarks. *(Briskly.)* "Final remarks. The work of the day is about to begin. You have been given your work and know what you are about to do. Let nothing interfere with your work. You can be inspected at any time. Remember: this is restricted ground. All trespassers are subject to the full force of the law and will be dealt with harshly. Sit down on the ground and wait for the sound of a bell. When the bell has rung, begin. Do not begin until you

---

13	15	17	18	16	14
7	9	11	12	10	8
5	3	1	2	4	6

have heard the bell. These are the orders. Do not forget the orders."

(Hardy closes the book and puts it in his satchel. They both sit down. Silence.)

LAUREL: *(Tentatively.)* Ollie?

HARDY: Not now. I'm listening for the bell.

LAUREL: Please?

HARDY: Don't interrupt. You'll break my concentration.

LAUREL: Just one thing. Please?

HARDY: *(Exasperated.)* Shh! Don't you know the rules?

LAUREL: *(Beginning to whimper. To himself.)* Why does it always have to be this way? I never get a chance to talk.

HARDY: *(With suppressed rage.)* Later!

LAUREL: *(Crying, his voice full of self-pity.)* You see what I mean? You're the one who's always telling me what I should do and what I shouldn't do and when I should do it and when I shouldn't. Who made you the boss, Ollie? Tell me, who made you so high-and-mighty that I'm not even allowed to ask you one little question?

HARDY: *(Boiling over.)* Oh, shut up, why don't you! You make me sick with all that whining of yours. Act like a man. If you'd only just stop that . . . that . . . noise . . . *(He is about to continue but is suddenly interrupted by the sound of the bell.)* Ah! There it is now. *(Stands up, relieved.)* Enough of this talk. Let's get to work.

(Laurel stands up slowly. The two of them walk to the heap. Each approaches a stone, and after many preparations—in the manner of weight lifters—they lift the stones. Grunts and groans, the strain of total exertion. Tottering under their burdens, they painfully make their way to stage center left, along the "wall line." They put their stones down—stones 1 and 2—groaning with relief, and then, without pause, carefully align them, side by side. Gasping for breath, they both flop to the ground.

They lie there motionless, holding on to the stones. A long moment.)

HARDY: This . . . can't . . . go . . . on . . . I can't . . . take it anymore.

(Silence. The sounds of their breathing.)

LAUREL: Is this the end?

HARDY: *(Pause.)* No. This is the beginning.

LAUREL: And if I stopped, if I simply stopped and walked away, it wouldn't be the end?

HARDY: There would be trouble. *(Pause.)* And then what would happen to you? How would you eat?

LAUREL: I could always do what I did before.

HARDY: *(Trying to remember.)* But you didn't do anything before.

LAUREL: What difference does that make? *(Pause.)* It was no worse than this.

HARDY: You just don't understand the work, that's all.

LAUREL: *(Heatedly.)* I understand—that my back hurts. I understand—that if I ever lift another stone, I'll never walk straight again. I understand—*(shouting)* that I'm going out of my mind!

HARDY: *(Annoyed.)* And you don't think I am? You don't think I might like having someone else to talk to now and then? *(Pause. Remembering.)* My life hasn't always been like this, you know. *(Meditatively.)* This is what you might call . . . an interim period . . . a time for taking stock . . . for gaining new strength.

LAUREL: *(Incredulous.)* Strength? You call this strength? If you go on like this, you won't have the strength to lift your finger and pick your nose!

HARDY: *(Quietly.)* I mean inner strength.

LAUREL: *(Contemptuously.)* Balls.

HARDY: *(To himself, ignoring Laurel. Lost in thought.)* I want to learn, once and for all, how to do the thing that has to be done. If I have to lift a stone, I want to learn how to think of nothing but the stone. I want to admire the stone for the strength it takes out of me. I want to understand that the energy I have lost now belongs to the stone. I want to love the stone. I want to learn how and why the stone is more powerful than I am. I want to remember, once and for all, that the stone will continue to exist long after I am dead.

(Silence. Hardy in a trance of contemplation. Laurel, unimpressed, stands up.)

LAUREL: Say, Ollie. Did you ever hear the one about the two men? *(No answer from Hardy.)* I said: Did you ever hear the one about the two men? *(No answer from Hardy. Laurel shrugs, pretends to be Hardy answering.)* No, Stan, which one is that? *(Shifts position. As himself.)* Well, two men pass each other on the way to work every day for twenty years and nod hello, but they never speak, never exchange so much as a word. Finally, one day one of the men stops the other and says: "For twenty years we've been passing each other on the street, and you've never once stopped me to ask how I am." "I'm sorry," says the other. "I didn't mean to be rude." He looks the man in the eye and says: "Well, old friend, how are you?" And the other one *(Laurel shifts position to impersonate the other one)* lets out a deep sigh and says: "Don't ask!" *(Shifts back into the imaginary Hardy. Laughs.)* Very good. *(Shifts back to himself.)* Not bad, huh? *(Laughs back and forth between imaginary Hardy and himself.)*

HARDY: *(Finally looking up. Puzzled, disdainful.)* What are you doing?

LAUREL: I'm laughing. Isn't it obvious? *(Laughs.)* I'm laughing.

HARDY: We have to get back to work.

LAUREL: What time is it?

HARDY: It's late. *(Consults watch.)* We're behind schedule.

LAUREL: No more farting around, huh?

HARDY: That's one way of putting it.

(They walk to the heap. Preparations to lift, as before. They lift. Enormous effort, as before. They carry their stones—stones 3 and 4—to the wall and put them in place. Again they collapse, out of breath, exhausted.)

HARDY: *(Gasping.)* Let's not stop. . . . Let's get up . . . and go on. . . . We could finish . . . the bottom row . . . right away . . . if we didn't stop.

LAUREL: *(Gasping and wheezing.)* No . . . I have . . . to rest. . . . My back . . . my lungs . . . my heart . . . I think . . . I'm going . . . to burst.

HARDY: *(Still struggling.)* All right . . . you stay there . . . and rest. . . . I think . . . I'll see what I can do . . . about another. *(Stands up with difficulty. Takes a few tottering steps toward the heap. Falls down. Crawls back to the wall. Looks over the wall at Laurel, who is lying flat on his back in front of it. Pause.)* Stanley? *(No answer. Pause. Louder.)* Stanley?

LAUREL: Yes?

HARDY: *(Reflectively.)* Do you think we're alone? *(No answer. Pause. Louder.)* Stanley?

LAUREL: Yes?

HARDY: Do you think we're alone, or do you think there are others like us? *(No answer. Pause. Louder.)* Stanley?

LAUREL: *(Long pause.)* Alone.

HARDY: I keep thinking there are others. I mean, how can the wall go up if there aren't others to build it? We can't be the only ones, can we? The work would never get finished. And why should work begin if it can't be finished? *(No answer. Pause. Louder.)* Stanley?

LAUREL: Yes?

HARDY: What do you think?

LAUREL: Nothing.

HARDY: *(Going on.)* If there are others, then they must not be far away. *(Pause.)* It's true that we've never seen anyone. But maybe we're working towards them. Closer and closer . . . a little bit at a time. *(Pause. Reflects.)* Unless we're working in the other direction, of course. *(Pause.)* Or unless the wall is so long that we'll have been replaced before we join up with the others . . . who in their turn will have been replaced as well. *(Pause.)* What do you think, Stanley? Do you think we're moving closer or farther away? *(No answer. Pause. Louder.)* Stanley?

LAUREL: Farther and farther away.

HARDY: Well, you can think what you like. *(Pause.)* But I think there's more to this than meets the eye. *(Pause. Reflects.)* When I think of the wall, it's as if I were going beyond what I can think. It's so big, so much bigger than anything else. *(Pause.)* And yet, in itself . . . in itself . . . it's just a wall. A wall can be many things, can't it? It can keep in or keep out. It can protect or destroy. It can help things . . . or make them worse. It can be part of something greater . . . or only what it is. Do you see what I mean? It all depends on how you look at it. *(Pause.)* Don't you agree? *(Pause. No answer. Louder.)* Stanley? *(No answer. Leans over the wall to look at Laurel. Laurel is sound asleep. Hardy shouts.)* Wake up, you fool! Time to get up!

(Laurel stands up slowly, parodying a somnambulist. Arms extended, as if hypnotized. Walks to heap. With no preparations, he squats down to lift a stone. He raises it with remarkable ease. Totally surprised, he abandons his pretend trance. He laughs. Tosses the stone cautiously in his arms, astounded by its lightness. He laughs again. Hardy, who has been watching him intently, is dumbfounded. As Laurel begins to carry the stone to the wall, Hardy goes to the heap and approaches another stone. He, too, lifts it with remarkable ease. Begins to laugh, more and more uncontrollably as he carries it to the wall. They put their stones—stones 5 and 6—in place. The bottom row is now finished. They begin laughing again, wildly, uproariously. They shake hands, gesture to the stones they have just put in place, mimic their actions of a moment ago. As their laughter subsides, Hardy turns to Laurel and bows. Laurel bows back.)

HARDY: Shall we continue, my lord?

LAUREL: By all means, my lord, let us continue.

(They bow to each other again and saunter back to the heap. Each approaches a stone. They exude confidence and nonchalance. But, contrary to expectations, these stones are as heavy as the earlier ones. Enormous effort, as previously.)

HARDY: *(Grunting and howling. As he lifts.)* Mercy on my bowels! Mercy on my bowels! *(Begins tottering toward the wall.)*

(Laurel progresses more slowly than Hardy. The stone he carries is so heavy that he cannot advance in a straight line. He begins circling and weaving around the stage, even as Hardy is putting his stone—stone 7—in place.)

LAUREL: *(Staggering.)* Help me. Help me. I can't see where I am.

HARDY: *(Directing Laurel. Gasping.)* To the right. . . . No, no, to *your* right. . . . Now to the left. . . . Not too much! . . . To the right. . . . Just a little. . . . Now straight ahead. . . . No, no, the other way. . . . Turn around. . . . Now to the left. . . . To the right. . . .

Straight ahead. . . .A little more. . . .A little more. . . . To the right. . . . To the left. . . . A little more. . . . Now stop.

(Laurel reaches the wall and stands behind stone 6. Hardy helps him ease his stone—stone 8—into place. They both collapse. Lying on their backs in front of the wall, breathing hard. A long moment. At last, they both sit up—simultaneously—and look at each other. Pause.)

HARDY: Do you want something to eat?

LAUREL: No.

HARDY: Neither do I.

LAUREL: I think I'm going to throw up.

HARDY: *(Pause.)* I think I'm going to crap in my pants.

LAUREL: *(Sniffing.)* I think you already have.

HARDY: *(Sniffing. Pause.)* I think so too.

LAUREL: What are you going to do about it?

HARDY: I don't know. *(Pause.)* What do you think I should do?

LAUREL: I don't know. *(Pause.)* It doesn't matter.

HARDY: You mean it doesn't matter to you.

LAUREL: Does it matter to you?

HARDY: *(Pause. Thinks.)* No, I suppose not.

LAUREL: Think of all the other things you have to put up with. Next to them, this is only a minor inconvenience. *(Pause.)* I wouldn't be surprised if you even came to enjoy it.

(Hardy stands up. Shakes one leg, tentatively. Shakes the other leg, tentatively. Gingerly bounces up and down. Repeats the process, with more assurance. Once again . . . until he is eventually moving his entire body, twisting with pleasure.)

HARDY: Not bad. . . . Not bad at all. It's almost . . . like playing . . . in the snow. *(Stops short. Stares right, as if peering into the distance. Surprised, excited. Shades his eyes in order to get a better view.)* Stan! Look! Come here!

(Laurel goes to where Hardy is standing. He, too, shades his eyes and looks into the distance.)

LAUREL: I don't see anything.

HARDY: Straight ahead. Where those two trees are standing together in the field.

LAUREL: What kind of trees?

HARDY: The elms. *(Pointing.)* Over there.

LAUREL: Are you sure they aren't oaks?

HARDY: *(Impatiently.)* Elms! Oaks! What difference does it make!

LAUREL: *(Looking hard.)* I still don't see anything.

HARDY: *(With a sudden inspiration.)* Wait a minute! Don't move. Just wait right there. *(Rushes off to his satchel. Excitedly pulls out a pair of binoculars.)* Look!

LAUREL: *(Still looking into the distance.)* I'm looking.

HARDY: No, no. Over here.

LAUREL: *(Turns. Pause.)* Binoculars?

HARDY: *(With swagger.)* What else?

LAUREL: But where did you get a pair of binoculars?

HARDY: Out of my sack.

LAUREL: *(Puzzled.)* But how did they get *into* your sack?

HARDY: I put them there. How else would they get into my sack?

LAUREL: You're not answering my question.

HARDY: You asked me how they got there, and I told you.

LAUREL: What I want to know is where you got the binoculars in the first place.

HARDY: Are you trying to say something?

LAUREL: *(Taking him literally.)* Of course I'm trying to say something. These are words *(pointing to his mouth)* and they're coming out of my mouth.

HARDY: I mean to say, are you trying to *say* something?

LAUREL: Oh, *say* something. Yes, I see what you mean. *Say* something. *(Pause.)* You tell me, Ollie. Am I trying to *say* something?

HARDY: *(Pause. Blurts out:)* I stole them.

LAUREL: *(Studying the binoculars.)* You what?

HARDY: *(Louder.)* I stole them.

LAUREL: *(In awe.)* You mean . . . you took what didn't belong to you?

HARDY: Am I supposed to worry about it?

LAUREL: *(Pause. Considers.)* No, I suppose not. *(Pause.)* Of course not. *(Holding out his hand.)* Let me see.

(Hardy gives him the binoculars. Laurel looks through them.)

LAUREL: Ah.

HARDY: *(Eagerly.)* Well?

LAUREL: *(Continuing to look.)* Ah.

HARDY: *(Impatiently.)* What do you see?

LAUREL: I see a man. . . .

HARDY: A man! What's he doing?

LAUREL: He's looking up into the trees.

HARDY: Into the trees? What else is he doing?

LAUREL: Nothing. *(Pause.)* No, wait, he seems to be spitting.

HARDY: Spitting? *(Pause.)* What does he look like?

LAUREL: He's little . . . he's bent over . . . he's wearing a long, dark coat . . . he looks like . . . a piece of . . . a piece of . . . human flotsam.

HARDY: *(Peeved.)* What are you talking about? *(Snatches the binoculars from Laurel.)* Human flotsam. There are too many opinions around here and not enough facts!

(Hardy looks through the binoculars.)

LAUREL: *(Smugly.)* Well?

HARDY: *(Conceding.)* I have to admit . . . the image from here . . . is not too impressive.

LAUREL: What's he doing now?

HARDY: It's hard to see . . . he's so far away. . . . Wait! Yes . . . he's talking to the tree. . . . He's shaking his fist. . . .

LAUREL: *(Apprehensive.)* His fist?

HARDY: Wait. He's stopped shaking his fist. . . . He's spinning around. . . . He's . . . falling. . . . He's standing up. . . . He's spinning around again. . . . Uh-oh. . . . He's . . . he's coming this way!

(Hardy lowers the binoculars and looks at Laurel. Silence.)

LAUREL: Do you think there's going to be trouble?

HARDY: *(Hopefully.)* Maybe he's coming to tell us what a good job we've been doing.

LAUREL: I doubt that. I don't see why a man would come all this way just to say hello and pat us on the back.

HARDY: Unless he has nothing to do with the wall. *(Pause.)* Maybe he's just a man out for a stroll, taking in the country air.

LAUREL: That's not possible.

HARDY: Why not?

LAUREL: This is restricted ground.

HARDY: *(Remembering.)* Ah.

(Silence.)

LAUREL: What do you think we should do?

HARDY: Maybe we could just . . . ignore him.

LAUREL: How can we ignore him when he's standing right in front of us?

HARDY: You know . . . pretend we're deaf and dumb.

LAUREL: *(Thinking it over.)* That wouldn't be polite.

HARDY: What does etiquette have to do with it?

LAUREL: We don't want to make a bad impression, do we? *(Pause.)* And besides, we'd never pull it off. You'd start laughing.

HARDY: Me? If anyone slipped up, it would be you. *(Pause.)* You'd probably start crying.

LAUREL: You don't know what you're talking about. I'm a terrific actor. Just give me a role, and I'm it.

HARDY: *(Scornfully.)* Is that all you think it takes to act? *(Mimicking Laurel.)* "Just give me a role, and I'm it." *(With emotion.)* You've got to feel it, man. You've got to get yourself into the skin of the character.

LAUREL: *(Calmly. Holding his ground.)* Once you've learned your lines, the rest is easy.

HARDY: You could never learn any lines. The moment you walked onstage, you'd go blank.

LAUREL: Want to try me?

HARDY: Try you?

LAUREL: Give me a person to be, and I'll show you.

HARDY: *(Dismissing it.)* There's no time for that now.

LAUREL: *(Alarmed.)* No time? What are you talking about? I want to learn my lines!

HARDY: Just be yourself. That's hard enough as it is.

LAUREL: But how are we going to fool that man? We have to get ready!

HARDY: There are no lines for that.

LAUREL: No lines? How can there be no lines? *(Pause.)* We have to learn our lines!

HARDY: Don't you remember?

LAUREL: Remember? How can I remember? I haven't been given my lines!

HARDY: There are no lines. We're supposed to play deaf and dumb.

LAUREL: *(Realizing.)* Ah.

(Silence.)

HARDY: Well, do you want to go through with it?

LAUREL: No, I'm not interested.

HARDY: Then what do you think we should do?

LAUREL: *(Pause. Considers.)* Nothing.

HARDY: Nothing!

LAUREL: What I mean is, maybe we shouldn't plan anything in advance. Maybe we should just . . . you know, play it by ear.

HARDY: *(Exasperated.)* That's simply one of the worst ideas I've ever heard.

LAUREL: Can you think of a better one?

(Hardy is about to answer—but realizes he has nothing to say. Beside himself with frustration, he stomps off to his satchel and puts away the binoculars. His back is turned to Laurel, and as he begins to speak he does not notice Laurel shuffle toward the heap. Laurel moves slowly, with resignation. He lifts a stone: an enormous effort, more terrible and painful than any before. As he carries the stone—stone 9—to the wall and puts it in place, it is as if every bit of strength is being crushed out of him. Hardy speaks as Laurel works.)

HARDY: *(In despair.)* It's no use. You break your back at something day after day, you give it everything you have, and then someone comes along to tell you it's no good, to tear it down, to make you begin all over again. They kill you with the work, and then, when you can't take it anymore, they bring you back to life and kill you all over again.

(By now Laurel has put the stone in place. Gasping for breath, he summons all his energy and without pause returns to the heap, barely able to stand up. He confronts another stone, lifts it, and carries it to the wall. Hardy finally notices him. He is awestruck by what he sees. Meanwhile, Laurel puts the second stone—stone 10—in place. He is completely spent. Still, he does not collapse. Like a drunken man, he totters around the stage, wild with bitterness, mustering all his forces in order to speak.)

LAUREL: *(Howling, jumping up and down, throwing his hat to the ground.)* Enough! Enough! Enough! This is the end! No more stones! No more wall! From this moment on . . . I refuse! I reject! I renounce! No more love! No more life! No more nothing! *(Stops the tirade suddenly and unexpectedly—as if coming out of a trance. Bends down, picks up his hat, dusts it off, and puts it carefully on his head. Straightens his clothes. In a normal, self-assured voice.)* What time is it, Ollie?

HARDY: *(Terrified by what he has just witnessed. Answers with difficulty.)* It's late. *(Consults his watch.)* It's getting later.

LAUREL: Shall we have our lunch?

HARDY: Our lunch? *(Pause.)* Of course. If you say so. *(Pause.)* By all means, let's have our lunch.

LAUREL: *(Stopping. Trying to remember something.)* Weren't we just talking about something important?

HARDY: *(Trying to remember.)* Yes . . . I think we were.

LAUREL: What was it?

HARDY: *(Searching.)* I can't remember.

LAUREL: I guess it wasn't so important after all.

HARDY: *(Still searching.)* No, I suppose not.

LAUREL: Shall we have our lunch?

HARDY: Good idea. Let's have our lunch.

(They go off to their satchels and sit down in front of the wall at opposite ends. Laurel takes out an enormous sandwich and begins to eat . . . slowly, contentedly. Hardy, more methodical, takes out a large red-and-white-checkered napkin and tucks it under his collar. One by one, he pulls out a hardboiled egg, a carrot, a stick of celery, a radish, a sandwich, another sandwich, a third sandwich, a quart bottle of beer, and sets them out neatly before him. Picks up the egg, opens his mouth, is about to eat. Stops. Sniffs the egg carefully. Shows disgust. Puts the egg back in the satchel. Picks up the carrot, opens his mouth, is about to eat. Stops. Examines the carrot carefully. Bends it back and forth. It is limp. Shows disgust. Puts the carrot back in the satchel. Picks up the celery stick, etc. The process is repeated with each article of food. After the carrot has been put away, Laurel stops eating and watches Hardy's performance. After Hardy has put away the last sandwich, he wipes his mouth with his napkin and puts the napkin back in the satchel. He sees the bottle of beer, picks it up, and is unscrewing the cap when—)

LAUREL: Has it ever occurred to you that we're already dead?

HARDY: *(Slow take.)* Dead? In what sense dead? *(Pause.)* Dead right? Dead wrong? Dead tired?

LAUREL: No, I mean dead. Really dead. Dead as a doornail. *(Pause.)* As two doornails.

HARDY: What kind of blather are you spouting now? Can dead people move? Can dead people talk? Can dead people breathe? *(Takes a deep breath and exhales by way of demonstration.)*

LAUREL: How do we know what happens after death? Maybe this is it. For all we know, we could be sitting in heaven at this very moment.

HARDY: Heaven?

LAUREL: Heaven, hell . . . the happy hunting grounds—whatever you want to call it. I only mean the place people go to after they're dead.

HARDY: Don't you think we'd know we were dead? *(Thinks.)* And besides, how is this any different from life?

LAUREL: It's not. That's just the point. It's the same.

HARDY: That's not a very happy thought. *(Pause.)* I'd rather be a pile of ashes.

LAUREL: Think of it another way. What can you remember? If you were alive, your head would be crammed with memories, wouldn't it? *(Long pause, looking at Hardy.)* Well, what can you remember?

HARDY: *(Upset.)* Why do you have to play around like this? Can't you see I'm exhausted? *(Hand to face, in a gesture of weariness.)* I don't want to think about it.

LAUREL: *(Compassionately.)* You see. You can't remember anything.

HARDY: *(Defensively.)* Of course I can.

LAUREL: What? Name one thing you can remember.

(Hardy concentrates, trying to come up with something. About to speak—then gives up, dejected. Silence. Laurel and Hardy look at each other for a long moment. Vital information is exchanged in this glance. Hardy puts the beer bottle back into the satchel. He stands up.)

HARDY: I think I'll check on the progress of . . . the stranger. He must be getting close by now.

LAUREL: Do you think he's the inspector?

HARDY: It's hard to imagine who else he could be.

LAUREL: Too much talk and not enough action, right?

HARDY: That's one way of putting it.

LAUREL: What do you think will happen to us?

HARDY: Nothing good. You can be sure of that. *(Climbs up onto the wall, takes out binoculars from the satchel, looks into the distance.)* What's this? *(Looks harder.)* Stan!

LAUREL: *(Excited.)* Is he here?

HARDY: *(Lowers binoculars and looks at Laurel. Amazed.)* He's gone!

LAUREL: Let me see. *(Climbs onto the wall, takes binoculars from Hardy, looks.)* Not a speck. Not a shadow. *(Lowers binoculars.)* He just . . . vanished into thin air.

HARDY: *(Jumping down from the wall. Enthusiastically.)* That's the best news we've had all day. Just think: we've been given another chance.

LAUREL: *(Climbing down from the wall slowly.)* What are you talking about?

HARDY: The inspector changed his mind and decided not to come. If we work quickly, we'll have just enough time to finish before the day ends.

LAUREL: What makes you so sure he was the inspector?

HARDY: You said so yourself. Who else could he have been?

LAUREL: Nothing is certain. *(Pause.)* He could have been a trespasser.

HARDY: Then *he* would have been in trouble. The orders say all trespassers will be dealt with harshly.

LAUREL: If he was a trespasser, yes. *(Pause.)* But nothing is certain.

HARDY: What are you trying to say?

LAUREL: Maybe he was something else.

HARDY: Either he was a trespasser or he was the inspector. There is no other possibility.

LAUREL: Anything is possible. *(Pause.)* He might have been someone like us. A builder of walls. Maybe he was trying to find us and got lost.

HARDY: But there is no one else. You said so yourself. We're alone.

LAUREL: I might have said that. But I also might have been wrong.

HARDY: You're going around in circles.

LAUREL: Perhaps.

HARDY: And besides, what difference does it make *what* he was?

LAUREL: It's just that we'll never know, that's all.

HARDY: Unless he decides to come back some day.

LAUREL: *(Thinks.)* Or doesn't. *(Shrugs.)* What time is it?

HARDY: It's late. *(Consults his watch.)* We have to get back to work.

LAUREL: Go ahead. I won't stop you.

HARDY: But we have to do it together.

LAUREL: No we don't. *(With resolve.)* I'm finished. This is the end.

HARDY: But you can't stop now. There won't be enough time if you don't help me.

LAUREL: *(Determined.)* I'm two up on you anyway.

HARDY: Two up on me?

LAUREL: Don't you remember?

HARDY: Of course I remember. *(Exasperated.)* But that doesn't matter now. It'll be getting dark soon, and if we don't finish, there's going to be trouble.

LAUREL: *(Stubbornly.)* This is the end, I tell you. *(Pause.)* I'm on strike.

(Silence.)

HARDY: *(Trying a gentler approach.)* Don't you care what happens to you, Stanley?

LAUREL: That's exactly what I do care about.

HARDY: Don't you have any pride in your work? In our work?

LAUREL: Stop trying to talk me into it, Ollie. I'm finished.

HARDY: And you won't even do it for my sake? For friendship's sake?

LAUREL: I'm telling you, there's nothing left. No more friendship. No more wall.

HARDY: *(Pacing frantically. Turning vicious.)* What am I going to do with you? *(Walks over to Laurel and pushes him to the ground with great force, utterly taking him by surprise. Shouts.)* What the hell am I going to do with you!

LAUREL: *(Stunned, humiliated.)* What are you doing?

HARDY: *(In a rage.)* I'm not going to let you run out on me, do you understand? I'm going to make you work, even if it kills you!

LAUREL: *(Beginning to sob.)* Ollie . . . what are you doing?

HARDY: *(Standing over Laurel.)* Stand up! *(Waits. Laurel does not move.)* Stand up! *(Laurel stands.)* You're going to work, do you hear me! *(Pushes Laurel violently to the ground.)* Stand up! *(Laurel stands.)* Don't play games with me! Do you understand? Do you understand! *(Pushes Laurel violently to the ground again. Laurel, sobbing, tries to crawl away. Hardy catches him, grabs him by the collar, and pulls him up.)* Now! You're going to work now!

LAUREL: *(Crying, but nevertheless determined.)* You can't make me do it. *(Louder.)* You can't make me do it! *(New burst of sobs.)* Go ahead and kill me. It doesn't matter. But I'm not going to do that work again. *(Sobbing and shouting.)* I'm finished! I'm finished!

(Hardy, still holding Laurel by the collar, throws him down in disgust. Storms off to the heap.)

HARDY: Suit yourself, traitor. It doesn't matter to me. *(Stops. Shouts.)* Nothing matters, goddammit!

(Hardy arrives at the heap. He works with furious energy. Nevertheless: an enormous effort and struggle. He puts one stone—stone 11—in the wall as Laurel's sobbing gradually subsides. As Hardy begins lifting another stone—stone 12—Laurel turns and watches him, his bitterness slowly turning into compassion. Hardy puts the stone in place and sinks to the ground, exhausted. A long moment.)

LAUREL: Are you all right, Ollie?

HARDY: As well as I'll ever be.

LAUREL: Maybe you should rest.

HARDY: I can't rest. There's no time for that.

LAUREL: Would you like me to help you?

HARDY: I don't need any help.

(Hardy lies there, breathing heavily. He makes no move to resume work. Silence.)

LAUREL: Ollie?

HARDY: Yes?

LAUREL: Do you think someone is watching us?

HARDY: I don't know, and I don't care. The only thing I want is to finish before time runs out.

LAUREL: But wouldn't you like to know, once and for all, exactly how we stand? *(Pause.)* I mean, don't you think we should put it to the test? If we both stopped working now, if we both just refused to go on, don't you think it would force them to act?

HARDY: It's too late for that now.

LAUREL: *(Anguished.)* Too late? *(Pause.)* It's never too late!

HARDY: Anything we did or didn't do now wouldn't make any difference. We've gone too far already. If we stopped now, they'd probably think we were tired and give us more work tomorrow to make up for it. *(Pause. Thinks.)* The only way to handle it is to start from the beginning. With the orders. We should refuse to open the book. Then they'd know what we were up to. That would be a real test! *(Savoring the thought.)*

LAUREL: But that's what you said yesterday. You said we would do that today.

HARDY: *(Startled. Remembering.)* You were supposed to remind me!

LAUREL: *(Suddenly remembering. Mortified.)* I forgot!

(Silence.)

HARDY: What difference does it make anyway?

LAUREL: It makes all the difference. All the difference in the world.

HARDY: Then why didn't you worry about it before?

LAUREL: It didn't occur to me.

HARDY: So why worry about it now?

LAUREL: Because it has occurred to me.

HARDY: Do you want me to weep for you?

LAUREL: I weep enough for myself. *(Pause.)* And for you too.

HARDY: For me? You weep for me? Don't make me laugh.

LAUREL: Yes, for you. *(Pause.)* Just look at you. You're falling apart. . . . You're wasting away. . . . You look like . . . a piece of . . . of . . . human flotsam.

HARDY: *(Offended.)* Well, you don't look so wonderful yourself.

LAUREL: *(Beside himself.)* Did I say I did? *(Pause.)* I look horrible. I feel horrible. *(Pause. Self-pitying.)* I'm turning into . . . I'm turning into . . . Christ, I don't even know what I am anymore. *(Pause. With revulsion.)* I disgust myself.

HARDY: *(Softly.)* You shouldn't have regrets, Stanley.

LAUREL: I don't. *(Pause.)* That's the problem. I don't have any regrets.

(Silence. They reflect. Laurel begins walking toward the heap.)

HARDY: Where are you going?

LAUREL: *(Stopping.)* Back to work.

HARDY: Don't let me stop you.

(Laurel continues walking toward heap. Stops.)

LAUREL: I won't.

(Laurel goes to the heap. Looks at the stones. Examines them as if he has never seen them before. Bends down to lift a stone. Changes his mind. Stands up. Examines the heap again. Scratches his head. Thinks.)

HARDY: *(Watching him.)* What's the matter?

LAUREL: I can't decide which one to choose.

HARDY: There's nothing to choose. They're all the same.

LAUREL: *(Examining them again.)* I'm not so sure of that.

HARDY: What are you talking about? They're all the same size, the same weight, the same color.

LAUREL: *(Perplexed.)* How can they be? Don't you remember what happened before?

HARDY: Before?

LAUREL: When we lifted those two stones and didn't have any trouble with them. *(Dreamily.)* They were so . . . light.

HARDY: *(Thinking.)* Yes, I remember. *(Pause. Relishing the memory.)* That was quite a moment, wasn't it?

LAUREL: You see. They were different. They were lighter.

HARDY: *(Thinks.)* They couldn't have been lighter. *(Pause.)* All the stones are the same weight.

LAUREL: *(Frustrated.)* But they were lighter. *(Pause. Remembering.)* It was like a miracle.

HARDY: It couldn't have been a miracle. *(Dismissing it.)* There are no miracles. *(Trying to solve the dilemma.)* It was all because of us.

LAUREL: Us?

HARDY: The stones were the same. Just like any other stones. *(Pause.)* We were the ones who were different.

(Silence. They reflect.)

LAUREL: Do you realize what you're saying?

HARDY: Of course I do. *(Pause.)* What am I saying?

LAUREL: That everything . . . depends on us.

HARDY: Us? *(Pause.)* That's impossible. We're the victims. *(Pause.)* I'm sure of it.

LAUREL: You can't be sure of anything.

HARDY: *(Emphatically.)* Believe me. *We* are the victims.

LAUREL: *(Not wanting to insist.)* You know something, Ollie?

HARDY: What?

LAUREL: You still haven't helped me pick out my stone.

HARDY: Ah yes. Your stone. *(Goes to the heap and examines stones with Laurel.)* Well . . . if you really want my opinion . . . *(Hesitates.)* I think you should pick . . . that one. *(Points.)*

LAUREL: *(Considering it.)* Mmm . . . not bad. But what about . . . that one? *(Points.)*

HARDY: *(Considering.)* Well . . . if you put it that way . . . it could be that the one over here *(points)* would be the best of all.

LAUREL: *(Examining it carefully.)* You know . . . you just may be right. Yes, I think you've done it, by God. *(Straightens up.)* Many thanks, Mr. Hardy. *(Shakes his hand.)* Many thanks indeed.

HARDY: My pleasure, Mr. Laurel. It's an honor.

(Laurel turns his attention to the heap. Approaches the stone and lifts. An enormous effort, but bravely sustained. He totters under the weight, weaving around the stage.)

LAUREL: *(Carrying the stone.)* I can do it! I can do it, I say! I can do it!

(Laurel puts the stone—stone 13—in place. Gasping for breath.)

HARDY: *(Impressed.)* Well done. Very well done. In all the time I've known you, I don't think you've ever handled one better.

LAUREL: *(Chest heaving. Triumphantly.)* Let their eyes fall out! Let them rot in their graves!

(Still panting, but with great determination, Laurel leads the way back to the heap. Hardy follows, close at his heels. They each approach a stone and lift. Same struggle as before. They stagger to the wall with the stones—stones 14 and 15—and put them in place. They collapse into each other's arms, propping each other up. Gasping for breath. A long moment. They separate.)

HARDY: *(Still panting.)* You know what I'd like to do? I'd like to kick the whole wall down . . . and then break up all the stones . . . into little stones . . . and I'd just wait here until someone came along—I don't care who . . . the goddamned inspector for all I care—and as soon as he got close enough . . . I'd let him have it! *(Gestures, as if throwing a stone.)*

LAUREL: Right between the eyes!

HARDY: I'd like to kick the whole fucking wall right down to the ground!

(Silence. They catch their breath.)

LAUREL: Ollie?

HARDY: Yes, Stanley?

LAUREL: Let's do it.

HARDY: Do what?

LAUREL: Kick the wall down.

HARDY: *(Startled. Reflects.)* If we kicked the wall down now, the whole day will have been wasted.

LAUREL: What difference does that make?

HARDY: It would be stupid, that's all. Why spend a whole day working on something . . . just to destroy it?

LAUREL: But how else can you destroy it? You have to build it first.

HARDY: *(Thinking.)* Believe me, I'm tempted.

LAUREL: We could knock down the whole damn thing.

HARDY: It's a beautiful thought, isn't it?

LAUREL: *(Relishing the prospect.)* It would make everything worthwhile.

(Silence. They reflect, dreamily.)

HARDY: Of course, they'd be down on our heads the minute we did it.

LAUREL: We could fight them off!

HARDY: With what?

LAUREL: With the little stones. We'll fight them off with the little stones.

HARDY: And where are we going to get the little stones?

LAUREL: From the big stones! We'll break the big stones into little stones!

HARDY: And how are we going to do that? *(Pause.)* We don't even have a hammer.

LAUREL: *(Clutching at straws.)* We'll fight them off with our fists!

HARDY: *(Imagining it.)* Stanley . . . do you want to die? *(Pause.)* Do you really want to die?

(Silence. Defeat. They sit down and think.)

LAUREL: What's going to happen to us?

HARDY: Nothing's going to happen to us.

LAUREL: Isn't that like being dead?

HARDY: Not really. It just means that nothing is going to happen.

LAUREL: We'll get back to work and finish, won't we?

HARDY: Yes. We'll get back to work and finish.

(Silence.)

LAUREL: We'll finish the wall and then go out tonight and get drunk, won't we?

HARDY: Probably. *(Pause.)* Yes, we'll probably get drunk.

LAUREL: And then we'll pass out or puke it up and that will be that.

(Silence. They reflect.)

HARDY: Well?

LAUREL: If you insist.

(They do not move.)

HARDY: Well, what do you say?

LAUREL: You first.

(They do not move.)

LAUREL: Well?

HARDY: I'm getting there. I'm getting there.

(A long moment. Hardy slowly stands up. Laurel slowly stands up. They go back to the heap. Same preparations as before. Same exertion and labor as before. They put the stones—stones 16 and 17—in place. Only one gap remains, in the middle of the top row. They stand in front of the wall, gasping for breath. Hardy goes behind the wall and pokes his head through the gap. A brief game of peek-a-boo follows. They both laugh. Hardy returns to the other side of the wall. They speak with their backs to the audience.)

HARDY: *(Admiring the wall.)* Well, it's nearly finished.

LAUREL: It's hard to imagine.

HARDY: We never thought we could do it.

LAUREL: We thought we could do it. And then we thought we could never do it. And then we did it.

HARDY: Imagine.

LAUREL: Yes. It's hard to imagine.

(Silence.)

LAUREL: *(Turning to Hardy.)* There's one more stone to go.

HARDY: Shall we do it together?

LAUREL: You took the words right out of my mouth.

(They go off to the last stone. They lift it together with a great effort. They approach the wall from behind, invisible to the audience. Nothing can be seen except the last stone being put into place. A long pause. They speak from behind the wall, in near darkness.)

LAUREL: What time is it, Ollie?

HARDY: It's late. It's time to go.

LAUREL: Can you see the stars?

HARDY: Yes. I can see the stars. I can feel the wind and I can see the stars.

LAUREL: Is that all there is, then? Is this the end?

HARDY: Yes. This is the end. Until tomorrow.

LAUREL: We should go, then. Do you remember the way?

HARDY: Yes, I remember the way.

LAUREL: Should we drink beer tonight and get drunk?

HARDY: We'll see. If you like.

LAUREL: I think that would be nice.

HARDY: We'll see, Stan. Whatever you like.

LAUREL: And what about tomorrow?

HARDY: We'll think about tomorrow tomorrow.

LAUREL: It's dark, isn't it?

HARDY: Yes, it's dark. But don't worry. Just follow me. We'll be there before you know it.

(Silence. Total darkness.)

(1976/77)

Blackouts

Characters

Green, a man about seventy years old
Black, a man about forty years old
Blue, a man about forty years old

An old-fashioned office, cluttered with papers, filing cabinets, etc. Stage right rear: a door with frosted glass panel, the word ENTRANCE *written in reverse. Stage center rear: a window. Stage left rear: a window. Stage right, at forty-five-degree angle facing out: Green's desk and chair. Stage left, at smaller angle facing out: Black's desk and chair. There is a third chair on the other side of Black's desk. Green's desk has a gray pencil sharpener attached to the top.*

Green wears a green suit. Black wears a black suit. Blue wears a blue suit.

Darkness. The sound of Green sharpening pencils. Four pencils. Lights gradually come on. Green is standing by his desk, sharpening pencils. Eight more pencils. Black is sitting at his desk, staring blankly ahead, as if lost in thought.

BLACK: Green. *(No response. Louder.)* Green!

GREEN: *(Stops sharpening.)* Yes?

BLACK: The pencils.

GREEN: *(Nods in agreement.)* The pencils. *(Resumes sharpening.)*

BLACK: Too loud. *(No response. Pause.)* Too loud!

GREEN: *(Stops sharpening.)* I beg your pardon?

BLACK: The pencils are too loud.

GREEN: *(Puzzled. Inspects pencils.)* The pencils? *(Pause.)* They are . . . mute.

BLACK: The ruckus . . . of that contraption.

GREEN: *(Pause. Considers. Tries sharpening pencils at various speeds. Stops.)* It can't be helped. It's in the nature . . . of the machine. The rotaries *(slight pause)* chew.

BLACK: Drop it.

GREEN: But I'm not ready. There aren't enough.

BLACK: *(Forcefully.)* You're ready.

GREEN: *(Pause. Humbled.)* As you wish. *(Takes already sharpened pencils and arranges them neatly on desk. Sits in chair.)*

BLACK: Are you ready?

GREEN: *(As if trying to remember.)* I note. Everything that is said is written. Even the silence must be marked . . . *(groping)* . . .

BLACK: Silence.

GREEN: . . . Silence. No talking unless asked. I am ears without mouth . . . nothing . . . but the hand that writes the words.

(Pause.)

BLACK: Who are you?

GREEN: *(Hesitates.)* Green. As previously. *(Pause.)* Executor . . . of the aforementioned.

(Pause.)

BLACK: Who am I? *(Green stares at him apprehensively. Pause. More forcefully.)* Who am I?

GREEN: Black.

BLACK: Since when?

GREEN: Since . . . the beginning.

BLACK: And so it will be—

GREEN: To the end. To the very end.

(Black sighs with satisfaction. Leans back in chair. Pause.)

BLACK: This is a great day, Green. A great and important day.

GREEN: I don't doubt it. *(Pause.)* But so is every day. A new beginning of all the days that remain.

BLACK: No. Today is different. Today is the day it ends.

GREEN: If you say so. *(Testing sharpness of pencils on his palm; wincing at the prick.)*

BLACK: I don't say so. It is written. *(Pause.)* A man will walk through that door, sit down in that chair across from me, and we will talk. By the time we have finished, there will be nothing left.

GREEN: There will be the words. I'll have written them down, one by one.

BLACK: That's beside the point.

GREEN: *(Confused.)* Then why am I here? What am I doing this for?

BLACK: You're here to make a record, to prove that what happened really happened. *(Pause.)* But it doesn't matter. One way or the other, it's beside the point.

GREEN: You're out of your mind.

BLACK: Not out, in. If anything, I'm too much in my mind. *(Pause.)* But that's only a detail. *(Longer pause. Turning to Green. Earnestly.)* Do you remember me?

GREEN: Of course I remember you. How could I forget you?

BLACK: Have I changed much?

GREEN: *(Thinks.)* You've grown older. *(Pause.)* But then so have I. *(Pause.)* I'd say you've become . . . more and more what you are.

BLACK: *(His spirits lifted.)* Do you think so? Is it really possible?

GREEN: Why shouldn't it be? It seems . . . almost inevitable.

BLACK: Not for me it isn't. *(Pause. Bitterly.)* You're making fun of me, aren't you?

GREEN: *(Trying to mollify.)* Listen, Charlie . . .

BLACK: *(Exploding.)* Don't ever call me that! Don't ever call me that again, do you hear!

GREEN: *(Mortified.)* I forgot.

BLACK: What is my name?

GREEN: Black. Black. From the very beginning. Black.

BLACK: You must never forget that, do you understand?

(Long pause.)

GREEN: Will he be here soon?

BLACK: Impossible to say. *(Pause.)* Perhaps he'll never come.

GREEN: When is he supposed to come?

BLACK: *(Consults watch.)* Any time now.

GREEN: What's his name?

BLACK: *(Looks Green in the eyes. Enunciates with deliberation.)* Blue.

(Green laughs with embarrassment. Long pause.)

GREEN: Is it over, then?

BLACK: Is what over?

GREEN: *(Pause.)* The story.

BLACK: Yes, it's over. *(Stands up. Walks to window behind his desk. Looks out.)* No doubt about that.

GREEN: *(Pause.)* Did you really believe in it that much?

BLACK: *(Looking out.)* It wasn't a question of belief. *(Pause.)* I really wanted to know what it would be like.

GREEN: For so long? For so many years?

BLACK: Once I started, it was hard to stop. *(Pause.)* I developed . . . a taste for it.

GREEN: *(Puzzled.)* For living like a ghost?

BLACK: Watch your tongue, old man.

GREEN: *(Pause. Wounded.)* I don't like it when you call me that.

BLACK: But that's what you are, isn't it? An old man.

GREEN: *(Angry.)* Are you forgetting who I am?

BLACK: *(Wearily.)* Hardly.

GREEN: *(Still angry.)* And that it was I who found *you?*

BLACK: *(Pause.)* Only because I wanted to be found.

(Long pause.)

GREEN: What will you do when it's over?

BLACK: I don't have many choices, do I?

GREEN: *(Tentatively.)* Did the little boy really die?

BLACK: *(Painfully.)* I can't remember anymore.

GREEN: Did White really disappear? Did Gray really disappear?

BLACK: You know the answer as well as I do.

GREEN: And Black. What's going to happen to him?

BLACK: *(Pause.)* There aren't many choices, are there?

(Long pause.)

GREEN: Will he be here soon?

BLACK: *(Not hearing him. Looking out window. Pause. Horrified.)* Oh my God.

(Lights out. Ten seconds. Lights on. Black and Green in same positions. A knock on the door. Black turns and looks at Green. They stare at each other. Pause. The knock is repeated. Black gestures for Green to open the door. Green shuffles to the door. Opens it very slowly. Blue is standing in the doorway. He is wearing a trench coat and a hat.)

GREEN: *(Tentatively, peering around the door.)* Yes?

BLUE: *(Matter-of-factly.)* Is it time?

GREEN: *(Turning to Black.)* He wants to know if it's time.

BLACK: *(To Green.)* Ask him his name.

GREEN: *(To Blue.)* He wants to know your name.

BLUE: *(To Green.)* Tell him I want to know if it's time.

GREEN: *(To Black.)* He wants to know if it's time.

BLACK: *(Pause.)* Yes. It's time.

GREEN: *(To Blue.)* He says it's time.

(Blue, hands in pockets, takes one large step across threshold into the room, and stops.)

BLACK: *(Gesturing to other chair at his desk.)* This chair will do.

(Blue puts hat on Black's desk, drapes coat over back of chair. They all sit down in their chairs. Long pause. Green writes whenever Black and Blue speak.)

BLUE: Aren't you going to ask me to identify myself again?

BLACK: I know who you are. *(Pause.)* The only thing I care about is your report.

BLUE: I have the report, no need to worry.

BLACK: *(Relieved.)* Does it surprise you that it should all come down to this?

BLUE: I've been on this case too long to be surprised by anything.

BLACK: You feel . . . no regrets?

BLUE: What I feel doesn't matter. *(Pause.)* Besides, you can't bring it back, can you?

BLACK: *(Reflects.)* Except now. We're bringing it back now.

BLUE: No. It's all gone. We're just putting it into words.

(Pause.)

BLACK: *(To Green.)* Did you get that last sentence? Let me hear it.

(Green continues to write. Silence. Looks up. Slowly realizes what has been asked of him.)

GREEN: *(Reads.)* "Let me hear it."

BLACK: That's what I asked you.

GREEN: *(Confused.)* And that's what I gave you.

BLACK: *(Realizing. Shouts.)* No, no! The one about the words!

GREEN: *(Searches. Reads.)* "We're just putting it into words."

BLACK: *(To Blue.)* Is that what you mean to say?

GREEN: *(To Black. Peeved.)* You shouldn't be so vague about it.

BLACK: *(Turning abruptly to Green. Angry.)* No talking! Don't you remember?

GREEN: *(Singing softly under his breath.)* The bear went over the mountain, the bear went over the mountain, the bear went over the mountain, to see what he could see.

BLACK: What did you say! *(Waits for response. Silence.)* What!

(Green purses his lips shut. Gestures to his mouth, as if to prove he cannot speak. Long pause. Black and Green glare at each other.)

BLUE: Yes. That's exactly what I mean to say.

BLACK: I'm sorry.

BLUE: *(Shrugs.)* I have all the time in the world.

BLACK: It would be nice to think so. *(Pause.)* Where were we?

BLUE: Nowhere. We haven't started yet.

BLACK: I suppose you'd like to get it over with quickly.

BLUE: As I said, I have all the time in the world.

BLACK: Do you think I'm afraid? Do you think I'm trying to delay? *(Pause. Slams palm down on desk in anger.)* Damn it! Say what you mean, goddammit!

BLUE: *(Calmly.)* Whatever I say, I mean. If you want me to begin, I'll begin. If you want me to wait, I'll wait. If you want me to leave, I'll leave and come back tomorrow.

BLACK: No, no, not tomorrow. It would be too late then.

(Pause.)

BLUE: Where were we?

BLACK: *(Pause.)* We were about to begin.

(Pause. A loud cheeping noise is heard in the room.)

BLACK: *(Nervously.)* What's that?

BLUE: *(After a moment.)* Sounds like mice.

GREEN: Yes. It's the mice.

BLACK: *(To Green.)* You mean there are mice in the walls and you didn't tell me?

GREEN: It's only . . . a detail. I didn't want to bother you with it.

BLACK: It's disgusting.

GREEN: There's no need to worry. I've taken care of it.

BLACK: What does that mean?

GREEN: *(Long pause.)* Poison.

BLACK: They'll die in the walls and begin to stink. Their bodies will rot in the walls.

GREEN: Not so. They eat the poison and then leave. They die outside.

BLACK: How can you be sure?

GREEN: The poison makes them thirsty. They eat the poison and begin to crave water. They get frantic, go outside, and look for a drink. But it doesn't do any good. Even as they drink, they die from thirst.

(Long pause.)

BLACK: *(Returning to himself.)* Where were we? *(Pause.)* Read me back the last sentence.

GREEN: *(Hunts through pages.)* "We were about to begin."

BLACK: Who said it?

GREEN: You did.

(Pause.)

BLACK: *(Turning to Blue. About to speak. Hesitates.)* Just a few questions.

BLUE: *(Shrugs.)* As you wish.

BLACK: *(Pause.)* Do you feel you've been well paid?

BLUE: I've been paid.

BLACK: I'm not sure I understand you.

BLUE: I've never had too much to be able to stop, and I've never had too little to want to quit.

BLACK: And you don't feel any . . . bitterness?

BLUE: For what? There wouldn't be any sense to that. . . .

BLACK: And yet?

BLUE: Well, of course, goddammit, what do you think? It wouldn't have been human not to.

BLACK: *(Backing down slightly.)* It's just that you took on the work with such . . . such ardor. Even when the investigation was going nowhere, you continued to devote yourself to an exhaustive . . . an exhaustive examination of the details, to record even the most peripheral references to the case. *(Picks up a handful of folders from a tall pile on his desk.)* Hardly the work of a man just doing his job. There's real . . . devotion in this.

BLUE: *(Pause. Hesitant.)* After a while . . . it kind of got under my skin. *(Pause.)* After all, what did I have to do? *(Pause.)* I had to watch this man and write down what I saw. It was so simple, it never made any sense.

BLACK: Did you ever try to find out who hired you?

BLUE: *(Pause.)* You know that as well as I do.

BLACK: You didn't answer my question.

BLUE: *(About to answer. Pause.)* I prefer not to.

(Pause.)

BLACK: Do you know why you were asked to come today?

BLUE: To give the report.

BLACK: But why are you willing to give the report to me?

BLUE: Because you're the one who's here. If it had been someone else, I would have given it to him.

BLACK: It doesn't bother you that I might be the wrong man?

BLUE: You didn't ask me to identify myself. That means you know who I am. And if you know me, I know you.

BLACK: But what if I know more about you than you know about me?

BLUE: I wouldn't count on it.

(Pause.)

BLACK: How did it work?

BLUE: I followed him. I watched what he did. Then I'd write my report. Every Sunday night.

BLACK: And then?

BLUE: I'd mail it to the post box number on Monday morning.

BLACK: Did you ever wonder what they thought?

BLUE: Sometimes. Of course I did. *(Pause.)* But since my check came every week, I figured they thought I was doing a good job.

BLACK: And the man. Did you ever wonder what he thought of you?

BLUE: He never saw me. *(Pause.)* That was the point, wasn't it? He wasn't supposed to know I was watching him.

BLACK: But didn't you ever feel like talking to him? Didn't you ever want . . . to know him?

BLUE: It made no difference to me. *(Pause.)* I thought: How much can I get to know just from watching him? It interested me . . . as a kind of puzzle. *(Pause.)* So I watched him. I'd plant myself outside his house in the morning and wait for him to come out. Most of the time, he never seemed to go anywhere. Nothing more than rudimentary kinds of things: grocery shopping, an occasional haircut, now and then a movie. But mostly he just wandered around the streets. *(Pause.)* He seemed to look at things in spurts. For a while, say, it would be buildings, craning his neck to catch a glimpse of the roofs, inspecting doors, running his hands over the facades . . . And then, for a week or two, he'd look at people . . . or the boats in the river . . . or the signs in the street. *(Pause.)* For a long time I thought he didn't have any kind of life at all. *(Pause.)* I mean, he didn't *do* anything. From everything I could gather, he lived alone. He never saw anyone, he didn't go to a job, it was an effort for him even to speak. *(Pause. Thinks.)* This went on for more than a year, maybe two. I can't remember. He was so blank, he hardly seemed to be there. *(Pause.)* In all that time, I learned nothing about him. *(Pause.)* Nothing. *(Pause.)* I could write down what he did, I could tell you what kind of soap he bought, what clothes he wore, but it didn't really amount to anything. *(Pause.)* I never had the slightest idea what he was thinking.

BLACK: Did it bother you?

BLUE: *(Shrugs.)* It made no difference to me. *(Pause.)* I was doing my job, I was getting paid, it made no difference at all.

BLACK: And then?

BLUE: *(Pause. Thinks. Remembers.)* Somehow or other, it started to change. I can't really say why. *(Pause.)* I think . . . I started to like him. *(Pause.)* One day I woke up, and I realized I couldn't wait to go out and watch him, to see what he did.

BLACK: You were having troubles of your own then, weren't you?

BLUE: What do you mean?

BLACK: *(Pause.)* Family troubles.

BLUE: You mean my wife.

BLACK: Your wife. Your children. *(Pause.)* They . . . disappeared.

BLUE: She walked out on me, if that's what you mean.

BLACK: More or less.

BLUE: Yes. My wife walked out on me. *(Pause.)* I admit it. *(Pause. Without emotion.)* I was a terrible husband. A terrible father.

BLACK: It's nothing to be ashamed of.

BLUE: *(Shrugs.)* A matter of opinion.

(For the past few sentences, Green has been breaking pencil points, tossing the broken pencil onto the floor and picking up a new one. He now breaks several points in rapid succession. Black and Blue stop talking and stare at him. Green smiles at them with embarrassment. Indicates he is ready to proceed again and gestures to them to continue.)

BLACK: And then?

BLUE: I had more time.

BLACK: You changed your life.

BLUE: My life?

BLACK: You moved, didn't you? Across the street *(pause)* from the man.

BLUE: It seemed like a practical thing to do. It was winter, after all. *(Pause.)* I could watch from the window, keep myself warm. Warm and hidden. *(Pause.)* When he went out, I went out.

BLACK: Is that when it started?

BLUE: What?

BLACK: To get . . . under your skin. *(Pause.)* I think those were your words.

BLUE: I didn't have anything else to do, you see. *(Pause.)* There was nothing else to think about.

BLACK: So you sat by the window and wrote *(pause)* about the man.

BLUE: I started to ask myself questions. I thought: No one could possibly be interested in this man. No one would pay me every week to do what I was doing, except . . . *(Slight pause, about to continue.)*

BLACK: Except?

BLUE: . . . the man himself.

BLACK: *(Nervously.)* But why would he do a thing like that?

BLUE: *(Shrugs.)* I have no idea. *(Pause.)* I'm just giving you the story. As it happened.

BLACK: And then?

BLUE: I thought it might be useful to see if he was the one who picked up my reports at the post office. I hung around there all week, each day in a different disguise. I like that kind of thing: the false mustaches, the wigs, the rubber noses, the makeup, the clothes. *(Pause.)* Brown, the man who broke me into the business twenty years ago, said I was one of the best he'd ever seen. *(Pause.)* Anyway, on the sixth day he finally came.

BLACK: Was it the man?

BLUE: *(Pause.)* I'm not sure. *(Pause.)* He was in disguise too.

BLACK: But couldn't you tell?

BLUE: I had my suspicions, but I couldn't be sure. *(Pause.)* He was wearing a mask. One of those things kids wear at Halloween. A big rubber mask of a goblin. *(Pause.)* What was I supposed to do? Go up and tear it off his face? *(Pause.)* I couldn't risk blowing my cover.

BLACK: Did you ever try again?

BLUE: A few more times. But nothing ever came of it. *(Pause.)* He was always wearing a different mask.

BLACK: You say "he." But it might have been "they," couldn't it? A different man each time. A different man in a different mask each time.

BLUE: Exactly.

BLACK: And then?

BLUE: Another year or so went by. I decided on a new approach. *(Pause.)* I thought I would make contact with him. *(Pause.)* I was itchy to get into disguise again, and he was beginning to drive me crazy. *(Pause.)* I mean, nothing ever changed. I felt trapped. As if, my God, this is going to go on forever.

BLACK: What did you do?

BLUE: I waited for my moments. The first time, I pretended to be a bum, begging nickels on the corner. He gave me a nickel and said, "God bless you." It was the first time I ever heard him speak. *(Pause.)* Another time, I pretended to be an out-of-town businessman, a blowhard in a polyester suit. I stopped him for directions and managed to talk my way into buying him a drink. We stayed for a few hours in that bar, the Algonquin I think it was. I can't remember. *(Gesturing to reports on Black's desk.)* It's all written down.

BLACK: Did you talk?

BLUE: We both talked.

BLACK: And?

BLUE: He told me he was a detective. For the past few years he'd been working on one case. He went on about it for half the evening. Following a man, he said, day in, day out, until he knew that man as well as he knew himself.

BLACK: Did you feel he was on to you then?

BLUE: Of course he was on to me. *(Pause.)* He was making fun of me.

BLACK: Did it make you uncomfortable?

BLUE: It made me feel like an idiot. *(Pause.)* I nearly quit right then and there.

BLACK: Why didn't you?

BLUE: *(Thinks.)* Because, even so, I had made several important discoveries. *(Pause.)* First of all, he was the man who had hired me. There was no question about that anymore. Second, he needed me. There was something he wanted me to know, and little by little he was letting me in on his secret.

BLACK: Couldn't you guess?

BLUE: No. *(Pause.)* The whole thing escaped me. *(Pause.)* All I knew was that he was calling the shots. Clues, legwork, investigative routine—all those things didn't matter anymore. I was on my own. *(Pause.)* At the same time, I had to keep up appearances . . . go about my business . . . do the job I was supposedly being paid to do.

BLACK: You played dumb.

BLUE: Very dumb.

BLACK: But of course he knew that.

BLUE: Of course.

BLACK: And then?

BLUE: Little by little, I began to lose patience again. *(Pause.)* I cooked up another scheme. *(Pause.)* But of course, by this time, I couldn't tell if it was my idea or his. *(Pause.)* I did the old routine of the Fuller brush man. I've always had luck with it. Knocked on his door and offered to show him my samples.

BLACK: Did he let you in?

BLUE: Of course he let me in.

BLACK: Why do you think?

BLUE: Because he was ready to have me come. He wanted me to be there.

BLACK: *(Reflective.)* Ah.

BLUE: The apartment was one large room. Nearly bare. A small, neatly made bed in one corner. A kitchenette in another corner. Also neat. Not a crumb to be seen. In the center of the room there was a wooden table with a single stiff-backed wooden chair. Pencils, pens, a typewriter. And then the piles of paper, manuscripts, neatly stacked around the edges of the table, on the floor by the legs of the table, and on the shelves of the bookcase that covered the entire north wall of the apartment. Other than that, nothing. No telephone, no radio, no books. Nothing. It wasn't a room you could really live in. A place to think, maybe. A place to write. But that's all. *(Pause.)* I realized that what I had seen was all there was. From the very beginning. *(Pause.)* The man had no life you could call a life.

BLACK: What did you talk about?

BLUE: The brushes. We had to keep up appearances, remember. That was part of the game.

BLACK: And then?

BLUE: Little by little, I began to ask him questions. About this, about that, very casually, part of my salesman's patter. *(Pause.)* He told me that he was a writer and that for a long time he had been working on a book. I asked him when I would get a chance to read his work. He said he didn't know. Maybe never, he said. He didn't know if he'd live to finish it.

BLACK: And then?

BLUE: *(Long pause.)* I made up my mind to steal the manuscripts.

BLACK: It sounds as if you were beginning . . . to overstep your bounds.

BLUE: No. He was asking me to take them.

BLACK: In so many words?

BLUE: Never in so many words. Of course not. Nothing said was ever what was meant. That was the point. *(Pause.)* It was a matter of understanding him in advance . . . of reading between the lines. *(Pause.)* Eventually I caught on.

BLACK: Did you go through with it?

BLUE: The next night. *(Pause.)* I knew what I was doing, you see. There was no need to waste time.

BLACK: Did you wait until he was out . . . or did you try some other method?

BLUE: I didn't bother about any of that. *(Pause. Emphatically.)* I knew what I was doing. *(Pause.)* It must have been about eight-thirty, nine o'clock. I had no trouble picking the lock. *(Pause. Remembering.)* Child's play. *(Pause.)*

I walked into the room, and there he was, sitting on the bed, as if . . . thinking. *(Pause.)* He was wearing the mask. The same one he had been wearing that first time in the post office.

(Black opens desk drawer, takes out Halloween mask, and puts it on.)

BLACK: Was it this mask?

BLUE: That's the one.

(Green starts giggling at the sight of the mask. Black and Blue turn to stare at him. A long moment. Green gestures for them to continue.)

BLACK: And then?

BLUE: He didn't say a word. He didn't move. *(Pause.)* I walked over to the table, picked up a pile of manuscripts at random, put them under my arm, and left the room.

BLACK: He did nothing to stop you?

BLUE: You still don't understand. *(Pause.)* He was waiting for me. He wanted me to take it. *(Pause.)* But I should have taken more. That was my only slip. *(Pause.)* So I went back the next night, and the next night after that.

BLACK: And what happened?

BLUE: The same thing. Nothing. Nothing happened.

BLACK: Did you read the manuscripts?

BLUE: Every word.

BLACK: And?

BLUE: The whole thing was there. *(Pause.)* More or less as I had imagined it.

BLACK: You weren't . . . disappointed?

BLUE: Not really. *(Pause.)* It seemed to make a kind of sense.

BLACK: *(Pause.)* And then?

BLUE: I went back one more time. *(Pause.)* But now it was different.

BLACK: In what way?

BLUE: He had a gun.

(Black takes a gun out of his inside breast pocket. Holds it up. Points it at Blue.)

BLACK: This gun?

BLUE: Yes. That's the one.

BLACK: And then?

BLUE: I opened the door, entered the room, and there he was, sitting on the bed, pointing that forty-five at my face. He said, "That's enough, my friend. You've taken it as far as it can go."

BLACK: And what did you say?

BLUE: Nothing. I didn't say a word. *(Pause.)* I snapped. Something inside me went crazy. *(Pause.)* I kicked the gun out of his hand, grabbed him by the collar, and started banging his head against the wall. I picked him up, threw him down, kicked him in the ribs, punched him in the face. I wanted to kill him.

BLACK: Did you?

BLUE: *(Pause.)* I'm not sure.

BLACK: *(Angry.)* Not sure? *(Pause.)* There's no middle ground, my friend. It's either life or death. There's nothing in between.

BLUE: I couldn't tell. He was still breathing when I left, but I didn't think he'd last much longer. He seemed to be bleeding inside, and he was unconscious.

BLACK: *(Enraged.)* And now? What is he now? Alive or dead?

BLUE: *(Hesitates.)* Alive.

BLACK: *(Shouting.)* Are you sure?

BLUE: *(Hesitates.)* Dead.

BLACK: *(Beside himself.)* Are you sure?

BLUE: No. I'm not sure. I'm not sure of anything.

(Lights out. Ten seconds. Lights on. All three in same positions. Black no longer wearing mask, no longer holding gun.)

BLUE: *(To Black.)* Are you finished now?

BLACK: Yes. It's finished.

BLUE: Nothing to add, nothing to take away?

BLACK: No. It's finished.

BLUE: Is it true that the boy died?

BLACK: I'm not sure.

BLUE: And the man, the one in the ditch. What was his name?

BLACK: White.

BLUE: Whatever happened to White?

BLACK: I'm not sure.

BLUE: And Gray? Is he alive or dead?

BLACK: Probably dead.

BLUE: Are you ready to talk about it?

BLACK: Later. I'll tell you the whole story later.

BLUE: And Green, what does he say?

BLACK: *(To Green.)* Green, what do you say?

GREEN: *(Pause. Looking up.)* What?

BLACK: What do you say, Green?

GREEN: *(Putting down his pencil. Clears throat, as if preparing for a long speech. Hesitates.)* Nothing. I don't say a thing.

BLACK: *(To Blue.)* Green doesn't say a thing.

BLUE: A pity.

BLACK: *(Takes gun from pocket and points it at Green.)* What do you say now, Green?

GREEN: *(Long pause, staring at gun.)* Nothing.

BLACK: Nothing?

GREEN: *(Slamming palm down on desk in anger. Shouting.)* Nothing!

BLUE: *(Sighs.)* Let's take it from the top again.

(Black puts gun back in pocket. Green resumes writing position.)

BLACK: I'm not sure there's anything to discuss.

BLUE: Let me be the judge of that. *(Pause. To Green.)* Are you ready, Green?

GREEN: *(Long pause. At last realizing he has been addressed.)* Are you speaking to me?

BLUE: Are you ready?

GREEN: Ready? Of course I'm ready. *(Holds up pencil.)* The pencil's ready. *(Holds up page.)* The paper's ready. *(Half stands up and gives brief bow.)* And Green's ready.

BLUE: Good. *(Pause. To Black.)* Is the little boy dead?

BLACK: Yes, he's dead. I don't think there's any doubt about it.

BLUE: And White?

BLACK: He was kicked to death.

BLUE: And Gray?

BLACK: He blew his brains out.

BLUE: And Black?

BLACK: What about Black?

BLUE: That's what I'm asking you. What about Black?

BLACK: *(Thinks.)* I don't know. *(Pause.)* Black doesn't count. *(Pause.)* Black is the one who isn't there.

BLUE: And what does Black say?

BLACK: *(Thinks.)* Black says he's tired. *(Pause.)* Black says he can't go on anymore. *(Pause.)* Black says nothing.

(Lights out. Ten seconds. Lights on. All three in same positions. Green is slowly tearing up the pages he has written, one by one. Blue and Black are watching him. A long moment.)

BLACK: *(To Green.)* Are you finished?

GREEN: *(Still tearing pages.)* Almost finished.

(Long pause. Green goes on tearing pages.)

BLACK: *(To Green.)* Are you finished now?

GREEN: *(Still tearing pages.)* Almost finished.

(Long pause. Green goes on tearing pages.)

BLACK: *(To Green.)* Are you finished now?

GREEN: *(Tearing last page.)* Finished.

BLUE: Good. I think we're ready to begin now. *(Pause. Turning to Green.)* Are you ready to begin, Mr. Green?

GREEN: Yes, I'm ready.

BLUE: *(To Black.)* And you, Mr. Black?

BLACK: I'm ready.

GREEN: And what about you, Mr. Blue?

BLUE: Yes, I'm ready.

BLACK: Good. Let's get on with it, then, shall we?

(Pause. Five seconds. Lights out.)

(1976)

Hide and Seek

Characters

MAN
WOMAN

Bare stage. Two rectangular boxes made of wood, standing upright, ten feet apart, stage center. Man occupies stage right box; Woman occupies stage left box. The boxes are approximately the size and shape of telephone booths. Each box is open on the front panel from waist level to roof and furnished with a dark velvet curtain, theater style, a shelf at thigh level for props within, and a drawstring that can be operated from within by the actors. The opening and closing of the curtains must be audible: a hard, distinctive grating sound. The stage is in darkness. Spotlights on each box, to remain until the end of the performance.

(Woman opens curtain. Pause, two beats. Man opens curtain.)

WOMAN: What did you say?

MAN: *(Thinks.)* I can't remember. *(Pause.)* Maybe I didn't say anything.

WOMAN: *(Shrugs.)* Suit yourself. *(Examines teeth in a pocket mirror.)* It makes no difference to me.

(Woman shuts curtain. Pause, two beats. Man shuts curtain. Pause. Eight beats. Man opens curtain.)

MAN: Do you think we'll ever find it?

(Woman opens curtain.)

WOMAN: What?

MAN: I said, "Do you think we'll ever find it?"

WOMAN: I heard what you said. Then I said, "What."

MAN: Oh. You mean *what.*

WOMAN: Yes, *what.*

MAN: Yes, yes, now I see. *What.*

WOMAN: Well?

MAN: *(Thinks.)* I can't remember. *(Pause.)* Maybe I wasn't asking anything.

WOMAN: *(Shrugs.)* Suit yourself. *(Flips through the pages of a magazine.)* It makes no difference to me.

(Woman shuts curtain. Pause, two beats. Man shuts curtain. Pause. Eight beats. Man opens curtain. Pause, one beat. Woman opens curtain.)

MAN: It's cold in here.

WOMAN: No it's not. It's quite warm.

MAN: Maybe for you. For me it's cold.

WOMAN: No. If it's warm for me, that means it's warm for both of us.

MAN: But . . . *(Exasperated.)* I'm shivering.

WOMAN: It's your imagination.

MAN: What are you talking about? It's my body. The cold is in my body.

WOMAN: *(Patiently.)* No, my love. It's in your mind.

MAN: Mind? *(Pause.)* Mind? You can't be serious. It's in my arms. My legs. My face. My chest. My feet. *(Pause.)* Mind!

WOMAN: *(Patiently.)* Are you finished?

MAN: Finished? What do you mean finished?

WOMAN: Finished with your . . . *(gropes)* . . . your ranting.

MAN: Yes. I suppose so. I mean . . . yes. *(Pause.)* I suppose so.

WOMAN: And?

MAN: *(Imitating her.)* And?

WOMAN: And how do you feel?

MAN: *(Thinks.)* Lonely. *(Pause.)* Unloved. *(Pause.)* Lonely and unloved.

WOMAN: That's not what I mean. I want to know if you're still cold.

MAN: Cold? *(Stops, touches his arms, his face, thinks.)* It's funny. I actually feel quite warm now.

WOMAN: Do you see?

MAN: *(Confused.)* See? Yes. Of course I can see. *(Peers out into the distance.)* I see people.

WOMAN: No, not that kind of seeing. I mean *see.* You know, with your mind.

MAN: With my mind? *(Pause.)* Yes. I see what you mean. See

with my mind . . . in the same way my mind can be cold. *(Smiles. Pause.)* See what with my mind?

WOMAN: How much I love you.

MAN: *(Pleased.)* Yes, my darling. Of course I see that. *(Pause.)* But what does that have to do with what we were talking about?

WOMAN: You said you were cold, didn't you?

MAN: Yes.

WOMAN: Well, I can't go over and take you in my arms, can I? I can't warm you with my body. *(Pause.)* Can I?

MAN: But you said it was all in my mind.

WOMAN: I had to say something. And what better way to warm you up than to get you angry? There's nothing like a vicious little spat to get the blood flowing again.

MAN: Ah. That was very clever of you.

WOMAN: You see what sacrifices a woman makes for the man she loves? I was willing to let you hate me—just to show my love.

MAN: I thought you hated *me.*

WOMAN: It's complicated, isn't it? But sometimes hate is really love.

MAN: *(Impressed, shaking his head.)* You're really a very clever woman.

WOMAN: *(Smiling.)* Of course I'm clever. *(Pause.)* I've needed to be, haven't I?

MAN: I don't deny it.

WOMAN: That's good.

MAN: Yes, I don't deny it.

WOMAN: *(A little puzzled.)* Deny what?

MAN: Anything. *(Pause.)* Everything. *(Pause.)* Anything and everything.

WOMAN: That's very clever of you.

MAN: *(Pleased.)* Well, you have to admit . . .

WOMAN: Yes, I do. *(Pause.)* In fact, I don't deny it.

MAN: Splendid. *(Reflects.)* I'm glad we agree.

WOMAN: *(Attention beginning to wander.)* I'm glad you're glad.

MAN: I'm glad you're glad I'm glad.

WOMAN: *(Pause. More abstracted.)* I'm glad you're glad I'm glad you're glad.

(Pause. Man listens. Closes curtain, as slowly and quietly as possible. Woman comes out of daze. Listens.)

WOMAN: Jimmy? *(Waits. No answer. Shrugs.)* Suit yourself. *(Takes out pocket mirror and examines her face.)* It makes no difference to me. *(Smiles at herself in mirror. Touches her face. Frowns. Looks more closely at herself in mirror. Smiles again. Still looking at herself, she absentmindedly reaches for cord and slowly closes curtain.)*

(Pause. Eight beats. Woman opens curtain. Pause, two beats. Man opens curtain.)

WOMAN: *(Thinking hard, as if trying to unravel a difficult logical problem.)* If you have nothing to say, maybe you just shouldn't bother to say it.

MAN: *(Shrugs.)* Speak for yourself.

WOMAN: On the other hand, if you have something to say, you should speak what's on your mind. *(Pause.)* That's what I think.

MAN: *(Sadly.)* It's all just words.

WOMAN: Of course it is. What else would it be? Words. That's what we're talking about.

MAN: You can't just say "words." That doesn't mean anything. You have to say one word or another. This word or that word.

WOMAN: But I don't want to say this word or that word. I want to say all words. Any word. Words. In the sense of *(pause)* words.

MAN: Yes, I see what you mean. *(Pause.)* But what if I were to say one word? What would you think then?

WOMAN: It depends on the word.

MAN: How about "blue"?

WOMAN: Ah yes, blue. *(Closes eyes, smiles.)* That's a very nice word.

MAN: Do you see what I mean?

WOMAN: Yes. *(Smiles with inward pleasure.)* I see . . . blue.

MAN: No. I mean . . . think of the *word* blue.

WOMAN: That's what I'm doing. And I see blue . . . beautiful blue.

MAN: But blue isn't a word like other words. *(Pause.)* It doesn't mean anything.

WOMAN: Of course it does. It means "blue."

MAN: But what can you really say about blue?

WOMAN: I can say . . . Blue . . . is blue. A color. I can say: blue is a color.

MAN: But that doesn't help, does it? I mean, it doesn't let you *see* blue.

WOMAN: All I have to do is say "blue" . . . and then I see blue.

MAN: Yes. But you see it only because you've already seen it.

WOMAN: *(Thinks. Long pause.)* Yes, I see what you mean. *(Pause.)* But just because I can't talk about blue, you're not trying to say there's no such thing as blue—are you?

MAN: No. There is blue. Blue exists. *(Pause.)* I believe in blue. I love blue. Of all the things in the world, blue is what I love best.

WOMAN: Me too. *(As if seeing it: contemplative, rapturous.)* A very blue blue. A blue bluer than the blue that is blue. The bluest of blues, a blue so blue it is beyond blue. A blissful, beautiful blue.

MAN: A blue that would be blue even if there were no blue.

WOMAN: A blue that would be blue even if there were no word for blue.

MAN: A blue that is green. A blue that is red. A blue that is green and red and blue.

WOMAN: A blue in the eye of all seeing, of all that is blue and not blue.

MAN: A blue of blues.

WOMAN: Yes. A blue of blues.

(Pause. Five beats. Letting the idea sink in. They slowly close their curtains in unison. Pause. Eight beats. They open their curtains quickly in unison.)

MAN: Do you remember the last time?

WOMAN: Which time was that?

MAN: The time we sang the song and danced the dance.

WOMAN: *(Remembering.)* Ah yes, That time. *(Remembering warmly.)* They loved us, didn't they?

MAN: We deserved it. We were wonderful.

WOMAN: I was deluged with flowers for a month.

MAN: I've never seen you so beautiful.

WOMAN: I had quite a voice in those days, didn't I? And you were so handsome.

MAN: We were in love.

WOMAN: It wasn't so long ago, was it, Jimmy?

MAN: I don't think so. At least not so terribly long ago.

WOMAN: Maybe things will pick up again. Maybe we'll get another break.

MAN: I'm not really counting on it, my love.

WOMAN: *(Reflects.)* No. I suppose not.

MAN: On the other hand, it could be worse.

WOMAN: Yes, at least we're working again. *(Pause.)* I know it's not much. But it's something, isn't it, Jimmy?

MAN: Yes, my love. It's something.

WOMAN: *(Smiling to herself.)* Do you remember Boston?

MAN: Yes. I remember Boston and I remember Kansas City.

WOMAN: Do you remember Chicago?

MAN: Yes. I remember Chicago and I remember San Francisco.

WOMAN: Do you remember Spokane?

MAN: Yes. I remember Spokane and I remember Atlanta.

WOMAN: Do you remember Minneapolis?

MAN: Yes. I remember Minneapolis and I remember New York.

(Pause. They reflect. Man takes out newspaper and starts reading. Woman remains wistful.)

WOMAN: Travel isn't the same today, is it?

MAN: *(Turning from his paper.)* Hardly.

WOMAN: I loved those old trains, with the berths, and the dining cars, and the sounds at night.

MAN: *(Turning from his paper.)* Clickety-clack. Clickety-clack.

WOMAN: And the silverware shivering on the table at breakfast, everything clinking together like little bells, and the trees and the air outside, always changing, always becoming more trees and more air, the whole thing always changing.

MAN: *(Turning from his paper.)* Clickety-clack. Clickety-clack.

WOMAN: Sometimes I would look out the window for hours on end. I'd always say to myself, "Try to remember this. Even though you're seeing it only once, try to remember it." But I never could. It all went by so fast, it became a blur in my head. *(Pause.)* That's what I see now. A beautiful blur.

MAN: *(Putting down his paper.)* Do you remember the last time?

WOMAN: Which time was that?

MAN: The time we sang the song and danced the dance.

WOMAN: *(Remembering.)* Ah yes. That time. *(Remembering warmly.)* I had quite a voice then, didn't I?

MAN: *(Remembering.)* It was quite a song.

WOMAN: *(Pause. Seeing it in her mind.)* It was quite a dance.

(Pause. Two beats. They both make gestures with their arms and shoulders, as if singing and dancing, moving their lips in silence, as if delivering the words of a song. Theatrical smiles. They finish, blow kisses to the audience, etc. They close curtains in unison. Pause. Eight beats. Man opens curtain quickly. Pause, one beat. Woman opens curtain quickly.)

MAN: *(Alarmed, excited.)* Have you noticed?

WOMAN: *(Also alarmed.)* Yes, yes, of course I've noticed.

MAN: What are we going to do about it?

WOMAN: I don't know. What *can* we do?

MAN: We can sue. We can protest. We can throw stones.

WOMAN: But that wouldn't solve anything. *(Pause.)* We've got to make them *listen.*

MAN: I know. But we don't have much time. We've got to act fast.

WOMAN: What if we don't? *(Pause.)* What will happen to us then?

MAN: Nothing good. *(Pause.)* I suppose the worst. *(Pause.)* Yes. Nothing but the worst.

WOMAN: The worst?

MAN: Yes.

WOMAN: That's bad, isn't it?

MAN: It's worse than bad. *(Pause.)* It's the worst.

WOMAN: The worst.

MAN: Are you all right?

WOMAN: To tell you the truth, no.

MAN: Do you have any ideas?

WOMAN: Yes.

MAN: What?

WOMAN: I'm going to scream.

MAN: When are you going to do it?

WOMAN: Right now.

MAN: Right now?

WOMAN: Yes. Right now.

(Man tenses for the scream. Woman building her courage. Man waits. Woman still building her courage. Man continues to wait. Finally gives up. Shrugs. Closes curtain.)

WOMAN: *(Meekly.)* Help. *(With more force.)* Help. *(With greater force.)* Help! *(With greatest force.)* Help! Help! Help!

(Man opens curtain.)

MAN: *(Screams.)* Help! Help! Help!

(They suddenly fall silent. Pause. Five beats, staring out blankly. Woman closes curtain. Pause, two beats. Man closes curtain. Pause. Eight beats. Man opens curtain.)

MAN: It begins like this. *(Recites.)* It was and it was and it was. It was and it was and it wasn't. It was and it wasn't and it wasn't. It wasn't and it wasn't and it wasn't. It wasn't and it wasn't and it was.

(Woman opens curtain. She is reading a magazine.)

WOMAN: *(Turning from her magazine.)* That's absurd.

MAN: You don't like it?

WOMAN: I can't stand that kind of stuff. *(Pause.)* Give me a good story any time.

MAN: *(Shrugs.)* People aren't interested in stories anymore.

WOMAN: That's absurd. *(Pause.)* I, for one, devour them.

MAN: Since when?

WOMAN: Since . . . since always.

MAN: I didn't know that.

WOMAN: There's a lot you don't know about me. I have my own life. I have my own life . . . and my own secrets.

MAN: Oh?

WOMAN: That's right. Since . . . since always.

MAN: What kind of secrets?

WOMAN: If I told you, then they wouldn't be secrets anymore, would they?

MAN: I suppose you mean that fellow in Baltimore. *(Pause.)* What was his name? That short one with the slicked-down hair. *(Pause.)* George.

WOMAN: George?

MAN: George. *(Pause.)* And then there was the one in Philadelphia. The tall fellow with the blond hair. *(Pause.)* The waiter. *(Pause.)* Oh yes. And the young woman in Washington. That redhead with the nice body. *(Pause.)* I remember her too.

WOMAN: You're being nasty again, Jimmy.

MAN: No I'm not, my love. I'm just telling you the story.

WOMAN: Well, I don't like it.

MAN: *(Shrugs.)* It makes no difference. *(Pause.)* Cocks and cunts have a life of their own. What they do and where they go has little to do with the people they belong to. *(Pause.)* It's always the same story.

WOMAN: But I like stories.

MAN: That's why I'm telling it to you.

WOMAN: Good. *(Pause.)* How does it go again?

MAN: What?

WOMAN: The thing about . . . about bodies.

MAN: *(Thinks. Has trouble remembering.)* Cocks *(pause)* and cunts *(pause)* have a life of their own.

WOMAN: That's right. I liked that very much.

MAN: You did?

WOMAN: Very much.

MAN: I made it up on the spot.

WOMAN: You see? When you let yourself go, you say the most brilliant things.

MAN: Perhaps. *(Pause.)* But it wasn't really a story.

WOMAN: It doesn't matter. I liked it.

MAN: It was just words.

WOMAN: So much the better.

MAN: Do you think so?

WOMAN: I know so.

MAN: *(Smiles.)* So much the better.

(They both laugh. They laugh again. They close curtains in unison at the peak of a third burst of laughter. Pause. Eight beats. Woman opens curtain.)

WOMAN: Have you noticed?

(Man opens curtain.)

MAN: *(Thinks.)* It's hard to say. *(Pause.)* Probably not. *(Pause.)* In fact, I'd say definitely not.

WOMAN: I find that hard to believe.

MAN: It's hardly hard. I can believe it quite easily.

WOMAN: Look. All you have to do is look.

MAN: *(Peers out into the distance before him.)* I'm looking.

WOMAN: And?

MAN: And what?

WOMAN: What do you see?

MAN: *(Looks even more intently.)* Nothing. *(Pause. Produces a pair of binoculars and looks through them.)* Absolutely nothing.

WOMAN: *Where* are you looking?

MAN: In front of me.

WOMAN: That's the problem. You're looking in the wrong place.

MAN: Where *should* I be looking?

WOMAN: To your left.

MAN: *(Looks to his left.)* All right. I'm looking to my left.

WOMAN: What do you see?

MAN: A wall.

WOMAN: Good. A wall. Now look to your right. What do you see?

MAN: *(Looks to his right.)* A wall.

WOMAN: Now look behind you. What do you see?

MAN: *(Looks behind.)* A wall.

WOMAN: Now look down, in front of you. What do you see?

MAN: *(Looks down.)* A wall. *(Pause. Considers.)* Half a wall. *(Pause.)* I would say I see half a wall.

WOMAN: So how many walls does that make?

MAN: *(Counting with his fingers.)* Four walls. *(Pause.)* No. Three and a half walls. *(Pause.)* There are three and a half walls.

WOMAN: And?

MAN: And what?

WOMAN: Have you noticed?

MAN: *(Thinks.)* I'm not sure I follow you.

WOMAN: Have you noticed that you're boxed in?

MAN: Oh. *(Pause. Thinks.)* Yes, I see what you mean. *(Thinks.)* So what else is new?

WOMAN: It doesn't bother you to be boxed in?

MAN: *(Reflects.)* I don't think so. *(Pause.)* Not particularly anyway.

WOMAN: Well, it bothers *me.* *(With emphasis.)* Very much.

MAN: You shouldn't let it get you down. After all, it won't go on very long.

WOMAN: *(Suspicious.)* Who told you that?

MAN: Isn't it obvious?

WOMAN: Not for me it isn't.

MAN: Don't you remember? We agreed to do it.

WOMAN: *(Thinks. Grudgingly.)* Vaguely. *(Pause. Angry.)* But I never thought it would be like this.

MAN: We're just here to help things along.

WOMAN: We could have helped in other ways, couldn't we? Boxes! *(Pause.)* It's so . . . demeaning.

MAN: We're in the boxes for a reason.

WOMAN: *(Sarcastic.)* Yeah? Name one.

MAN: What I think doesn't matter.

WOMAN: You see? You can't even come up with one.

MAN: That's not true. How about this? *(Pause. Thinks.)* The boxes are our bodies, and our bodies inside them are our souls?

WOMAN: Rubbish.

MAN: How about . . . We are all alone, walled off from each other in darkness . . . *(waxing eloquent)* . . . in the darkness of an unappeasable solitude?

WOMAN: Piffle.

MAN: How about . . . *(Groping.)* The boxes are just here, and we're just here inside them . . . to help things along?

WOMAN: You see! When you come right down to it, there's no reason at all.

MAN: *(Considers.)* Mmm . . . I see what you mean. *(Pause.)* I'll have to think about that.

WOMAN: Well, don't be long. I don't have all night. There are things I want to do, and I can't do them standing in this box.

(Woman shuts curtain. Man thinks. Three beats. Man shuts curtain. Pause. Eight beats. They open curtains quickly in unison. Pause. Three beats.)

MAN: In answer to your question . . .

WOMAN: Yes?

MAN: In answer to your question about . . . these enclosures . . .

WOMAN: Yes?

MAN: I think . . .

WOMAN: Yes?

MAN: I think . . . there is only one thing to be done. . . .

WOMAN: Which is?

MAN: To do what we have to do.

WOMAN: Aren't you repeating yourself?

MAN: No, there's a difference.

WOMAN: Which is?

MAN: To put it another way . . .

WOMAN: Yes?

MAN: It all comes down to this . . .

WOMAN: Yes?

MAN: To say what we have to say, to do what we have to do, to act in the way we have to act.

WOMAN: And then?

MAN: There is no then. That's it.

WOMAN: Ah. *(Smiles.)* What a soothing thought. *(Pause.)* And how kind everyone has been to us tonight.

MAN: You almost seem to be . . . happy.

WOMAN: I'm very happy. Wonderfully and blissfully happy.

MAN: You never fail to astonish me.

WOMAN: I never fail to astonish myself.

MAN: Ah yes. I see what you mean.

WOMAN: Funny, isn't it?

MAN: Yes, it's funny.

WOMAN: And sad too.

MAN: Yes, I suppose it's sad too.

WOMAN: And many other things as well.

MAN: Yes. And many other things.

WOMAN: And life just goes on, doesn't it? With us or without us.

MAN: That's true. With us or without us.

WOMAN: That's why I'm so happy.

MAN: What a lovely thought. I couldn't agree with you more.

WOMAN: I'm glad.

MAN: I wish I could kiss you.

WOMAN: There will be time for that later.

MAN: I hope so.

WOMAN: Hope is the air we breathe. Hope is everywhere.

MAN: Very well put.

WOMAN: Yes. I sometimes have a gift for saying beautiful things.

MAN: *(Pause. Looks at his watch.)* I think we have to stop now. This little part is over.

WOMAN: Oh, that's too bad. I was just getting warmed up.

MAN: There's always the next time.

WOMAN: I suppose so. But it might not be the same. One has one's moments . . . of inspiration.

MAN: *(Looks at watch nervously.)* Darling, I really think we'll have to put this off until later. Time is up.

(Man shuts curtain suddenly.)

WOMAN: It's such a pleasure to feel the words rolling off your tongue, to feel them flowing out from you, into the air, into the world, into the ears of others. It's such a pleasure to hear yourself speaking the words that come from your mouth, to feel your mouth moving with the sounds you make. It's such a pleasure—

(Man opens curtain suddenly.)

MAN: Darling!

WOMAN: Yes, dear. I'm coming.

MAN: Now!

WOMAN: *(Sighs.)* Yes, dear.

(Woman closes curtain. Man, listening to be sure she has done it, then closes his curtain. Pause. Eight beats. Man opens curtain. Woman opens curtain.)

WOMAN: Do you think we'll ever find it?

MAN: It depends on what we're looking for.

WOMAN: It doesn't matter. Anything.

MAN: A door to open, a door to shut. A place to put our heads.

WOMAN: Yes. And those things as well. *(Pause.)* But it doesn't really matter.

MAN: No. It makes no difference at all.

(Pause. Four beats. They think.)

WOMAN: Do you think we'll ever find it?

MAN: We can't count on it too heavily.

WOMAN: Does that mean we've given up?

MAN: Not exactly. But as time goes on, we invent new ways of looking for it.

WOMAN: Like closing our eyes.

MAN: Yes. That should be mentioned. But that is only one example.

WOMAN: One could also include: keeping your eyes open, blinking your eyes, wearing dark glasses, wearing no glasses, or any of the above in any or all of their combinations.

MAN: That's a beginning, yes. But it's too early to tell if something will come of it.

(Pause. Four beats. They think.)

WOMAN: Do you think we'll ever find it?

MAN: What makes you so sure we haven't found it already?

WOMAN: My bones. I feel it in my bones.

MAN: Maybe bones have nothing to do with it. Maybe we've

been surrounded by it from the very beginning and have been too distracted to notice.

WOMAN: Do you mean it doesn't have to be somewhere else? It can also be here, right in front of us?

MAN: I only mean that we shouldn't ignore the evidence.

(Pause. Four beats. They think.)

WOMAN: Do you think we'll ever find it?

MAN: First you must leave, and then you must be on your way, and then, if a door happens to appear before you, so much the better. But there is nothing that says you must open the door.

WOMAN: And if you open the door anyway?

MAN: Then you have simply opened the door.

WOMAN: To stand in an empty room. Or else, to discover that this is where you live.

MAN: Or else, it is simply a door, standing in the road. You open it, step over the sill, and discover there is no room at all. Nothing but more road, stretching before you. And so you just move on, putting one foot in front of the other, continuing on your way.

WOMAN: Until you come to another door.

MAN: Or a wall without a door.

WOMAN: Or a hole in the ground.

MAN: Or a hole in the sky.

(Pause. Four beats. They think.)

WOMAN: And if none of this ever happened?

MAN: It would happen anyway.

WOMAN: *(Dejected.)* I'm so tired. I don't want to think about it anymore.

MAN: That's part of what happens too. *(Pause.)* It all has to end some time.

WOMAN: Which means . . . it can end at any moment.

MAN: *(Sighs.)* Most likely. *(Pause.)* It probably means it will end at any moment.

(Pause. Four beats. They think.)

WOMAN: Do you think we'll ever find it?

(Pause. Four beats. Man shuts curtain. Pause. Four beats. Woman is about to speak, then says nothing. She shuts curtain. Long pause. Darkness.)

(1976)

Appendix 2
ACTION BASEBALL

Description

Action Baseball is a card game for 1 or 2 players, consisting of two decks of 96 cards, a playing field with pegs, and a scoreboard. It is suitable for both children and adults, and one game can be played in approximately twenty minutes.

Without elaborate charts or complicated rules, Action Baseball simulates baseball as it is played on the field and allows players to make all the important strategy decisions of a big-league manager. Pitch by pitch, the results are uncannily true to life, and every outcome reflects the statistical possibilities of real baseball. From the final score to the ratio between balls and strikes, from the number of hits and errors amassed by each team to the number of successful and unsuccessful stolen bases, sacrifice bunts, and double plays, Action Baseball unfolds with all the excitement of a flesh-and-blood game.

How to Play

The traditional rules of baseball are followed at all times. There are nine innings in each game, three outs in an inning, three strikes for a strikeout, four balls for a walk.

Each card has a triple function: for the pitcher, for the batter, and for strategy situations. The diamond in the center of the card indicates "ball" (green), "strike" (red), or "swing" (black). The second area of information on the card gives the result of a batted ball: groundout to the shortstop, single, fly out to deep left field, error, double, etc. The third area of information deals with strategic maneuvers.

The players decide who will represent the home team and who will represent the visiting team. Home team takes the red deck; visiting team takes the green deck. The home team pitches first; the visiting team bats first.

The pitcher turns over his cards one by one, calling out balls and strikes as they appear. When a "swing" card turns up, the player at bat turns over his top card and reads off the result.

The player at bat keeps track of balls, strikes, and outs on the scoreboard and puts his pegs in the appropriate bases as batters reach base. After three outs have been made, the pitcher becomes the batter and the batter becomes the pitcher.

The cards are shuffled at the beginning of each game and at the end of the fifth inning. If a player comes to the end of his deck before the fifth inning is over, both players reshuffle at that point and the action resumes without interruption. If the game goes into extra innings, the cards are shuffled again after the ninth inning.

Reading the Cards

The red and green diamond cards ("strikes" and "balls") are numbered 1 through 9. Each number represents a different player position: 1 = Pitcher; 2 = Catcher; 3 = First Base; 4 = Second

Base; 5 = Third Base; 6 = Shortstop; 7 = Left Field; 8 = Center Field; 9 = Right Field. Green 1, 2, 3, 4, 5, 6 indicate ground balls. Red 1, 2, 3, 4, 5, 6 indicate either pop-ups or line drives. Green 7, 8, 9 indicate shallow fly balls. Red 7, 8, 9 indicate deep fly balls.

The black diamond cards ("swing") include singles, doubles, triples, home runs, and foul balls. Red singles advance runners two bases; green singles advance runners one base. Red doubles advance runners three bases; green doubles advance runners two bases. When the player at bat turns over a "foul ball" card, it is counted as a strike, except when there are two strikes, in which case the count remains the same—as in real baseball.

TAKING A PITCH: The player at bat can declare that he wants to take a pitch (not swing), in which case a "swing" card counts as a strike.

HIT AND RUN: With a runner on first base, the player at bat can declare "Hit and Run." If a "swing" card is turned over, a force out is avoided on a ground ball. The runner advances to second base, and the play is to first. On a single or double, the runner advances one more base than indicated on the card. If a "ball" or "strike" card is turned over by the pitcher, the player at bat must then turn over a card and consult the Stolen Base section at the bottom—SB (2)—to see if the runner is out or safe at second. A green dot indicates safe; a red dot indicates out.

WILD PITCH: With no runners on base, the Wild Pitch is counted as a ball. When it turns up with runners on base, they advance one base. There is no extra advance for runners if it turns up as the fourth ball.

THREE-AND-TWO PITCH WITH TWO OUTS AND RUN-

NER ON FIRST, RUNNERS ON FIRST AND SECOND, OR BASES LOADED: If a "single" or "double" card is turned over by the player at bat, the runner or runners advance one more base than is indicated on the card.

Reading the Strategy Symbols

E (ERROR): If the player at bat turns over an "Error" card, the pitcher then turns over a card and refers to the E section at the bottom. Green indicates a one-base error, red a two-base error. The number refers to the position of the player responsible for the error.

DP (DOUBLE PLAY): With no outs or one out and a runner on first base. If the player at bat turns over a ground ball card (green 1, 2, 3, 4, 5, 6), the pitcher then turns over a card and refers to the DP section at the bottom. A green dot indicates that the runner is forced out at second base and the batter is safe at first (no double play). A red dot indicates a successful double play: both the runner and the batter are out. Runners on second and/or third base advance one base on a double play attempt.

- With runners on first and second, the pitcher can go for an automatic force out at third or declare "Double Play," in which case the runner on second advances to third.

LDDP (LINE DRIVE DOUBLE PLAY): With no outs or one out and one or more runners on base. If the batter turns over a "line drive" card (red 1, 2, 3, 4, 5, 6), the pitcher then turns over a card and refers to the LDDP section at the bottom. A green dot indicates that all runners are safe, and only one out is recorded on the play. A red dot indicates a double play. With more than one runner on base, it is always the *least* advanced runner who is out.

SacB (SACRIFICE BUNT): With no outs or one out and a runner

on first base. Before the pitcher turns over any cards, the batter declares that he wishes to attempt a sacrifice bunt. He then turns over a card and refers to the SacB section at the bottom. A green dot indicates a successful sacrifice: the runner advances from first to second, and the batter is out at first. A red dot indicates an unsuccessful sacrifice: the runner is forced out at second, and the batter is safe at first. A red dot followed by "(DP)" indicates a force out at second and a possible double play: the pitcher then turns over a card and refers to the DP section for the result.

SB (STOLEN BASE): With runner on first base or second base. The batter declares that he wishes to attempt a steal, turns over a card, and refers to the SB section at the bottom. A green dot indicates that the runner is safe; a red dot indicates that the runner is out. The chances of stealing second base—"SB (2)"—are better than those of stealing third—"SB (3)." There are no double steals or steals of home.

SacF (SACRIFICE FLY): With no outs or one out and a runner on third base. If the batter turns over a fly ball card (7, 8, 9), he can attempt to score the runner. He declares "Sacrifice Fly," turns over a card, and refers to the green or red SacF section, depending on whether the fly ball is deep (red) or shallow (green). On a deep fly, the chances of scoring the runner are good; on a shallow fly, the chances are poor. A green dot indicates a successful sacrifice: the runner scores, and one out is recorded on the play. A red dot indicates an unsuccessful sacrifice: the runner is thrown out at home, and two outs are recorded on the play.

EB (TAKING EXTRA BASE ON HIT): After a "single," "double," or "triple," the batter declares that he wants to try to stretch the hit by an extra base. He turns over a card and consults the EB section at the bottom. A red dot indicates that the runner is out; a green dot indicates that the runner is safe. If there is a runner on base at the time of the hit, the red or green dot refers to *that* runner. The batter takes an extra base automatically, whether the runner is safe or out.

Inf In (3) (INFIELD IN WITH RUNNER ON THIRD BASE): With no outs or one out and a runner on third base. The pitcher can choose to play his infield in to prevent the runner on third from scoring on a ground ball. If the batter turns over a "ground ball" card (green 1, 2, 3, 4, 5, 6), he can declare that he wants to send the runner home—in which case the pitcher turns over a card and refers to the "Inf In (3)" section at the bottom. A red dot indicates that the runner is out at home; a green dot indicates that the runner is safe at home. On a play at home, whether out or safe, the batter is always safe at first. NOTE: With the infield in, certain ground ball outs become singles—which are indicated at the edges of the central area of the card.

- With no outs or one out and runners on first and third. If the batter chooses *not* to attempt to score the runner from third, the pitcher cannot attempt a double play. The batter is out at first base.

- With no outs or one out and bases loaded. On a ground ball, the force out at home is automatic. The pitcher need not consult the "Inf In (3)" section.

2 to 3 (ADVANCING RUNNER FROM SECOND BASE TO THIRD BASE ON GROUND BALL): With no outs or one out and a runner on second. On a ground ball to the infield (green 1, 2, 3, 4, 5, 6), the player at bat can declare that he wants to try to advance the runner from second to third. The pitcher then turns over a card and refers to the "2 to 3" section at the bottom. A red dot indicates that the runner is out; a green dot indicates that the

runner is safe. If safe, the batter is out at first. If out, the batter is safe at first.

Ground Balls with Runner on Third Base and Infield Back with No Outs or One Out

- Runner on third: Runner scores; batter out at first.

- Runners on second and third: Runner on third scores; runner on second advances to third; batter out at first.

- Runners on first and third: Runner on third scores; normal double play attempt.

- Bases loaded: Runner on third scores; runner on second advances to third; normal double play attempt.

(1978)

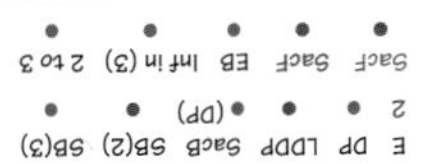

2

FOUL OUT TO C

E	DP	LDDP	SacB	SB(2)	SB(3)
2	•	•	•(DP)	•	•
SacF	SacF	EB	Inf in (3)	2 to 3	
•	•	•	•	•	

5

GROUND OUT TO 3B

E	DP	LDDP	SacB	SB(2)	SB(3)
5	•	•	•	•	•
SacF	SacF	EB	Inf in (3)	2 to 3	
•	•	•	•	•	

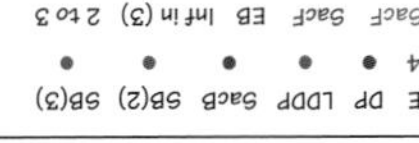

4

GROUND OUT TO 2B

E	DP	LDDP	SacB	SB(2)	SB(3)
4	•	•	•	•	•
SacF	SacF	EB	Inf in (3)	2 to 3	
•	•	•	•	•	

FOUL BALL

E	DP	LDDP	SacB	SB(2)	SB(3)
6	•	•	•	•	•
SacF	SacF	EB	Inf in (3)	2 to 3	
•	•	•	•	•	

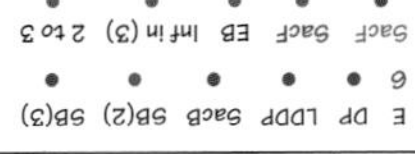

SINGLE

Runners advance 2 bases

E	DP	LDDP	SacB	SB(2)	SB(3)
6	•	•	•	•	•
SacF	SacF	EB	Inf in (3)	2 to 3	
•	•	•	•	•	

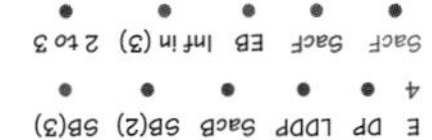

SINGLE

Runners advance 1 base

E	DP	LDDP	SacB	SB(2)	SB(3)
4	•	•	•	•	•
SacF	SacF	EB	Inf in (3)	2 to 3	
•	•	•	•	•	

6

GROUND OUT TO SS

E	DP	LDDP	SacB	SB(2)	SB(3)
6	•	•	•	•	•
SacF	SacF	EB	Inf in (3)	2 to 3	
•	•	•	•	•	

1

GROUND OUT TO P

E	DP	LDDP	SacB	SB(2)	SB(3)
1	•	•	•	•	•
SacF	SacF	EB	Inf in (3)	2 to 3	
•	•	•	•	•	

E	DP	LDDP	SacB	SB(2)	SB(3)
4 •	•	•	•(DP)	•	•
SacF	SacF	EB	Inf in (3)	2 to 3	
•	•	•	•	•	

FLY OUT TO SHALLOW LF

7

7

FLY OUT TO SHALLOW LF

E	DP	LDDP	SacB	SB(2)	SB(3)
4	•	•	•(DP)	•	•
SacF	SacF	EB	Inf in (3)	2 to 3	
•	•	•	•	•	

E	DP	LDDP	SacB	SB(2)	SB(3)
5	•	•	•	•	•
SacF	SacF	EB	Inf in (3)	2 to 3	
•	•	•	•	•	

LINE OUT TO 3B

5

5

LINE OUT TO 3B

E	DP	LDDP	SacB	SB(2)	SB(3)
5	•	•	•	•	•
SacF	SacF	EB	Inf in (3)	2 to 3	
•	•	•	•	•	

E	DP	LDDP	SacB	SB(2)	SB(3)
8	•	•	•(DP)	•	•
SacF	SacF	EB	Inf in (3)	2 to 3	
•	•	•	•	•	

FLY OUT TO DEEP CF

8

8

FLY OUT TO DEEP CF

E	DP	LDDP	SacB	SB(2)	SB(3)
8	•	•	•(DP)	•	•
SacF	SacF	EB	Inf in (3)	2 to 3	
•	•	•	•	•	

E	DP	LDDP	SacB	SB(2)	SB(3)
5	•	•	•	•	•
SacF	SacF	EB	Inf in (3)	2 to 3	
•	•	•	•	•	

GROUND OUT TO 3B

5

5

GROUND OUT TO 3B

E	DP	LDDP	SacB	SB(2)	SB(3)
5	•	•	•	•	•
SacF	SacF	EB	Inf in (3)	2 to 3	
•	•	•	•	•	

E	DP	LDDP	SacB	SB(2)	SB(3)
4	•	•	•	•	•
SacF	SacF	EB	Inf in (3)	2 to 3	
•	•	•	•	•	

ERROR

ERROR

E	DP	LDDP	SacB	SB(2)	SB(3)
4	•	•	•	•	•
SacF	SacF	EB	Inf in (3)	2 to 3	
•	•	•	•	•	

E	DP	LDDP	SacB	SB(2)	SB(3)
3	•	•	•	•	•
SacF	SacF	EB	Inf in (3)	2 to 3	
•	•	•	•	•	

POP OUT TO 1B

3

3

POP OUT TO 1B

E	DP	LDDP	SacB	SB(2)	SB(3)
3	•	•	•	•	•
SacF	SacF	EB	Inf in (3)	2 to 3	
•	•	•	•	•	

E	DP	LDDP	SacB	SB(2)	SB(3)
6	•	•	•	•	•
SacF	SacF	EB	Inf in (3)	2 to 3	
•	•	•	•	•	

FLY OUT TO SHALLOW CF

8

8

FLY OUT TO SHALLOW CF

E	DP	LDDP	SacB	SB(2)	SB(3)
6	•	•	•	•	•
SacF	SacF	EB	Inf in (3)	2 to 3	
•	•	•	•	•	

E	DP	LDDP	SacB	SB(2)	SB(3)
3	•	•	•	•	•
SacF	SacF	EB	Inf in (3)	2 to 3	
•	•	•	•	•	

GROUND OUT TO 1B

3

3

GROUND OUT TO 1B

E	DP	LDDP	SacB	SB(2)	SB(3)
3	•	•	•	•	•
SacF	SacF	EB	Inf in (3)	2 to 3	
•	•	•	•	•	

HOME RUN

HOME RUN

E	DP	LDDP	SacB	SB(2)	SB(3)
6	•	•	•	•	•
SacF	SacF	EB	Inf in (3)	2 to 3	
•	•	•	•	•	

GROUND OUT TO SS

6

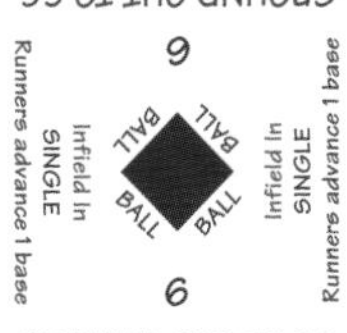

6

GROUND OUT TO SS

E	DP	LDDP	SacB	SB(2)	SB(3)
6	•	•	•	•	•
SacF	SacF	EB	Inf in (3)	2 to 3	
•	•	•	•	•	

FLY OUT TO SHALLOW RF

9

9

FLY OUT TO SHALLOW RF

E	DP	LDDP	SacB	SB(2)	SB(3)
6	•	•	•	•	•
SacF	SacF	EB	Inf in (3)	2 to 3	
•	•	•	•	•	

FLY OUT TO DEEP LF

7

7

FLY OUT TO DEEP LF

E	DP	LDDP	SacB	SB(2)	SB(3)
7	•	•	•	•	•
SacF	SacF	EB	Inf in (3)	2 to 3	
•	•	•	•	•	

SINGLE
Runners advance 2 bases

SINGLE
Runners advance 2 bases

E	DP	LDDP	SacB	SB(2)	SB(3)
5	•	•	•	•	•
SacF	SacF	EB	Inf in (3)	2 to 3	
•	•	•	•	•	

DOUBLE
Runners advance 3 bases

DOUBLE
Runners advance 3 bases

E	DP	LDDP	SacB	SB(2)	SB(3)
5	•	•	•	•	•
SacF	SacF	EB	Inf in (3)	2 to 3	
•	•	•	•	•	

SINGLE
Runners advance 1 base

SINGLE
Runners advance 1 base

E	DP	LDDP	SacB	SB(2)	SB(3)
3	•	•	•	•	•
SacF	SacF	EB	Inf in (3)	2 to 3	
•	•	•	•	•	

FLY OUT TO SHALLOW CF

8

8

FLY OUT TO SHALLOW CF

E	DP	LDDP	SacB	SB(2)	SB(3)
6	•	•	•	• (E-2)	•
SacF	SacF	EB	Inf in (3)	2 to 3	
•	•	•	•	•	

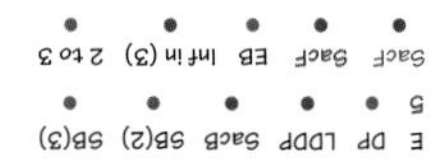

SINGLE

Runners advance 1 base

E	DP	LDDP	SacB	SB(2)	SB(3)
5	•	•	•	•	•

SacF	SacF	EB	Inf in (3)	2 to 3
•	•	•	•	•

8

8

FLY OUT TO SHALLOW CF

E	DP	LDDP	SacB	SB(2)	SB(3)
4	•	•	•	•	•

SacF	SacF	EB	Inf in (3)	2 to 3
•	•	•	•	•

4

4

POP OUT TO 2B

E	DP	LDDP	SacB	SB(2)	SB(3)
4	•	•	•	•	•

SacF	SacF	EB	Inf in (3)	2 to 3
•	•	•	•	•

DOUBLE

Runners advance 3 bases

E	DP	LDDP	SacB	SB(2)	SB(3)
6	•	•	•	•	•

SacF	SacF	EB	Inf in (3)	2 to 3
•	•	•	•	•

2

2

GROUND OUT CHOPPER TO C

E	DP	LDDP	SacB	SB(2)	SB(3)
2	•	•	•	•	•

SacF	SacF	EB	Inf in (3)	2 to 3
•	•	•	•	•

5

Infield In SINGLE Runners advance 1 base

BALL BALL BALL BALL

Infield In SINGLE Runners advance 1 base

5

GROUND OUT TO 3B

E	DP	LDDP	SacB	SB(2)	SB(3)
5	•	•	•	•	•

SacF	SacF	EB	Inf in (3)	2 to 3
•	•	•	•	•

ERROR

E	DP	LDDP	SacB	SB(2)	SB(3)
3	•	•	•	•	•

SacF	SacF	EB	Inf in (3)	2 to 3
•	•	•	•	•

1

1

GROUND OUT TO P

E	DP	LDDP	SacB	SB(2)	SB(3)
1	•	•	•	•	•

SacF	SacF	EB	Inf in (3)	2 to 3
•	•	•	•	•

E DP LDDP SacB SB(2) SB(3) 4
SacF SacF EB Inf in (3) 2 to 3
FOUL BALL

FOUL BALL

E	DP	LDDP	SacB	SB(2)	SB(3)
4	•	•	•	•	•
SacF	SacF	EB	Inf in (3)	2 to 3	
•	•	•	•	•	

E DP LDDP SacB SB(2) SB(3) 3
SacF SacF EB Inf in (3) 2 to 3
TRIPLE

TRIPLE

E	DP	LDDP	SacB	SB(2)	SB(3)
3	•	•	•	•	•
SacF	SacF	EB	Inf in (3)	2 to 3	
•	•	•	•	•	

E DP LDDP SacB SB(2) SB(3) 9
SacF SacF EB Inf in (3) 2 to 3
FLY OUT TO DEEP RF
9

9

FLY OUT TO DEEP RF

E	DP	LDDP	SacB	SB(2)	SB(3)
9	•	•	•	•	•
SacF	SacF	EB	Inf in (3)	2 to 3	
•	•	•	•	•	

E DP LDDP SacB SB(2) SB(3) 6
SacF SacF EB Inf in (3) 2 to 3
LINE OUT TO SS
6

6

LINE OUT TO SS

E	DP	LDDP	SacB	SB(2)	SB(3)
6	•	•	•	•	•
SacF	SacF	EB	Inf in (3)	2 to 3	
•	•	•	•	•	

E DP LDDP SacB SB(2) SB(3) 1
SacF SacF EB Inf in (3) 2 to 3
LINE OUT TO P
1

1

LINE OUT TO P

E	DP	LDDP	SacB	SB(2)	SB(3)
1	•	•	•	•	•
SacF	SacF	EB	Inf in (3)	2 to 3	
•	•	•	•	•	

E DP LDDP SacB SB(2) SB(3) 4
SacF SacF EB Inf in (3) 2 to 3
GROUND OUT TO 2B
4

4

GROUND OUT TO 2B

E	DP	LDDP	SacB	SB(2)	SB(3)
4	•	•	•	•	•
SacF	SacF	EB	Inf in (3)	2 to 3	
•	•	•	•	•	

E DP LDDP SacB SB(2) SB(3) 4
SacF SacF EB Inf in (3) 2 to 3
LINE OUT TO 2B
4

4

LINE OUT TO 2B

E	DP	LDDP	SacB	SB(2)	SB(3)
4	•	•	•	•	•
SacF	SacF	EB	Inf in (3)	2 to 3	
•	•	•	•	•	

E DP LDDP SacB SB(2) SB(3) 7
SacF SacF EB Inf in (3) 2 to 3
FLY OUT TO DEEP LF
7

7

FLY OUT TO DEEP LF

E	DP	LDDP	SacB	SB(2)	SB(3)
7	•	•	•	•	•
SacF	SacF	EB	Inf in (3)	2 to 3	
•	•	•	•	•	

DOUBLE

Runners advance 3 bases

E DP LDDP SacB SB(2) SB(3)
4 • • • • •
SacF SacF EB Inf in (3) 2 to 3
• • • • •

7

FLY OUT TO SHALLOW LF

E DP LDDP SacB SB(2) SB(3)
4 • • • • •
SacF SacF EB Inf in (3) 2 to 3
• • • • •

3

POP OUT TO 1B

E DP LDDP SacB SB(2) SB(3)
3 • • • • •
SacF SacF EB Inf in (3) 2 to 3
• • • • •

SINGLE

Runners advance 2 bases

E DP LDDP SacB SB(2) SB(3)
6 • • • •(E-2) •
SacF SacF EB Inf in (3) 2 to 3
• • • • •

SINGLE

Runners advance 2 bases

E DP LDDP SacB SB(2) SB(3)
2 • • • • •
SacF SacF EB Inf in (3) 2 to 3
• • • • •

7

FLY OUT TO DEEP LF

E DP LDDP SacB SB(2) SB(3)
7 • • • • •
SacF SacF EB Inf in (3) 2 to 3
• • • • •

9

FLY OUT TO SHALLOW RF

E DP LDDP SacB SB(2) SB(3)
6 • • • • •
SacF SacF EB Inf in (3) 2 to 3
• • • • •

FOUL BALL

E DP LDDP SacB SB(2) SB(3)
4 • • • • •
SacF SacF EB Inf in (3) 2 to 3
• • • • •

E DP LDDP SacB SB(2) SB(3)
9 • • • • •
SacF SacF EB Inf in (3) 2 to 3
• • • • •
FLY OUT TO DEEP RF
9

9

FLY OUT TO DEEP RF

E	DP	LDDP	SacB	SB(2)	SB(3)
9	•	•	•	•	•
SacF	SacF	EB	Inf in (3)	2 to 3	
•	•	•	•	•	

E DP LDDP SacB SB(2) SB(3)
9 • • • • •
SacF SacF EB Inf in (3) 2 to 3
• • • • •
FLY OUT TO SHALLOW RF
9

9

FLY OUT TO SHALLOW RF

E	DP	LDDP	SacB	SB(2)	SB(3)
9	•	•	•	•	•
SacF	SacF	EB	Inf in (3)	2 to 3	
•	•	•	•	•	

E DP LDDP SacB SB(2) SB(3)
7 • • • • •
SacF SacF EB Inf in (3) 2 to 3
• • • • •
FLY OUT TO DEEP LF
7

7

FLY OUT TO DEEP LF

E	DP	LDDP	SacB	SB(2)	SB(3)
7	•	•	•	•	•
SacF	SacF	EB	Inf in (3)	2 to 3	
•	•	•	•	•	

E DP LDDP SacB SB(2) SB(3)
4 • • • • •
SacF SacF EB Inf in (3) 2 to 3
• • • • •
Runners advance 2 bases
SINGLE

SINGLE

Runners advance 2 bases

E	DP	LDDP	SacB	SB(2)	SB(3)
4	•	•	•	•	•
SacF	SacF	EB	Inf in (3)	2 to 3	
•	•	•	•	•	

E DP LDDP SacB SB(2) SB(3)
9 • • • • •
SacF SacF EB Inf in (3) 2 to 3
• • • • •
FLY OUT TO DEEP RF
9

9

FLY OUT TO DEEP RF

E	DP	LDDP	SacB	SB(2)	SB(3)
9	•	•	•	•	•
SacF	SacF	EB	Inf in (3)	2 to 3	
•	•	•	•	•	

E DP LDDP SacB SB(2) SB(3)
4 • • • • •
SacF SacF EB Inf in (3) 2 to 3
• • • • •
GROUND OUT TO 2B
4

4

GROUND OUT TO 2B

E	DP	LDDP	SacB	SB(2)	SB(3)
4	•	•	•	•	•
SacF	SacF	EB	Inf in (3)	2 to 3	
•	•	•	•	•	

E DP LDDP SacB SB(2) SB(3)
6 • • •(DP) • •
SacF SacF EB Inf in (3) 2 to 3
• • • • •
GROUND OUT TO SS
6

6

GROUND OUT TO SS

E	DP	LDDP	SacB	SB(2)	SB(3)
6	•	•	•(DP)	•	•
SacF	SacF	EB	Inf in (3)	2 to 3	
•	•	•	•	•	

E DP LDDP SacB SB(2) SB(3)
3 • • • • •
SacF SacF EB Inf in (3) 2 to 3
• • • • •
LINE OUT TO 1B
3

3

LINE OUT TO 1B

E	DP	LDDP	SacB	SB(2)	SB(3)
3	•	•	•	•	•
SacF	SacF	EB	Inf in (3)	2 to 3	
•	•	•	•	•	

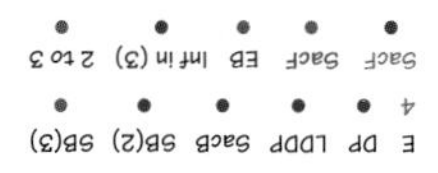

E DP LDDP SacB SB(2) SB(3)
4 ● ● ● ● ●
SacF SacF EB Inf in (3) 2 to 3
● ● ● ● ●
LINE OUT TO 2B
4

4

LINE OUT TO 2B

E DP LDDP SacB SB(2) SB(3)
4 ● ● ● ● ●
SacF SacF EB Inf in (3) 2 to 3
● ● ● ● ●

E DP LDDP SacB SB(2) SB(3)
3 ● ● ● ● ●
SacF SacF EB Inf in (3) 2 to 3
● ● ● ● ●
SINGLE
Runners advance 1 base

SINGLE

Runners advance 1 base

E DP LDDP SacB SB(2) SB(3)
3 ● ● ● ● ●
SacF SacF EB Inf in (3) 2 to 3
● ● ● ● ●

E DP LDDP SacB SB(2) SB(3)
3 ● ● ● ● ●
SacF SacF EB Inf in (3) 2 to 3
● ● ● ● ●
GROUND OUT TO 1B
3

3

GROUND OUT TO 1B

E DP LDDP SacB SB(2) SB(3)
3 ● ● ● ● ●
SacF SacF EB Inf in (3) 2 to 3
● ● ● ● ●

E DP LDDP SacB SB(2) SB(3)
8 ● ● ● ● ●
SacF SacF EB Inf in (3) 2 to 3
● ● ● ● ●
FLY OUT TO DEEP CF
8

8

FLY OUT TO DEEP CF

E DP LDDP SacB SB(2) SB(3)
8 ● ● ● ● ●
SacF SacF EB Inf in (3) 2 to 3
● ● ● ● ●

E DP LDDP SacB SB(2) SB(3)
3 ● ● ● ● ●
SacF SacF EB Inf in (3) 2 to 3
● ● ● ● ●
GROUND OUT TO 1B
3

3

GROUND OUT TO 1B

E DP LDDP SacB SB(2) SB(3)
3 ● ● ● ● ●
SacF SacF EB Inf in (3) 2 to 3
● ● ● ● ●

E DP LDDP SacB SB(2) SB(3)
5 ● ● ● ● ●
SacF SacF EB Inf in (3) 2 to 3
● ● ● ● ●
POP OUT TO 3B
5

5

POP OUT TO 3B

E DP LDDP SacB SB(2) SB(3)
5 ● ● ● ● ●
SacF SacF EB Inf in (3) 2 to 3
● ● ● ● ●

E DP LDDP SacB SB(2) SB(3)
6 ● ● ● ● ●
SacF SacF EB Inf in (3) 2 to 3
● ● ● ● ●
SINGLE
Runners advance 2 bases

SINGLE

Runners advance 2 bases

E DP LDDP SacB SB(2) SB(3)
6 ● ● ● ● ●
SacF SacF EB Inf in (3) 2 to 3
● ● ● ● ●

E DP LDDP SacB SB(2) SB(3)
6 ● ● ● ● ●
SacF SacF EB Inf in (3) 2 to 3
● ● ● ● ●
POP OUT TO SS
6

6

POP OUT TO SS

E DP LDDP SacB SB(2) SB(3)
6 ● ● ● ● ●
SacF SacF EB Inf in (3) 2 to 3
● ● ● ● ●

E DP LDDP SacB SB(2) SB(3)
3 • • • • •
SacF SacF EB Inf in (3) 2 to 3
• • • • •

SINGLE
Runners advance 2 bases

SINGLE
Runners advance 2 bases

E DP LDDP SacB SB(2) SB(3)
3 • • • • •
SacF SacF EB Inf in (3) 2 to 3
• • • • •

E DP LDDP SacB SB(2) SB(3)
4 • • • • •
SacF SacF EB Inf in (3) 2 to 3
• • • • •

SINGLE
Runners advance 1 base

SINGLE
Runners advance 1 base

E DP LDDP SacB SB(2) SB(3)
4 • • • • •
SacF SacF EB Inf in (3) 2 to 3
• • • • •

E DP LDDP SacB SB(2) SB(3)
6 • • • • •
SacF SacF EB Inf in (3) 2 to 3
• • • • •

LINE OUT TO SS
6

6
LINE OUT TO SS

E DP LDDP SacB SB(2) SB(3)
6 • • • • •
SacF SacF EB Inf in (3) 2 to 3
• • • • •

E DP LDDP SacB SB(2) SB(3)
5 • • • • •
SacF SacF EB Inf in (3) 2 to 3
• • • • •

SINGLE
Runners advance 2 bases

SINGLE
Runners advance 2 bases

E DP LDDP SacB SB(2) SB(3)
5 • • • • •
SacF SacF EB Inf in (3) 2 to 3
• • • • •

E DP LDDP SacB SB(2) SB(3)
1 • • • • •
SacF SacF EB Inf in (3) 2 to 3
• • • • •

SINGLE
Runners advance 2 bases

SINGLE
Runners advance 2 bases

E DP LDDP SacB SB(2) SB(3)
1 • • • • •
SacF SacF EB Inf in (3) 2 to 3
• • • • •

E DP LDDP SacB SB(2) SB(3)
4 • • • • •
SacF SacF EB Inf in (3) 2 to 3
• • • • •

FLY OUT TO SHALLOW LF
7

7
FLY OUT TO SHALLOW LF

E DP LDDP SacB SB(2) SB(3)
4 • • • • •
SacF SacF EB Inf in (3) 2 to 3
• • • • •

E DP LDDP SacB SB(2) SB(3)
5 • • • • •
SacF SacF EB Inf in (3) 2 to 3
• • • • •

LINE OUT TO 3B
5

5
LINE OUT TO 3B

E DP LDDP SacB SB(2) SB(3)
5 • • • • •
SacF SacF EB Inf in (3) 2 to 3
• • • • •

E DP LDDP SacB SB(2) SB(3)
5 • • • • •
SacF SacF EB Inf in (3) 2 to 3
• • • • •

FOUL BALL

FOUL BALL

E DP LDDP SacB SB(2) SB(3)
5 • • • • •
SacF SacF EB Inf in (3) 2 to 3
• • • • •

E DP LDDP SacB SB(2) SB(3)
8
SacF SacF EB Inf in (3) 2 to 3
FLY OUT TO DEEP CF
8

8

FLY OUT TO DEEP CF

E DP LDDP SacB SB(2) SB(3)
8
SacF SacF EB Inf in (3) 2 to 3

E DP LDDP SacB SB(2) SB(3)
4
SacF SacF EB Inf in (3) 2 to 3
GROUND OUT TO 2B
4

4

GROUND OUT TO 2B

E DP LDDP SacB SB(2) SB(3)
4
SacF SacF EB Inf in (3) 2 to 3

E DP LDDP SacB SB(2) SB(3)
5
SacF SacF EB Inf in (3) 2 to 3
GROUND OUT TO 3B
5

5

GROUND OUT TO 3B

E DP LDDP SacB SB(2) SB(3)
5
SacF SacF EB Inf in (3) 2 to 3

E DP LDDP SacB SB(2) SB(3)
5
SacF SacF EB Inf in (3) 2 to 3
Runners advance 2 bases
SINGLE

SINGLE

Runners advance 2 bases

E DP LDDP SacB SB(2) SB(3)
5
SacF SacF EB Inf in (3) 2 to 3

E DP LDDP SacB SB(2) SB(3)
3
SacF SacF EB Inf in (3) 2 to 3
Runners advance 3 bases
DOUBLE

DOUBLE

Runners advance 3 bases

E DP LDDP SacB SB(2) SB(3)
3
SacF SacF EB Inf in (3) 2 to 3

E DP LDDP SacB SB(2) SB(3)
9
SacF SacF EB Inf in (3) 2 to 3
FLY OUT TO DEEP RF
9

9

FLY OUT TO DEEP RF

E DP LDDP SacB SB(2) SB(3)
9
SacF SacF EB Inf in (3) 2 to 3

E DP LDDP SacB SB(2) SB(3)
6
SacF SacF EB Inf in (3) 2 to 3
FLY OUT TO SHALLOW RF
9

9

FLY OUT TO SHALLOW RF

E DP LDDP SacB SB(2) SB(3)
6
SacF SacF EB Inf in (3) 2 to 3

E DP LDDP SacB SB(2) SB(3)
4 (DP)
SacF SacF EB Inf in (3) 2 to 3
Runners advance 1 base
SINGLE

SINGLE

Runners advance 1 base

E DP LDDP SacB SB(2) SB(3)
4 (DP)
SacF SacF EB Inf in (3) 2 to 3

E DP LDDP SacB SB(2) SB(3)
3 • • • • •
SacF SacF EB Inf in (3) 2 to 3
• • • • •
GROUND OUT TO 1B
3

Infield In
SINGLE
Runners advance 1 base

Infield In
SINGLE
Runners advance 1 base

3

GROUND OUT TO 1B

E	DP	LDDP	SacB	SB(2)	SB(3)
3	•	•	•	•	•
SacF	SacF	EB	Inf in (3)	2 to 3	
•	•	•	•	•	

E DP LDDP SacB SB(2) SB(3)
6 • • • • •
SacF SacF EB Inf in (3) 2 to 3
• • • • •
POP OUT TO SS
6

6

POP OUT TO SS

E	DP	LDDP	SacB	SB(2)	SB(3)
6	•	•	•	•	•
SacF	SacF	EB	Inf in (3)	2 to 3	
•	•	•	•	•	

E DP LDDP SacB SB(2) SB(3)
4 • • • • •
SacF SacF EB Inf in (3) 2 to 3
• • • • •
POP OUT TO 2B
4

4

POP OUT TO 2B

E	DP	LDDP	SacB	SB(2)	SB(3)
4	•	•	•	•	•
SacF	SacF	EB	Inf in (3)	2 to 3	
•	•	•	•	•	

E DP LDDP SacB SB(2) SB(3)
3 • • • • •
SacF SacF EB Inf in (3) 2 to 3
• • • • •
Runners advance 2 bases
SINGLE

SINGLE
Runners advance 2 bases

E	DP	LDDP	SacB	SB(2)	SB(3)
3	•	•	•	•	•
SacF	SacF	EB	Inf in (3)	2 to 3	
•	•	•	•	•	

E DP LDDP SacB SB(2) SB(3)
5 • • • • •
SacF SacF EB Inf in (3) 2 to 3
• • • • •
Runners advance 2 bases
SINGLE

SINGLE
Runners advance 2 bases

E	DP	LDDP	SacB	SB(2)	SB(3)
5	•	•	•	•	•
SacF	SacF	EB	Inf in (3)	2 to 3	
•	•	•	•	•	

E DP LDDP SacB SB(2) SB(3)
6 • • • • •
SacF SacF EB Inf in (3) 2 to 3
• • • • •
Runners advance 2 bases
DOUBLE

DOUBLE
Runners advance 2 bases

E	DP	LDDP	SacB	SB(2)	SB(3)
6	•	•	•	•	•
SacF	SacF	EB	Inf in (3)	2 to 3	
•	•	•	•	•	

E DP LDDP SacB SB(2) SB(3)
6 • • • • •
SacF SacF EB Inf in (3) 2 to 3
• • • • •
FOUL BALL

FOUL BALL

E	DP	LDDP	SacB	SB(2)	SB(3)
6	•	•	•	•	•
SacF	SacF	EB	Inf in (3)	2 to 3	
•	•	•	•	•	

E DP LDDP SacB SB(2) SB(3)
4 • • • • •
SacF SacF EB Inf in (3) 2 to 3
• • • • •
FLY OUT TO SHALLOW LF
7

7

FLY OUT TO SHALLOW LF

E	DP	LDDP	SacB	SB(2)	SB(3)
4	•	•	•	•	•
SacF	SacF	EB	Inf in (3)	2 to 3	
•	•	•	•	•	

SINGLE
Runners advance 2 bases

E	DP	LDDP	SacB	SB(2)	SB(3)
5	•	•	•	•	•
SacF	SacF	EB	Inf in (3)	2 to 3	
•	•	•	•	•	

5
POP OUT TO 3B

E	DP	LDDP	SacB	SB(2)	SB(3)
5	•	•	•	•	•
SacF	SacF	EB	Inf in (3)	2 to 3	
•	•	•	•	•	

3
LINE OUT TO 1B

E	DP	LDDP	SacB	SB(2)	SB(3)
3	•	•	•	•	•
SacF	SacF	EB	Inf in (3)	2 to 3	
•	•	•	•	•	

6
GROUND OUT TO SS

E	DP	LDDP	SacB	SB(2)	SB(3)
6	•	•	•	•	•
SacF	SacF	EB	Inf in (3)	2 to 3	
•	•	•	•	•	

8
FLY OUT TO SHALLOW CF

E	DP	LDDP	SacB	SB(2)	SB(3)
4	•	•	•	•	•
SacF	SacF	EB	Inf in (3)	2 to 3	
•	•	•	•	•	

8
FLY OUT TO DEEP CF

E	DP	LDDP	SacB	SB(2)	SB(3)
8	•	•	•	•	•
SacF	SacF	EB	Inf in (3)	2 to 3	
•	•	•	•	•	

FOUL BALL

E	DP	LDDP	SacB	SB(2)	SB(3)
3	•	•	•	•	•
SacF	SacF	EB	Inf in (3)	2 to 3	
•	•	•	•	•	

HOME RUN

E	DP	LDDP	SacB	SB(2)	SB(3)
4	•	•	•	•	•
SacF	SacF	EB	Inf in (3)	2 to 3	
•	•	•	•	•	

Appendix 3
SQUEEZE PLAY

by

"PAUL BENJAMIN"

1

IT WAS THE SECOND Tuesday in May when George Chapman called me. He had been given my name by his lawyer, Brian Contini, and he wanted to know if I was available to take on a case. If it had been anyone else, I probably would have said no. I had just spent three tedious weeks looking for the nineteen-year-old daughter of a wealthy suburban family, and the last thing I wanted at the moment was a new client. After going down a dozen dead ends I had finally found the girl in Boston, working as a Combat Zone hooker. The only words she said to me were, "Fuck off, fuzz. I don't got no mommy and daddy, you dig? I got born last week when you screwed some dog up the ass."

I was tired, and I needed some time off. The parents had given me a bonus when they learned their daughter was still alive, and I was thinking about blowing the money on a trip to Paris. But when Chapman called, I decided to let it wait. I sensed that whatever it was he wanted to talk about was more important than looking at paintings in the Louvre. There was something desperate in his voice, and his reluctance to talk about it over the phone made me curious. Chapman was in trouble, and I wanted to know what it was. I told him to meet me in my office at nine o'clock the next morning.

Five years earlier, George Chapman had done everything a baseball player can possibly do in one season. He batted for a .348 average, hit forty-four home runs, knocked in one hundred thirty-seven runs, and was given the Gold Glove at third base. The New York Americans won it all that year. The division title, the pennant, and the World Series. And when it was over, Chapman was named the Most Valuable Player in the league.

It was almost unreal. Every time you opened a paper, it seemed that Chapman was getting headlines for a ninth inning home run or a superhuman play in the field. In a year of garbage strikes, political scandals, and foul weather, Chapman became the hottest story in town. His picture was printed so often you started seeing his face in your sleep. Even the junkies on the Lower East Side knew his name, and a poll conducted by one of the local radio stations found that he could be identified by more people than the secretary of state.

Chapman himself was almost too perfect a hero. He was big and handsome, he always talked openly to reporters, and he never turned down a kid for an autograph. What was more, he had gone to Dartmouth as a history major, had a beautiful and sophisticated wife, and actually did things other than play baseball. This wasn't the kind of guy you'd look for to turn up in a deodorant commercial. When Chapman appeared on television, it was to do a plug for the Metropolitan Museum of Art or to solicit donations for refugee children. That winter after Chapman's great season, he and his wife made the covers of all the magazines, and the American people learned what books the Chapmans read and what operas they went to, how Mrs. Chapman prepared *poulet chasseur,* and when they were planning to have children. He was twenty-eight years old at the time, and she was twenty-five. They had become everyone's favorite couple.

I remembered Chapman's season all too well. It had been a bad year for me. My marriage was breaking up, my job in the D.A.'s office had gone stale, and I was up to my eyeballs in debt. Every time I turned around, a black ox was standing there ready to stomp me. When spring came I found myself retreating into my childhood, trying to put some order in my world by immersing myself in a time when life still seemed full of promise. One of the things I started to get interested in again was baseball. The very unreality of it was soothing to me. It didn't matter that I was using it as a way to avoid having to face the mess I was in. I had had enough of prosecuting black teenagers for nickel and dime robberies, of hanging around courtrooms with fat, sweaty cops, of dealing with crimes that turned everyone into a victim. And I had had enough bickering with my wife, enough pretending that we could still make it work. I was lying low, getting ready to abandon ship.

As the season wore on, I got more and more wrapped up in following the Americans, poring over the box scores every morning and catching the games on radio or television whenever I could. Chapman interested me more than any of the other players because we had played against each other in college. At the same time Chapman had been doing his number at third base for Dartmouth, I had been plodding along at third for Columbia. I was never much of a prospect. I batted something like .245 for my college career and led the league in errors at my position for three straight years. While Chapman was destroying college pitching and getting ready to sign a major-league contract, I just hung in there, playing for the fun of it and preparing to drift into law school when it was over. Following Chapman during his great season, I somehow thought of him as my alter ego, as an imaginary part of myself that had been inoculated against failure. We were the same age, the same size, and had been through the same Ivy League education. The only difference was anatomical: he had the world at his feet and the world had me by the balls. When he stepped up to the plate at the stadium, I sometimes found myself rooting for him so hard that I became embarrassed. It was as though his success could save me, and the idea of transferring so many private hopes to another person frightened me. Of course, I had gone a little crazy that year. And Chapman went on doing so well, day after day, that in some sense I suppose he really did keep me from going off the deep end. I probably also hated the guy's guts.

As it turned out, that was Chapman's last season in the major leagues. Whatever secret jealousy I felt toward him disappeared one night in February just before the start of spring training. Driving back to the city in his Porsche from a baseball banquet upstate, Chapman collided head-on with a trailer truck. At first it didn't look like he'd survive. And then, when he did survive, he came out of it minus his left leg.

For a year or two after that you didn't hear much about George Chapman. A little story now and then—"Chapman Fitted with Artificial Leg" or "Chapman Visits Disabled"—and nothing more. But then, just as it seemed he was going to slip out of sight permanently, he published a book about his experiences, *Standing on My Own,* which made a big splash and put him back in the public eye. If there's one thing America worships more than a celebrity, it's a celebrity who makes a comeback. The talented and beautiful are always admired, but they are a little remote from us, existing in a sphere that never touches the real world. Tragedy makes a star more human, proves that he is vulnerable like the rest of us, and when he is able to pick himself up again and return to the stage, we reserve a special place for him in our minds. Chapman certainly had the knack, you couldn't deny him that. There weren't too many people around who could turn an amputated leg into a new career. But from the moment he came back, he stayed in the limelight. He had become one of the leading advocates for handicapped people's rights, sponsoring wheelchair Olympics, appearing at congressional hearings, and doing special television programs. Now that a vacancy had opened up for one of New

York's United States Senate seats, some of the important Democrats were pushing Chapman as a possible candidate. The word was that he was going to announce before the month was out.

HE ARRIVED A few minutes early, striding in stiffly with his silver-handled cane and shaking my hand with the formality of a diplomat. I pointed to a chair, and he sat down without smiling, perfectly erect, the cane between his legs. Chapman's face was broad and muscular, with an almost Apache-like slant to the eyes, and the neatness of his sandy brown hair told me he was someone who took his own image seriously. He still looked to be in top condition. Except for a touch of gray around the temples, he had lost none of his youth, none of the physical authority of an athlete. And yet, behind it all, there was something in his face that made me wary. The brown eyes didn't seem to respond. I felt they were too determined, too fixed, as if he had somehow willed them never to betray the slightest spontaneity. Chapman appeared to be a man who made up his mind never to give an inch, and if you didn't want to play it his way, then you just didn't play. It wasn't the attitude you'd expect from an aspiring politician. More than anything else, he reminded me of a tin soldier.

He made it obvious that he wasn't very happy to be in my office, and as he sat down and glanced over the room, he had the look of someone who suddenly finds himself alone at night in the wrong neighborhood. I didn't let it bother me. Most people who walk into my office feel rather uncomfortable, and Chapman probably had better reason than most. He didn't waste any time in telling me why he had come. It seemed that someone was planning to kill him.

"Brian Contini told me you were intelligent and that you work quickly," he said.

"Chip Contini always had an inflated idea of my intelligence," I answered. "That's because we got the same grades in law school and I worked only half as hard as he did." Chapman was in no mood for lighthearted reminiscences. He looked at me impatiently, fidgeting with the handle of his cane. "I'm flattered that you called me," I went on, "but why didn't you take it to the police? They're better equipped for this sort of thing than I am, and they'd do everything they could for you. You're an important man, Mr. Chapman, and I'm sure you'd be given special treatment."

"I don't want this thing to get out into the open. It would cause a lot of idiotic publicity and divert attention away from more important things."

"We're talking about your life," I said. "There's nothing more important than that."

"There's a right way and a wrong way to handle this, Mr. Klein, and I want to do it the right way. I know what I'm doing."

I leaned back in my chair and waited for the silence to build up and make the atmosphere slightly unpleasant. Chapman's approach was putting me in a bad humor, and I wanted him to understand exactly what he was getting into. "When you say someone is trying to kill you, do you mean that someone has tried to push you out of a window? That someone's taken a shot at you? That you've seen someone slip arsenic into your martini?"

"I mean this letter," Chapman said coolly. "It came Monday, the day before yesterday."

He reached into the inside breast pocket of his tan cashmere jacket. Chapman's clothes were casual and elegant, in a way that only the well-heeled can be casual and elegant. Most ball players dress as if they've just stepped out of a Hawaiian singles bar, but Chapman was pure Madison Avenue, right down to his charcoal-gray pants and hundred-dollar shoes. I imagined that he probably spent more each year on underwear and socks than I did on my entire wardrobe.

Chapman took out a plain white business-size envelope and handed it across the desk to me. It was addressed to his East Side apartment and had been sent from the main post office in the city. The address had been typed out on an electric typewriter, possibly an IBM Selectric. I opened the envelope and read the letter inside. It had been typed on the same machine and was one page long.

Dear George

Remember Feb. 22 five yeares ago?

The way youve been acting lately it seems you dont. You were lucky that nite to be alive when they pride you from the reck. Maybe next time you wont be.

Your a smart boy George so we dont have to spell it out. We had an agreemint and your supposed to stick to it. And that means or else.

They say your going to be a candidate. The way it looks now the only thing your a candidate for is the deep freez.

A friend

I looked up at Chapman, who had been watching me with steely eyes as I read the letter.

"It doesn't take a genius to tell you that it sounds like blackmail," I said. "What about it, Chapman? Has someone been putting the bite on you?"

"That's just it," he said. "I don't know what the letter's talking about. The implication is that I've reneged on some kind of agreement. But I never made an agreement with anyone in the first place."

"It also seems to imply that the accident wasn't an accident after all."

Chapman shook his head back and forth, as if trying to clear his mind and make the thought of that night five years ago retreat back into the shadows. For a brief moment he looked older, almost spent. The effort to recall the past was difficult for him, and for the first time I saw the suffering in his face that until now he had managed to keep hidden.

"Believe me," he said slowly, "it was an accident. I skidded on some ice to avoid a fallen branch and went straight into the truck in the opposite lane. It's all too improbable to have been planned.

And why would anyone have gone to the trouble?"

"What about the driver of the truck?" I asked, pursuing a line of thought. "Do you remember his name?"

"Papano . . . Prozello . . ." He paused. "I can't remember it exactly. An Italian name that begins with P. But it's too far-fetched to think there's anything in it. The man was sincerely upset when he found out I was the person in the car. He came to me in the hospital and begged me to forgive him, even though it wasn't his fault."

"Where did the accident take place?"

"In Dutchess County, on Route 44 near Millbrook."

"But the banquet was up in Albany, wasn't it? Why weren't you on the Thruway, or at least the Taconic?"

Chapman suddenly seemed at a loss. "Why do you ask?"

"It's a long drive from Albany to New York. I'm curious to know how you wound up on a small country road."

"Well, actually," he said, recovering awkwardly, "I was fairly tired, and I thought that if I got off the big highway I would have an easier time with the driving." He paused melodramatically. "Obviously I was wrong."

I didn't want to sidetrack the discussion at an early stage, so I filed away this little detail for future reflection. I said, "There's something that rings false about the letter. It seems to come on very hard, and yet the overall effect is somehow too vague. If, as you say, you don't know anything about the agreement it refers to, then the letter hardly even makes sense. I wonder if you've considered the possibility of a hoax, something written by a crank, or maybe even a practical joke from one of your friends."

"If I thought the letter was a hoax," Chapman said, "I wouldn't have called you yesterday, and I certainly wouldn't have come down to see you in this office of yours at nine o'clock today. Naturally, I've considered all the possibilities. But in the end it doesn't make any difference. The letter is a fact, and the only way to handle it is to assume it's the real thing. I don't want to go around thinking it's a prank and then wind up murdered in some alley because I made a bad guess."

"Let's put it another way. From all I can gather, you've always been a highly successful and well-liked man. Is there anyone who hates you, anyone who hates you so much that he or she would consider the world a better place if you were removed from it?"

"I've spent the last two days trying to answer that question. But I honestly can't think of anyone."

"Let's put it still another way, then. How is your marriage? How is your sex life? How is your money situation? How is the work you've been doing?"

Chapman cut me short. "Don't be snide," he said. "I'm not here to give you my life story. I'm here to hire you to track down the person who wants to kill me."

"Listen, Chapman," I snapped back at him, "I haven't even decided to work for you yet. But if I do, I'll need your full cooperation all along the line. People don't decide to make murder threats out of pure whim, you know. There are reasons, cold, hard reasons, and they usually have to do with sex, money, or one of the other things no one likes to talk about. If you want me to find the person responsible for this letter, then you'll have to be willing to let me turn your life inside out, because more than likely the answer is buried there. It might not be very pleasant for you, but it might keep you alive. And I assume that's the object."

As a rule, I don't like to talk this way to my clients. But sometimes it becomes necessary, especially when things get off to a shaky start. Investigative work is a dirty business, but so is crime, and it's just as well to let people know that even if they are helped, they are going to get hurt a little too. It's a game which no one wins and everyone loses. The only difference is that some people lose more than others.

Chapman was contrite, and he apologized with good grace as I'd hoped he would. Even though he had a less steady grip on himself than he pretended to have—which continually put him on the defensive—I found myself unable to dislike him. He was a curious mixture of shrewdness and stupidity, a man with a hundred blind spots who was capable of seeing things with surprising clarity, and the contradictions in his character interested me. Behind his pose of self-assurance there was something almost pathetic about him, as if he had not yet fully come to terms with himself. I had no desire to become his friend, but I did feel like trying to help him. I realized that I wanted the case.

"I'm sorry," he said. "You're absolutely right. These past two days have put a strain on me, and I'm not myself. In general, I'm a very happy man. I know it seems hard to believe, but in many ways losing my leg was good for me, and I think it's made me a better person. I have a sense of real purpose now, and I'm working for things that are important to me. My wife is a marvelous woman who saw me through the difficult times after the accident, and I love her deeply. I am not fooling around with anyone else, my money situation is good, and I find my work satisfying—to answer your questions. The only thing I want to know is why in God's name would anyone want to kill me?"

He looked at me with a lost expression, his face full of sincerity and bewilderment. Either Chapman was a very good actor or he really did lead a totally blameless life. I didn't know what to think. He seemed almost too sincere, too eager to convince me with his soft speech. I wanted to believe him, and yet something in my gut resisted. If I accepted Chapman's account of his life, then I had nothing to begin the case with. And someone, after all, wanted him dead.

"What about the political angle?" I asked. "Maybe someone doesn't like the idea of your becoming a senator."

"But I haven't even announced yet. How can I be a threat to anyone when I'm not even a candidate?"

"Are you planning to run?"

"I was planning to make my final decision by the end of next week. But now that this business has come along, everything's up in the air again. I don't know what I'm going to do."

"And then there's your baseball career," I said, throwing out another possibility. "A ball player comes in contact with dozens of crazy characters—gamblers, hustlers, the so-called undesirable element. Maybe you got involved with something or someone and weren't even aware of it."

"That was a long time ago. People hardly remember me as a ball player anymore."

"You'd be surprised. A guy who handles the stick the way you did isn't forgotten so easily."

Chapman smiled for the first time since entering my office. "Thanks for the compliment," he said. "But again, there's nothing in it, nothing in the baseball idea. I never got to know any of those people."

It went on like this for a little while longer. I would ask Chapman a question, and he would answer that he couldn't see anything in it, that there was no connection with the letter. Since my display of temper, he had become more polite and agreeable, but I suspected it was merely a change of tactics on his part. The results were the same, and they added up to nothing. I couldn't figure out the game he was playing with me. He was genuinely shaken by the letter, and yet he was acting as though his sole purpose was to prevent me from doing anything about it. He was offering me the case, and at the same time he was snatching it away from me. I felt like a man who is given an expensive watch as a present and then discovers the watch has no hands.

The interview wound down to its conclusion and I got him to give me a list of names, addresses, and phone numbers, which I wrote down in my pocket notebook. I had no idea how useful the names would be, but I didn't want to take anything for granted. As things were shaping up now, I had a lot of legwork in front of me.

"I get a hundred fifty dollars a day plus expenses," I said. "Three days in advance. When the job is finished I'll supply you with an itemized list of expenses."

Chapman took out his checkbook, put it on the desk, and began writing with his Mont Blanc fountain pen. "Pay to the order of Max Klein," he said. "Any middle initial?"

"Just plain Max Klein."

"I'm making this out for fifteen hundred dollars, which will cover me for the first ten days. I'm hoping to be around at least that long." He grinned across the desk at me. "If you happen to solve the problem before then, you can keep the difference."

Like a lot of people when they spend money, Chapman was oddly jovial. By giving me so much in advance, he probably felt he was taking positive action, that he was writing out a protection policy on his life. As they say, money talks. But I had yet to see the dollar bill that could stop a bullet.

"I have a few ideas," I said. "I'll call you tomorrow morning when I see how it's going. I'll probably want to have another discussion with you then."

He ripped the check out of the book and handed it to me. Then he stood up, deftly putting his weight on his cane and pushing down on it. I imagined it was a gesture that had become automatic for him. I saw him to the door, we shook hands, and I watched him limp his way down the hallway to the elevator. Our conversation had lasted less than forty-five minutes.

I hadn't bothered to mention to Chapman that we had played against each other in college. It didn't seem to matter very much at this point. I also hadn't bothered to mention that his lawyer's father, Victor Contini, was one of the heads of the East Coast mob. Or that Chip Contini had grown up in the town of Millbrook in Dutchess County. As the letter said, George was a smart guy. He probably knew these things already.

2

MY OFFICE WAS on the third floor of an ancient West Broadway building two blocks south of the Chambers Street subway station. It consisted of one room that measured approximately fifteen by twenty feet—too cramped to rent out as a dance hall but large enough for me to breathe in comfortably if I didn't chain-smoke. The ceiling was high, patterned into rectangles with embossed swirls inside them, and here and there the plaster had bubbled below the weary plumbing, leaving certain spots that reminded me of Alka-Seltzer dregs whenever I looked up at them.

The sun did not flood through the two wire-mesh windows on the east wall; they hadn't been touched with a sponge since the day Mr. Clean went bald, and I kept the overhead light on at all times. For furniture I had a scarred oak desk as solid as a Stonehenge boulder, a few chairs, a black imitation-leather couch with yellowed foam creeping out of the seams, two filing cabinets, an old refrigerator, and a spanking new one-burner electric hot plate for making coffee.

My upstairs neighbor was an artist named Dennis Redman. A few years ago he had given me three of his early paintings to put on the walls, and for about six months the look of the office was definitely improved. But then a jealous wife came in and pumped four bullet holes into one of the paintings, and the next day her husband showed up and slashed one of the other paintings with a hunting knife. It seems that people find modern art a satisfying outlet for their frustrations. I returned the paintings to Dennis and tacked up a big color reproduction of Brueghel's *Tower of Babel,* which was being given away by my neighborhood bookstore uptown with every purchase of two or more books. Within a couple of months I had accumulated nine of the prints, and all of them had wound up hanging on my walls. It struck me as an admirable solution to my decorating problems. I found the painting an inexhaustible source of pleasure, and now I could look at it from any angle in the office—sitting, standing, or lying down on the couch. On slow days I spent a lot of time studying it. The picture shows the nearly finished tower reaching up toward the sky and scores of tiny workers and animals toiling away at the construction, diligently laboring over the most colossal monument to human presumption ever built. The painting never failed to make me think of New York, and it helped to remind me how our sweat and agony will always come to nothing in the end. It was my way of keeping things in perspective.

I put Chapman's check and the letter in the wall safe behind my desk and then sat down and made a call to the sociology department of Columbia University. I asked for William Briles.

"I'm sorry," said the female voice on the other end. "Professor Briles isn't in yet. Would you care to leave a message? I could have him call you back later. He should be in his office between eleven and twelve."

"My name is Max Klein," I said. "The professor doesn't know me, but it's rather important that I get to speak to him today. Could you make an appointment for me to see him at about eleven-thirty?"

"I'm sorry," said the voice. Apparently that was the only way she knew how to begin a remark. "I don't make appointments for the faculty. We're getting to the end of the semester now, and Professor Briles probably has several conferences scheduled with students."

"I'm sorry too," I said. "And I'm especially sorry that you're sorry. But I would appreciate it if you told Professor Briles that I'll be coming to see him about a matter of life and death at eleven-thirty and that if he doesn't plan to let me in he'll have to install a set of new locks in his door before I get there."

The voice went silent for a few moments. When it spoke again, it had turned into a whine. "You'd better tone down your act, mister. This is a university, you know, not a pool hall."

"Just give him the message, and don't worry your pretty head about it."

"You're damn straight I'll give him the message. And don't call me pretty. No one gave you any right to call me pretty."

"A thousand pardons," I said. "I'll never call you pretty again."

She slammed down the receiver, putting an end to our chat. I was in a frisky mood, eager to get started with the case. William Briles was a friend of Chapman's who had once collaborated with him on a book, *Sports and Society,* and I thought he might be able to tell me something interesting about my client. I was planning to go up to Columbia anyway for a look at the microfilm files, and I didn't want to waste the time on another trip later.

There were two ways of getting up and down the building. You could take the elevator, a decrepit machine that moved about as fast as a Wagner opera, or you could take the stairs, the city's answer to cave crawling. I usually took the elevator up and the stairs down. On the second floor there was a yoga studio run by a fortyish ex-beatnik by the name of Sylvia Coffin, and as I steered myself around the landing I could hear Sylvia instructing her nine o'clock class to forget they lived on the planet Earth, to leave behind their petty concerns and become one with the universe. It was all a matter of breathing correctly. I told myself I would keep that in mind.

When I reached the ground floor I hung around in the doorway for a moment, squinting out at the street and giving my eyes a chance to adjust to the sunlight. It was a beautiful May morning. Dazzling brightness, a touch of chill on the face, and everywhere those sudden gusts of wind that send paper scraps flying, taking them off in a way that seems to give the world a sense of purpose.

I walked the two blocks to the subway station, bought a *Times* at the corner, and went back down into the darkness. The token vendor was a sullen black man who sat hunched over the racing forms in his cage. From the expression on his face, it looked as though he hadn't had a winner in six or seven years. When the train came I settled into a corner seat and made a few halfhearted tries at tackling the paper. The only news that mattered to me anymore was Chapman. Until the case was over, I was going to have trouble thinking about anything else.

I got off at 116th Street, the Columbia-Barnard stop. It never gave me much pleasure to return to Morningside Heights. I had spent seven years of my life there, and after seven years even the sweetest of relationships can go sour. Institutions are dreary places at best, and Columbia was not one of the best. The imposing pseudoclassical architecture that crowded the small campus looked like a herd of elephants trying to hold a cocktail party on a tennis court, and the new buildings that had gone up in the past fifteen or twenty years were no better. The law school, for example, looked like a toaster. Students walked in as fresh pieces of bread and came out three years later as packages of crumbs.

The files of *The New York Times* were kept in the Barnard library. I showed my Columbia alumni card to a uniformed guard drowsing over a rumpled copy of the *News* and walked up to the main room on the second floor. A few coeds were bent over their books at long reading tables in the middle of the room, but at this hour the place was more or less empty. I dug out the box that contained the papers from February of five years ago, sat down at a viewing machine, and hooked up the film to the spools. I turned the handle quickly, watching the events of three weeks race past my eyes without reading, and then stopped at the twenty-third. Chapman's accident was on the bottom of the front page, a small story that had just managed to make the final edition.

Looking at a microfilm gives you an eerie feeling. Everything is reversed. Instead of black on white, the words are white on black, and it makes you think of an X ray, as if you were looking into the insides of time, as if somehow the past was a secret dimension of the world that couldn't be recovered unless you lured it out with tricks and mirrors. It's a little like discovering a fossil. The fern leaf has disintegrated millions of years ago, and yet its image is sitting in your hand. It's somehow both there and not there at the same time, lost forever and yet found.

BASEBALL STAR INJURED IN AUTOMOBILE ACCIDENT
Special to The New York Times

George Chapman, the all-star third baseman of the New York Americans, was injured early this morning when his car collided with a transport truck on Route 44 in Millbrook, N.Y. Authorities did not reveal the extent of his injuries, but they are believed to be serious.

Chapman had attended a baseball banquet held in his honor last night at the YMCA in Albany. He was taken by ambulance to Sharon Hospital in Sharon, Conn.

The driver of the truck, Bruno Pignato of Irvingville, N.J., reportedly suffered minor injuries.

This gave me what I had come for, but I kept turning the crank to read the follow-up stories for the rest of the month. As soon as it became clear that Chapman would not play baseball again, there were articles for several days in a row by nearly all the writers on the sports staff. They mentioned the highlights of his short career, talked about his character as a man, and eulogized the special grace and style he brought to the playing field. The writers seemed to feel cheated by not being able to see him play anymore. What interested me most were the figures. In his five seasons as a player, Chapman had averaged .312, hit 157 home runs, and driven in 536 runs, and each season had been an improvement on the one before. If he had been around for another six or eight years, the results would have been staggering.

I packed up the film and went downstairs to put in a phone call to Dave McBell at the D.A.'s office from the pay booth in the lobby. McBell and I had started working there at the same time, and he was good for a favor now and then if I didn't push too hard. Of all the people in the D.A.'s office, he was the only one who still thought I was a human being.

"Dave. Max Klein."

"The man himself," he quipped in his W. C. Fields voice.

"I need a little information. It shouldn't be too hard to get."

"Right down to business as always," he said in his normal voice. "You might ask how things are going."

"Well, how are they going?"

"Ugh," he said, pausing for maximum effect. "Don't ask." He burst into raucous laughter at the joke.

"Not bad. I'll try to remember that one for the next meeting of my Kiwanis Club in Jamaica."

"What can I do for you, Max?"

"Do you remember the accident five years ago—when George Chapman lost his leg?"

"I never forget a disaster. That guy could really pick it at third."

"I'm interested in finding out about the driver of the truck Chapman crashed into. Name of Bruno Pignato, lived in Irvingville, New Jersey five years ago."

"What do you want to know?"

"Mainly if he has any kind of record. And also if there's anything to connect him with Victor Contini."

"I guess I can manage it. Why don't you call me back in a few hours."

"Thanks a lot, Dave."

"Sure, sure. And you'll do the same for me one day, I know." He paused for a second. "Are you onto something hot?"

"I don't know yet. I'm just digging around for the moment."

"Well, if you stumble onto any gold, don't forget McBell."

"Don't worry. You wouldn't let me."

"Hey, Max."

"Yeah?"

"Ever hear the one about the castrated cop?"

"You told it to me a few months ago."

"Shit."

We hung up.

3

SHE WAS ONE OF the skinniest girls I had ever seen. She was sitting at her desk, reading a copy of *Prevention* magazine with a smug expression on her face and reaching for a sliced carrot stick from a pile that lay on her blotter. I guessed her age at around twenty-five. To judge by her looks, she was destined to wind up playing the role of skeleton in somebody's closet. She was all bones and angles, and her blue and red peasant dress hung on her like a sheet on an abandoned coatrack. One of the headlines on the magazine cover read: "Smokers Are Criminals." I took out my Gauloises and lit my fifth cigarette of the day.

"Hi," I said. "I'm Max Klein. I'm here to see Professor Briles."

She looked up, annoyed at being distracted from her reading, and gave me a cold stare.

"The tough guy," she said, as if to herself. "You'll have to wait a minute. I'll go see if he's free."

Her desk was in a small reception room, with the closed doors of professors' offices on the three walls behind her. The spaces between the doors were taken up by filing cabinets and bulletin boards with university announcements on them. She stood up slowly with pursed lips, resenting the effort, as if I had just asked her to eat a chocolate layer cake. In spite of her slouch, she was a good six feet tall, which put her eye-to-eye with me. She went to one of the doors, gave a quick knock, and poked her head into the office. A few mumbled words were exchanged, and then she shuffled back to her desk and sat down. Instead of saying anything to me, she picked up her magazine and started reading again.

"Well?" I said at last.

"Well what?" she answered, not lifting her eyes from the page.

"Can I go in to see him?"

"Not yet. He's with a student. It'll be a few more minutes."

"Thanks for telling me. I might have barged in there by mistake."

She put down her magazine with feigned weariness and sighed deeply. She gave me another one of those hard stares with her sad brown eyes.

"The trouble with you tough guys," she said, "is that you have no patience. And do you know why? A lack of B vitamins. If you ate more whole grains, you'd feel a lot calmer. You wouldn't be so pushy. You'd let things take their course, let yourself become one with the flow."

"The flow?"

"The flow of nature."

"Is that like becoming one with the universe?"

"Not really," she said, suddenly very serious. "Nothing so cosmic. It's more like being in touch with your body, the functioning of your organs."

"But I like to be in touch with other people's bodies," I said.

She looked at me carefully again and then shook her head with exasperation.

"You see," she said. "You begin to talk about something important and then you get embarrassed and all you can do is make wisecracks." She shook her head again. "Sick. Very sick."

I was no longer a possible convert, and therefore she had lost interest in me. She started reading again, groped blindly for a carrot with her right hand, and stuck it in her mouth. The room filled with the sound of her crunching.

The door of Briles' office opened, and a young man in jeans and a plaid work shirt walked out. He was carrying a pile of books and notebooks under his arm, and he looked like he had just been told he had only six months to live.

"Don't worry," I said to him as he walked by, "it's only one course."

He looked up, surprised to see me standing there, and made an attempt at a smile. "Don't tell that to Professor Briles," he said.

He went on out, his head bowed, conjuring up visions of what it would be like to spend vacation in summer school.

Briles appeared in the doorway of his office. He was about forty, a shade over six one, and he wore the kind of thin tortoiseshell glasses that had recently come back into fashion. Briles had a reputation as a polished and prolific writer, and he had made his name with a series of books on the marginal figures of society: prostitutes, thieves, homosexuals, gamblers, and so on. A latter-day Mayhew. I had read a few of them and had been sufficiently impressed. I figured him to be one of the showboat professors who perform before packed classes of awed, tittering students, a man who prizes every word he speaks, which also meant he was probably something of a tyrant, if the kid who had just walked out was any indication. The academic as superstar. There were always a few of them in every university.

"Mr. Klein?" He gestured for me to enter the office, closed the door when we were both inside, and pointed to a heavy wooden chair with a slatted back for me to sit in. The room was cluttered with piles of papers and books, and every inch of the walls was lined with bookshelves. Sun poured in through the windows and glared against Briles' glasses so that I couldn't see his eyes behind the lenses. It made him look slightly less than human, as though he were a creature who had been born without the ability to see. Five stories below, students were beginning to gather in the center of the campus for outdoor lunches, and faintly, through the half-opened windows, I could hear the shout of a Frisbee player, the barking of a dog, the hum of the warming day.

"I don't know who you are," Briles began pompously, taking his seat behind his desk, "and I don't really care. But I would like an explanation for the way you talked to Miss Gross this morning on the phone. We're accustomed to dealing with civilized people here, and frankly I'm inclined to look on your presence as a most unwelcome invasion."

"The explanation is simple," I said. "She wouldn't give me a straight answer, so I yelled at her. I'm sure you would have done the same thing in my place."

Briles looked at me as though I was some kind of curious sociological specimen. "What exactly do you want?" he asked with distaste.

"I want to talk about George Chapman," I said. I took out my investigator's license and showed it to him. "I have reason to believe he's in some danger."

"George Chapman?" Briles had been taken completely by surprise. "What in the world can I tell you about George Chapman?"

"Well, you did do that book with him seven or eight years ago, and I assumed you might be able to give me some of your impressions of him."

"First of all, Mr. Klein, I've published some eleven books in the past twelve years, and *Sports and Society* is the least substantial of the lot. It is not an important book. It is not even an interesting book. George Chapman was a student of mine at Dartmouth when I taught there. After his first year in the major leagues he got in touch with me and suggested we do a book together on the impact of professional sports on the athletes who play them. Because of his connections, George had easy access to the athletes and was able to arrange interviews with them. I wrote the commentaries and interpretations. He did a conscientious job of questioning, and I did what I could to organize the materials. But the book was a rush job. The publisher wanted it out during the next baseball season to capitalize on George's name. As it turned out, the sales were excellent. But it was still a bad book. I haven't been in close touch with George since that time. We see each other once or twice a year, no more."

"Is that a fact?" I asked, not trying to hide my sarcasm.

"I'm beginning to wonder what your motives are, Mr. Klein. It occurs to me that you've come here looking for dirt on George Chapman, and I refuse to be part of it. What are you trying to do, smear his name to hurt his chances of getting the Senate nomination? Or are you simply interested in dirt for its own sake? Hasn't that man suffered enough?"

The interview was rapidly slipping away from me. I had tried to be straightforward with Briles, but he was not having any of it. Still, I didn't want to let go. I felt that if I got nothing from him now, the tiny path I was opening would close up around me and Briles would be lost to me for the rest of the case. I tried changing my strategy.

"Yes," I said, "I agree with you that George Chapman has suffered enough already. But right now he's having some difficulties, and I'm doing my best to try to help him."

"And what is that supposed to mean?"

"It means that I'm asking for your help. I know very little about George Chapman except what everyone knows from reading the paper. To get him out of his predicament I need something more, something that might lead me to the heart of the problem."

"And naturally you aren't in a position to tell me about his predicament," Briles said. "Believe me, Mr. Klein, I've always been very fond of George and would do anything to help him. But unless I know what this is about, I'm afraid I won't be able to cooperate with you."

"It wouldn't be ethical for me to talk about it. You know that, Professor. I'm only asking for some background so that I can locate myself and not waste time floundering around. But as to what I do with the information you give me, you'll just have to trust me."

"Let me put it this way, Klein. George Chapman is a very important man to many people in this city and state. And important men, no matter how upright they may be in their private and public lives, are always vulnerable men. Until now you've said nothing to make me believe that you, or whoever it is you work for, are not planning to attack George in some way. You ask me to trust you. But how am I to know you haven't been lying to me from the moment you stepped into this office?"

"If you're interested in checking out my credentials, why don't you call Dave McBell in the D.A.'s office? We used to work together there, and he knows the kinds of things I've been doing for the past five years. I think he would vouch for my honesty."

"Mr. Klein," he said in his best lecturing voice, as if rebutting a naive remark by a student, "I have no doubt that in the past you've performed honorably on numerous occasions. But I simply do not see what your past activities have to do with the matter at hand. People in your line of work are subject to all sorts of pressures and temptations, and you could very conceivably have been turned by the promise of money, power, or whatever it is you value most. I'm sorry, Mr. Klein," he concluded, leaning back and putting his fingertips together with a disdainful expression, "but I'm afraid we'll have to terminate this talk."

Strictly speaking, Briles was correct. I had not given him any solid proof that I was working in Chapman's interests. And it was true that Chapman was particularly vulnerable at this moment because of his political ambitions. On the other hand, I had not asked Briles any specific questions and certainly nothing that could have compromised him. When people are told that someone they know is in trouble, they are usually quick to offer help.

But Briles had balked from the start, steering the conversation away from Chapman by challenging my motives. Not only was he reluctant to talk, he was lying. And doing a very poor job of it.

It's all a matter of details, coincidence, the chance gesture, the unconsciously spoken word. You have to be alert at every moment, on the lookout for the slightest note of discord, the most subtle hint that things are not what they seem to be. You go off in one direction, hoping to find one small thing, and instead find another thing, which sends you off in yet another direction. If you're not careful, you can get lost in the labyrinth of other people's lives and never find a way out. But those are the risks. Once you get involved with human beings, there are no straight roads anymore.

"You're a very impressive man, Professor Briles," I said. "A leader in your field, author of eleven books, an important figure on campus. But you forget that I'm not just some quaking undergraduate in here to ask your opinion of Weber's Puritan Ethic. You've sat here for the past fifteen minutes playing cat and mouse with me, refusing to answer the simplest questions. There wasn't any need. I came here to get some help, and now you've made me think I've chanced onto something. As they used to say in the sixties, you're either part of the solution or part of the problem. And you certainly haven't been very eager to give me a solution. In fact, Professor, I've rarely encountered a more unconvincing liar than you are. It's a matter of public record that you're a close friend of George Chapman, that you've spent weekends with him and his wife in the country, that you've been to the opera with them, that you invited Chapman to give a talk here at Columbia a few months ago. You pretend that you're just a casual acquaintance, when all you had to say was that you didn't want to talk. I would have accepted that. But to lie first and then refuse to talk doesn't make sense unless you're trying to hide something."

Briles sat there unmoving, indifferent, without the slightest trace of emotion. "Is that all?" he finally said. His voice sounded like a machine.

"That's all. But you can expect more from me later." I stood up. "Don't bother to see me to the door."

I left him there sitting at his desk in the sun-drenched room.

4

I WAVED DOWN a cab on Broadway and told the driver to take me to West Seventy-first Street. His name was J. Daniels, and he handled his hack like a failed bronco buster from a previous incarnation. He was about fifty, with crooked teeth and wild eyebrows that sat perched on his forehead like a pair of tiny forests. As we rattled and lurched our way downtown, I was thankful I had eaten a small breakfast.

We stopped for a light at 110th Street, and he said, "Aren't you going to ask me?"

"Ask you what?"

"What nine out of every ten goddamn people who step into this cab ask me."

"I hear you talking. But the only thing I get is static."

"The J in J. Daniels," he said, as if any fool should have known. "Everybody wants to find out what the J in J. Daniels stands for. Don't you want to ask me?"

"Not particularly."

"Aw, come on, why don't you take a guess? It helps pass the time." The light went green and we barreled ahead.

"All right," I said. "I give up."

"No, no, make a real guess. It's no fun if you don't try."

He wasn't going to let go until I relented, so I finally decided to humor him. I wished I had been as persistent in my questioning of Briles.

"Since there's only one obvious answer," I said, "I suppose it can't be that. And if it's not Jack, then it's got to be something odd." I paused for a moment. "How about Jeremiah? You look like a man with a lot to complain about."

"Wrong!" he bellowed, letting out an enormous laugh. "You lose. It don't stand for nothing! My name is just plain J., period. My goddamn parents couldn't think of anything to call me." His voice turned philosophical. "But that's okay. What the hell do I care? You can call me Jack. Lots of people do."

We made the rest of the trip in silence, and I didn't call him anything. The myth of the New York cabdriver had never held much water in my experience. Cabbies are just people, and when they talk they say the same stupid things other people say. J. Daniels had come on with an original line, and now that the joke was over, I didn't feel like hearing the rest of his repertoire. As I was climbing out of the cab at Seventy-first Street, he poked his head through the open window and gave me his parting shot.

"You know, mister," he said, "I've been driving a cab for twenty-three years, and not one person, not one goddamn person, has ever guessed what the J stands for." He laughed his enormous laugh once again and sped off eastward into the jungle of New York traffic to look for his next victim.

I lived in one of those classic West Side buildings, a kind of Noah's Ark that housed almost every New York species in existence. There were white people, black people, yellow people, and several shades in between. There were families, couples of men and women, two couples of men, one couple of women, and people who lived alone. There were professional people, wage earners, and people who did not work. Among them were a poet, a journalist, a three-hundred-pound soprano, two oboe students from Juilliard, a black homosexual art dealer, a dry cleaner, a post office clerk, a social worker, and a private investigator, to mention just a few. The whole operation was under the control of Arthur, the plump Puerto Rican superintendent. He had four kids and a wry sense of humor, and he took his job seriously. He was almost always around, either in the lobby or just outside the door, waiting with a baseball bat in his right hand and carefully scrutinizing every stranger who tried to enter the building. He cleaned up in tips at Christmastime.

I stopped at my mailbox in the lobby to collect some bills and junk mail and then rode the creaking brown-and-white-speckled elevator to the ninth floor. My apartment had two dark rooms that overlooked the courtyard and a kitchen just large enough for me to enter and exit if I remembered to hold my breath. They called it a kitchen nook, but the true word for it was cranny. For the past several years I had been telling myself that next week I was going to start looking for a better apartment, but I still hadn't managed to get around to it. I had probably grown too attached to the place to leave it.

I put on a record of one of the Mozart quartets dedicated to Haydn and made myself a ham and cheese sandwich on rye with two slices of Gruyère, a leaf of Boston lettuce, and a spoonful of Poupon mustard. I took a bottle of Beck's beer from the refrigerator and carried everything out to the round table in the living room.

Ten minutes later I called Dave McBell.

"You ring none too soon," he said. "I was just about to walk out for lunch."

"You don't need any lunch," I answered. "That's supposed to be for human beings. I thought you knew that only machines worked in the D.A.'s office."

"Well, this little machine needs a grease job, and then maybe a couple of beers to flush out the sludge."

"Any word?" I asked.

"No problem. Your man Pignato has been around. Nothing

too heavy, though. What you might call a bit player. He also seems to have a few dusty corners upstairs. But no history of violence. Been in and out of nuthouses the past four or five years, has a wife and three kids."

"What about Contini?"

"Patience, patience. I'm getting to it. Pignato's been clean for quite a while, since the accident with Chapman. Mainly he's a driver. The last time he was arrested, it was for driving a truck with a headlight missing."

"That doesn't sound too serious."

"Yeah. But when they opened the truck they found about twenty thousand dollars' worth of black market cigarettes from North Carolina stashed in the back. The charges didn't stick, of course, but he was working for Contini. He's been on the payroll for fifteen years."

"And before that?"

"The usual stuff. A few car snatches. Worked as the driver in a few holdups. Reform school as a kid. He's been in the can three times, but never for more than a few months."

"Do you have an address?"

"The same town as before, Irvingville. 815 Seventeenth Street. His wife's name is Marie."

"Thanks, Dave. I guess that should do it."

"Good. Now maybe I can leave this place before my stomach crawls out of my body and strangles me."

"Remember to watch the calories."

"Yeah. And you remember to watch yourself, Max. Contini may be getting old, but he's still no pussycat."

"Don't worry about me," I said. "I'm the last of the hard-boiled Yids."

I didn't move from my chair. For a few minutes I just sat there, watching a couple of pigeons strut back and forth on the window ledge outside. One of them, all puffed up with male pride, kept trying to mount the other, but the female managed to elude him each time he approached. Desire among pigeons is remorseless and robot-like. They seem compelled to do one thing again and again all their lives without showing the slightest awareness of what they are about. There is no true love among them, as there is among sparrows. Pigeons are exemplary New Yorkers, and they display all the best-known characteristics of the city: sex without soul, gluttony, nastiness, and disease. In France they are bred with special care and eaten as a delicacy. But then the French are supposed to know how to enjoy life more than we do.

Things were breaking nicely for me so far. I had my first lead, and it seemed to be a good one. The important thing was to avoid rushing to conclusions. I had been toying with the idea that Chapman's accident had in fact been a deliberate attempt to murder him, but I was hesitant just now to consider this as anything more than a possibility. A hunch is not evidence, and I still had nothing tangible to take hold of. It was at this point that I had to begin earning the money that Chapman had given me.

I went over the names on Chapman's list and then put in a call to Abe Callahan, one of the Democratic Party leaders who had been touting Chapman as a candidate. He was one of the so-called new breed who looked, acted, and smelled very much like the so-called old breed. His secretary said he was in Washington and wouldn't be returning until Monday. I left my name and told her I would call back then.

My next call was to Charles Light, the owner of the Americans, and through his secretary I managed to set up an appointment with him for early the next day. I was a little surprised to be given the appointment so easily, but I chalked it up to the innate charm of my telephone voice. This was going to be my lucky day.

I dialed the number of my answering service to find out if there were any messages for me. There was only one. From Mrs. George Chapman, and it was urgent. She was going to be waiting for me in my office at two-thirty. I always left my office unlocked, and since there was no secretary, I had given the women at the answering service instructions to make appointments for me. I checked my watch. It was pushing two o'clock. If I hustled out of my apartment, I might get there just in time.

I carried my lunch plate to the kitchen and threw it into the sink with the other dirty dishes, telling myself I would take care of them when I got back. The cockroaches would be grateful, and I liked to stay on good terms with my tenants.

I went into the bathroom, splashed cold water on my face, straightened my tie, brushed some crumbs off my green corduroy jacket, and combed my hair. When I looked at myself in the mirror my face seemed eager; it was the face of a teenager getting ready to go out on a hot date. I supposed I was excited about meeting Judith Chapman. But that was only part of it. My case was beginning now, and I could feel the tension building up in the pit of my stomach. The adrenaline was flowing.

I was just about to leave, when there was a knock on the door. It wasn't one of those polite, tentative knocks a neighbor gives when he wants to borrow the salt shaker, but a loud, insistent banging that told me I wasn't going to make my two-thirty appointment, no matter how hard I tried. They knew I was in there, and they didn't want to be kept waiting. My last thought before opening the door was to wonder how they had managed to get past Arthur downstairs.

There were two of them, as there always are. One of them was very big and the other was just big. Very Big was dressed in a blue and red Madras sport jacket, a purple tie, a yellow wash-and-wear shirt, and pale-green double-knit slacks. It was a nightmare combination, like something cooked up by a demented circus barker. He was wearing wraparound sunglasses, and the idiot smirk on his smooth, beefy face indicated that he was happy with his work. Big was slightly more distinguished. His synthetic brown suit looked as if he had debated over it a moment or two at the racks in Sears, and his powder-blue "American Bicentennial" tie showed that if nothing else, at least he was a patriot. But I didn't like his eyes. They were the same color as the tie and had that hard, hungry look eyes get when they've seen everything and keep wanting to go back for more. I hadn't been expecting anything like this to happen so quickly, and it scared me. Men of this sort never drop by for casual visits. They come with a purpose, and they usually don't leave until they have what they want. It was a dangerous situation, and they had caught me off guard. I told myself to stay calm.

It was Big who broke the ice. "Max Klein?" he asked. It was a voice that had come straight from Newark by way of the Pulaski Skyway and then got lost in the traffic somewhere on Tenth Avenue.

"I'm sorry," I said. "I'm just the cleaning woman. Mr. Klein is on vacation in Europe."

"A funny guy," said Very Big. He seemed pleased by this, as if it would make his visit more enjoyable.

"You'll have to excuse me, gentlemen," I said. "I'm already late for an appointment. Why don't you come back in about three years? We can talk about it then."

I made a move to get through the door, but they stood there impassively, like two Easter Island statues.

"This won't take but a few minutes of your time, Mr. Klein," said Big. He was all business, and he wasn't giving me any choice.

"All right," I said at last. "Come on in. But mind you don't put your cigarettes out on the floor."

"We don't smoke," said Very Big in dead earnest.

I let them in. Big sat on the couch and I took a seat at the table. Very Big wandered around the room, inspecting the books and records. He made me think of a truckdriver who had made a wrong turn and wound up in a museum by mistake.

"We know who you are," Big began. "So you don't have to play games with us. We know how you made a big stink in the D.A.'s office a few years back over the Banks case. We know how you blabbed the whole thing to the papers when you quit. And we know that you don't have too many friends left in this city." He sounded as if he had sat down and memorized his speech from three-by-five index cards.

"I'm glad you know these things," I said. "I wouldn't want to have any secrets from you. But I don't see what it has to do with the price of pizza in the Bronx."

"It means we have more friends than you do, Klein. Which means you would be very stupid not to cooperate with us."

"Let's hear it, then. The suspense is killing me."

Big leaned back on the couch and gave me one of those looks that are supposed to stop tigers cold in their tracks. The fact was he did a pretty good job of it. Lucky for me I wasn't a tiger.

"Stay away from George Chapman," he said in a dry monotone.

"Oh, I see," I said sarcastically. "You barge in here and tell me the kind of company I should keep, and I'm supposed to nod my head and thank you for keeping me on the path of virtue."

"Something like that," he said.

Over in the corner by the stereo machine, Very Big was studying the record I had been playing earlier. "Who's this guy?" he asked, holding up the record jacket and looking at Mozart's portrait on the cover. "Looks like some kind of fag creep to me."

"That guy, as you put it," I said, "has been dead for nearly two hundred years. At the age of three, he had more intelligence in his kneecap than you have in your entire gorilla brain."

"Shit," said Very Big. "You sure have a way with words." He slipped the record out of its jacket, examined it carefully on both sides, and snapped it in two. He idly tossed the pieces onto the floor.

"For that," I said, "you'll languish in the ninth circle of hell for a thousand years."

"Sorry," he said, staring down at his open palms with feigned bewilderment. "My hands must have slipped."

"All right," I said to Big, "why don't you and your friend run along now. I've got your message. There's nothing more to discuss."

"Yes, there is," he said. "I've given you the message, but you haven't given me an answer."

Very Big went over to the bookcase, chucked a few books onto the floor, and then reached his long arm into the shelf and in one smooth motion swept off the rest of the books. They tumbled down, clattering onto the clear plastic top of the record player, and landed on the floor. Big paid no attention to these antics. It neither amused nor offended him. He had his job to do, and his partner had his.

"Jesus," Very Big said. "I don't know what's wrong with me today. I must be getting awfully clumsy."

Very Big seemed to have aspirations as an interior decorator. No doubt he spent his free evenings combing the latest issue of *House Beautiful* for new ideas. In a matter of minutes he had nearly redesigned my entire living room, and by the time he was finished I was sure he would have it exactly as he wanted it. It was called the scatter approach, and it lent the room the kind of informal charm you find only in the best homes.

I let it pass. I wasn't going to allow anything to disturb me. This was my lucky day, and you're not supposed to tamper with fate. I hadn't been born a Jew for nothing. You learn how to take the good with the bad from an early age. And you also learn how to count. No matter how I looked at it, two against one struck me as a convincing argument.

"Let's put it this way," I said to Big, as Very Big got to work on the second bookshelf. "Why the hell should I do anything you ask me to do? You tell me to drop a client I only started working for this morning, but I don't know you from a ping-pong ball. You forget that I'm trying to make a living, that I can't just take on a case one minute and quit the next. If you want to take bread out of my mouth, you'll have to offer me some cake instead."

Big broke into a broad smile. I was talking a language he could understand now. We were both professionals, working on opposite sides, perhaps, but nevertheless united by the same cynicism, the same philosophy that always gives the buck the last word.

"I knew you were one of those smart lawyer types, Klein," he said. "It pains me to see you get such a sweet deal, but I'm only the messenger boy around here." He paused, as if with envy at my good fortune. "You stay away from Chapman and you get five thousand, no questions asked."

"And where does this money come from?"

"Like I said, no questions asked. Five grand seems like enough for no questions."

"All right, no questions. How am I supposed to get the money?"

"In cash. Everything's been arranged."

"And what if I decide not to?"

"You don't decide nothing. You just do. Am I making myself clear?"

"Not terribly. I still would like to know what happens if I send you back to your boss with a message to take those five bills and shove them up his ass."

"You don't say that unless you want to wind up with a pair of broken legs."

"But that's precisely what I am saying."

Big was incredulous. It was beyond his comprehension that anyone could even entertain the possibility of rejecting such an offer. Our momentary rapport had been destroyed, and he no longer knew where he stood with me. I was a stranger again.

"Are you saying no? Are you fucking saying no?" His voice had gone up a full octave.

"That's right, I'm saying no. And I don't want you to forget my message. Up his ass. The whole five thousand."

I was taking a big risk, and I knew I would probably have to pay for it. But refusing the money was the only way I would be able to find out who was behind the offer. Someone was very serious about keeping me away from Chapman, and that meant I had even less time than I had thought. If I didn't work fast, Chapman's life wouldn't be worth the ink on a canceled stamp.

"You're a dead man," Big said. "You just wrote yourself a ticket to the happy hunting ground."

Very Big had stopped his wrecking operation and was watching Big with the expectant look of an attack dog. He was waiting for a sign.

"Let's get out of here, Angel," Big said. "This bastard's got to be the stupidest fuck in New York."

"Yeah, I know," Angel answered. "He's a funny guy. I told you that when we got here, Teddy." Angel grinned at me and then walked over to where I was sitting. "He reminds me of one of them clowns with the big red noses. You know what I mean, Teddy? A real Bozo." Without any warning he yanked me out of my chair and flung me like a beach ball onto the pile of books on the other side of the room. "A regular barrel of monkeys. Just like one of them stand-up comedians on the TV. Only this guy ain't standing up so good right now." Before I had a chance to catch my breath, he was on top of me again, jerking me back to my feet. I tried to double up into a crouch, but he was too quick for me, and by the time I realized I should give him my shoulder, he had sent a short, incredibly powerful right hand into my gut. It felt like the IRT had been derailed in my bowels. I went down, unable to breathe, unable to move. The whole world was turning black, and whatever light was left in it sputtered fitfully, as cheerless as a candle in the rain.

"That's enough, Angel," Teddy said. "It's time to go."

"I just wanted to give this creep a taste of things to come," Angel said, standing over me with his fists still clenched. "Something juicy to think about the next time he takes a crap."

I didn't notice them leave. I was somewhere down at the bottom of the ocean, looking for an iron lung. By the time I was able to breathe again, they had probably driven off in their car, stopped for a late lunch, and made it halfway back to Brooklyn. Or wherever it was they came from.

5

IT WAS AFTER three-thirty when I made it down to my office. I was a little surprised to find Judith Chapman still waiting for me. I had called the office from my apartment before leaving and no one had picked up the phone, which gave me the answering service again—and they had no new messages to report. I figured she had given up on me.

"I was late too," she said, turning around in her chair to greet me. It was the same chair her husband had sat in that morning. "So I suppose I can't hold it against you." She smiled with gentle irony, as if to say we were both guilty and therefore both innocent.

I sat down behind my desk and smiled back at her. I appreciated the way she had tried to put us on an equal footing.

"What can I do for you, Mrs. Chapman? My answering service said it was urgent."

I liked Judith Chapman's face. It wasn't pretty in the classical sense, perhaps not even beautiful, but compelling, the kind of face it's almost impossible to stop looking at. Her nose was a little too big, her jaw was too broad, and her lips were slightly too full. But somehow it all fit together, and when you looked into her round brown eyes they almost startled you with their intelligence and sense of humor. She seemed to be one of those rare women who fit comfortably into themselves and the world, a woman who could go to the ballet one night and play poker with the guys the next night and find them equally enjoyable experiences. She was sophisticated but not brittle, and her dark wavy hair gave her a sensuousness you don't usually find in rich women. She was wearing a simple white knit dress with colorful embroidery around the neck. There was little jewelry on her hands and wrists and only a touch of makeup around her eyes. She reached into her large brown leather bag and pulled out a Merit, which she lit with a sleek gold lighter before I had a chance to strike a match for her. She did it with the automatic gestures of someone who smokes a pack or two a day.

"It's about my husband, George," she said. "I know he came here this morning to see you, and I'm worried that something serious has happened."

"Nothing serious has happened. Not yet. We talked about how we might keep it from happening."

"Then there is something to worry about." She looked as if whatever it was that was on her mind had been bothering her a lot longer than since this morning.

"Hasn't your husband talked to you about it?"

"My husband and I don't talk about much of anything to each other, Mr. Klein." There was no bitterness in her voice. It was simply a statement, a fact of life.

"If you didn't talk to your husband, then how did you find out he came here?"

She hesitated for a moment, as though trying to make a decision. I felt she was suddenly having second thoughts about coming to my office.

"Bill Briles told me."

I leaned back in my chair and gazed up at the ceiling. In my most serenely innocent voice I asked, "That wouldn't be Professor William Briles, would it? Member of the sociology department of Columbia University and author of some eleven books?" I swung my chair forward and grinned at her.

"Don't be sarcastic, Mr. Klein," she said, with her first display of bad humor. "You know who he is. You saw him yourself just a few hours ago."

"What exactly did Briles tell you?"

"He called me at about noon in a total panic. He said you were conducting some kind of investigation involving George, that you had threatened him and said you were going to keep after him."

"He wasn't particularly cooperative. I had the feeling he was trying to hide something. And I'm a curious person. I like to know why people do the things they do."

"Maybe he was scared." Her voice had taken on an edgy, defensive tone.

"I only wanted to ask him a few questions that would help me to protect a friend of his."

"That's exactly why he would be scared. Anything to do with George is rather difficult for Bill to deal with."

"And why is that?"

Again she hesitated, as if afraid to say the wrong thing.

"It's complicated," she said.

"That's all right. I'm in no rush. You can explain it to me."

She took a deep breath to build up her courage. Then she leaned forward and stubbed out her cigarette in the ashtray on my desk. As she spoke she continued to stare at the ashtray, as though she was speaking to it rather than to me. The dead cigarette was an uncritical audience.

"I don't suppose it matters now," she said. "Maybe it would be of some help if I told you." She took another deep breath and waited for her body to relax. I could hear the rumblings of the afternoon traffic outside, the sound of water running in Dennis Redman's studio upstairs, the ubiquitous cooing of pigeons on the window ledge, all the little noises that live inside the silences of the city. "You see," she went on, "Bill Briles and I were lovers for a long time. That would probably explain why he was so nervous with you today. He just didn't know what you were after. I think we did a pretty good job of keeping it secret from the public. But you can never be sure."

"You and your husband always come across as admirably devoted to each other," I said. "You're the model couple."

"It's terrible, isn't it," she said, "living a lie, knowing you're a complete hypocrite. My marriage with George fell apart after three years. But we just went on, appearing in public together, pretending nothing had happened, and all the while leading separate lives."

"When did the affair with Briles start?"

"About two years before George's accident."

"And it went on the same way after the accident?"

"More or less. Bill and I stopped seeing each other for a while, but it wasn't really over. It was just a pause."

"But it's over now."

"Yes, we finally broke it off about six months ago. I decided to make a fresh start with George. He said he desperately wanted me back, and I believed him. Things were fine for a while, but then it all blew up in our faces again. George Chapman is an extremely difficult man to get along with, Mr. Klein."

"He told me this morning that he loved you very deeply, that you were the support of his life."

"That's not unlike him. One of his greatest problems is that he always says the expected and conventional thing rather than reveal his emotions. He's always been like that, but even more so since the accident. It's difficult for me to talk about this. But you've got to understand that I was only a child when I married George. I was twenty-one, just out of college, and I thought he was the most extraordinary man I had ever met. I didn't know anything about baseball or what it was like to be a ball player's wife. When the season started, I hardly ever saw him. You must know something about athletes when they're on the road. George had a woman in every city. It took me a few years to figure it out, but he didn't really want a wife, he wanted me as a showpiece. I gave him a good image. That's why he pleaded with me to go back with him last winter. He was thinking of getting into politics, and he knew that a pretty wife is a great asset for a politician. It was also a way to avoid a political scandal if anyone ever found out about my relationship with Bill. George has a way of always playing both ends at once. He doesn't like to take risks."

"I don't mean to pry," I said, "but didn't you ever think of getting a divorce?"

"Of course I did. Bill and I went to him several times, but he swore he'd kill us both. And I believed him. George has a great capacity for violence. Everything is so bottled up in him, it periodically explodes in terrible rages. He got used to the fact that Bill and I were lovers. He decided it was all right for me to see Bill—as long as no one else knew about it. It's perverse, I know, but that's the way George is. I don't mean to make him out to be an evil man. He's a very complex and difficult person. In his own strange way I think he still loves me—to whatever extent he's capable of loving anyone. And in spite of everything, I find I still have some feelings for him. Pity . . . affection . . . I don't know what to call it. We've been through a lot together, and I suppose that creates a bond. And yet, I needed something more . . . I still need something more. . . ."

I stood up from my chair, walked to the other side of the room, and sat down on the windowsill. I was puzzled why she had chosen to confide in me like this. After keeping her affair with Briles a secret for so long, it didn't make sense for her to talk about it with such candor. At the same time, I was pleased that she had opened up to me. I was hungry for information about Chapman, and in just a few minutes she had given me something that might have taken me weeks to discover on my own. I considered it a lucky break.

"You're a good listener, Mr. Klein," she said. "I guess I've been wanting to tell this to someone for a long time." She smiled with embarrassment. "And you, as it turned out, were it."

"You can call me Max," I said. "Everyone does. Even the people who think my name is Mud."

"If you put it that way," she said with another smile, this one a genuine show of warmth that made her eyes dance, "then my name is Judy."

We studied each other carefully, sizing each other up as human beings for the first time. The atmosphere in the office changed, suddenly and ineffably. We were no longer complete strangers. Something intimate had passed between us.

I went on looking her in the eyes.

"Tell me," I said, "has George had any affairs of his own since the accident?"

She shook her head. "I don't think so. At least not that I know of."

"Did the accident have any lasting physical effects . . . besides the loss of his leg?"

"If you're asking the question I think you are," she said, "the answer is no. George is perfectly capable of having sex."

"Then why doesn't he have it? I'm not talking about falling in love. I just mean someone to satisfy his needs."

"George's needs are not like those of other men," she said quietly. "Even before the accident, sex was more of a duty for him than a pleasure. I think he's afraid of it, afraid of the emotions it creates."

I thought about that for a while, trying to fit it into the picture I had begun to form of Chapman. Things didn't necessarily make sense, but they were there, out in the open, and I had to live with them now and try to make them a part of me.

I said, "Your husband came to see me this morning because he received a letter threatening his life."

Judy Chapman looked at me as if I had just spoken to her in Chinese. "I don't understand," she said. "What are you talking about?"

"Someone sent George a letter. The letter said that if George didn't do certain things, then George would be ushered from the world of the living. The only trouble is that George doesn't know what these things are. So that even if he wanted to cooperate, he can't. And that puts him in a rather precarious position."

"Oh my God," she said. Her voice was barely audible. "Oh my God."

"I have nothing definite to go on yet, but I'm working on a lead that might turn out to be fairly solid." I paused, giving her a little time to compose herself. "Does the name Victor Contini mean anything to you?"

"He's the father of George's lawyer, Brian Contini."

"Have you ever met him?"

"No, never."

"What about George?"

"He never mentioned him, as far as I can remember." She looked up at me with a quizzical expression. "Isn't Victor Contini some kind of mobster?"

I nodded. "One of the worst."

She held her eyes on me for a moment, as if hoping I would break into a smile and tell her it was all a joke. When my expression didn't change, she said, "I can't believe this is happening. It's just not real."

I didn't say anything to reassure her. Telling her that it was all going to work out in the end would have been a lie, and I didn't want to make false promises. It was real, and because it was real anything could happen.

"Tell me a little about George's finances," I said. "Is he spending more than he brings in?"

"No, just the opposite. He has more money than he knows what to do with. The book sold very well, and there's still quite a bit coming in from that. Then there are the talks he gives on the lecture circuit, the investments he's made, and the salary he still gets from the Americans. He signed a long-term contract before the accident, you know."

"Yes, I know. For eight years."

"That money would be more than enough. It amounts to a considerable fortune, more than most people make in their whole lives."

"Two hundred and fifty thousand a year, isn't it?"

"Not quite. But you're pretty close."

"And what about Charles Light? I would imagine he'd resent parting with all that money every year without getting anything in return."

"There's no question that he resents it. But he's bound by the contract, and there's nothing he can do about it. For the first few years he was very persistent about trying to arrange some kind of compromise settlement, but George stuck to his guns, and finally he gave up."

"Is there anyone else besides Light who could possibly have a grudge against George?"

"I'm sure there are many people who dislike George. He has a very strong personality, and that rubs some people the wrong way. But that doesn't mean they would want to kill him."

"What about William Briles?"

She stopped short and looked at me closely. "Impossible. Bill Briles is not that kind of man. For one thing, he abhors the idea of violence. For another, he's too afraid of George even to consider such a thing." She spoke incisively, as if to banish the thought from my mind. It seemed that she was trying to sweep Briles off the stage once and for all, and I wondered if she was doing it for her own benefit or if it was an indirect way of telling me she was available. This wasn't the moment for me to try to find out.

"One last question," I said. "Has George ever spoken to you about why he was driving on a small country road the night of the accident?"

The question confused her. She had no idea what I was talking about. "What difference in the world would it make what kind of a road he was on?"

"It strikes me as odd, something of a loose end. And anything that doesn't fit into a normal pattern, I have to pull out and examine as closely as I can."

"But what does the accident of five years ago have to do with what's happening now?"

"I don't know," I said. "That's what I'm going to try to find out."

Judy Chapman sat lost in thought, slowly shaking her head back and forth. It seemed that the whole business was finally beginning to sink in. "Poor George," she muttered, almost to herself. "Poor, poor George."

"Will I be able to reach you at home?" I asked. "I'll probably want to call you if I chance onto anything relevant."

"Yes, I'll be home. And you can always leave a message on the machine if I happen to be out."

She got up to leave. I found myself liking the way she carried herself in her lean body. Her clothes didn't form the kind of armor around her that they do around some attractive women. They seemed to enhance her presence, to remind you that she was alive inside them and didn't have to flaunt herself to be desirable. She made it all seem so effortless. I was beginning to wonder if I had ever met anyone like her.

As we were about to walk out the door toward the elevator, she turned around and looked back into the room at the nine Towers of Babel on the walls.

"I'll say one thing about your decorations," she deadpanned. "They don't compromise."

"I'm a guy who doesn't like too many things," I said. "So when I discover a good thing, I like to hang on to it."

We were talking to each other in a strange, truncated code, feeling each other out with an almost Victorian delicacy. No word was exactly what it seemed to be, and even the most trivial remark had a double meaning, a hidden purpose. She smiled at me with amusement. I had just paid her a compliment, and she had recognized it for what it was. It made me glad to know we were on the same wavelength.

We waited for the elevator in silence. When it finally came she touched me on the arm and said, "Take care of yourself, Max."

I told her I would.

6

LUIS RAMIREZ was the day man at the Big Apple parking lot across the street. I had been keeping my 1971 Saab there for the past five years, and in that time I had come to know Luis fairly well. He was a small, thin man in his early thirties who always wore a blue hooded sweatshirt, and he spent his spare moments in a dilapidated wooden shack about the size of a telephone booth, reading every baseball publication known to man—from *The Sporting News* to *Sport,* the *Baseball Digest,* the *Baseball Monthly,* the *Baseball Quarterly,* and Street and Smith's *Baseball Annual.* Whenever he had a car to move, he would rev up the engine until it roared, back out with a screech of rubber and flying gravel, and maneuver the car into position with the abrupt, speeded-up motions of an old silent film. In the five years I had known him he had fathered three sons, and each one had been named after a different Latin ball player: Luis Aparicio Ramirez, Minnie Minoso Ramirez, and Roberto Clemente Ramirez. Whenever I saw him we talked baseball. His knowledge of the game was staggering. What Berenson was to art and Tovey was to music, Luis Ramirez was to baseball.

"Hey, big guy," he said to me, looking up from the list of

Pacific Coast League averages on the back pages of *The Sporting News.* "You want your wheels?"

"That's right," I said, "all four of them. But from the way the car is sandwiched in there, it'll probably take you twenty minutes to get it out."

"You kidding?" He was happy to take on my challenge. "Three minutes. You watch. No more than three minutes."

He grabbed the keys from the peg board on the wall, and I watched him go into his Keystone Cop routine with a Ford Mustang, a VW Bug, and a new Chrysler. By the time the dust had settled, a good four and a half minutes had gone by.

He opened the door of my Saab for me and laughed. "What I tell you, man? Four minutes. When I give a time I always make it. Four and a half minutes!"

I got into the car and rolled down the window. "Who's going to win the game tonight, Luis?"

His face became serious. "It depends. If they throw Middleton, the Americans have a chance. He likes this weather. But his slider's no good yet. If they go with Lopez, then forget it, man. That dude can't keep the fastball away from those Detroit hitters. I say Detroit wins, but it'll be close. Six to four, seven to five, something like that."

If Luis Ramirez had been a betting man, he probably could have spent the rest of his life on a golf course in southern California, driving around in one of those electric carts. But he was a purist, and the idea of making money from baseball upset him. You didn't try to turn an art form into a business. It would kill the pleasure.

I pulled out of the lot and started to make my way uptown to the Lincoln Tunnel. It was four-thirty, a bad time to contend with New York traffic, much less to try to get out of the city. But I didn't want to wait until tomorrow. I needed to get hold of Pignato right away.

Under normal conditions it's a thirty-five- or forty-minute

drive to Irvingville. I had grown up in New Jersey and was familiar with the terrain. After you get out of the tunnel, you take one of those highways that have given New Jersey its reputation as the armpit of the Western world. Although there are no more pigs in Secaucus, there is enough industrial stench along the way to make you think you've traveled through a time warp back into nineteenth-century England. Thick white smoke charges out of giant factory chimneys, polluting the grotesque landscape of swamps and abandoned brick warehouses. You see hundreds of seagulls circling hills of garbage and the rusted hulks of a thousand burned-out cars. In a low mood, it's enough to make you want to live as a hermit in the Maine woods, feeding off wild berries and the roots of trees. But people are wrong to say this is a preview of the end of civilization. It is the essence of civilization, the exact price we pay for being what we are and wanting what we want.

The traffic was heavy when I reached the Garden State Parkway, but it moved steadily. It wasn't hot enough yet to be the season of overheated radiators and bald-tire blowouts, and the beautiful weather seemed to urge the drivers on. They probably were hurrying home to spend the rest of the spring afternoon in their backyards, planting tomatoes or drinking beer, rushing to flee the scene of their monotonous days and make a stab at pretending to be alive. It was twenty to six when I reached the ramp for the Irvingville exit.

Like most of the towns and small cities around Newark, Irvingville was a down-at-the-heels working-class community. Its better days were behind it, and even those had been nothing to rave about. Unlike the neighboring cities, however, all of which had become predominantly black in the past twenty years, Irvingville was still almost completely white. It was a little alcove of reactionary fervor in the midst of a changing world. Back in the thirties, there had been a Nazi Bund in Irvingville, and its cops were well known to be the most brutal in the county. The town was inhabited by Poles and Italians, and most of them had never had anything better than grueling factory jobs and desperate, exhausted lives. These were the people who stood just a half step away from the welfare office, a half step away from the black man's poverty, and because of this threat, many of them found release in a particularly vicious kind of racism. It was a rough place, a depressing place. You didn't want to be there unless you had to.

Seventeenth Street was a neighborhood of two-family houses, bravely trying to keep a smile on its face as it went under. Most of the houses were covered with gravelly maroon or green tar shingles, and many of them had flower boxes in the windows, filled with bright red geraniums. Old people sat on the porches and gazed out at the kids swarming over the sidewalks below, shouting and screaming at their games.

The Pignato house was no better or worse than any of the other houses on the street. I walked up the rickety steps, saw their name on the black tin mailbox beside the left-hand door, and knocked. Nothing happened for thirty seconds. I knocked again, this time much harder. From inside the house a woman's voice called out wearily, "I'm coming, I'm coming." It sounded as though she expected it to be one of the neighborhood kids coming to beg for a cookie.

I heard the sound of slippered feet padding toward me, and then the door jerked open. Marie Pignato was a dark, sallow-faced woman in her early forties. She stood at about five three, her stomach and voluminous hips bulging in tight black stretch pants. There were fluffy pink mules on her feet, and she wore a yellow smock-like blouse with a small silver cross hanging from a chain around her neck. She had that washed-out expression that told you she had stopped waiting for her ship to come in a long time ago. From the dark bags under her eyes, it looked as if she hadn't had a decent night's sleep in years.

"Mrs. Pignato?"

"Yes?" Her voice was tentative, unsure of itself. She seemed a little taken aback to find a stranger standing at her door.

"My name is Max Klein. I'm an attorney representing the Graymoor Insurance Company." I took out one of my old attorney-at-law cards and handed it to her. "Do you think it would be possible for me to see Mr. Pignato?"

"We don't want no insurance," she said.

"I'm not selling insurance, Mrs. Pignato. I represent the insurance company. It seems that your husband has come into some luck, and I'd like to tell him about it."

She looked at my face, then down at the card in her hand, and then back at my face. "What are you, some kind of lawyer?"

"That's right," I said with a smile, "I'm a lawyer. And if I could just see your husband for a few minutes, I'm sure you wouldn't regret it."

"Well, Bruno isn't in," she said, still skeptical, but softening.

"Do you know when he'll be back?"

She shrugged. "How do I know? Bruno comes and goes, you can't keep no tabs on him. He's on disability, you know, so he don't have to work." She made it sound as though a job was the only thing that kept a man coming home every night.

"Was he around today?"

"Yeah. He was here before. But then he went out." She paused, shook her head, and sighed, as if trying to cope with the behavior of a difficult child. "Sometimes he don't come back for days at a time."

"I hear your husband hasn't been well."

"No, he ain't been well. Not for four or five years, ever since his accident. They have to take him away every once in a while for a rest."

"What kind of accident was that?"

"With his truck. There wasn't nothing wrong with him. But mentally he ain't been the same since."

"Do you know where I might find him, Mrs. Pignato? This is rather important, and I'd hate to leave without trying to find him."

"Well, you could go over to Angie's on Fifteenth and Grand. He sometimes goes there for a beer."

"I think I will," I said. "Thank you for your help."

I turned around to leave.

"Hey, mister," she said, "you forgot your card." She held it out to me, not knowing what to do with it. It was a foreign object to her, and she almost seemed afraid of it.

"That's all right. You can keep it."

She looked down at the card once again. "Is there going to be money in this for us?" she asked timidly, not wanting to expect too much.

"There's money," I said. "I don't think it's a lot, but I'm sure there will be something."

I smiled at her, and again she looked down at the card. It seemed to exert a magical force over her, as if it were somehow more real than I was.

Fifteenth and Grand was only a few blocks away, but I decided to take my car. I didn't want to leave it there with its New York license plates as a temptation for the kids on Seventeenth Street. Driving along with the window down, I passed more rows of two-family houses, a vacant lot filled with weeds and stray dogs, and a schoolyard in which a pickup softball game was going on. The pitcher had just released the ball and the batter was drawing back his arms to swing as I went by, but before I could see what happened I was gone, my view blocked by the brick wall of the school. It was a moment frozen in time, and the image of the white ball hanging in the air stayed with me, like a vision of eternal expectation.

The neighborhood became more commercial on Grand Avenue, and I found Angie's Palace sitting between a liquor store and a corner Gulf station. I parked my car a few doors down in front of a beauty parlor. A red and blue hand-painted sign in the window announced: Dolores is Back. I hoped she wouldn't regret her decision.

In spite of its name, Angie's Palace was just a local bar, like a thousand others on a thousand streets like this one. Neon beer signs in the window, peeling green paint on the facade, and a battered red door that had been pushed open by a million thirsty hands. Over the door there was a sign displaying two tilted martini glasses with bubbles coming out of them. The lettering for the word "Lounge" had been reduced to a dismal L U G.

It was dark inside, like the inside of a fish's brain, and it took a few moments for my eyes to adjust. The only moving things in the bar were the undulating purple lights of the jukebox, and they danced with incongruous gaiety as a mournful song of rejection and despair poured from the machine. There were only five or six customers in the place. Two of them, dressed in the gray uniforms of telephone repairmen, sat hunched over their beers at the bar, talking about the relative merits of BMWs and Audis. A few others were sitting alone at wooden tables in the room reading copies of the *Newark Star-Ledger*. The bartender, dressed in a short-sleeved white shirt and a white apron, looked like a former defensive tackle who had gone to fat reminiscing over too many beers with his customers.

I went up to the bar and ordered a Bud. When the bartender returned with the beer and a glass, I put down a dollar and said, "I'm looking for Bruno Pignato. His wife said I might find him here."

"You're not a cop, are you?" It was a matter-of-fact question, and he wasn't trying to make an issue of it. But he had his customers to protect, and he didn't know my face.

"No, I'm a lawyer. I just want to talk to him."

The bartender looked me over, testing me with his eyes, and then gestured to the back corner of the room. A man was sitting there at a table with a full glass of beer in front of him and staring off into space.

"Thanks," I said. I picked up my drink and walked over.

Because of the name Bruno, I had been imagining a large, powerfully built man. But Pignato was small and frail, hardly bigger than a jockey. His dark, curly hair had receded a third of the way back on his head, and his face had the pointy, bug-eyed look of an underground creature. He had almost no chin, which made his long nose seem to jut out even further than it did, and every inch of him exuded unhappiness. Bruno Pignato gave off the smell of failure in the same way that George Chapman gave off the smell of success. He was wearing an inappropriately loud Hawaiian shirt, and his skinny white arms had the pathetic, unused look you find in hospital patients. I realized I would have to throw out the tactics I had been planning for our encounter. I sat down at the table.

"Hello, Bruno. My name is Max Klein. Your wife told me you would be here."

He turned and looked at me with indifferent eyes. "Hi, Max. Have a drink."

"I don't want to take up much of your time, Bruno. But I do have a few questions I would like to ask you."

"Sure, Max. What can I do for you?"

"I'd like to talk to you about five years ago and what happened to you the night of your accident."

His placid face became troubled. It was as if I had pushed a button, automatically changing his mood. Any person with normal feelings would have stopped there and not tried to press him. But I was working on a case, and a man's life was at stake. I hated myself for what this conversation might do to Pignato. But even so, I went on with it.

"That was bad," he said, "very bad. A guy got hurt that night real bad."

"Yes, I know, Bruno. Real bad."

"Do you know who that guy was?" His voice was beginning to waver out of control. "George Chapman. The baseball player." He stared down at the table and drew in his breath. "Christ, could he play ball!"

"Can you tell me how it happened, Bruno?"

He shook his head despondently, trying not to remember. "I don't think I want to talk about it. I don't like to talk about it anymore."

"I know it's hard, Bruno. But it's important for you to try. Victor Contini wants to do something bad to George Chapman again, and unless you help me, he's going to get away with it."

Pignato's eyes flickered with recognition. He studied me carefully for the first time and then said in a querulous voice, "I don't think I know you, do I? What do you want to talk against Mr. Contini for? He's a great man, Mr. Contini. You shouldn't say nothing against him."

"I'm not saying anything against him, Bruno. I'm only saying that I need your help. You don't want anything bad to happen to George Chapman again, do you?"

"No," he said submissively, easing back into his torpor. "But I swear I didn't want him to get hurt. I mean, that guy could sure hit the ball, couldn't he?"

"What happened that night, Bruno? What did they tell you to do? Believe me, it's very important."

"They didn't tell me to do nothing, really. They just wanted me to stop on the road so they could put some stuff in the truck. I don't know, I can't remember too good. But Mr. Contini was always real nice to me."

"Did they ever come with the stuff?"

"What stuff is that?"

"Did they ever come with the stuff they said they were going to put in the truck?"

"I don't think so." Pignato looked into his hands, as if the answer was somehow waiting for him there. "But I don't remember too good anymore."

There was a long silence. I took out a fifty-dollar bill from my wallet and put it on the table in front of him.

"Here, Bruno, I'd like you to have this."

He picked up the money and examined it closely, in much the same way his wife had examined my card earlier. After turning it around for a while, he put it back on the table.

"What do you want to give me this for?"

"Because you've been a big help to me."

He hesitated, then picked up the bill and looked at it again. He was thinking, trying to come to a decision. After a moment he slapped the money on the table and pushed it away at arm's length.

"I don't think I want to take your money," he said.

"If you don't want it, why don't you give it to your wife? I'm sure she would like to have it."

"Marie? What's this got to do with her?" He was becoming petulant. "I thought we were having a talk. You know, man to man."

"That's right, Bruno. Man to man."

"Then why do you want me to give the money to Marie? I don't want to give her money," he shouted. He picked up the fifty-dollar bill and with hasty, violent motions tore it into little pieces. "It's not right for you to make me give money to Marie."

I had unintentionally hit a raw nerve. He had transferred much of his resentment against himself and his illness to his wife, the person who took care of him. It was a humiliating situation for him, an impossible situation for her. I hated to think of what daily life was like for them.

"Don't give it to her, then," I said. "You don't have to do anything you don't want to do."

"That's right," he said, "I don't have to do nothing." It sounded as though he was making a general defense of his life.

I had hoped the fifty dollars would make him more willing to talk, but I had made a mistake. With the uncanny perception of many schizophrenics, he had seen through my gesture, and it had put him on his guard. I would have to try again some other time. At least I had made a start.

"I'm going to leave now, Bruno," I said. "I don't think we should talk about these things anymore today."

He stared at me with bewilderment and hatred, his mouth quivering. "I don't like you," he said. "You're a no-good person."

I stood up from my seat and started to walk away from the table.

"You're a bad man," he shouted after me. "I hate you! You're a bad man!"

Everyone in the bar was staring at me, watching me in the same cold and curious way you look at an animal in the zoo. I just kept walking and didn't turn around. When I got to the street and started toward my car, I could hear that Pignato had followed me outside.

"You're a bad man!" he kept shouting in his high, broken voice. "You're a bad man!"

I reached my car and unlocked the door to get in. I turned around for a last look and saw him standing in front of Angie's Palace, no longer screaming at me but at the whole world, his tiny white body in those ridiculous clothes weaving back and forth in the dusk like an emaciated bird without wings.

7

IN THE FIVE YEARS since the breakup of our marriage, Cathy and I had gradually learned how to become friends again. Once the bitterness wore off, we both came to realize that we still meant something to each other. But that had taken time. The marriage had fallen apart because of me, because of a job I didn't believe in, and I could hardly blame Cathy for leaving me when she did. I had almost goaded her into it, in some way secretly trying to sabotage the marriage—as if I had to prove my life really was in a shambles before I could begin to change it. I wanted to feel sorry for myself, and I wound up doing a very good job of it. Cathy took a job as a music teacher in a private school for girls and refused to accept any help from me. We weren't even tied together by the usual alimony string. Although I told myself that I knew better, I couldn't help feeling hurt by this as yet another rejection. Not even my money was good. The day of the divorce was probably the low point of my life.

Things didn't start to improve for me until a few months later, when I finally convinced myself that I hadn't been cut out to be a lawyer after all and went into detective work on my own. The Banks case gave me a convenient excuse to get out from under as assistant district attorney.

Jo Jo Banks was a twelve-year-old black boy from Harlem who had been shot and killed by a thirty-seven-year-old white cop by the name of Ralph Winter. Winter claimed the boy had pulled a gun on him. As in most of these cases, the matter probably would have ended there. Winter would have been given a brief suspension, and everyone eventually would have forgotten about it. But Jo Jo Banks' father, as it turned out, was no elementary school janitor willing to resign himself to his son's death as the natural consequence of being black and poor. James Banks worked as a journalist for the *Amsterdam News,* and he wasn't about to let the public forget that his son had been murdered in cold blood one Saturday afternoon by a drunken off-duty cop. As the pressure started mounting on the police department, Banks suddenly found himself accused of pushing drugs. Thirty thousand dollars' worth of heroin was discovered in his apartment. When the case came up, I was given the assignment of prosecuting him. I refused. And later that same day I quit. Winter was guilty, Banks had been framed, and I didn't want to be part of a police snow job on the city. I gave quite a few interviews to the papers that week, and it did me a lot of good to get things off my chest. It didn't matter that every cop in the city hated my guts and that the D.A. considered me a left-wing subversive. I had done it according to my own rules, and my self-esteem had been restored. Six months later, Winter was kicked off the force for another incident and wound up drifting into construction work. He died eighteen months after that when he fell off a steel girder on the twenty-first floor of an office building that was going up on Third Avenue. He had been drunk on the job.

The day after the story of my resignation hit the papers, Cathy called to congratulate me. We had a pleasant talk, and it was the first time in more than a year that we had spoken to each other without quarreling. We had reached a kind of emotional truce, and I felt we were both finally cured of all the resentments that had followed the divorce. It was the moment for us to forget the past, to walk out of each other's lives for good. If it hadn't been for our little boy, Richie, we probably never would have seen each other again. But he was there, and I kept coming around every week to see him. Cathy had never been very convinced of my abilities or dedication as a father, and in the beginning she was always out when I came to pick up Richie, leaving her mother to take care of him before I got there and after I dropped him off. It took her a while to understand that I cared about him as much as she did. When that happened, we started to trust each other again.

For the past eight or ten months, all three of us had been having dinner together every Wednesday night. Cathy had decided it would be good for Richie if he could see both of us at the same time. Relations between us had become warmer, more relaxed, and she figured we could do it without too much strain. We could. We had been through the wars together, and the friendship that had come out of it meant a great deal to both of us. We counted on each other now for the kinds of things no one else could give us. But at the same time, neither one of us wanted to get too close, to presume too much. We were afraid of hurting ourselves and destroying what we had managed to build up again. We never asked each other who we were seeing, who we were sleeping with. We got together because of Richie and because we liked being together. But we had no holds over each other.

Richie was nine years old now. Not long ago he had been into dinosaurs. After that it was bugs, and soon after that Greek mythology. One day last summer we went for a drive in my car, and when we returned to the parking lot Richie got into a conversation about baseball with Luis Ramirez. Luis took Richie into his shack and showed him his baseball books and magazines. It was like being initiated into a mystical universe of arcane numbers, obscure personalities, and cabalistic strategies, and Richie became hooked. Luis became his Virgil, his guide through this land of gods, demigods, and mortals, and an outing with me was no longer complete for Richie unless he could have his conference with Luis in the parking lot. Richie had memorized two-thirds of the Baseball Encyclopedia I had given him for his birthday, and he rarely went anywhere without his collection of baseball cards.

It was quarter to nine when I rang the bell at the East Eighty-third Street apartment. Richie answered the door in his pajamas.

"Mom says the dinner's ruined," he announced.

"I hope you didn't wait for me," I said.

"She didn't let me. I had a hamburger and spinach at six-thirty."

Cathy appeared in the living room. She was wearing blue jeans and a light-gray sweater with the sleeves pushed up to her elbows. Her long blonde hair hung loose, falling down to her shoulders, and I was a little startled by how young she looked. My stomach had begun to ache with the aftereffects of Angel's punch, and I was feeling particularly old and worn out. For a moment I imagined I had come to visit my daughter and grandson. But when Cathy came up and kissed me on the cheek, I saw that she looked tired around the eyes, and it reassured me. It somehow meant that she had been marked by this day too, that the two of us were traveling through life at the same pace. I wondered what we would be like in thirty years.

"We'd pretty much given up on you," she said.

"I'm sorry," I said, trying to think of a plausible lie. "I thought I was going to make it, but there was a big accident on the Garden State Parkway."

"Was anybody killed?" Richie asked. He was at an age when the thought of violent death was exciting, as unreal as an explosion on TV. I wondered if he would still find it so fascinating if one day I suddenly didn't show up anymore.

"Nobody killed," I said. "But a lot of smashed-up cars."

"Boy," he said, trying to imagine the scene. "I wish I could have been there."

I put the bottle of Beaujolais I had brought on the coffee table and took off my jacket.

"There's not much to eat," Cathy said. "I had everything ready for six-thirty. But it's all turned to leather now."

"What was it called before it expired?"

"Veal saltimbocca."

"And now you're going to punish me by never making it again."

"That's right," she said, half smiling and half annoyed at having her efforts go to waste. "From now on you get only TV dinners."

We settled on a meal of odds and ends. Lentil soup, a tin of pâté, salad, and some cheese. Beginnings and endings, as Cathy said, with nothing in between. Richie was allowed to stay up past his normal bedtime, and he sat with us at the table with a glass of milk and a pile of graham crackers. It was difficult for Cathy and me to say much of anything to each other, since Richie had decided he was going to run the show tonight. We were all going to play Baseball Quiz, and he was the master of ceremonies. The only problem was that his questions were impossible to answer. Who was the last player on the Cleveland Indians to win the American League batting championship? Bobby Avila, 1954. Who led the National League in stolen bases more times—Maury Wills or Lou Brock? Brock, eight times. Wills led six. And on and on. It seemed it was never going to end.

"I think you've proved to us," Cathy said at last, "that you know more about baseball than anyone else in this room."

"That's not saying much," he offered modestly. "The day I know more than Luis, then I'll have something to brag about."

"I'm sure you've already passed him," I said. "After all, he has a job to go to and a family to support, and he doesn't have as much time as you do for all this stuff."

"Well, I have to go to school," Richie said, "and that takes a big chunk out of my day."

He realized his mistake almost as soon as the words were out of his mouth, but it was too late. Cathy had been willing to let his bedtime slide a little, but now that the subject had come up, he was a doomed man. After some feeble protests, including a statement that Einstein slept only four hours a night, he gave in without much of a struggle. It was quarter past ten.

I supervised him as he went through the motions of brushing his teeth and washing his face. He dealt with the water in that tentative way kids go about things when they don't fully believe in what they're doing. When I got him into bed and asked him if he wanted me to go on with *Treasure Island,* he said he'd grown tired of waiting for me to finish it and had gone on and read the end himself. He wanted to talk instead. I had bought tickets for Saturday's game at the stadium, and he was having trouble thinking about anything else. It was going to be his first trip to a major-league game.

"When we go to the game," he asked, "are we going to be on television?"

"The game is on television. But chances are they won't show us."

"I told my friend Jimmy I was going to be on television. He'll think I'm a liar."

"All you have to do is show him your ticket stub," I said. "That will prove you were there. It's not your fault if the cameras don't pick up your face."

That seemed to reassure him. "Are we going to a doubleheader?" he asked.

"No, only one game. But that should be enough. If there were two, you'd probably wind up in the hospital with stomach poisoning. Those hot dogs are lethal."

"Mom doesn't let me eat hot dogs," he said glumly. "But I think they're pretty good."

"Your mother is a smart lady, Richie. You should do what she tells you."

He looked at me with sleepy eyes and said, "Do you love Mom, Dad?"

"Yes, very much," I said.

"Then why don't you come back and live with us?"

"We've talked about this before, Richie. It just can't be. That's the way it is."

"I know. I was only asking." His eyes were closed now, but then he opened them again, one last time. "I don't understand grownups," he said. "I don't understand them at all."

"I don't either, Richie."

I sat there watching him sleep for a few minutes. When I got back to the living room, Cathy had already finished the dishes and was sitting in a chair beside the piano, smoking one of her infrequent after-dinner cigarettes. I opened a new bottle of Beaujolais and sat down on the couch. I liked sitting in that room. Cathy had arranged it in a way that didn't impose itself on you, that made you feel the walls and furniture and pictures were somehow trying to work for you and put you at your ease. The fact that she always kept a good supply of wine on hand didn't hurt either.

We talked for a while about some of the things that had been happening to us in the past week. Cathy said the school year had been a difficult one and that she was looking forward to the summer vacation in six weeks. I told her about my plans to go to Paris and how I had delayed them because of a new case I was working on. When we were halfway through the bottle of Beaujolais she got up from her chair, came over to the couch, and curled up with her head in my lap. It was her first gesture of physical affection toward me in over five years.

"I've got to talk to you, Max," she said. "I need your advice about something."

I stroked her soft blonde hair with my hand. Her body seemed tense, and she tucked herself into a fetal position, the way a child does at night in a strange house.

"Why do we have to talk?" I said. "I like being slightly drunk on this couch with your head on my lap."

"I have a decision to make, and I don't know what to do."

"You've made a lot of decisions in the past five years without my help. Most of them have been good ones."

"This is different. And I'm scared that I'm about to make a big mistake."

"The last time you were scared of anything," I said, "was the day you forgot your lines in the fourth-grade play."

"No, I really am scared, Max." She hesitated. "You see, someone wants to marry me. And I just don't know what to do."

It was a little like being thrown into a freezing river in the middle of December. Every time I tried to come up for air, I kept banging my head on a piece of floating ice. One voice in me was frantically saying that this was none of my business, that she could do whatever she liked, and another was trying to persuade me to get up and smash everything in the room.

"I think maybe you've come to the wrong person for that kind of advice, Cath," I said. That was about the best I could manage.

"I know, Max. It's not fair. But there's no one else I can turn to."

"Who's the lucky man?" I asked. "Do you love him? Is he rich? Will he offer you a life of leisure and distinction?"

"No, he's not rich. He's a teacher, an English professor at the University of New Hampshire, and he loves me very much."

"But do you love him?"

"I think so. But I'm not sure."

"If you're not sure, then maybe you should wait."

"But if I wait, I might blow the whole thing. And I keep thinking it would be good for Richie. Good for him to have a man around all the time. Good for him to live in the country, away from all this New York madness."

"And what does Richie say?"

"He says to me, 'Mom, if it will make you happy, then I'll be happy.' I don't know where he picked up that line. Probably from some old movie on TV. I don't really know how he feels."

"It sounds like it's up to you."

"I know. And I know I should probably go ahead with it. But I just keep thinking . . ." She let her sentence hang in the air. We didn't say anything for half a minute.

"Thinking what?" I asked.

"I don't know . . . It's hard for me to say it." She paused again. When she spoke, her voice sounded a thousand miles away. "That maybe you and I could eventually get back together again."

"Would you want that, Cathy?"

"I've thought about it a lot lately. Deep down inside, I think that's really what I want."

"And you're able to forget everything that happened five years ago?"

"I'll never forget it. It's just that we're different now. We've finally grown up."

This was one of the most difficult conversations of our lives, and we were both afraid to look at each other, as if eye contact would break the mood and prevent us from speaking our thoughts. And speaking honestly was crucial now; everything depended on it. Cathy kept her head buried in my lap, and I stared out at the light switch beside the doorway to the kitchen, somehow hoping it would provide me with the words I needed to say.

"You're not thinking about the work I do now, Cathy," I said. "You don't know what it would be like waiting up for me every night, worrying about whether you were going to have to go down to the morgue at three A.M. to identify my body. That's no kind of life for you and Richie."

"Other women live with it," she said. "Think of policemen's wives. They go through the same thing. We're all going to die someday, Max. Life is full of risks, but it shouldn't stop us from living."

"It's not the same as being married to a cop. They have regular jobs with regular hours, and once they're through for the day they go home and forget about their work. But when I'm on a case, it's a total commitment, twenty-four hours straight. I'd bring it home with me, all the ugliness, all the brutality. You wouldn't be able to stand it. And eventually you'd be after me to quit, to go into something else."

"No, I wouldn't, Max. I understand what you need now, and I wouldn't interfere."

"You say that now. But after a year or two it would be too much for you. You need good things, Cathy, steady things, music and books, nice food, and a man who will be there when you need him. I couldn't give you any of that. You'd be miserable."

"You don't want me anymore, do you, Max?"

"You can't possibly know how much I do want you. But I've already lost you once, and I don't want to lose you again. I wasted a lot of years of my life before I discovered what I liked doing. This work means something to me, and I can't get out of it now. But that's what I'd have to do if we got back together. And without my work, we'd gradually slip back into the same scene we lived through before the divorce. At least this way I don't have to lose you again, not really. We'll still be as close as we are now."

Faintly, at first so faintly that I hardly noticed, she began crying. As I talked I could feel her body trembling under my hand, and each wave traveled into my bones like the echo of some distant tremor from the core of the earth. When I was finished, she sat up and looked at me with tears streaming down her face.

"Oh, God, Max. Why does it have to be this way? Why can't we just love each other again?"

She threw her arms around me and clung to me as hard as she could, weeping out of control. I held her tightly, praying to myself that I hadn't just made the worst mistake of my life. I couldn't tell if I was really doing it for her own good, or if I was simply too afraid to commit myself again. It was the kind of choice that never stops haunting you.

I kissed her on the mouth, and she gave herself willingly to me, as if in this closeness we could cancel out the terrible decision I had just forced on us. When we made love, it was not the beginning of anything, not the promise of a new start, but a kind of farewell, a desperate leave-taking of all we had lived through together in the past. Cathy couldn't stop crying, and when it was over neither one of us had found release from our unhappiness. The flesh has no solutions. It can be a place of infinite sadness.

It was after two o'clock when I unlocked the door of my apartment. For more than an hour I methodically cleaned up the havoc left by my afternoon visitors. My mind was blank, and I craved order. When I finally went to bed, I couldn't sleep. And when at last I did sleep, I dreamt that Cathy and Richie were standing in my room with anger in their faces. They were screaming at me, "You're a bad man, Max Klein. You're a bad man."

8

I WOKE UP feeling as though I had spent the night in a steam shovel. It was seven-thirty, and the gray gloom in the apartment told me it was going to be a cloudy day. With all the enthusiasm of an arthritic tap dancer, I crawled out of bed and groped my way into the bathroom, where I turned on the shower and stepped into the steam. The hot water felt good on my tired body. By the time I toweled myself down and started shaving, I was beginning to think about auditioning for a role in the human race. If I got lucky, maybe they would give me a walk-on part.

I put on my bathrobe, went into the kitchen, and got busy making the morning's coffee. My system was to use a number 6 Melitta filter on top of a wide-mouthed thermos bottle. I usually had a supply of Melitta filter papers on hand, but my box had run out, so I tore off a couple of paper towels and used them instead. I put up some water to boil, took out the bag of Bustelo from the refrigerator, and measured out four level tablespoons. When the water started bubbling I poured a little over the coffee and then waited. The trick is to wait. Thirty seconds, maybe forty. If you can hold off from dumping all the water in at once, the coffee will have time to expand with the moisture and give off its full aroma. Only then do you pour the rest of the water through. When everything was ready I put the thermos on a tray along with a cup, a spoon, a carton of milk, and the sugar bowl, and then carried it all into the living room. After the third cup I persuaded myself to get dressed.

At nine o'clock I called the Chapman apartment. It was Judy Chapman who answered.

"Hi," I said. "Max Klein."

"I know." She sounded pleased. "I never forget a voice."

"I'm not waking you up, am I?"

"Are you kidding? I've already done my five miles in Central Park, baked a batch of croissants, and read the last two hundred pages of *Crime and Punishment.*"

I gathered she had just woken up.

"I know it's a little early," I said. "But it's going to be a busy day."

"How are things going?"

"They're going. But it's hard to say in what direction."

"It sounds as though you've been working."

"I try. If I keep at it, one of these days I might actually accomplish something."

"You know what they say about Jack."

"I know. But my name isn't Jack. It's Max."

"And fortunately you're not dull either."

"That depends on who you talk to. Take my accountant, Mr. Birnbaum. He considers me the dullest man he's ever met."

"What do accountants know?"

"Arithmetic."

She laughed. "This is a nice way to greet the day. Maybe you should call me every morning. I could hire you as my wake-up service."

"Next time I'll give you breakfast in bed too. It's all included in the one charge. You have to pay extra for the second cup of coffee, though."

"I'm looking forward to it already," she said. "The only trouble is that I don't usually eat breakfast."

"So much the better."

She laughed again. "You're really wicked, aren't you?"

"Only on Thursday mornings. I spend the rest of the week spinning my prayer wheel."

"I hope you pray for George," she said, suddenly very serious.

"Why do you say that? Nothing's happened, has it?"

"No. It's just that I'm worried. I hope you solve this thing quickly, Max."

"So do I. I don't want to drag it on. Time always increases the dangers."

"Do you want to speak to George?"

"That's why I called."

"Just a minute. I'll go tell him you're on the line."

She put down the phone and went to get him. A minute later I heard the click of another phone being taken off the hook, and Chapman's voice came on. The first phone was never hung up.

"Hello, Klein," he said. "What's the word?"

"Everything and nothing."

"Which means nothing, I assume."

"Not exactly. If you put it that way, it's more like everything."

He sounded anxious. "What have you found?"

"I'd rather not talk about it over the phone. Would it be all right if I came by your apartment between eleven and eleven-thirty?"

"Yes, that will be fine. I'll be in."

"I just want you to know," I said, "that I don't think you've been playing straight with me."

There was a pause at the other end. Chapman was peeved. "That's not true, and I resent your saying it. I've been as open and honest with you as any man in my situation could possibly be."

"We'll discuss it later, Mr. Chapman." I hung up.

AT TEN MINUTES TO TEN I was sitting in an oatmeal-colored designer chair facing the receptionist's desk in the offices of Light Enterprises on Madison Avenue. I had put on my best lawyer's pinstripes for the occasion and had even made sure that my shoes were shined. After all, I was paying a visit on several hundred million dollars, and I thought the least I could do was to show some respect.

The offices of Light Enterprises didn't so much suggest a place of work as an environment, someone's vision of what life will be like when we no longer inhabit our bodies. You felt as though you were sitting in a twenty-third-century hotel lobby and that any moment a Martian was going to walk up and ask you if you wanted to play a game of extrasensory checkers. Nothing was real. The thick beige carpeting muffled every sound, and I had to put my watch against my ear to make sure I hadn't gone deaf. People glided in and out like apparitions, and when the chic, long-legged receptionist dressed in a two-hundred-dollar imitation of a parachutist's costume took my name, I was surprised to learn that she could speak. I had thought she was a piece of furniture. In any case, it seemed likely that she had been hired by the interior decorator. Beyond sitting at her modular desk and looking stylish as she smoked a cigarette about fifteen inches long, she didn't seem to have any work to do. The nameplate on her desk read Constance Grimm, Receptionist, and that seemed to say it all. I wondered if she would cry real tears if I pinched her cheek.

Charles Light had inherited his family's shipbuilding business thirty-five years ago. In that time he had diversified into airplane parts, computer equipment, magazine publishing, fast food, and coal mining. The activities of Light Enterprises now extended into forty-one of the fifty states, and branch offices had been opened in Chicago, Los Angeles, and Hong Kong. Light had bought the New York Americans twelve years ago when they were struggling along in fourth place, and within a couple of seasons he had turned them into division champions. Ever since then the team had been at or near the top. With the club now firmly established, he had begun toying with another hobby in the past year or two—politics, specifically conservative politics. Although it would take longer to accomplish, he was hoping to use his money for the right-wing cause in the same way he had already used it for baseball: to produce a winner. Light was the kind of man who nearly always got what he wanted, and no matter how unlikely his views might have seemed, he had to be taken seriously. He was sixty-two years old, a physical fitness buff, and the father of five children who had in turn given him eleven grandchildren. He was celebrated for his ability never to forget a face and had once written an article for *Reader's Digest* on the art of memory. His stamp collection was said to be one of the largest in America.

I found him a pleasant enough looking man, about five nine, stockily built, with the watery blue eyes of a New York patrician. His graying hair was just the right length to make him look at home at a conservative banquet in Texas or a cotillion ball in New York. He had a deceptive moon face that wasn't quite as bland as you thought at first, but it was somehow featureless. It gave him a chameleon-like quality, as if his success had been built on being able to adapt to the different kinds of people he had to deal with and to blend quietly into his surroundings. Like many powerful men, he was an actor in the drama of his own life, and he seemed to savor each new encounter as a challenge to the acting talent he had cultivated so carefully in himself. I realized it was going to be difficult to get much out of him that he didn't want to give.

His private office was roughly the size of the state of Rhode Island, and by the time you got halfway to his desk you almost expected to see a sign announcing a Howard Johnson's a mile up the road. The office had one virtue, though, which was that it made a point of belonging to the present rather than the future. The decor extolled traditional masculine values. The walls were made of dark oak paneling, there were Persian rugs on the floor, and the furniture was rather stuffy and old-fashioned. The walls were covered with nineteenth-century paintings of the ships built by Light's ancestors, pictures of the modern products manufactured by Light Enterprises, and several dozen photographs of former players for the Americans. I didn't see George Chapman's face among them.

Charles Light stood up when I reached his desk, shook my hand vigorously, and gestured to a vast red velvet wing chair for me to sit in.

"I'm not usually able to see people on such short notice, Mr. Klein," he said, settling into the chair behind his desk. "But when my secretary told me you were a private investigator, I decided to cancel my ten o'clock appointment to find out what it was all about. To tell you the truth, I was intrigued." He smiled broadly.

"I hope I don't disappoint you," I said. "It's a minor matter really, one small detail in a rather complicated case I've been working on. It has to do with a series of bomb scares over the past six months, and some evidence has turned up that suggests a possible connection with the person who made the call threatening George Chapman's life five years ago during the World Series. I understand it was you who took the call, and I wonder if you remember anything about it—the caller's voice, what he said, and so on. It just might help me find the missing link I've been looking for."

Charles Light reared back his head and laughed heartily, as if I had just told a very amusing joke. "Very good, Mr. Klein. Very, very good," he said, gradually subsiding and wiping the tears from his eyes. "I was curious to know what kind of story you were going to invent for me when you walked in here. But I had no idea you would concoct such a far-fetched tale. You must have spent some time working on that one."

"I'm glad you find it so entertaining," I said. "I wouldn't want you to think I lacked imagination."

All traces of Light's good humor suddenly vanished. It was like seeing a blackboard wiped clean. His face closed off, and his voice became hard, sarcastic, irritated. "Come, come, Mr. Klein. You don't have to play games with me. I know why you're here today, and I know everything about you that I care to know. I know where you were born, what schools you went to, and how much money you make. I know about your brief and inglorious career as assistant district attorney. I know where you live, where you buy your groceries, and that you have an ex-wife and a nine-year-old son." He paused for a moment. "You lead a very boring life, Mr. Klein."

"You find it boring," I said, "because you don't know anything about it. What about all my dark secrets? My hundred-dollar-a-day habit, for example. Or my penchant for twelve-year-old girls. Not to speak of the compromising pictures I take of all my clients. I think you should hire yourself a new research assistant. The one you've got now has been sleeping on the job."

"You can joke all you like. But the fact is that I'm three steps ahead of you, Klein. I make it my business to know the people I deal with. Don't think you can play with me, because I guarantee you that you're going to lose."

"Okay," I said. "You're Chief Hard-as-Nails, and I'm trembling in my boots. But there's still one point that confuses me. If you know so much already, why did you agree to see me today?"

"That's simple. I wanted to give you a lecture."

"Sounds exciting," I said. "Do you want me to take notes?"

"That won't be necessary. What I have to say is so simple you won't have any trouble remembering it."

"Does your lecture have a title?"

Light's eyes narrowed. "Let's call it 'Background Material for a Study of George Chapman—with Incidental References to a Private Investigator Named Klein.' " He leaned forward and paused, waiting until he was sure he had my full attention. "I want to talk about George Chapman with you because I know you've been hired by him and I want you to hear my side of the story. I am a man with a great deal of money, Mr. Klein, and I use my wealth for a wide variety of purposes. Most of it is put to work to make even more money for me, but a portion of it, a very small portion of it, I spend for my own amusement. Over the years, one of my greatest entertainments has been owning a major-league baseball team. I like the competition of sports, I like the recognition the team gives me, and I enjoy getting to know the athletes who work for me. They're like big children, and I find their innocence of the real world touching. Deprived of their skills, ninety percent of them would probably be working as filling station attendants or farmhands. But the peculiar economics of professional sports turns them into rich men and gives them a prestige way out of proportion to what they contribute to society. But such is life, and I have no qualms about it. In fact, I've probably helped to create this situation as much as anyone else. No doubt you know that the salaries I pay the Americans are among the most generous in baseball. I want my players to be happy, and I've always had excellent relations with them. Every once in a while, however, a player comes along who tries to take advantage of me and abuse my trust. Most often the young man in question soon finds himself playing somewhere else, in a city like Cleveland or Milwaukee. George Chapman was such a player. But I was unable to trade or sell him because of his value to the team on the field and his popularity with the people of this city. If I had gotten rid of him, I would have been hanged in effigy, and that would hardly have been good for business. So I swallowed my pride and did my best to come to terms with Chapman. Unlike most of his colleagues, he was not stupid. Everyone knows this, and I would be the last person to deny it. I first met him when he was twenty-one, and already he knew exactly what he wanted out of life. He knew that sports are a limited and limiting occupation, but he also knew that he had been blessed with an extraordinary gift. George Chapman, I believe, derived no pleasure from playing baseball, but he realized he could use it as a stepping-stone for bigger and better things. Not long after his fifth season with the club, we began negotiating a long-term contract. His demands were totally outrageous, but eventually we worked out a compromise, a compromise that still made Chapman one of the highest-paid players in the history of baseball. My better judgment told me I was being a fool, but I'm sometimes susceptible to the grand gesture—a tragic flaw, you might say. Then, a mere two weeks later, just twelve days after the signing of the contract, Chapman was involved in the auto accident that ended his days as a ball player. Believe me, I was as devastated as the next man. Whatever my personal feelings for Chapman, it's a terrible thing to see a young man's career cut short in such a violent manner. After the initial impact wore off, however, I realized that I was in a particularly difficult situation. I had committed myself to paying Chapman an enormous sum of money over an eight-year period, and now he wasn't even going to play. And my hands were tied because of an injury clause in the contract. It was not a just arrangement, given the unforeseen events that had occurred, and I suggested to Chapman that we work out a settlement. He refused. I asked him to manage the team. He refused. I asked him to take over as general manager. He refused. I offered him a job as president of the team. He refused. I believe George Chapman was secretly glad to be out of baseball. And he didn't even have the common decency to deal with me fairly. I have conceived a most inordinate loathing of George Chapman. The man is a charlatan, an out-and-out impostor, and I can think of no one in the world I would rather see fall on his face. My moment has finally come, Mr. Klein, and I'm going to break Chapman. Now that he's involved in politics, I'm going to break him into little pieces."

He leaned back with a self-satisfied smile, reveling in his own cleverness and pedantic turns of phrase. I had just heard the world according to Light, and now I was supposed to roll over dead, foaming at the mouth. I had never seen a bigger ham in all my life.

"Very interesting," I said. "But none of this has anything to do with me. It's strictly between you and Chapman. And I'm still waiting for the references to a private investigator named Klein."

"I'm coming to that. But first I wanted you to know the kind of man you're working for."

"It may be difficult for you to understand, but I don't choose my clients, and I'm in no position to pass judgment on their moral qualities. They come to me with specific problems, and I do my best to try to solve them. I don't require them to give me a list of character references."

Light had no interest in the subtleties of my profession. It was as though he hadn't even heard me. He folded his hands together and spoke in a measured voice.

"I'm only going to say this once, so listen carefully, Mr. Klein. I'm declaring war on George Chapman, and I'm not going to be satisfied until I've won. It's going to be a very messy affair with many casualties and skirmishes. I realize you're only an innocent bystander, but by working for Chapman I'm forced to consider you an enemy. Unless you relish the idea of getting caught in the crossfire, I suggest you terminate your relationship with Chapman at once. Even though you and I seem to disagree about most things, I have nothing against you personally. You're a man of spirit, and I wouldn't want to see you get hurt in a matter that doesn't concern you."

"Aren't you going to offer me any money?" I asked. "I thought this was the part where money always comes into it."

"I'm willing to give you five thousand dollars."

"It seems I've heard that figure mentioned before."

"Five thousand dollars. That's my one and only offer."

"Thanks," I said. "But no thanks."

Light shrugged. "Suit yourself."

That was the end of it. Our interview was over. Light put on his horn-rimmed glasses and began studying various papers on his desk with great concentration. The curtain had come down on the play, all the actors had gone home, and I was just another inanimate prop collecting dust backstage. I stood up from my chair and started walking toward the door.

"You should remember," I said, turning around, "that I'm not in the habit of giving in to threats."

Light looked up from his papers, pushed his glasses down to the tip of his nose, and peered at me over the frames. He seemed surprised that I was still in the room.

"I realize that," he said. "That's why I chose not to threaten you. I merely presented you with the facts. You can deal with them as you see fit. Your decision is of no concern to me."

9

I BOUGHT A PACK of cigarettes at the cigar counter in the lobby and went to look for a cab. My watch said ten past eleven, and outside it was raining hard. People were crowded in around the doorway waiting for it to pass. In the street it was all wind and weather, one of those torrential spring rains that hit the city like an act of divine vengeance. The rain was bouncing up from the pavement with such force that it looked as though it was raining upside down. A bus pulled up by the curb in front of the building with wings of water, gliding in like a speedboat.

I waited in the doorway with the other people, breathing in the pleasant smells of damp wool, perfume, and tobacco smoke. A short woman of about fifty with bleached blonde hair and a pink raincoat was saying that the raindrops looked like bullets. "In India," she said, "when the monsoons come it rains so hard you can get killed if you go out." Her companion, a chunky brunette in a black raincoat and a clear plastic hat, nodded her head in agreement. "I can believe it," she said. "India is a terrible place."

I lit a Gauloise, took two drags, and put it to my lips for a third. At that moment a hand appeared before my face and ripped the cigarette out of my mouth. I looked up and saw that it was Angel, my friend from yesterday, along with his keeper, Teddy.

"You shouldn't smoke, funny man," he smiled. "It's bad for your health."

"Thanks," I said. "It's nice to know that somebody cares."

"We didn't want you to forget about us," Teddy said. "So we thought we'd say hello."

"You underestimate the impression you make," I answered. "Guys like you never fade."

I took out another cigarette and lit it.

"How's the old gut feeling today?" Angel asked.

"Terrific," I said. "I had a stomach transplant at Roosevelt Hospital last night, and I'm fit as a pin."

The cloudburst was over, and the rain had turned to a drizzle. Some of the people in the doorway decided to venture outside.

"You can expect to be seeing a lot of us," Teddy said.

"That should be fun," I said. "Maybe next time we can all play tennis. I'll bet you two look cute in shorts."

Angel took a glance at the street through the glass door. "Those were some cats and dogs, eh, funny man?"

"It's good for the flowers," I said.

"That's right," he said. "Good for the flowers they make into funeral wreaths. Right, Teddy?"

"Just count yourself lucky, Klein," Teddy said. "Every day you go on living is a gift from heaven."

"I'll remember to say my prayers."

"You do that. And pray real hard. Because you're gonna need a lot of help."

"Hang loose, gumshoe," Angel said. "Until next time."

He blew me a kiss, and then the two of them went out through the revolving door, waddling off down the street like a pair of baby hippos. I could sense their frustration. Angel and Teddy were conscientious workers, and they didn't like being held back. But whoever was giving them orders had decided to wait before moving in on me. This meant that he still wasn't quite sure what I was up to, and it gave me a little more time to play with. I hoped I would use the time wisely.

I turned in the opposite direction, walked uptown for a couple of blocks and managed to find a cab that was dropping off a load of passengers. I climbed in and gave the driver the Chapmans' address in the Seventies off Lexington Avenue.

George and Judy Chapman lived in one of those luxury high-rise apartments that have been going up on the East Side for the past few years. Their neighbors were people who supported the ballet, kept Bloomingdale's in the black, and drove the finely tooled cars that made being an auto mechanic one of the highest-paying jobs this side of the law. To walk by a building like this one was enough to create the illusion that New York was still in business.

The door was tended by a tall Irishman with woebegone eyes who appeared to have been standing there without a coffee break since the last Memorial Day parade. He was sweating under a heavy blue coat with red trim that resembled something from a Polish cavalry uniform, and on his head he wore a matching military hat with the address of the building stitched onto the peak. As he gazed out at the traffic with his hands in his pockets, it looked as though he was dreaming about the horse they had forgotten to deliver with the uniform. His face brightened when I gave my name.

"Mr. Klein," he said, pulling an envelope from his pocket. "Mr. Chapman wanted you to have the keys to the apartment so that you could let yourself in. He said he was going to be taking a bath sometime late this morning and was afraid he might not be able to get out of the tub if you rang. It's apartment eleven-F."

It was a bizarre kind of arrangement, and it puzzled me. Something seemed to be going on, but I had no idea what it was.

"And Mrs. Chapman isn't in?" I asked.

"She went out about an hour ago."

"Did Mr. Chapman come down and give you the keys himself?"

"No, he called down on the house phone and gave me the instructions. We keep spare sets of keys for all the apartments in the basement."

"When did he call?"

"Shortly after Mrs. Chapman left."

I thanked him, walked through the mirrored lobby, and rode the elevator upstairs. My watch read precisely twenty to twelve. The eleventh floor was decorated with bright Miró and Calder exhibition posters, and I wandered through the long carpeted halls like a rat in a maze. When I found the apartment I rang the bell a few times just to be sure Chapman wasn't up and about. I waited for an answer and then let myself in with the keys.

The apartment was quiet. I closed the door behind me and walked into the living room. It was an impressively furnished place, not at all the chrome and glass coldness you see in the pages of *New York* magazine, but something softer, more subtle, that showed definite signs of intelligence behind it. At the same time, there was an unlived-in feeling to the room. It made me think of a beautiful painting an artist had labored over for several months and then stored away in a closet as soon as it was finished. There were no books or magazines on the coffee table, no cigarette butts in the ashtrays, no dents in the pillows on the couch. I imagined that the Chapmans spent most of their time at opposite ends of the apartment and avoided meeting on the common ground of the living room. It had become a no-man's-land.

I walked in and out of the various rooms, keeping my ears open for the sound of sloshing water from the bathroom. I tried to visualize how Chapman went about taking a bath and wondered whether it was painful for him or just a matter of routine now after so many years. In what was obviously his study, I browsed through the books on his shelves, mostly works of history and political science, and found a few titles by William Briles, one of them inscribed "To my good friend, George Chapman—W.B." A set of weights was on the floor in one corner of the room, which helped to explain why Chapman was still in such good shape. I took a glance at some papers on his desk and discovered what seemed to be a draft of the speech announcing his Senate candidacy. It wasn't dated, and I couldn't tell how recently he had been working on it. What struck me most about the room was the absence of baseball memorabilia. There were no trophies or photographs on display, nothing to indicate Chapman had ever played baseball. Maybe Charles Light had spoken the truth when he said that Chapman had not been happy as a professional athlete. Or maybe it had meant everything to him and he simply found it too difficult now to be reminded of it.

I was getting restless. It made no sense for Chapman to take a bath when he knew I was coming. I was aware of the fact that I fell into the category of hired help for him, but there were less elaborate ways of being rude to someone who's working for you. I found the bathroom door and pressed my ear against it. No sound came from inside. I knocked softly and got no response. I tried the doorknob, felt it click open, and decided to chance a look inside. The room was empty. Unless George Chapman was the neatest man who ever lived, no one had taken a bath in there today. Fresh blue towels with white GC monograms hung in perfect order on the racks, and there was not a drop of water in the tub or on the floor.

I walked through all the rooms of the apartment again. It wasn't until I tried the kitchen that I found him. He was lying facedown under the table, and he was motionless. There was a stench of vomit and feces coming from his body, and the moment I saw him I knew that he was dead. There is a particular kind of inertness about a dead body, an almost supernatural stillness that tells you no one is there anymore, that what you are seeing is just flesh and bones, a body without a soul. I knelt down, turned him over, and felt for a pulse. Everything was silence, everything was death.

Chapman had died fighting terrible pain. His face was a rictus of agony, and his eyes seemed locked on some distant object, as if in the far reaches of nothingness he had chanced upon a hideous, untellable truth. His clothes were covered with blood-speckled vomit. He had literally coughed up his guts, and I couldn't bear to look at it any longer than I had to. There didn't seem to be any doubt that he had been poisoned.

The table had been set for two. In the center stood an almost full pot of coffee, a plate of cold uneaten toast, an open jar of orange marmalade, and a stick of butter that had begun to go soft. There was an empty coffee cup on one place mat, a full cup on the other. It looked as though Chapman had been eating breakfast with someone about two hours ago—probably his wife. I turned the scene over in my mind and came up with several possibilities, none of which seemed very convincing. Accidental poisoning was out of the question. A lethal dose of whatever it was Chapman had swallowed could not have passed unnoticed. I rejected suicide as well. Chapman had too many things to live for—and I had a fifteen-hundred-dollar check in my office safe to prove that he wanted to stay alive. Nor did I think a suicide would have opted for such a gruesome death. Chapman had probably suffered for more than an hour, and I was certain he had not done it out of choice. That left murder. When Judy Chapman left the apartment, her husband had still been alive; the doorman had talked to him on the phone. Someone else might have entered the apartment soon after. But the doorman had not mentioned any other visitors. And would Chapman have sat down calmly to coffee and toast with a person who was planning to kill him? There was no sign of struggle, nothing to indicate the presence of another person. It didn't make sense to me, and I felt lost, like a blind man stumbling around in a darkened house. Even if I was given back my sight, I still wouldn't have been able to see anything.

I went into the living room and called the police. It wouldn't take them long to arrive. It never does when someone is already dead. I lit a cigarette and flicked the match into one of the pristine ashtrays on the coffee table. My thoughts at that moment were not pretty. A man had asked me to help prevent him from being murdered, and I had agreed to do it. Now, a little more than twenty-four hours later, he was dead. I hadn't done my job. Chapman had trusted me with his life, and I had let him down. The damage was mortal, irreparable. I studied the matchbook cover in my hand. It advertised a correspondence course in television repair, and I wondered if I shouldn't send away for the brochure. Maybe I was in the wrong line of work after all.

Lieutenant Grimes of Homicide led the delegation from the police. I had encountered him on a case once before, and we had not hit it off. His attitude toward me was the same as a watchdog toward the mailman. He knew I had a job to do, but he couldn't stop himself from barking. It was something in his blood, a result of his breeding. Grimes was about fifty, heavyset, with thick eyebrows, and he walked around with the rumpled, weary look of a chronic insomniac. In spite of our personality differences, I considered him to be a good cop. He was accompanied by two young sergeants I hadn't seen before. Both of them were named Smith, but they didn't have beards, and they didn't look like brothers. The photographers and lab men followed.

"When I heard you were the one who called it in," Grimes said by way of greeting, "I was going to give the case to Metropolis. But then it turned out he had a pressing engagement at the hospital to have a bullet taken out of his side." He pinched the bridge of his nose with fatigue. "It's been a rough week, Klein, so don't get too close."

"Don't worry," I said. "There's a collapsible ten-foot pole in the trunk of my car, and I'll let you hold it every time we have to talk."

"Just don't breathe on me, that's all I ask. There's enough pollution in this city already."

"You should talk," I said. "I could smell your pastrami sandwich before you came through the door."

"Corned beef. I don't eat pastrami. It doesn't agree with me."

We went into the kitchen to have a look at Chapman's body. Grimes stood there for a while without saying anything and then shook his head. "I remember that guy when he used to play for the Americans," he said. "Best goddamn natural hitter in twenty years. He made it all look so easy, as if he didn't even care. And now he's just a piece of dead meat." He shook his head again. "The funny thing is that I was probably going to vote for him if he ever ran."

"A lot of people were going to vote for him," I said. "Until this morning, he was on his way to big things."

Grimes let out an enormous sigh. "The shit is going to hit the fucking fan with this one."

He wanted to talk to me, and we went back into the living room while the technicians went about their business in the kitchen. I told him how Chapman had come to see me in my office yesterday and described the threatening letter. I also explained how I had been given the keys by the doorman downstairs, so that Grimes would know I had entered the apartment legitimately. I said nothing about anything else. Contini and Pignato, Briles and Judy Chapman, Angel and Teddy, Charles Light—nothing. They were my leads, and this was my case. I owed it to Chapman and to my own pride to pursue it. I had been paid for ten days' work, and I wanted to earn the money. I didn't want to have to think of myself as one of those guys who back off when no one is looking. And then there was the matter of being able to look Richie in the eyes when I told him about the kind of work I did. Grimes was going to make his own case, and if he needed to know these things, he would find them out. The last thing he wanted from me was advice.

"I'm going to have to get that letter from you," he said.

"It's sitting in my office safe. We can go down for it now if you like."

"It probably doesn't mean a damn thing, though," he speculated.

"At the moment it's the only thing we've got," I said.

"Until I talk to Chapman's wife. Because if it's poison—which it sure as hell looks to be—then she's got to be number one. Unless, of course, someone else was sitting at that breakfast table. But that seems pretty unlikely."

"You forget that Chapman was alive after she left. He called the doorman about the keys."

"Poison takes time. He might have called too soon afterwards, before he knew anything was wrong."

"It still doesn't figure," I said. "Why would she leave all her dishes on the table? If she poisoned Chapman, she would have cleaned up after herself to make it look as though she hadn't been there."

"She probably panicked. Rich women are sensitive types, Klein. They like to think their wicked thoughts, but as soon as they do something naughty they get all upset." Grimes started walking toward the front door. "Let's get out of here and take a look at that letter. The Smith boys can handle all the questioning in the building without me."

We went downtown in a patrol car driven by a young cop with a bad case of acne. He seemed terrified of Grimes, and his driving showed it. He missed every green light, kept hitting the brakes too hard, and took three or four wrong turns. Grimes stared out the window, muttering under his breath.

We left the driver outside in the car and took the elevator up to my office. Once inside, Grimes began looking over the place like a prospective tenant.

"This is one hell of a dump you've got here," he said.

"I know it's not much. But home is where the heart is."

Grimes ran his finger over the dust on the filing cabinet. "I mean, Jesus, I wouldn't wish this place on a caveman. I thought you were making out all right. But from the looks of this hole, you're a prime contender for the poorhouse."

"You forget that I'm a man with responsibilities, Lieutenant. I've got an ex-wife and a son to support, as well as a couple of old parents, a maiden aunt with epilepsy, and six young cousins I'm seeing through college. And I always make a point of giving away half of what I earn to charity. I couldn't live with myself otherwise."

"I'm glad you could find someone to live with you. If I had to look at that face in the mirror every day, I'd walk around in bandages."

I walked over to the wall safe and opened the combination lock. When I reached my hand in for the letter, I couldn't find it. I took out Chapman's check and the few things I usually kept in there—a bottle of Chivas Regal, my passport, my two diplomas, and the Smith & Wesson .38 I was lucky enough not to have carried in almost a year. I put them on the desk one by one and then reached my hand back into the safe. It was empty.

"The letter's gone," I said.

Grimes looked up at the ceiling sarcastically, as if begging for help. "I should have known," he sighed. "Nothing in this life is ever simple. God wants me to suffer because I'm so good-looking."

I was angrier than I had been in a long time. "The letter was here yesterday," I almost shouted. "Chapman left it with me in the morning after our interview. I immediately locked it away, and I haven't touched it since. There's no way anyone could have taken it except by cracking the safe. There are no signs of forcing, and the combination isn't written down."

"Sure, sure," Grimes said. "You want me to believe in this letter, so you drag me halfway down to goddamn Mississippi to make me think you've got it. But there is no letter, there never was."

"There's no letter now. But I give you my word it was here yesterday."

"Your word isn't worth much, Klein."

"I'm not going to stand around here arguing about it. I know there's a letter, and you know there's a letter. The important thing is to get it back. The fact that it's missing means it's crucial to the case."

"Nothing's stopping you from going off to look for it. At least that will keep you out of my hair."

"And you'd better pray that I find it. Because if I don't, your case is going to look about as promising as a rainy weekend at the beach."

"I never go to the beach," Grimes said. "I like the mountains. Much better for your health."

10

As soon as Grimes was gone, I sat down and put in a call to Chip Contini. He was the one who had sent Chapman to me in the first place, and I wanted to use him as a means for getting to his father. Men like Victor Contini are not in the habit of making appointments with strangers over the telephone, and I didn't have time to start cultivating his friendship. I needed to have a long, quiet talk with him, and I needed to have it as soon as possible.

I hadn't spoken to Chip for several years, and for the first few minutes of the conversation we caught up on each other's news, mostly his. Things were going well for him, and he wasn't too bashful to let me know it. Like most insecure people, Chip felt a constant need to justify his life, to make it seem exciting and enviable. He had spent his first thirty-odd years trying to get out from under the burden of his father, and even though he had made a success of himself, I suspected he still walked around with the feeling that a building might fall on top of him at any moment.

"I was hoping you'd call," he said.

"I'm curious about why you sent Chapman to me."

"I thought you could probably use the business. When George told me about the letter he received on Monday, I figured it might be best for someone to investigate it. It doesn't look like anything too serious to me, but George was scared and I wanted to take some action so that he wouldn't worry so much."

"He had reason to be scared," I said.

"Why? Have you found out who wrote the letter?"

"No, I haven't found out. But Chapman is dead. He was murdered in his apartment this morning."

"Don't put me on, Max."

"I'm not. Chapman is dead. They're probably already talking about it on the radio."

"Jesus Christ."

"You're going to be pretty busy. From the looks of things, Judy Chapman is the leading suspect."

"That's ridiculous. I've never heard anything so stupid."

"You're probably right. But tell that to Lieutenant Grimes of Homicide. In the meantime, she's going to need a lawyer."

"What a mess," he groaned. "What a god-awful mess."

"Before you start feeling sorry for yourself," I said sharply, "maybe you can give me a little help."

He was chastened and took hold of himself. "Anything I can do I will, Max."

"For starters I want you to set up a meeting between me and your father. Right away. For today or tomorrow."

"What in the world for? My father has nothing to do with George."

"Not so. I've found a definite link concerning the accident five years ago, and I need to talk to your father."

"Bullshit," Chip said angrily. "Just because of my father's past, people assume he's responsible for everything that happens. He's an old man, and he's been out of the rackets for years."

"Maybe that's what you tell yourself to soothe your conscience, Chip. That's your privilege, and it's none of my business. But we both know it isn't true. Your father's old, yes, but he hasn't retired. He's only slowed down a bit. I wouldn't have brought it up unless I was sure. A man is already dead, and before this thing gets out of hand I've got to do something about it."

"All right. I'll call him and try to set it up."

"You'll do more than try. You'll do it. There's no more time for diddling around."

I gave him my number and told him I would sit there until he called back. Two cigarettes and about fifteen minutes later, the phone rang.

"Ten-thirty tomorrow morning in my office," Chip said.

"Did you tell him what it was about?"

"I gave him a rough outline. He's going to stay with us for the weekend and spend some time with the kids."

"I appreciate it, Chip."

"I still think you're making a big mistake, Max. My father has nothing to do with Chapman."

"Then he wouldn't have agreed to see me. I know I'm right now, and all the wishing in the world isn't going to change it."

I PUT EVERYTHING back into the safe except the Smith & Wesson. I loaded the revolver, stuck it in my shoulder holster, and put the whole business on. I wasn't used to wearing it anymore, and it felt bulky and uncomfortable. But I was going up against the big boys now, and I wanted some sense of security. My neck was the only collateral I had left.

Down in the parking lot, Luis was full of last night's game. Detroit had won six to five in twelve innings, and he was bemoaning the Americans' lack of stable relief pitching and their inability to hit with men on base.

"Two times they get bases loaded with no outs, and they don't get nothing." He spat out the words in disgust.

"Don't worry, Luis. It's only May. Things don't start getting serious until August."

"By then it's too late."

For a true fan a loss or a win can color the mood for an entire day. Your team wins, and every tuft of grass pushing through the pavement is a beautiful wildflower, a testimonial to the perseverance of nature. Your team loses, and you're surrounded by weeds, cracked asphalt, and ugliness. Luis was suffering. I didn't bother to tell him it was only a game.

The drive to Irvingville was easier this time. The midday traffic moved quickly, and it looked as though the weather was clearing. The rain had stopped more than an hour ago, and although the sky was still cloudy, you could see the sun bravely trying to fight its way through. This was May, after all, and the sun had a reputation to uphold.

I turned on the car radio to one of the all-news stations. When the half-hour headline report came on, Chapman's death was the lead story. They didn't have much yet. George Chapman had been found dead in his apartment by a private detective, and the police suspected foul play. They went on to talk about Chapman's baseball career and how he had been planning to announce his candidacy for the Senate. I moved the dial up to WQXR and found myself listening to Richter's version of the *Wanderer Fantasy.* I stuck with Schubert and didn't go back to the news.

It was going to be a tough case for Grimes. It always is when a well-known person is involved. The press refuses to sit still, crackpot theories multiply like fruit flies, and the police wind up conducting an investigation in the middle of Grand Central Station. Pressure builds up. The mayor feels the heat from the public, the D.A. feels the heat from the mayor, the chief of Homicide feels it from the D.A., and the lieutenant in charge feels it from the chief. I wondered how long it would be before Grimes buckled under. He had a lot of experience, but I had never seen how he handled himself in a tight situation. It usually brought out the worst in a man. For Judy Chapman's sake, I hoped his skin was as thick as it looked.

It was after two-thirty, and I realized that I was hungry. I found a place on the highway called the Coach Lantern Diner and pulled into the parking lot. It was one of those modern, pretentiously rigged out diners with flashy chrome, marbleized Formica, and imitation-brass lamps that are supposed to make you think you've just climbed off the Canterbury–London coach and stepped into an eighteenth-century English inn. There were about twenty pies on display shelves behind glass. They were so puffed up they looked like they had gone through a series of silicone injections. I found them about as appetizing as a row of basketballs.

It was an off hour, and the place was nearly empty. I sat down at the counter and studied the menu, an outsized affair with more entries than the Milwaukee phone book. A squat waitress in a starched red uniform bounced over to take my order. Her dyed red hair was a shade or two darker than the dress, and the way it stayed in place a foot and a half above her head defied every law of Newtonian physics. With her false eyelashes, bright gold earrings, and clattering bracelets, she somehow reminded me of a sports car. Her name was Andrea and she called me honey.

I ordered a hot turkey sandwich, and three minutes later it was sitting in front of me. There was so much gravy on the plate that for a moment I thought I had been given an aquarium to eat. But I was too hungry to care. It wasn't until the last few bites that I realized it actually didn't taste bad. The waitress said I was the fastest eater she had ever seen, and I gave her a dollar tip. I was a big shot who spent his time making everybody happy. Santa Claus was my middle name. I walked out of the place sucking on a mentholated toothpick.

At ten past three I found a parking space a few blocks up from the Pignato house on Seventeenth Street. It was a little too early for the kids to be back from school, and the wet weather had kept the old people inside. The neighborhood felt deserted, as if it had been evacuated for a disaster. I wondered if I was that disaster or if it had already struck. Water dripped slowly from the branches of the trees. The world was dark under those trees, and the sky glowed through them eerily, as if from another planet. Nothing felt right. I had that sinking sensation you get when you walk into the wrong movie. I had put down my money for Buster Keaton, and they were giving me John Wayne instead.

No one came to open the door after I knocked. I knocked again, waited two, three, four minutes, and still no one came. I tested the door. It was unlocked. I opened it softly, slipped inside, and shut it behind me. Doors had been opening for me all day, and behind them I had been finding nothing but myself. I knew I was too late. As soon as I stepped across the threshold, I knew what I was going to find. I was reliving the same experiences of a few hours ago, and it made me feel as though I had been locked into some cruel dream, condemned to go on discovering images of death.

It was a shabby house, and it stank of poverty. Children's toys were scattered over the floors, and the unwashed dishes of several meals were piled high in the kitchen sink. There were religious pictures hanging in most of the rooms. Tacked onto the wall over the color television set in the living room was a big red, white, and blue tapestry portrait of John F. Kennedy that looked as if it had been bought in some novelty shop on Times Square. All the shades were drawn, as though the unhappiness of the house could be prevented from leaking out and contaminating the rest of the neighborhood. I found myself thinking about Pignato's children, wondering if they would miss their father, or if his death would free them from this darkness.

He was in the bedroom, stretched out on the unmade bed with half his face blown away. There was a pool of blood on the pillow, and blood was splattered on the wall behind him. On the bureau a few feet from the bed, a portable television was tuned to a soap opera, with the sound on very softly. The whispering phantoms were sitting in a bourgeois living room, drinking from delicate teacups and talking about their neuroses, their love affairs, and how they were going to spend their summer vacations. In a peculiar way, they seemed to represent the dead man's thoughts. It was as if he had already gone to heaven and from now on would be able to lead the same life they did.

There was nothing to be done. I went back into the kitchen and called the police. I was getting very good at calling the police. Pretty soon they were going to give me my own special hot line so I wouldn't have to go to the trouble of dialing anymore.

Pignato's murder looked like a professional job. One quick bullet, and that was the end of it. A split second of incredible pain, and then nothing, nothing at all. The killer had chosen his moment carefully, making sure that Pignato's family was out of the house when he arrived. I wondered if Pignato had been expecting him, lying on his bed watching television until he came. It seemed logical to assume that Pignato had called Victor Contini after my visit yesterday and that Contini had sent someone over to silence the man who had let out the secret of George Chapman's accident. It was logical, but logic doesn't always count for much.

The police arrived noisily, barging into the house like a bunch of invading Goths. I immediately regretted not ducking out after I made the phone call. For the past two days it seemed I had been doing nothing but making wrong decisions.

Captain Gorinski was in charge. He was a bull of a man in his early forties, still solid, with a bit of a paunch that spilled out over his belt buckle. He had the erratic eyes of a drinker, and from the disheveled clothes he wore, I gathered he had personal problems. I didn't want to become one of them.

He seemed unmoved by the sight of Pignato's corpse. When he walked into the bedroom and saw the body, his only comment was, "Nobody's going to fuck on those sheets anymore." It was all hard-guy stuff, a way of looking at the world with the mind of a reptile. Compared to him, Grimes was as gentle as a den mother.

He asked me who I was and what I was doing there. I answered the first question by showing him my investigator's license. He studied it with contempt, as if I had just handed him a pornographic picture.

"A Jew-boy shamus from the big city," he said.

"That's right," I answered. "I come from a long line of rabbis. All those people you see walking around in the funny hats and long beards are my cousins. At night I sprout horns and a tail, and every spring at Passover I kill a Christian baby to use its blood in a secret ritual. I'm a Wall Street millionaire and a Communist, and I was there when they nailed Christ to the cross."

"Shut the fuck up, Klein," he snapped, "or I'll break your goddamn neck."

"Just watch the way you talk to me, Captain," I came back at him. "There's no way I'm going to cooperate with you unless you act like a human being."

"You assholes from New York are all the same. You think you're the toughest, smartest guys that ever came down the pike, but just let somebody call your bluff, and you go screaming for a lawyer. This ain't New York, Mr. Rabbi, it's Irvingville. This is my town, and I'll act any goddamn way I want to."

"Suit yourself," I said. "I had this crazy idea that maybe you wanted to do something about solving a murder. There's a dead man lying in the next room, and while you stand here talking about your beautiful town, the murderer is getting farther and farther away."

"That's where you're wrong, sweetheart," he said with a sadistic grin. "The murderer ain't going nowhere. I'm standing here with him right now."

"That's quite a clever theory you've got," I said. "Let me see. I walk in here and shoot Pignato in the face. Then, instead of running out, I stroll into the kitchen, call the police, and offer to help them. Yeah, I see what you mean. It makes a lot of sense. You must be some kind of genius, Captain."

"Mike," Gorinski barked at one of the cops watching our conversation, "come over here and take this joker's gun away from him."

Mike was a young one, no more than twenty-five or twenty-six, and he was having a good time. He seemed to think Gorinski was Irvingville's answer to Sherlock Holmes, and he was all too happy to do his bit. He sauntered over to me and stuck out his hand.

"All right, Klein, let's have it."

"This gun hasn't been fired in months," I said. "All you have to do is smell it to know I haven't used it today."

I opened my jacket, put my hand on the butt, and was about to pull the revolver out of its strap when Gorinski rushed over and struck a tremendous blow on the side of my head. I went down like a collapsible chair, my ear ringing with the impact. I sat up after a moment in a half daze to find Gorinski standing over me and screaming.

"Don't you know it's against the law to pull a gun on a police officer, you idiot! I could have put you away a long time for that stunt. Mike," he said, turning again to his faithful assistant, "put the cuffs on him. We're all going to have ourselves a little discussion down at the station."

Mike did as he was told, and then the two of them marched me out of the house and into one of the squad cars outside. It didn't take more than ten minutes to get to the station. I told Gorinski to call Lieutenant Grimes in New York, and he told me to go fuck myself. That was one of the things I liked about him. He had an original remark for every situation.

They threw me into an interrogation room and spent the next several minutes kicking me around. I had heard of the third degree before, but in their hands it was a fine art, more like the nth degree, or a lesson in how to play soccer without a ball.

It seemed to put them in good spirits, because every time Gorinski knocked me out of my chair, it got a big laugh from Mike. Naturally, I didn't fight back. They were the police after all, officers of the law. And I happened to be in handcuffs. I tried to separate my mind from my body, to pretend that what was happening to me was actually happening to someone else. It's a method for fighting pain that's supposed to work very well in the dentist's chair. Unfortunately, it doesn't work in police stations.

Eventually they got down to business. They wanted to know who had hired me to kill Pignato, how much money I was being paid, and what other jobs like this one I had done recently. They called me kike, faggot, and commie. I told them I was working on the Chapman murder case and that they should call Louis Grimes of Homicide in New York. I couldn't be sure that Grimes would stand up for me, but I figured it was my only chance of getting out of Irvingville before the year two thousand.

It didn't make much difference what I said. They knew I hadn't killed Pignato, but they went through the charade because they enjoyed it. It made them feel like important men. They were good, red-blooded Americans, and it wasn't every day an easy target like me fell into their hands. Besides, they knew they were never going to solve the case anyway. Pignato had been connected with the Contini mob, and the killing was a matter of internal politics. In a place like Irvingville, gangland executions weren't considered murders. They were part of the local scenery, the same as the Fourth of July fireworks or the policemen's ball. They didn't get solved, they got ignored. Gorinski wasn't about to do anything to upset Victor Contini. As the saying goes, you don't bite the hand that feeds you.

What finally rescued me was Gorinski's stomach. It was getting on toward dinnertime, and after an hour of going through the same comedy again and again, I could see that he was beginning to lose interest. The thought of eating appealed to him more than turning me into ground chuck. He left the room, and Mike carried on without him. Fifteen minutes later he returned.

"You're a lucky man, Klein," he said. "I just spoke to Grimes in New York. Make yourself scarce. We don't want you around here."

"I don't know how to thank you," I answered. "You've made my stay in your town such a pleasant one, I almost don't want to leave. I sure hope I can come back soon. Maybe I'll bring the wife and kids next time."

"You so much as show your face around here," Gorinski said, "and I'll turn it into spackling. I'll make you so unhappy you'll wish the hospital went up in flames the day you were born."

Mike took out a key and unlocked the handcuffs. I tried to get the blood flowing again, but I couldn't feel a thing. I was dead from the elbows to the fingertips.

"You're a courageous man, Gorinski," I said, "and a credit to every police force in the country. Without guys like you, the streets wouldn't be safe for ordinary citizens like me. I just want you to know how grateful I am. I thank you. I thank you from the bottom of my heart."

Gorinski muttered something to himself, turned on his heel, and walked out of the room. Mike escorted me to the front desk.

"I'll give you one thing," he said. "You sure know how to take a punch."

It was all a sport for him, and he wanted to thank me for being a worthy competitor. It didn't matter that the game had been rigged, that they hadn't given me a chance. I refused to shake his hand when he held it out to me.

"That's quite a hero you've picked for yourself," I said. "Is that what you're planning to be like when you grow up?"

"He's really not such a bad guy once you get to know him."

"Sure," I said. "And Hitler loved children. It's the same old story. In every brute there's a humanitarian crying to get out."

Mike's eyes turned hard again. "Just be glad you got off as easy as you did, Klein."

"I'll try to remember. Every time I walk by a church I'll go in and light a candle for Gorinski. And maybe one for you too."

It was six o'clock. I called for a cab from the pay phone and arranged to be taken back to Seventeenth Street to pick up my car. My body was going to hurt for the next few days, but I would survive. That was more than George Chapman or Bruno Pignato could say.

11

THERE WERE THREE MEN hanging around my car on Seventeenth Street. They were waiting for me, and I knew it wasn't because they were interested in talking about 1971 Saabs. I could have told the cabdriver to go on past them and take me to the bus station. There were other ways of getting back to the city. But I was curious. If they wanted something from me, then maybe I could get something from them. I was realistic enough not to expect an equal exchange. I only hoped I wouldn't be too far behind when it was all over.

They were an odd group. One of them, dressed in blue jeans, a leather jacket, and motorcycle boots, looked like a recent youth gang graduate. He was leaning against the car with his hands folded across his chest and chewing gum, the expression in his eyes as empty as a bullet hole in a tin can. The second was in his thirties, neatly appointed in a powder-blue leisure suit and spotless white loafers. He was smoking a cigarette and pacing back and forth, lost in his own thoughts. He was obviously the idea man. The third was the oldest, somewhere in his mid-forties, and more conservatively dressed, in a brown suit, brown shirt, and white tie. He was smoking a cigar and kept looking at his watch. They were all about my size. Except for the differences in their clothes, they seemed to be images of each other at various stages of life. It was a group portrait of three generations of hoods.

I paid off the driver, got out of the cab, and walked across the street. All three of them followed me with their eyes.

"Nice car, isn't it?" I said to White Tie. "I'll give you a good deal on it and throw in the snow tires to boot."

"Let's go, Klein," Leisure Suit said. "You've got a rendezvous with destiny."

"Sounds like a redhead," I replied. "Is she good-looking?"

"She's a dog," said Leather Jacket, getting into the act. "But you're just going to have to take it as it comes."

They had it all worked out. Leather Jacket took my gun from me and went off to fetch a green Buick that was parked down the street. The other two told me to get into the driver's seat of the Saab and then climbed into the car after me. Leisure Suit sat in the back, and White Tie sat next to me in the front.

"Before I buy any car," White Tie said, "I gotta see how it handles. I don't wanna get stuck with a lemon."

"Just tell me where you want to go," I said, "and I'll take you there."

Leisure Suit leaned forward in the back seat. "Do you know the North Mountain Reservation?"

"I know it."

"Well, that's where we're going. And no monkey business, Klein. I've got a thirty-eight pointed at the back of your head.

Any tricks, and your brain is going to decorate the windshield."

I started the car and pulled out. The Buick followed right behind me. For the moment at least, I knew I was safe. In spite of Leisure Suit's threat, he wasn't about to pull the trigger while I was driving. As long as we were in the car, nothing was going to happen.

The situation seemed clear to me. These were Contini's men, and they were taking me off to finish what had been started earlier in the day with Pignato's murder. I was the one person who knew about Chapman's accident, and with me out of the way, Contini would be home free. The answer to the most important question still eluded me, however. Why had Contini wanted Chapman dead in the first place? I had been hoping to find that out in my meeting with him tomorrow. But now I wasn't so sure I was going to be around tomorrow. Or any other tomorrow, for that matter.

"I don't suppose you'd like to give me a hint about why you find it so important to be with me this evening," I said to White Tie.

"You're a troublemaker, that's why," Leisure Suit answered for him. "You don't know how to keep your nose out of other people's business. Sooner or later a guy like you is bound to come down with a bad case of grief. And this is the day, lover boy, this day is it."

"You seem to have lots of answers," I said. "Here's another question. Who do you work for?"

"I've got six big answers sitting in the palm of my hand," Leisure Suit sneered, "and any one of them can put an immediate end to this conversation."

"You've sure got a quick tongue. You go through clichés as fast as a baby goes through diapers." I looked at him in the rearview mirror. "Maybe you should lay off all those comic books."

"Just drive, Mr. Snoop. When I want your opinion I'll write you a letter."

I drove. We went west for several miles along Spring Avenue, the main commercial street in Irvingville, and up toward the brighter, wealthier towns beyond. The scenery changed. From factories and warehouses we moved on to a stretch of used-car lots and Dairy Queens, and then through modest residential neighborhoods, which gradually turned into plush suburbs with vast, manicured lawns, three-car garages, and kidney-shaped swimming pools. We were climbing up into the mountains, away from the dirt of cities and into a never-never land of doctors, executives, and slumlords. This was the world in which people played golf at the country club, fooled around with each other's wives, and sent their kids off to expensive summer camps with three thousand dollars' worth of orthodonture work in their mouths. It gave me a strange feeling to be driving past these mansions with a gun pointed at the back of my head. It was as though I had passed into another dimension, a place of absurd juxtapositions and nursery-rhyme logic. Fear was a black Lincoln speeding through a red light. Violence was a hunchbacked gardener methodically pruning a rhododendron. Death was the punch line of a joke told over cocktails on the terrace. Everything was something else, and nothing was what it was supposed to be.

The North Mountain Reservation consisted of several hundred acres of woods, picnic areas, and hiking trails at the top of the hill. At quarter to seven, it was almost completely deserted. White Tie told me to turn off onto a small dirt road which ran through the oak and maple woods. The green Buick followed close behind us. After about half a mile we came to a large meadow on our right, and Leisure Suit told me to pull off the road and go up onto the grass. I followed his instructions. It was going to be almost impossible for me to break away from them. I would be out in the open and an easy target if I tried to make a move. My only chance was the woods on the other side of the road, but they were more than two hundred yards off. I wondered why I had ever decided to get out of the cab on Seventeenth Street.

I stopped the car when they told me to, and the three of us climbed out. Leather Jacket pulled up, cut the engine of the Buick, and came over to join us. For a moment we all stood there in the tall grass and orange light of dusk without saying anything. I felt as though we had become human shadows, motionless figures locked in the spectral landscape of a De Chirico painting.

"I don't think I like the car, Klein," White Tie finally said. "It's got no pickup, and the engine knocks."

"That's all right," I said. "I decided I don't want to sell it after all."

Leather Jacket opened the trunk of the Buick and took out a sledgehammer. He walked over to the Saab and examined it with a sarcastic leer. "The trouble with foreign jobs like this," he said, "is that they're not built to last." He swung the hammer over his head and brought it down on the windshield. The glass shattered to pieces. "See what I mean? One little tap, and the whole thing falls apart."

"That was pretty good," I said. "Maybe you should apply for a job on a chain gang breaking up stones."

"Shit," he said, "that was nothing. Watch this."

Again he swung the hammer over his head, and in quick succession he knocked out all the other windows in the car. White Tie and Leisure Suit grinned. They seemed glad to be letting youth have its day.

"You see, Klein," Leather Jacket went on, "you were going to sell this car to a friend of mine, and I think you were trying to stick him with a bummer. I just want him to see what a piece of junk you were peddling."

His words became self-fulfilling prophecy. Whatever life had been left in the Saab when the day began was battered out of it forever. In fifteen minutes the car was literally turned into a piece of junk. He smashed the doors, put several holes in the hood, cracked the steering wheel to bits, and then ripped up the upholstery and slashed the tires with a switchblade. It no longer resembled a car. It had become a piece of exotic sculpture.

Leather Jacket had worked up a sweat, and when he was finished he stood there panting with a triumphant smile on his face. Leisure Suit clapped with mock politeness.

"That's the end of act one," he said. "Not a bad performance, eh, Klein?"

"Olivier was better in *Wuthering Heights,*" I said. "Your pal here doesn't know how to emote. It's hard to believe in him as a character."

"You'll believe him, all right," White Tie said. "Show him something he can believe in, Andy."

Leather Jacket was just getting warmed up. He had that maniacal kamikaze glare in his eyes, and all his attention was focused on me. It flashed through my mind that maybe he was on drugs, in which case I knew I could take him. He charged at me with a wild right I could see coming all the way from Pittsburgh. I blocked it with my left forearm and countered with a hard right into his belly. He gave out a loud grunt and doubled over. That punch gave me infinite satisfaction. After being pushed around for two days, I was at last fighting back, and my body responded to the situation with more fury than I thought was in me. Leather Jacket was only temporarily stunned, and he came up smiling.

"That's all you get," he said. "One punch. Now it's my turn."

He rushed at me again, with the same overconfident abandon. He must have thought he was invincible, that no matter what he did he couldn't be touched. This time I ducked his right and came up with a sharp left to the jaw. It was a wicked shot that sent waves of pain from my knuckles to my shoulder. He went staggering back five or six steps and then fell. He wasn't out, but he was down, and before he could rush me again I wheeled around to protect myself from behind. Leisure Suit was standing there with his gun pointed at my stomach. White Tie calmly lit another panatela.

"A waste of time, lover boy," he said without emotion. "All this is going to get you is a sore hand."

"It's in a good cause, though," I said, breathing hard. "I like to see friends of yours fall on their ass."

And then the sun set very rapidly. It had been there, just behind Leisure Suit's shoulder, a huge disk of red fire, and then it wasn't there anymore. The blow struck at the back of my head, and I went down like a Raggedy Ann doll. For a long time I was a coal miner digging under the earth. The lantern on my helmet projected a beam of light down a tunnel twenty miles long. I had to keep walking. When I reached the end of the tunnel I would find the biggest lump of coal in recorded history and get my picture in the newspaper. I started wondering if my high school graduation picture would be appropriate, and then suddenly I wasn't a coal miner anymore. I had become a corpse. The undertakers were carrying me to the cemetery, and no one had come to mourn me. They were going to put me in a pauper's grave and throw stones at my body just for the fun of it. I heard one of them say, "It never hurts to make sure. What if he decides to wake up?"

I opened my eyes. I was on my back, and the whole world was shaking under me. I puzzled over that for a little while, wondering how I could be moving and yet lying perfectly still at the same time. Then I realized I was lying on the floor in the back of a car. I was very impressed by this discovery, and for a few moments I treated it with all the enthusiasm of a major scientific breakthrough. Then I noticed that my hands were tied together with a piece of rope. Outside, it was dark. Night had come in my absence.

"Rip Van Winkle's about to return to civilization," Leisure Suit said from the back seat. White Tie turned around from the front and looked down at me. That left Leather Jacket as the driver.

"Too bad," White Tie commented. "You missed most of the ride. We're almost there."

I moved my head slightly and groaned. I felt like an artichoke whose leaves had been plucked. My brain was exposed to the air and had the same consistency as a bowl of warm jello.

"Just catching up on my beauty sleep," I said.

"The way you snore," Leisure Suit answered, "it's more like ugly sleep."

"That's because I was dreaming of you," I said. "And now I wake up to find out it all really happened. It's just like a fairy tale. You know the one I mean—Beauty and the Beast."

"I'll tell you another bedtime story later," Leisure Suit said. "Maybe if I make it real good, you won't wake up again."

Five minutes later the car slowed down to make a turn, and then we were driving over gravel. After what seemed to be a quarter of a mile, the car stopped.

"End of the line," Leisure Suit said. "This is where all the deadbeats get off."

He opened the door, climbed out, and then he and Leather Jacket yanked me from the car onto the ground. The gravel cut into my back as though I'd been raked over a bed of knives. They told me to stand up. I gave it my best effort, but apparently it wasn't good enough. Leisure Suit gave me a kick in the kidneys with one of his white shoes, and that slowed down my progress a little. After a few more tries and a few more kicks, I eventually made it to my feet. My head felt as heavy as a bowling ball, and it took me a while to learn how to cope with this new distribution of my weight.

The situation didn't look good for me, but nevertheless I was getting my confidence back. I had been with them for nearly two hours, and I was still breathing. If their instructions had been to kill me, I would have been long dead by now. It seemed that Contini was willing to let me live. He just wanted to make things difficult for me, to put me out of commission until the Chapman investigation was over. Maybe the old man was going soft, I thought to myself. Or maybe it had something to do with my phone call to Chip. If I turned up dead, then Chip would know his father had been responsible. Contini wasn't afraid of the law, and I'm sure he didn't give a damn about my life. But he didn't want his son to know he was a murderer. Strange how morality creeps into the most unlikely places. A man will do almost anything to gain the respect of his son. I had done quite a bit of thinking about it myself.

The four of us walked for ten minutes. White Tie held a flashlight to guide us over the stones, and Leisure Suit held a gun in my back. I made a guess that we were in Kern's Quarry, an old gravel excavation that had gone out of business about seven years ago. It was no more than twelve miles from the reservation, and it was probably as good a place as any to keep someone out of sight for a while. When we started climbing up the gravel slope and walking around the rim of the excavation, I saw that I had guessed correctly. A small triumph. But at least I knew where I was.

We came to an abandoned foreman's shed. White Tie opened the door and said, "This is your new house, Klein. You're gonna get to know it real good in the next week or two."

"That's swell," I said. "When can you have my piano sent over? I don't want my fingers to get rusty."

"I wouldn't joke if I were you," Leisure Suit said. "You don't realize how lucky you are. I mean, you're so goddamn lucky it makes me want to puke. By all rights in a situation like this, you get whacked. But for some reason the old man wants you alive."

"I guess that makes him a candidate for the Nobel Peace Prize."

Leisure Suit went on as if I hadn't said anything. "He wants you alive, but that doesn't mean it's going to be much fun for you. There are ways of keeping a guy alive that are a lot worse than dying. You step out of line, and you'll start begging for a bullet in the head. It'll seem like a vacation to Bermuda compared to what we can do to you."

It was a bare, dusty room, damp with the smell of rotting wood, and it measured about eight by fifteen feet. As the flashlight panned over it, I saw a table, a few chairs, and a couple of old ledger books. It was the kind of place that hangs out welcome signs for the rats, and I didn't like the setup at all. There wasn't going to be much room for me to maneuver, especially with a gun pointed at me the whole time. I was beginning to resign myself to the thought of a long stay. But then I got a break. Leisure Suit and White Tie left. They told Leather Jacket they were going out for some food and that they would be back in an hour. Leather Jacket asked them to buy him a sausage hero and a six-pack of beer, and off they went, just like that. That left me alone with the kid. The odds had improved considerably, but they still weren't good. I had to figure out a way to pick a fight without getting my head blown off.

He sat in one of the chairs by the door, a flashlight pointed at my face in one hand and the gun pointed at my face in the other. I sat on the floor in the corner, looking the other way to avoid the light. Outside, the crickets were chirping to the moon, and every now and then a bullfrog croaked, sounding like a strange Chinese instrument with only one string. We didn't say anything for five or six minutes. I listened to the kid work over his chewing gum.

"Hey, Andy," I said. "There's something that's been bothering me. I wonder if you can help me figure it out."

"What's that, Klein?"

"I just want you to tell me how it feels."

"How what feels?"

"Being a fag."

"I don't know what you're talking about."

"Sure you do, Andy. You try to come on as a muscle man, but you've got sissy written all over you."

"I don't have to take none of your crap, dumbbell."

"Just try to stop me. I can open my mouth any time I please. A pansy like you doesn't have the balls to try to close it. You're too afraid of messing up your pretty face."

"One more word and you'll be sorry."

"Little faggy Andy's getting upset," I pouted.

By way of response he fired a bullet into the wall above my head.

"Boo-hoo," I went on. "I don't think Mr. Fruitcake likes me."

"Any more shit, and I'll aim lower next time."

"You wouldn't have the guts to shoot me. You're supposed to keep me alive. If you go against orders, your life won't be worth two cents. And you can go to the bank with that."

"That's what you think, big-mouth. Nobody tells me what to do. If I emptied this gun into you, they'd probably give me a medal."

"Why don't you try it, then, pussyfoot? I mean, it must make you feel mighty tough holding a gun on a man with his hands tied. It's just the kind of arrangement a punk like you has to have. Everything stacked in your favor."

"Any time, any place, Klein, I'll beat you to a bloody pulp."

"Why not now, pimple-face? Or are you afraid you might get the shit kicked out of you again? You look pretty terrific smashing up a car that can't fight back, but boy, are you a sucker for a punch. You couldn't hit your way out of a bag of vomit."

I had begun to lose hope. He was never going to give in, and I would be sitting there spouting these insults at him until Leisure Suit and White Tie came back. But it finally worked. I had managed to push him over the edge. He put the flashlight on the table so that it was shining on me, stood up, and tucked the gun under his belt. Then he walked over to where I was sitting.

"Get up, motherfucker!" he screamed at me, beyond all patience. "I'm going to teach you a lesson you'll never forget."

I stood up and faced him. With the light coming from behind him, only the outline of his body was visible. I couldn't see his eyes. But I didn't have to see them to know what was coming. He pulled back his right hand and brought it down full force into my jaw. It was a good punch, and for a moment I thought he had broken something in my face. I tottered backward and banged into the wall, but somehow I was able to keep my balance. That was what I wanted. More than anything else in the world, I wanted to stay on my feet. I knew that if I could take his best punch without falling down, I was going to have him. And he knew it too.

"If that's all you can deliver, Andy boy," I said through the pain, "then you'd better write away to Charles Atlas for the crash course in body building. A punch like that wouldn't hurt my grandmother. And she weighs ninety pounds."

He was incensed. In all his years of beating people up, he probably had never come up against anyone who could hold his ground against him. That's the trouble with bullies. They spend so much of their time picking on people smaller than they are that they get a false idea of their own strength. I wasn't some old guy who ran the corner grocery store. I was a little bigger than Andy, and I had a lot more experience than he did. It was enough to destroy his pride, to make him plunge on and make more mistakes, instead of quitting while he was still ahead.

"Nobody talks like that to me!" he ranted. "Do you hear me? Nobody can get away with that kind of shit around me!"

In the same way he had overreacted in the reservation earlier, he now came around so wide with his second punch that I was able to duck under it and come up at him from below. My bound hands were like a double fist, and I put everything I had into it. He caught it on the chin and went flying back into the table, knocking off the flashlight and throwing the room into darkness. I rushed for the door, but he was able to stick out his arm and trip me as I was crossing the threshold. I went down hard onto the gravel, unable to break the fall with my hands, and then scrambled quickly to my feet, my lungs fighting for air. I knew that if I gave him enough time to stand and draw the gun, it would be all over. It was a clear night, lit by a half-moon, and there were no trees to hide behind. I had to put as much space between us as I could.

I started running. But the kid was faster than I was, and I

could hear him gaining on me as our feet crunched wildly over the stones. I realized I wasn't going to get away. Suddenly, impulsively, I made a decision to stop. If I couldn't outrun him, then I would have to surprise him. I skidded to a halt, planted my feet as firmly as I could, and then drew my hands back as if I was about to swing a baseball bat. I aimed for his head. He ran straight into it, and I felt the bones in his face shatter into little pieces. It was as though he had crashed into a brick wall, and he went down straight, fast, and screaming. But still he didn't know when to quit. Like a wounded animal fighting for its life, he had become pure instinct. He got up in blind pain and came at me once again. By now my eyes had adjusted to the darkness, and I could see where we were standing. But there was no time to move away. I sidestepped his charging body, and that was all. He was already over the edge of the excavation, falling to the bottom seventy-five feet below.

For a few minutes I didn't do anything. I just stood there panting like a pig under the half-moon, trying to get my breath back. Then I started to shake. It wasn't anything I wanted to do, but my body decided to go ahead and do it without me. For a moment I thought I was going to faint, so I sat down on the ground, and then promptly retched up everything inside me. I wasn't really sure if I was throwing up or sobbing. It was the same violence in the chest, the same breathless scald in the lungs. If I hadn't stopped running when I did, I said to myself, I would have gone over the edge first. It almost didn't matter. There had been too much death today, and I was sick of it, sick of my life, sick of everything I had done to myself in order to stay alive. I had become a destroyer, and I didn't know who I was anymore.

It took me a good ten or fifteen minutes to settle down. By then I was rational enough to know I couldn't stay where I was. The other two would be coming back any moment, and I realized I couldn't face any more. It wasn't that I cared about what happened to me. But I knew I couldn't go through the same thing again. I had come to the limit of myself, and there was nothing left.

I got the hell out of there.

12

I WAS DREAMING of a city with no one in it but me. Everyone had vanished because of a strange and devastating power that had taken hold of my voice. Whenever I spoke to anyone, he would disappear. All I had to do was open my mouth, and everyone around me would be gone. People started running away from me whenever I approached, but I would shout after them, trying to explain that it wasn't my fault, and suddenly they too would evaporate into thin air. Eventually there was no one left. I had become the last man in the world. I sat down in a hotel lobby somewhere, filled with grief and self-pity. I wondered if there was any way to undo the damage I had caused and concluded there was none, that the people would never reappear. I resolved never to say another word, to atone by taking a lifelong vow of silence. Then I heard a hammering noise from one of the upper floors of the hotel. I got out of my seat and started climbing the stairs. There was still another person in the world, and if I could manage to find him, I would be saved. Hour after hour I climbed the stairs, and the noise kept getting closer.

Just as I was about to reach the top, I opened my eyes. Someone was knocking on the apartment door. I made a move to get up and heard all the muscles in my body howl with outrage. I felt as if I had been used to fill a pothole in the West Side Highway. I was never going to walk again, and for the rest of my life I would be confined to this room, attended by an old wrinkled nurse in a white uniform who would feed me nothing but chicken broth. The knocking continued, and I told whoever it was that I was coming. I looked at my watch and saw that it was ten past eight. I had been asleep for less than five hours.

Three weeks later I made it to the front door. It took me another four days to undo the locks and at least six hours to pull open the door, but at last my visitor was standing before me. It was Grimes.

"Sweet Jesus," he said. "Your face looks like a contour map of the Rocky Mountains."

"Yeah, and I'm lucky too. I almost wound up in Death Valley."

I let him into the apartment. This time he didn't try to make any witty remarks about the furniture. We were beyond the stage where jokes mattered now. It had become all business.

"I won't be able to put two sentences together until I get some coffee inside me, Lieutenant," I explained. "You're welcome to join me if you like."

I went into the kitchen, turned on the cold water, and stuck my head under the faucet. I kept it there for a good three or four minutes, trying to will myself back into one piece. As I toweled down my head, I set about preparing the coffee.

"Seeing that I had breakfast two hours ago," Grimes said, "I guess I won't refuse. You private dicks sure do lead the life. You get up any time you want, and then if you feel like it you can take the day off and lie around in bed eating chocolates and reading French novels."

"I'm out of chocolates today, but anytime you want to borrow a book, feel free. I'd recommend starting off with *The Red and the Black.* Stendhal would help get your mind off your work."

"How about *The Black and the Blue?* I always wanted to read your autobiography. Maybe I could learn a few of your secrets. Like who gave you your first boxing lesson. And why you disappear into New

Jersey when you're supposedly working on a case in New York."

As soon as the coffee was ready, I put the thermos on a tray, along with two mugs, two spoons, a couple of paper napkins, the sugar box, and a half-empty carton of milk, and carried it into the living room. Nobody could say I wasn't a gracious host.

Grimes liked the coffee, which both pleased and surprised me. I found myself beginning to like him.

"I suppose I should thank you for bailing me out yesterday," I said, lighting a cigarette with my bruised and swollen hand. "It seems so long ago, I had almost forgotten about it."

"I nearly told Gorinski that I didn't know you. But then I remembered what Irvingville is like, and I decided that maybe you needed a little help."

"I was hoping you would. I didn't know who else to call."

Grimes drank off the last of his coffee and put down his mug. "I'm glad I could do you a favor, Klein, I really am. But now you've got to tell me what you were doing out there in the first place."

"I was following down a lead on the Chapman murder. I still don't know who did it, but I've got something almost as good."

I told him about Chapman's accident five years ago, about Victor Contini's involvement in it and how Bruno Pignato had worked for Contini. I gave him the story of both my trips to New Jersey, describing how I had found Pignato dead in his house and then going on to outline my experiences with Captain Gorinski. I finished off with an account of my car and what had happened during the night. Grimes poured himself another cup of coffee.

"If you'd told me about this yesterday," he said, "you could have spared yourself a lot of lumps."

"I didn't think things were going to happen so fast. I was waiting for something really solid before I told you about it."

"It's not for you to decide what's solid and what's not solid, Klein. When you've got a lead on a case like this, it's police business, do you understand? You come straight to me with it. No snooping around on your own. That guy Pignato might still be alive if you'd opened your mouth yesterday."

"That's just talk, Lieutenant, and you know it. Yesterday you weren't interested in a thing I had to say. You treated the letter as if I'd made it up."

"The letter doesn't exist until I see it. It's not evidence, it's not a lead, it's not anything." Grimes got up from his chair and began walking around the room. "The mistake you're making with this thing is that you want it to be too complicated. You think it's all part of a big plot that goes back to the moment Chapman was born. You spend your time worrying about what happened five years ago, when you should be using your clever Jewish brain to think about what happened yesterday. That's when Chapman got murdered, if you remember, and today's the day to do something about it."

"I believe Victor Contini is mixed up in what happened yesterday. The letter sent to Chapman made explicit references to the accident five years ago. If I find out exactly what took place in the past, it stands to reason I'll know a lot more about the present. I'm not just talking about some minor coincidence. I'm talking about a definite connection. And I think you're a fool if you can't see it."

Grimes threw up his hands and slapped them disgustedly against his sides. We weren't only talking about Chapman, we were examining basic principles, and he wanted to convince me that he was right.

"Look," he said, "I'm not saying Contini didn't have anything to do with the accident. I'll put someone on it today. But you know as well as I do it's going to be next to impossible to get anything to stick on that guy. In the last thirty-five years he hasn't come up for anything worse than a parking ticket." He held up his hands to silence me, wanting to go on with his argument without interruption. "Okay. Say we find out that Contini set up Chapman five years ago. Where does that get us? Does it mean that Contini had Chapman murdered yesterday? Maybe yes, maybe no. We can discuss it all you like, but we've still got a dead man on our hands, and that's what we have to start with. You're going about it ass backwards, Klein. You should try looking at what's in front of your nose before you take out your telescope. It doesn't take a genius to solve a murder—it takes hard work."

"The difference between us," I said, "is that I'm interested in finding out why Chapman was murdered, and what you care about is how. I want real answers, and you want a conviction."

"That's what I get paid for," Grimes said. "That's what police work is all about."

"I guess I'm in a different business, then."

"That's right. And you're not going to get a pension either."

"So how have you been earning your money lately, Lieutenant?"

"I thought you'd never ask." Grimes paused, walked back to the table, and sat down again. He was smiling. "In fact, that's why I came to see you. I wanted to tell you about the arrest we made yesterday."

"And I suppose you're going to tell me it's Judy Chapman."

"You're damn straight I am. Because she did it. That woman's guilty as hell."

I didn't like it. It was all too easy, and it didn't make sense. At nine o'clock yesterday morning I had talked to Judy Chapman on the phone. After making a few jokes, she had stopped short and told me how worried she was about her husband. Her voice had been genuine, concerned. It wasn't the voice of someone who was about to become a murderer.

"I don't know what kind of evidence you think you have against her," I said, "but I guarantee you she didn't do it."

"Bullshit," Grimes retorted. "You want evidence, I'll give you evidence. Number one, she admits to having breakfast with her husband. Number two, her fingerprints are not only all over her cup but on the cup Chapman drank out of too. Number three, we found the bottle of poison in the kitchen cabinet, and it was bought at a hardware store on Monday by Mrs. Chapman herself. Number four, she was fooling around with that Columbia professor, Briles. She wanted a divorce from Chapman, and he wouldn't give it to her. Do you want me to go on?"

"Where is the Chapman woman now?" I asked.

"At home. Out on bail."

"Is Brian Contini working for her?"

"Yeah. But he won't be handling the case in court. He's no trial lawyer, and they're going to need someone pretty good. I hear he's going to hire Burleson for her, one of the hotshot criminal guys."

I decided to give it one more stab. "And it doesn't seem a little curious to you that the son of the man who arranged the accident five years ago was Chapman's lawyer?"

Grimes was bored with the argument, and he let out a sigh of irritation. "It won't wash, Klein. You can't hold someone responsible for the man who signed his birth certificate. Brian Contini is just a normal guy who had the bad luck not to be able to choose his father. I know that smart types like you and me don't get born unless we have a say in the matter. But all the other slobs have to settle for what they get." He waved his hand impatiently, as if trying to chase away all these idle words. "Forget it. Let the whole thing drop. It's an open-and-shut case, and it's finished."

"That's just the trouble. It's all too pat, too simple. The case shuts before it even opens. There's almost too much evidence. It looks more like a frame-up than straight murder. For Judy Chapman to have left behind all the clues you say she did, she must have been in some kind of trance."

"A guilty conscience, maybe. It could be she wanted to get caught."

"That's too easy."

"Well, life is easy once in a while too," Grimes said, standing up from his chair. "Just because most cases are hard, it doesn't mean we should turn up our noses when an easy one comes our way." He started walking toward the door. "I've got to run along now, Klein. I just thought you'd appreciate it if I stopped by to tell you what's been happening."

"I do appreciate it, Lieutenant. Without you as an alarm clock, I might never have woken up today."

Grimes smiled, got halfway out the door, and then poked his head back into the room. "Hey, Klein," he said. "Thanks for the coffee. It wasn't bad at all. If you ever get tired of detective work, you might think about opening one of those espresso shops down in the Village."

He didn't wait for an answer. His head disappeared into the hallway, the door shut, and he was gone.

I remained in my chair, studying the dregs at the bottom of my coffee cup. They didn't tell me anything I wanted to know. I lit a cigarette and spent the next few minutes blowing smoke rings into the room. But they didn't give me any answers either. I got up, walked around the room until I had counted ninety-nine steps, and then sat down on the couch. My mind was blank. It seemed to be getting into the habit of deserting me whenever I needed it most.

The whole business had taken a wrong turn, and I was suddenly in danger of being left behind. For the past two days I had been struggling to fit together a complex puzzle of motives, personalities, and relationships, and now Grimes had come along and swept it all off the table. I wondered if there would be enough time for me to pick up the pieces. I wondered if there would be any pieces left.

Almost unconsciously, I found myself thinking about Chapman. I watched myself trying to crawl inside his skin, trying to see the world through his eyes. After a little while it slowly began to dawn on me that he had never really been in control of himself. He had been a prisoner of his own talent. I tried to imagine what it felt like to be better at something than anyone else, to be so very good at one particular thing that you would come to resent it. Chapman had achieved every possible success—and yet in some way he had not done it himself. His talent had done it, a kind of monster that lived inside him, using him only as an instrument to further its own ends. He must have felt detached from himself, somehow separated from his own life, as if he were a fraud, a substitute Chapman who had abdicated responsibility for his own actions. The monster was in command. The monster had given him everything—and taken everything away.

And then, suddenly, the monster was slain. Would it have freed him, or would it have engulfed him in a new and more terrifying emptiness? If his whole existence had been defined in terms of the monster, where would he begin to look for himself now? A man like Chapman would have felt unreal, as if the essential part of him had never truly been born. He would have been lost, stranded somewhere between the self that had been stolen from him and the self he would never be able to find. I saw the bitter contract dispute with Light as a way of getting back at the monster for all it had done to him. It was a blood debt, and Chapman had been determined to exact payment.

I wasn't going to let it drop. No matter what Grimes might have thought, the case still wasn't over, and I wanted to see it through to the end. The only thing I needed was a client. I decided to offer my services to Judy Chapman.

It was an older woman who answered the phone. "Judith is not taking any calls," she said. "It's quite impossible to speak to her now." I assumed it was Judy's mother. Only parents call their children by their full names.

"Please tell her it's Max Klein. The last thing I want to do is intrude. But this is extremely important, and I think she'd be willing to talk to me."

She said she would ask. Less than a minute later, Judy came to the phone.

"Oh, God, Max. I'm so glad you called. It's so awful. You can't believe what's been happening." Her voice had lost all its assurance. In the past twenty-four hours she had been through the ordeals of death and false accusation, and she was scared.

"I know," I said. "Things look very bad right now. But the way to do something about it is to fight it, and I want to help you, Judy."

She took a deep breath, as if struggling for air, as if it required a special effort for her to keep breathing. "When can you come? I want you to be here."

"Soon. There's something I've got to do first. But I should make it by twelve."

"Don't be late."

"I'll be there as close to noon as I can."

"I'll be waiting."

"Me too."

We hung up, leaving everything else unsaid. I had promised to help her, and yet I had not given her anything tangible to hold on to. I wondered how long she would be able to stand up to the pressures she now had to deal with. A woman like Judy Chapman had no frame of reference for coping with a murder charge. She wanted to lean on someone, and I had given her my arm. I wondered if I would be able to clear her. And if I did, I wondered if she would still want to lean on me.

I went off to get ready for my meeting with Victor Contini. Looking at myself in the mirror, I saw that my face wasn't quite as bad as I thought it would be. There was an ugly welt on my left cheek, but for the most part the injuries were inside, where they didn't show. The back of my head was still tender, and my ribs smarted every time I moved too quickly. But there was nothing that wouldn't heal. I counted my blessings.

I was just starting to loop my tie around my neck when the phone rang. I automatically made a move to go answer it, got halfway there, and then decided to leave it alone. I returned to the bathroom on the fourth ring, started to reconsider my decision on the sixth, and went back to answer it on the ninth. The caller was obviously determined, and I thought it might be something important. One of the facts of modern life is our belief in the sanctity of the telephone. People will interrupt passionate love-making or suspend a violent quarrel just to obey its command. Refusal to answer is equated with anarchy, an assault on the very structure of society. I picked up the phone on the eleventh ring. Pavlov would have been pleased.

"Klein?" The voice was muffled, throaty, menacing. It sounded as though it was coming through a handkerchief, and I didn't recognize it.

"That's right," I said. "What can I do for you?"

"It's not what you can do for me, it's what you can do for yourself, Klein."

"Such as what?"

"Such as disappearing."

"I already tried that. But the magic potion I took wasn't strong enough. My nose kept sticking through."

"Let me say, Klein, that if you do not disappear of your own accord, you will be made to disappear—in a way that will have permanent effects. I would like to tell you that you will regret your stubbornness. But a dead man doesn't have any regrets, does he, Klein?"

"Look, if you're trying to move in on my subscription to *The New Yorker,* you can forget it. It ran out in February, and I didn't renew."

"I'm not trying to move in on anything, Klein. I'm only interested in seeing you move out. Out of the Chapman case, out of everything to do with George and Judith Chapman."

"In the past three days everyone I've met has said that. They're all so worried about my health, they think I should go away on vacation. But I like it where I am. There are only two or three decent months each year in New York, and May happens to be one of them. Why don't you call back in November? Maybe I'll be more interested then."

"November will be too late, Klein. You'll be dead."

"And so will the poppies. The World Series will be over, and the birds will be flying south. What else is new?"

"Good-bye, Klein. You are an ignorant man."

"Same to you, Muffle Mouth. It was a pleasure."

And so began my day. I wasn't going to let it bother me. There had been too many threats for me to get alarmed anymore. I had filled my alarm quotient for the week, and from now on it would be one step at a time. There was no more room for me to look back. And in front of me there was a wall. My problem at the moment was figuring out how to get through it, especially since there was no door in sight.

13

CHIP HAD PUT ON weight since I had last seen him, and he had taken to wearing glasses. You always notice changes when you meet up with an old friend after a long interval, but the years had been particularly hard on Chip. The thickness around the belly was probably not unusual for a man moving into his mid-thirties, but there was something in him that had already become old, used up, and for a split second I almost didn't recognize him. He had lost some hair, and a lot of gray had crept into his temples, but that wasn't what confused me. It was more a kind of stodginess or resignation, a feeling he gave off that told you he wasn't interested in conquering new worlds anymore, that he would be content to spend the rest of his life holding on to what he had already won. He was a good family man with three kids and a nice-looking wife, and they lived in an expensive house in Westport. He had become a solid citizen, a commuter, and a man who made money. I didn't know whether I should call him Chip anymore. He didn't look like the kind of person who would use a nickname.

He came out to the receptionist's desk wearing a dark-blue three-piece suit, and we exchanged the usual smiles, handshakes, and back slaps. Underneath it, though, I could see that he was worried. The situation was upsetting to him, and he wasn't sure if I had come as a friend or an enemy.

We went on talking for a few minutes, making conversation about the past. He wanted to know how long it had been since we'd seen each other, and I told him four years. He didn't want to believe me, but I remembered the restaurant where we had eaten lunch that day, and he finally remembered too.

"That was two kids and thirty pounds ago," he said. He made it sound as though he was talking about another century.

He led me out of the reception room down a hallway with thick burgundy carpeting, stylish spotlights, and expensively framed seventeenth-century etchings. The place had been redecorated since my last visit. Ryan and Baldwin, the two senior partners, were both ready to retire, and Chip had become the head man. The office had been remodeled to keep up with the times, and the decor served as a kind of advertisement to the clients, as if to say this was a first-class operation and naturally the fees were going to be high.

Halfway down the hall, Chip took me gently by the elbow and stopped. He wanted to talk to me before we walked in on his father, who was waiting in Chip's private office. I felt like a boxer being told the rules by a referee before the first round of a fight. The only thing Chip didn't know was that his father had already gone a few rounds with me in absentia.

He no longer seemed so glad to see me, and all the forced cheer of his greeting was gone. His face had become pinched with apprehension, as if I was some kind of bomb about to explode at any moment. He spoke to me almost in a whisper.

"Listen, Max, I don't know what you're up to, but go easy, okay? I don't want any trouble."

"I'm not here to cause trouble. The trouble started a long time ago, before I ever arrived on the scene."

"I mean, don't push too hard. My father has a bad heart, and I don't want anything to upset him."

"You don't have to worry about that. Guys like me can't upset your father. You should be worried about me, not him."

"Just remember that I did you a favor by setting this up."

"I've already put you in my will, so cool it, Chip. I'm not calling the shots, your father is."

Chip pursed his lips unhappily. He realized it was out of his control. "I knew it was a mistake," he said. "I knew I shouldn't have done it."

Before we went in, I changed the subject. "What's happening with Judy Chapman?"

"I've gotten Burleson for her." He looked at his watch. "They're probably meeting together right now."

"I'm going over there myself a little later. We're on the same side, Chip. Try to remember that."

"I know, I know," he groaned. "I just wish I wasn't on any side. I'm not cut out for this sort of thing."

"Buck up, lad," I said, clapping his shoulder. "Discomfort is good for you. It makes you tough."

Chip grimaced and opened the door of the office. His father was sitting in a leather lounge chair and staring out the window. Victor Contini was a short, pudgy man in his late sixties, who looked no more dangerous than a toad. He was dressed in casual clothes, with a flowery shirt under a navy-blue golf sweater, red and blue plaid slacks, and white shoes. If you didn't know who he was, you might have taken him for a senior citizen reclining in the sun at Miami Beach. The only thing that gave any hint he wasn't living on social security checks was the large diamond ring he wore on the pinkie of his left hand. He didn't get up when we entered.

"This is Max Klein, Pop," Chip said.

"Pleased to meet you, Mr. Klein," the old man said. He couldn't have cared less.

"Max and I went to law school together. He used to be quite a ball player in his day," Chip continued.

"Very nice," the old man replied. He made it sound as though he had just been handed a finger painting by a three-year-old. "Why don't you run along now, Chipper. Mr. Klein and I have business to discuss."

Chip blushed with embarrassment. He had been treated this way a thousand times by his father, and yet each time it came as a fresh humiliation. Instead of standing up to it years ago when it would have mattered, he had allowed himself to be dominated, and now it was too late for the relationship to change. Chip's solution had been to make himself into everything his father wasn't: studious, sincere, straightforward. In one way it had made his father proud of him. But in another way it had made it impossible for him ever to gain his father's respect. He had managed to make it on his own, but he was still nothing more than the obedient boy who brought home straight A's from school. He would never be treated as an equal.

"I'd rather stay, Pop," he said, making a token defense of his rights. "Max and I are old friends. We don't have any secrets from each other."

The old man spoke gently but firmly. "This is private stuff, Chip, and I don't think you should be here. It'll only take a few minutes."

Chip looked at me with an expression of hopelessness and envy, and then left the room without saying anything.

When he had gone, Victor Contini said, "Brian is a good boy, but he's an innocent. I don't like him getting mixed up in my business. There's business and then there's family, and my son is family. You shouldn't have called him to arrange this meeting, Klein. That's not playing by the rules, and a guy like you should know better."

"Maybe you should send me a copy of your rule book," I said. "It seems there are a lot of twists in the game you play. Like sending three against one. Like agreeing to come here today and then booking reservations for me in an abandoned quarry to make sure I'd never show up."

"Okay, so you're a big tough guy," Contini said in his hoarse, expressionless voice. "But from the looks of your face, you're not a well man, Klein. Maybe you should see a doctor."

I walked across the room and sat down on the window ledge behind Chip's desk, about four feet from Contini. I wanted to be face-to-face with him while we spoke. It was like looking at a sculpture of a bulldog. Contini's liver-spotted jowls hung in loose folds down the sides of his face, and his tiny dark eyes seemed to repel all light. There was too much shrewdness in them to betray any emotion. He had it down to a science.

"If you think my face looks bad," I said, "you should see the other guy. He's at the bottom of a big hole, keeping company with a bunch of stones."

"So I heard." Contini looked so relaxed that I kept expecting him to open up a newspaper and start reading as we talked. "But that was yesterday, and today is today. I'm not interested in the past."

"With a past like yours, I wouldn't think you'd like to do much looking back. But I'm asking you to make an exception for me. I want you to help me understand some things that happened five years ago. You see, Mr. Contini, the past sometimes has a funny way of catching up with the present."

"Maybe for some people, but not for me. If you want to talk about five years ago, okay, I'll talk about five years ago. But there's not much to say about the present. I could tell you about my golf scores, maybe, or about the restaurants I like best, but that's about all. I had open-heart surgery two years ago, and I don't do much business now. It's mostly family. You know, the kids, the grandchildren, picnics on Sunday, bedtime stories, boat rides, things like that."

"Sounds terrific. Too bad I didn't grow up in your family. Think of all the things I missed."

"I'm really not such a bad guy, Klein. Everybody loves me. I do people favors, and they remember me for my kindness."

"Like Bruno Pignato, I suppose. There's a man who was literally killed with kindness."

Contini met my eyes for the first time. He didn't care for my joke, and my insinuation seemed to offend him. "I don't like that kind of talk," he said in the same unmodulated voice. "Bruno Pignato was the son of a second cousin of mine, and I looked after him all his life. He was a very unhappy person, with lots of problems. Whoever whacked him had to be a real creep, one of them sick perverts."

"You mean to say you didn't have Pignato killed?"

"That's what I'm telling you—I didn't have him killed. Why would I have killed him when I treated him like my own son? Who do you think paid his doctor bills, gave him money for his medicine, and got him into one of those fancy private hospitals with the green grass and pretty nurses? That stuff ain't cheap, you know. I really cared about Bruno. I'd like to get my hands on the creep that did it to him."

"And now I suppose you're going to tell me Pignato never called you two days ago about seeing me?"

"I'm not going to tell you that, because it's not true. You know that, and I know that, so why beat around the bush? Bruno called me and told me about talking to you. You really upset him, Klein. It took me twenty minutes before I could figure out what he was saying, he was talking so crazy."

"We talked about five years ago," I said. "In particular, George Chapman's accident. And that's what I want to discuss with you too. If you can give me some decent answers, maybe I'll decide to leave you alone. But if you fool around with me, then I'll start digging even deeper. I've already found enough dirt to make a lot of trouble for you. If I go any farther, I'll probably have enough to put you away for a long time, Contini. You might think a guy like me doesn't count for much, but I've got two things going for me. I'm persistent, and I have a hard head."

Contini took out a huge cigar from his shirt pocket and studied it casually. "I don't like your act, Klein. You come on too strong when you don't have to, and you don't know what you're talking about. That's two things going against you. You think you're some kind of a smart aleck because you got out of a little scrape last night. But I was doing you a favor, and you shouldn't forget it. One word from me, and you don't breathe anymore. You owe me one, Klein, and I can make you pay up any time I want to."

"You're avoiding the subject, Contini. I asked you about George Chapman, not your opinion of me. When I decide to change my style, I'll ask you to write me a recommendation for a scholarship to the Dale Carnegie School."

"There's not much to say about George Chapman," Contini answered. "He's dead."

"You're very astute."

"So they tell me."

I stood up from the window ledge and walked back and forth in front of the old man's chair. He followed me lazily with his eyes, as if each time I came into view I was a different passerby, a new stranger deserving of a mildly curious glance.

"I want it all, Contini, from the very beginning. How you met Chapman. What kind of business you had with him. Why you arranged the accident five years ago. Why you sent him a threatening letter earlier this week. And why you had him killed in his apartment. The facts, Contini, from top to bottom, and everything in between."

Contini raised his right hand. "Slow down, cowboy—you're

going too fast. First you say you want to talk about five years ago, and I say okay, I'll talk about five years ago. But before I get a chance to say anything, you start asking me about last week. Now, I already told you to forget about recent things. I'm not involved, do you understand? I spend my time playing golf, and that's it. If you knew anything about anything, you'd know you were asking stupid questions. When business is over it's over, and that's the end of it. Sure I knew Chapman—what's the big deal? We did some business together, settled up, and that was that. The rest you can figure out for yourself. I'm not going to sit around here and give you my life story. You can go to the library and read about it there."

"How did you meet Chapman in the first place?"

"Chapman was a big man, right? And I was a big man, right? So it was only natural for us to get together. In a place like New York, it was only a matter of time."

"Forgive me if I sound a little incredulous," I said, "but I find it hard to imagine a guy with Chapman's class wanting to hang around with a mug like you."

Contini smiled, not so much at me, but inwardly, as if enjoying a private joke with himself. "What do you know about class, Mr. Private Detective? You think just because a guy is good-looking, wears nice clothes, and doesn't say 'ain't' that he's got class? You take a type like Chapman and scratch the surface, he's just like everybody else, maybe even a little worse. It's the ugly ones like me who've got all the class. We are what we are, and we don't pretend we're something else. We're the ones with character. Guys like Chapman aren't worth a tinker's fart."

"What were you into him for, Contini? What kind of blackmail scheme had you worked out? And why did you want him dead?"

"No blackmail," he said, waving off the word with his cigar. "Never any blackmail. I'm a businessman. Nothing more, nothing less. I don't go screwing around in people's private lives. Like

I said, Chapman and I had business. We settled up, and then the business was over."

"You mean you settled up. Chapman reneged on something, and you decided to arrange the accident to teach him a lesson. Nobody reneges on Victor Contini. A deal's a deal, and if you try to back out of it, you get burned. Isn't that right?"

"Whatever. You're the one with all the bright answers. Why bother to ask me?"

"It won't take me long to find out what you were working on with Chapman. And when I do, I'm going to blow the thing open. It's going to be a lot of fun for me to see you have your day in court."

Contini laughed. It wasn't much of a laugh, hardly more than a grunt. But for him it was just short of rolling in the aisles. The situation was too fraught with irony for him to contain himself.

"The only trouble with your plan is that there's never going to be any day in court. You're forgetting about my heart. No court doctor would ever let me go to trial. It would be bad for my health, too much of a strain on me. You can find out all you like about five years ago, but it's not going to do you any good. You can't touch me."

"It doesn't make any difference," I said. "I'll expose you, give it to all the papers, and the effect will be the same."

"Rumors, gossip, hearsay," Contini said with complete indifference. "I've been through it before, and it doesn't bother me. If you took all the things they've printed about me and put them in a book, I'd come out looking worse than what's-his-name, Nixon. Let them think what they want. I know how to live with myself, and that's all that matters. How your grandchildren feel about you, that's what counts."

"You're not only one of the great golfers of our time," I said, "but you're also a Zen master. How do you find enough time in the day to pursue so much wisdom?"

He ignored my remark and went on with his own train of thought. "I'll tell you what, Klein. Maybe we can get together after all. You find out who killed Bruno, and I'll give you two grand, straight across the table."

"So you can send your boys after the guy who did it?"

"I'm going to find out anyway, so it doesn't matter. I just thought you'd like to make some extra cash. It's no skin off my back who does the work."

"Thanks, I appreciate the offer. But I don't want to have to cover up all the mirrors in my house. I'm still going to need them when I shave."

"Whatever you say, Klein. No hard feelings."

"That's right. No hard feelings. No feelings at all."

Contini closed his eyes and didn't say anything for a while. I was beginning to think he had drifted off to sleep.

"This has been a pleasant conversation, Klein," he said at last, opening his eyes. "But it's getting late, and it's time for my pills. I've got so many pills it sometimes takes me ten minutes to get them all down. But I do what the doctor says. I stick to my diet, and I don't smoke these cigars anymore." He held up the cigar and examined it wistfully. "Two dollars apiece, and I just play with them in my mouth. But that's the way it goes. I take care of myself because I'm planning to stick around for a few more years. That's what you call character."

I left him there on the lounge chair, looking at his cigar. His whole life had become one long leisure moment spent by the side of an imaginary swimming pool, and nothing could faze him anymore. It had amused him to talk to me for a while, but in the end it had left him cold. He had been through it so many times before, he could have done it in his sleep. I wished him luck with his pills and walked out the door. Chip wasn't in sight when I reached the reception room, and I didn't have time to go looking for him. He probably didn't want to speak to me anyway.

14

THE SAME DOORMAN was on duty in front of the Chapmans' building. He had put his overcoat in mothballs for the summer and was now dressed in a lightweight uniform. Otherwise, he looked the same, if a trifle less substantial. He greeted me with a sad smile.

"That was a nasty business you walked in on yesterday, Mr. Klein," he said.

I nodded. "It's not the kind of thing you expect to find when you go calling on someone."

"No, I wouldn't think so. At least not in a building like this one." He seemed to be one of those people who thought of violence as a disease that struck only the lower classes.

"I was wondering," I said, "if anyone came to see Mr. Chapman between the time Mrs. Chapman went out and the time I got here."

"I've already talked to the police about that," he said, studying the bruises on my face but not daring to mention them. "There was no one."

"Is there another way of getting into the building besides the front door?"

"There's the service entrance downstairs around the side, but that door is usually locked."

"Was it locked two days ago?"

"Not in the morning. Some workers from Con Edison were here, and they were running in and out for several hours."

"Who's responsible for keeping the door locked?"

"The superintendent."

"Is he the only one with a key?"

"No, everyone in the building has a key. It's convenient to use that door when there's something bulky to take upstairs. There's more room in the service elevator."

"Thanks. This will be a help."

"But I already told this to the police yesterday."

"I'm sure you did. But the police sometimes forget what they're told."

He called the Chapman apartment on the intercom phone, and I went inside to get the elevator to the eleventh floor. It was quarter past twelve.

The door was opened by an older version of Judy, a woman of about fifty-five with the same large brown eyes and lean, athletic body as her daughter. She was puffy around the eyes and was wearing slightly too much makeup. I imagined she had done a lot of crying since yesterday. She looked at me as if I had just stepped off a flying saucer.

"Yes?" It was the same voice that had spoken to me on the phone earlier.

"I'm Max Klein. The doorman just called up with my name."

"Of course." She was too distracted to feel embarrassed by her lack of hospitality. "Come right in, please."

Judy was sitting at a round table in the far corner of the living room with a gray-haired man I took to be Burleson and a younger man who was probably one of his associates. Judy was wearing a simple cotton dress with blue and white checks, and it made her look very young, more like a college student than a thirty-year-old widow. I had somehow been imagining her dressed in black, displaying all the traditional signs of mourning. But then this was not an ordinary situation. Her back was to the wall, and she was fighting for her life. No sooner had she absorbed the shock of her husband's death than she was forced to defend herself for his murder. The simple dress and schoolgirl look were a badge of innocence she had put on to prove the accusation wrong. No woman who looked like that could possibly be a murderer. I wondered if she was wearing it for the benefit of her lawyer or to reassure herself, and I wondered if she had done it consciously or not. In the end, it probably didn't make any difference.

She smiled when she saw me and stood up from her chair. I walked over to the table, and Burleson and his associate stood up as well. Judy introduced me to the two men, and we all shook hands. They had already been told who I was, and they greeted me more as a colleague than a stranger. We were all in it together, they seemed to be saying, so let's get down to work. I was encouraged that Burleson didn't resent my presence, which had often been my experience with lawyers. He was one of the best in the business, and he knew that someone like me on the case could be a big help to him.

He was a curious mixture of flamboyance and reserve. His dark-gray suit was expensive, subdued, and perfectly tailored, which showed that he was a man of the world, someone for whom success came naturally. At the same time, he sported an almost foppish mane of long silvery hair, which showed that he was an eccentric, perhaps even a genius, who could dazzle you with unpredictable brilliance in the courtroom. It was a carefully studied image, and he gave off the kind of self-confidence that seemed calculated to soothe the nerves of his clients. It wasn't a style I either liked or felt comfortable with, but I wasn't about to pick a quarrel with him. He had made a career out of winning highly publicized trials, and it was only natural for him to be something of a performer. The only thing I cared about was that he get Judy acquitted.

"I wonder if I could have a word with Max in private, Mr. Burleson," Judy said. "There are some things I want to discuss with him before the three of you sit down together."

"Go right ahead," Burleson answered. "Harlow and I have a lot to go over. Take your time."

Judy led me out of the living room, down the hallway, and into her bedroom. She closed the door quietly, and then without a word came over to me and put her arms around my body.

"Hold me tight," she said. "I'm so scared I don't think I can stand up anymore."

I wrapped my arms around her and let her put all her weight against me. We stood there for a moment in silence, her head leaning on my chest. I kissed her on the forehead and cheeks and told her not to worry, that it would be all cleared up soon. She closed her eyes and parted her lips, asking me to kiss her, wanting me to take her, as if she could wipe out the reality of the situation by losing herself in my body. I made myself back off.

"We've got to talk, Judy. There's no time now."

"I just wish I didn't have to think about it," she almost whispered. "I just wish this had never happened."

"But it has happened, and now we have to do something about it."

I walked her slowly to the bed and sat her down. She held on to my hand, unwilling to let go. It was as if I had become a source of electricity and could keep her functioning even though there was no life left in her. She looked up at me and seemed to notice the condition of my face for the first time. It brought her back to earth.

"Good Lord! What happened to you? You look awful."

"It's a long story," I said. "You remember my asking you about Chip Contini's father the other day. This was done by a few of the surgeons who work for him."

"Then he's involved in this after all, isn't he?"

"He's involved, but to what extent I can't say. There's no question that he arranged your husband's accident five years ago. I know that now beyond the slightest doubt. I don't think he was the one who sent the threatening letter, and I'm fairly certain he's not responsible for what happened in this apartment yesterday."

She reached for her cigarettes on the bedside table, lit one with trembling hands, and took a deep drag. "You mean George's accident wasn't an accident? Are you saying that Victor Contini was trying to kill him?"

For five years she had been living with the assumption that her husband's crash was a freak occurrence, an act of God. Now she had learned that it was the act of a single man, and this new knowledge frightened her. It was like discovering you've been living with a defective furnace for five years and that at any moment your house could have blown up. It was the horror of hindsight.

"Nearly everything I've discovered about George has been unexpected," I said. "And Contini isn't the only one who had it in for him. No one I've spoken to has had anything nice to say about your husband."

"I told you he's a difficult person," she said, and then stopped, momentarily confused. "I mean was. Was, damn it. George is dead, isn't he? I still can't get used to it." She looked up at the door, as if half expecting him to walk into the room.

"I know you've probably been through it a hundred times already with the police and Burleson, but I want you to tell me what happened here yesterday morning. The D.A. will be building his case on the fact that you had breakfast with George in the kitchen and that you were seen leaving the building very close to the time he swallowed the poison. I've got to know what really happened, or else I'm not going to be able to do much."

She put out her cigarette in the ashtray and then immediately lit another one. She was chain-smoking in the way some people drink. She didn't know she was doing it. "It's very simple," she said, "and I tried to explain it to that man Grimes, but he just wouldn't believe me." She paused and took a deep breath. "George and I had an argument. He had heard me talking on the phone to you, and he got very angry. He flew into a rage, saying that I was meddling in his business, and that if I ever did it again he would kill me. It was one of our typical fights, I suppose. I thought it might calm George down if I offered to make him breakfast. He apologized, and for a few minutes it looked like the whole thing had blown over. But then, as soon as we sat down at the table, he started in on me again. He was like a crazy man. He said that I was throwing myself at you, that I was acting like a cheap slut. He said some terrible things, Max, and I couldn't listen anymore. I just turned around and ran out of the apartment. When I got back a few hours later, the police were there and George was dead."

"What about the poison? Grimes says he has definite proof that it was bought by you."

"It's true. I did buy it." She raised her shoulders and let them drop with a painful smile. "That's the trouble. The more I tell the truth, the worse it looks."

"Why did you buy it?"

"George asked me to. He said there were mice in the kitchen at night and he wanted to get rid of them."

"Were there any?"

"I don't think so. I don't remember that George ever really used the poison. And I'm positive that he didn't keep it in the kitchen cabinet, because I know I never saw it there."

I got up from the bed and walked around the room, trying to assimilate this new information, trying to fit it into the new pattern I sensed was gradually taking shape. I knew I would have to begin looking at Chapman's murder from a completely different perspective, but I didn't yet know how. Judy watched me with a worried expression and finally asked me if anything was wrong. I avoided answering her question directly.

"It's going to be a difficult case for Burleson," I said slowly. "Everything stacks up so neatly against you. The police are satisfied that you did it and are no longer working on the case. It's with the district attorney now. Which means the pressure is off the real murderer and he can just sit back and wait for you to be convicted."

"I trust Burleson. He won't let me get convicted."

"I don't trust anyone. Not in a case like this. The evidence is just too good, and I don't like to think of what a jury might do to you.

Your husband was a very popular man, and when they find out about your affair with Briles, they'll have the motive they need."

She lit yet another cigarette and stared down at the bed. "It does look bad, doesn't it?"

"It's bad unless I can find the person who did it."

She looked up with a flickering of hope in her eyes. "But won't it count for something when they find out that Bill and I broke it off six months ago?"

"They'll also find out that you broke off once before and managed to get back together again. But more importantly, they'll know you weren't a faithful and devoted wife."

"And it doesn't matter that I tried to be," she said glumly.

"Tell me a little about Briles," I asked, wanting to jar her from her thoughts.

"What do you mean?"

"How did he take it six months ago when you told him you were calling it off?"

"He was very upset. He begged me not to."

"Is he someone given to jealousy?"

"No, I don't think so. Bill is an intellectual, and he usually manages to rationalize his feelings, to see every issue from the other person's side. That's why he's such a good sociologist. If he has any failing, it's a lack of aggressiveness. He's not the type to get very heated up about anything."

"Does he still love you?"

"I'm sure he does."

"And what about you? How do you feel?"

She looked up at me with those big brown eyes, which seemed to have been robbed of all their radiance. "It's all over, Max. I'm not going back to him, no matter what happens."

I RETURNED TO the living room, and Judy went off to the kitchen to be with her mother. I outlined for Burleson and Harlow what had been happening to me since George Chapman walked into my office Wednesday morning. The important thing, I explained to them, was for me to go on with my investigation as before. If I could turn up something that proved Judy's innocence, then the case would never have to go to court. In the meantime, they would prepare their defense. Burleson asked what I thought my chances were of turning up anything, and I said they weren't good. He and Harlow were not too optimistic about their own prospects either. We all agreed that we would have to get lucky. We shook hands and promised to stay in touch.

As I was walking down the front hall on my way out of the apartment, the doorbell rang and I opened the door. It was Briles. He looked me over with a sour face.

"What are you doing here?" he asked.

"I was just going to ask you the same thing."

"I came to see Mrs. Chapman. I'm a good friend of hers."

"That's not what you told me the other day. I thought you hardly knew her."

"I don't like your tone, Klein. You shouldn't butt into things that don't concern you."

"But it does concern me. I'm working on the case. If you'd been a little more forthcoming with me the other day, maybe Chapman would still be alive."

"You have no idea what you're talking about."

"But then again," I went on, "maybe it doesn't matter to you that Chapman is dead. With the husband out of the picture, you can come back and try to make another play for the grieving widow. Maybe this time you can win her over."

Briles' face tensed with anger, and for a second I thought he was going to react with his fists. "I'm not a violent man, Klein. But I can be pushed just so far. I find your comments obscene. You have no right to speak to me that way."

"Why don't you try to make something of it, Professor?" I

said, continuing to bait him. "You might feel better if you let it all explode."

I wasn't sure why Briles' presence had triggered off such hostility in me. It was almost as though I considered him a rival, a threat to the way I felt about Judy. I was allowing my own emotions to interfere with the case, and I knew I was acting stupidly. But I couldn't help myself. I felt an almost chemical desire to tangle with him.

I never got to find out what his breaking point was. At that moment Judy appeared in the hallway.

"Bill. What in the world are you doing here?"

"Hello, Judy," he said, forcing a smile. "I was coming in to see you, but then this thug decided to block my way."

"We were just having a conversation," I explained. "About what motivates people's behavior."

Judy was upset by the anger in our voices, and she reacted with anger of her own. "I don't care what you were talking about. It's stupid for two adult men to carry on like children. Why don't you leave him alone, Max? He hasn't done anything to you. There are enough problems in this house without bringing in a shouting match."

"It's all over now," I said. "I was just leaving."

As I walked out the door, I turned to catch a last glimpse of Judy's face. She was looking at Briles, and her expression was one of both hatred and pity. There was a darkness in her eyes I had never seen before, a depth of passion that was almost frightening. I bore the image of that face in my mind for the rest of the day.

15

I STARTED ALL OVER again. I decided to forget what I had learned, to unteach myself the lessons of the past few days, to go back to zero. From the very beginning, I realized, I had been running around in circles. Chapman had come to me with a threatening letter, and after his murder I had gone on assuming that the letter writer and the murderer were the same person. But that was making things too simple for myself. There was nothing to say that only one person was involved. The letter writer seemed to have gained access to some secret Chapman wanted to protect. And if one person knew the secret, it was possible that another person knew it as well. In fact, it was more than likely. Chapman had received the threat on Monday, and just three days later—too soon for him to begin getting scared—he had been poisoned. The letter writer would not have acted so quickly. It had to mean that Chapman was being squeezed from the other end, that something else was going on at the same time. From all I had learned about Chapman, this made sense. He was a man who had been involved in many things, had known many people, and had made many enemies. Any one of them could have wanted him dead.

The thing I needed most was Chapman's secret. I hadn't known what I was looking for during my first encounters with Light and Contini, but now that I did, I wouldn't let them hold out on me again. In the meantime, I decided to cover some ground. If I studied the map carefully, maybe I would find a road to get me off the detour I had been following since Wednesday. I was tired of eating dust.

I got back to my office at two-thirty with a fresh pack of cigarettes, a couple of sandwiches, and a few beers in a paper bag. I settled into the chair behind the desk, laid out my lunch, and got busy with the telephone.

I called Abe Callahan first. Chapman's death had brought him back to New York early, and I figured he might be willing to talk to me. The first thing he said was that he remembered me from the Banks case. It seemed that everyone remembered me from the Banks case and that for the past five years I had ceased to exist. I had been news for a couple of days, like one of those characters who mountain climbs to the top of the World Trade Center or walks across the Brooklyn Bridge on his hands, and then I had vanished into the smog. Pretty soon my name would be mentioned in one of those "Where Are They Now?" columns.

Callahan didn't say if he was pleased or displeased by the memory, and I didn't ask him. I told him I was working on the Chapman case.

"There is no Chapman case," he said. "Or don't you read the papers? His wife was arrested yesterday, and everybody's talking about what a great job the police did. Everybody but me, that is. Not only did we lose one of the best-looking candidates this country's seen in a long time, but we also lost one hell of a fine man."

"I read the papers. But as I said, I'm working on the Chapman case."

"What are you, one of those believers in lost causes?"

"I don't give myself labels. I just go about my work until it's finished. And at the moment it's far from finished. I'm calling you for some information."

"What kind?"

"Private information. I'd like to know if you ran any security checks on Chapman in the past few months, and if so, whether you turned up anything questionable."

There was a pause at the other end. "A lot of reporters would cut off their right arms for that kind of stuff. Why should I give it to you when I wouldn't dream of giving it to them?"

"Because a reporter doesn't care about anything but a good byline, and because I won't pass on what you tell me. Because I care about cracking this thing, and because I don't have much time left."

There was another pause, and I could almost feel Callahan wrestling with the decision. I took another sip of beer.

"All right, Klein, here it is, for whatever it's worth. We did do an investigation, but only because the political climate is what it is. Five or six years ago this kind of thing would have been unthinkable. But you know what happens today when there's the slightest hint of scandal. A political party has to be very cautious. In some sense we're almost doing a disservice to the people we represent."

"You don't have to give me a preamble. I'm aware of the situation. Just the facts will do."

"Well, the facts are these. We discovered that George was involved in a potentially dangerous situation over a contract dispute with Charles Light, the owner of the Americans."

"I know about that. Was there anything else?"

"We also discovered that George's marriage was liable to blow up right in the middle of the campaign."

"Everyone knows about his marriage now. I'm thinking more in terms of something that had to be hidden at all costs. Something criminal, maybe, or at least something so dubious that it would have discredited him."

"No, there was nothing like that. The two things I mentioned were serious enough. But we decided that George could handle it if either one became an issue."

"Who did the investigation for you?"

"One of the men from the Dampler Agency. A guy by the name of Wallace Smart. And he did a good job too. Stayed on it for more than a month."

"You really thought Chapman was going to win, didn't you?"

"Let's put it this way. All our private polls put him at sixty-three percent against the strongest Republican, and that's almost unheard of. George was a natural. He had all the instincts, all the moves. I wouldn't have been surprised to see him run for President one day."

"Interesting."

"Interesting, my ass. It's a tragedy, that's what it is. A goddamn brutal tragedy."

I CALLED THE Dampler Agency and asked to speak to Wallace Smart. That was impossible, I was told. Mr. Smart had left the agency three weeks ago. Did they know where he could be reached? No, he had retired from detective work altogether. He had come into a small inheritance and had decided to pull up stakes. The word was he had gone off to Hawaii. I asked if he had any family in the city I might contact to find out his address. No, Mr. Smart's wife and children had been killed in a car accident ten or twelve years ago. He had no living relatives.

I took out a blank sheet of paper from my desk drawer and wrote down Wallace Smart's name in large block letters. The number of people who knew Chapman's secret had now been increased to three. Smart had retired on his so-called inheritance, which meant that he had sold his information to someone who could meet his price, someone with money to spare. Charles Light, for example. If all else failed, I could always go off looking for Smart. Mr. Wally Smart: ex-detective, ex–New Yorker, a seller of secrets. My ace in the hole.

I finished my second sandwich and then spent five minutes in intimate conversation with a sweet, drawling operator from Charleston, South Carolina. She very patiently helped me track down the name of a restaurant owned by Randy Phibbs. It turned out to be Dandy Randy's: Ribs by Phibbs. As she flipped through the book, she asked me what the weather was like in New York, called me "Sugar," and said I had the sweetest accent she'd ever heard, just like one of those actors on television. She sounded so pretty, so engaging, that I was reluctant to hang up. It didn't matter that she was probably a sixty-year-old grandmother with lumbago.

Five years ago Randy Phibbs had been an aging utility infielder for the Americans. Of all the players on the team, he was the only one who had managed to form any kind of friendship with Chapman. Phibbs spent most of his time on the bench, but he could still do a solid job at second base for a couple of weeks if necessary. In the World Series five years ago, he wound up playing the last three games, got four or five hits, and turned in some sparkling fielding plays. It was an impressive enough performance to prolong his career for one more season. He was a player who did it with desire rather than talent, and I had always enjoyed watching him stuff his cheek with tobacco, pound his glove in an old-fashioned gung-ho way, and scream at the umpires until the veins in his neck stood out like snakes. He and Chapman made an unlikely pair of friends. But Phibbs was probably the only player on the team not intimidated by Chapman's being an Ivy League intellectual and a possible Hall of Famer. He came from a universe in which these things simply didn't matter. Phibbs was a good ol' boy, and as far as he was concerned, Chapman was a good ol' boy too.

It took him a few minutes to understand why I had called. He had heard about Chapman's murder on television last night, and he also knew about Judy's arrest from a report on the radio today. He called her a nice little swatch of woman and was damned if he knew why she'd want to do in poor ol' George. George was his great buddy, and they still sent each other Christmas cards every year.

"I want you to think back to George's last season five years ago, Randy."

"I'm with you, buddy," he said. "Five years ago would be when George hit all them home runs."

"You were his best friend, Randy, so you would be able to tell me better than anyone else what I need to know."

"I wasn't just his best friend," Phibbs said matter-of-factly. "I was the only damned friend George had on the whole team. He never said more than but a few words to the rest of them, like as if he really didn't want to be there. George was a tough one. Never would take no shit from nobody. But he and me, we hit it off just fine. I think he liked the way I talked."

"Can you remember if George acted at all differently that last year, whether there seemed to be anything weighing on his mind?"

"There was always something weighing on George's mind, mister. He had one of them big minds, if you know what I mean, and everything that got inside it made itself real comfortable and settled in there for a long time. George did more thinking than any two men I ever saw."

"But did you notice anything special about that last year? Did he seem to be pressing more than he had in the past?"

"George was always what you call a presser. He took that ol' game of baseball mighty serious, sort of like it wasn't a game no more, but real work. I don't think he ever got much fun out of it, he was always concentrating so hard. A dumb cracker like me, it just tickled me every time I walked out on the field."

"So there was no real change in the last year?"

"Well, I'm just thinking . . . though I don't know if it's much for a dee-tective like you to sink your teeth into. But George did act a little strange at times. Long about the middle of the season he'd start coming up to me before the game and say, 'Randy, today I'm going to go three for four,' and damn if he didn't get angry at hisself if he went two for four. Once he hit a frigging two-run double in the ninth inning to win a game and come back to the clubhouse shaking his head, saying it should have been a home run."

"Did he seem more interested in his own performance than in how the team did?"

"No, I wouldn't say that. George always wanted to win as much as the next fella. It was just that he had these high standards, you know, like he had to carry the whole team on his back. When you come to think of it, I guess he did."

There was a short pause, and I asked, "How's the restaurant business, Randy?"

"Real fine, real fine. I gave the hometown folks a lot of thrills when I was playing up North, and they remember ol' Randy Phibbs."

"If I ever get to Charleston, I'll be sure to stop in for dinner."

"You do that," he said enthusiastically. "You'll get a plate of ribs that'll stick to your ribs and make you the happiest damn Yankee that ever stepped foot in this place."

AFTER CHARLESTON I dialed San Diego and spoke to the Mexican housekeeper who worked for Chapman's parents. The phone had been ringing steadily since yesterday morning, and both the mother and father had stopped taking calls. In between the housekeeper's ranting about what a terrible thing had happened, I managed to learn that arrangements were being made to have Chapman's body flown back to California and that the funeral would take place in San Diego.

My next call was to Minnesota. Chapman seemed to have no real friends, no one he confided in, and I wondered if he hadn't kept in touch with his older brother, Alan, a doctor who lived in Bloomington. The nurse at Alan Chapman's office told me the doctor had gone to San Diego last night. There had been a tragedy in the family, she explained. Yes, I said, I had heard something about it.

My answering service had two messages for me. One was from Alex Vogel, a reporter from the *Post,* and the other had come from Brian Contini just minutes before I returned to my office. I figured Vogel had gotten my name from a contact in the police department and that he wanted a story from me about discovering Chapman's body. The *Post* was very big on doing background scoops connected with the bloody stuff on the front page. It had become the kind of paper that treated every murder, fire, and mugging as the first spark of the apocalypse, and I tried to stay away from it now on principle. If Vogel wanted to talk to me, he would have to keep trying.

Chip was gone from his office when I called, gone for the day, the secretary said. I asked her if she knew why he had called me, and in one of those bored, I-only-work-here voices, she said she didn't. I guessed that he and his father had taken off early for their family weekend in Westport. It disappointed me that Chip was leaving everything to Burleson in preparing Judy's defense. The practice of law had become a cozy refuge of documents, contracts, and hearty handshakes for him, and he had become too timid to venture outside it. Like the roll of soft flesh that had developed around his middle, there were now several layers of fat around his mind that helped to insulate him from the real world. And this was the same man who had talked about going straight into the Legal Aid Society after he graduated from law school. I wondered how long it would be before his arteries hardened.

I had just put my hand on the receiver to make another call when the phone rang, sending its metallic vibrations into my palm. After dialing out so many times in the past hour and a half, it seemed almost unnatural that anyone should want to call me. I hoped it wasn't the reporter from the *Post,* and my wish came true. It was Muffle Mouth.

"You don't give up easily, do you?" I said.

"And neither do you, Klein. You have been watched for the entire day, and my conclusion is that you have no intention of doing what you were asked to do."

"I've been going through travel brochures ever since I got back to my office. You wouldn't believe the number of places you can go to these days on the American plan. But you'll be happy to know that I've finally made my decision. I want to spend my vacation in Anchorage, Alaska. The problem is that the only way to get there from New York is by tramp steamer through the Panama Canal, and the next ship doesn't leave for another six months."

"I suggest you pick another vacation spot."

"Well, I do have a second choice. New York City. They say it's a great place to visit, even though most people don't want to live there."

"You won't be living anywhere if you decide to stay."

"You must be the nervous type. I already got the message this morning. It's not going to get any clearer if you keep repeating it."

"Then why don't you listen?"

"For two good reasons. I have work to do here, and I'm not afraid of you."

"You'll be sorry you said that. Just remember that you've been warned."

"I'll go right out now and buy some string to tie around my finger."

"Walking the streets is going to be dangerous for you from now on. Any step you take might well be your last."

"It's pretty dangerous for the hookers too, but they seem to make out all right. Maybe I'll get lucky."

"Impossible, Klein. Your luck has just run out."

"Thanks for the tip. I was going to put some money on a horse tomorrow, but maybe I won't bother now."

"There are a lot of things you won't be bothering about, Mr. Klein. Your future has suddenly become so short it wouldn't stand knee-high to a midget."

"A pretty image," I said. "I'll have to use that one sometime."

But Muffle Mouth didn't hear me. He had already hung up.

I SWEPT THE CRUMBS off my desk and threw the sandwich wrappers and beer cans into the trash. It was four-fifteen. I started to open the safe to get out my .38 in case Muffle Mouth was waiting for me outside, but then I remembered that I didn't have a gun anymore. It had been taken away from me last night and lost somewhere in the quarry. I wondered if it would come back to haunt me.

There was no one lurking about the street, but I decided to take a cab anyway, just to be cautious. It took twenty minutes to reach the Eighth Street Bookstore. Along with the Gotham Book Mart and a handful of other places in the city, the Eighth Street was dedicated to the idea that books live in their own special time and do not suddenly wither away when the new spring list arrives. You didn't rush in there to plunk your money down for the latest nine-hundred-page saga written by a computer masquerading as a lady novelist from Beverly Hills, you came to make your own choices. There were some books of poetry that hung around on the shelf for six or seven years before the right buyer came along. The idea was that good books manage to survive us all.

I told myself there was no time to do any browsing and went straight up to the third floor, where the books on history, sociology, and psychology were kept. Six of William Briles' eleven books were available in paperback. I looked over the titles and finally decided on three of them, *In and Out: The Life of a Professional Thief; The Other Side of the Law: Investigations into Criminal Behavior;* and *The Gangster in the Gray Flannel Suit: The Mafia Leader as Businessman.*

The young man behind the cash register was wearing an army fatigue shirt and had the open-eyed expression of someone new on the job. He seemed amused by my choice of reading matter. I must not have looked like the studious type to him.

"Actually, I'm thinking of a career in crime," I said, "and I thought I would do a little boning up before I got started."

He smiled, happy to play along. "What are you going to do for your first job?"

"I was planning to rob a bank. What do you think?"

He shook his head. "Too risky. I'd go in for something a little more respectable. Maybe blackmail."

"The only problem is that you have to find a victim first, and that could run into a lot of work."

He waved his arm in a broad gesture that included all the customers in the store. "Everyone's a victim," he said. "Just take your pick. I'll bet you there's not one person in this whole city who doesn't have something to hide."

"You sound like you just came out of a Jimmy Cagney movie."

"Yeah." He nodded sheepishly. "I go to a lot of flicks."

The bill came to more than fifteen dollars. I wondered how much of it would go into Briles' pocket and solaced myself with the thought that I could write it off as an expense.

Forty minutes later I was back in my office armed with a takeout pizza, a few more cans of beer, and my books. I sprawled out on the couch, made myself comfortable, and spent the next several hours reading. I felt the night gradually come on as the street emptied of sounds and traffic. West Broadway was a daytime neighborhood, and by dinner hour there was nothing left to it but darkness. I no longer felt the presence of the city, and I read with the quickness and attention of a student cramming for a final exam.

By nine-thirty I decided I had had enough for one evening. I washed up in the basin, brushed the lint off my jacket, and got ready to go out again. It seemed as good a time as any to pay an unannounced call on Charles Light.

The weather had turned cool, and I walked uptown at a brisk pace, hoping a cab would show up in the deserted street. I had gone about a block and a half when the first shot came humming by my ear and landed in the brick wall to my left. I fell to the pavement without thinking—as if by ducking after the shot I could avoid being hit. Panic sometimes makes the body act before the brain has time to give it instructions. I was still on the ground, realizing that I had to get up and away from there, when the second shot was fired. It churned up the sidewalk and sent concrete dust flying into my face. I rolled toward the darkness of the building and heard the third shot go through the window above my head. Shattered glass fell on top of me, and a burglar alarm immediately went off inside. It was probably the noise of the alarm that saved me. I had nowhere to hide, and if the gunman had moved in on me then, it would have been all over. But the noise scared him off. I heard the sound of running footsteps across the street, and for a moment I couldn't believe they were running away. But then they were gone. In less than thirty seconds, I had passed from life into death and then back into life again. I said a little prayer of thanks to the owner of the electrical parts shop whose window had been broken. Muffle Mouth had been wrong. I wasn't at the end of my luck yet. And I had my beating heart to prove it.

16

IT WAS ONE OF THOSE New York mansions Henry James might have written about. Standing in floodlit dignity on a side street off Park Avenue, it made you think of women in long white dresses, musical soirees, and grim black-suited men discussing why Teddy Roosevelt's foreign policy was good for business. The Light House, as it was called, had been in the family for generations, and it was a monument to a lost age of imperialism, hard currency, and cheap labor. The tour buses usually made a stop there so the people from Wichita could go back home with a lasting impression of what New York wealth looked like. This was not your quick postwar-boom money from Houston and Los Angeles that drove around in white Cadillacs. The Light money was so old it had to be pushed around in a wheelchair. Little matter that the wheelchair was slightly larger than the *Titanic.* Someone could always be hired to push it.

The servants, of course, were no longer around at this hour to answer the door. I stood in front of the massive grillwork that guarded the entrance and pushed the bell. It was connected to an intercom system that looked like something from a radio control tower. I waited, looked at my watch, and rang again after a minute. I repeated the process. Just when I was debating whether to push the button a fourth time, Light's voice came through the speaker. There was no static or crackling in the machine, and I could hear him as clearly as if he had been standing next to me.

"Go away, or I'll call the police," he said.

"It's Klein, Mr. Light. I've got to talk to you."

"We did all our talking yesterday. There's nothing more to say."

"Just ten minutes, that's all I ask. It can't make much difference to you now. The game with Chapman is over, and you've come out on top."

Instead of answering, Light rang the buzzer that automatically unlatched the door, and I let myself in. I walked up the vestibule stairs, and another buzzer went off, opening the inner door. I crossed the threshold and found myself standing in an entrance hall as big as the whole first floor of a normal house. There were black and white square tiles on the floor and a huge cut-glass chandelier on the ceiling about twenty feet up. It was the kind of room that had been built for the sole purpose of impressing anyone who walked into it. I let myself be impressed.

Light entered the hall wearing khaki pants, slippers, and a green pullover, looking like someone who had spent the day cruising on a yacht. He eyed me with amusement and said, "You seem to have been busy since I saw you last."

I glanced down at my jacket and saw that it was torn at the elbow. "Yeah," I said. "Yesterday I accidentally got mixed up with the lions' food at the Central Park Zoo, and then tonight I thought it would be too boring to take a cab over here, so I decided to crawl. It's fun, but a little rough on clothes."

Light grinned vaguely, turned on his heel, and led me through the living room, through another room, and then down a hallway that brought us to a small room under the back stairs. One wall was lined with glassed-in shelves that held black stamp binders arranged in alphabetical order. There were several gaps in the rows for special displays of framed stamps and first day cover items. A ten-foot-long light table occupied most of the opposite wall, and in the middle of the room there was a round oak table cluttered with open stamp binders, loose stamps, a set of tweezers, glassine envelopes, and a magnifying glass. I had never seen a room like this in a house before. It was like walking into a mausoleum.

"This, as you may have gathered," he said with unmistakable pride, "is the stamp room. The temperature and humidity are controlled to guard against moisture damage. Take a look around. This is probably the most valuable collection in the country."

"Very interesting," I said, browsing at the displays behind the glass. "It must be wonderful to be able to lose yourself in such a stimulating hobby." He didn't hear the irony in my voice.

"Yes. I try to give it at least a few hours a week. It's a way for me to commune with myself and keep in touch with the past. The whole history of the modern world is in stamps. They are the one thing in everyday life that contains a record of the important events that define a period." He stopped abruptly, suddenly aware of himself. "But of course you're not interested in stamps."

"On the contrary. I'm interested in everything you're interested in, Mr. Light. I've been spending a lot of time lately trying to understand you. Nothing is irrelevant to me where you're concerned."

"You do tend to push rather hard, don't you?" he said pompously. "Ringing my bell at ten o'clock is something I could easily have you arrested for, if I felt like it. Fortunately for you, I don't feel like it tonight. That's because I'm in an excellent mood. I'm celebrating George Chapman's death, which has given me no end of joy."

"You don't have to put on an act for my benefit, Mr. Light. Celebrating is actually the last thing in the world you feel like doing tonight. You're upset that Chapman is dead. You win the game, yes, but at the same time you're denied the pleasure of playing. It's more like a forfeit. You were looking forward to destroying George Chapman in public. It meant so much to you that you were willing to run over anyone who stood in your way. And now suddenly you're very confused about how things have turned out. That's the only reason you let me in tonight. You think I might have something important to tell you."

Light sat down in an armchair to the side of the round table and studied me carefully. "You're a clever man, Mr. Klein," he said quietly. "I believe I've underestimated you."

"I'm not that clever. If I was really clever, it wouldn't have taken me two days to figure it out, and maybe Chapman would still be alive."

"Ridiculous. Chapman was killed by his wife. His death had nothing to do with anything." He picked up the magnifying glass from the table and began playing with it nervously. "It was strictly a family affair."

"That's the official version. It makes for a good story, but unfortunately there's no truth in it. Judy Chapman is no more guilty than Mahatma Gandhi."

Light seemed to take this as a veiled accusation. "Just what are you trying to say, Klein? That you're on the prowl for suspects and you think you can somehow drag me into this?" He waved the magnifying glass at me in a gesture of disgust. "I'm completely out of it. My hands are clean."

"I'm not saying you had Chapman killed. I just finished

explaining why. But your hands are not clean, Mr. Light. In fact, they're just about as dirty as your mind." I walked around the table slowly, wanting to leave him hanging for a moment, and then stopped at the display case. I lit a cigarette and threw the match on the floor. Light looked aghast when he saw that I was about to smoke. No one ever smoked in his stamp room. I waited for him to protest, and when he didn't, I went on. He was too afraid of what I was going to tell him to say anything. "Of course, you were prepared to kill Chapman if you had to. But that would have been much later. For the time being you were much more eager to pursue your plan of public humiliation. You're obviously not a man who needs money, but in every other respect you're no better than the tawdriest blackmailer. Everything was going along fine until I appeared on the scene. Chapman was going to announce his candidacy and win the primary. That much was almost certain. And that was just where you wanted him to be—out in the open, at his most vulnerable. But when Chapman hired me, you assumed he knew what you were up to and that therefore I was also in on the secret you were planning to expose. It didn't really matter that Chapman knew, because like all victims of blackmail he was in a double bind. To protect himself from you would have meant letting out the secret, and that was the one thing he had to hide. But it did matter that I knew. And so you started to apply the pressure. You sent your two thugs around to buy me off the case, but that didn't work. Then you tried to threaten me off, but that didn't work either. In a way it was almost lucky for me that Chapman died when he did. You probably would have sent Angel and Teddy to kill me in just a few days. You were so afraid I would cross Chapman and let out the secret that you were willing to see me dead."

Light sat there without moving. I had hit too close to the truth for him to be able to formulate a quick response. I put out my cigarette on the counter of the display case, and he didn't react. His voice came softly, distantly, as if from some remote corner of himself, and it seemed that he spoke almost unconsciously.

"What is it you want?" he asked.

"I want to make a trade with you."

"Money? I thought you weren't interested in money." He sighed with disappointment and exhaustion.

"I said a trade, not money. You give me the information I want, and I promise to keep silent."

"I don't understand what you mean."

"I realize you're a very powerful man, Mr. Light, and that no matter what I did, a person like me can't cause you much permanent harm. But I can create considerable unpleasantness for you, and I can damage your reputation. Now that you're in politics, your reputation is your most valuable asset. All I have to do is tell one of my friends at the *Times* about the dirty tricks you've been up to, and you'll be spending so many hours with your stamps it will make you sick just to look at them."

"You goddamn liberals are all the same," he said resentfully, his brashness beginning to return. "Politics is power, and power is a dirty business. Whenever a Democrat does something, he's being pragmatic. But just let a Conservative do the same thing, and he's committed a terrible crime. And meanwhile this whole country of ours is playing right into the hands of the Reds."

"This wasn't politics," I said. "It was pure personal hatred. I know that you're committed to your cause and that in your eyes the government is run by a conspiracy of card-carrying Communists who can't get up in the morning without permission from the Kremlin, but you weren't thinking about your ideals when you decided to go after Chapman. You didn't want to defeat him in an election; you wanted to crucify him."

"And I would have too. Then people would have seen what you socialists are really like."

"The funny thing is that if you hadn't done anything, you wouldn't be in this mess now. But you overreacted, in the same way you overreact in politics. You see, I resent it that you sent those two imbeciles to my apartment. They walked in and destroyed my living room, roughed me up, and thought it was all some kind of outing to an amusement park. You should have it happen to you sometime and see how much you like it."

I slid open the door of the display case and took out one of the binders. It threw Light into a panic. "What the hell are you doing!" he screamed.

I tossed the binder onto the floor and said, "This is the slow-motion replay of what happened. It helps to see it with your own eyes, doesn't it? Much more vivid than the radio commentary."

I threw another binder onto the floor. I did it gently, with a kind of feigned negligence. I wasn't interested in damaging the collection, but I wanted to upset him, to make him understand that he was no longer in control of the situation.

Light sprang out of his chair and came at me with an almost hysterical anger. He was an old man but very fit and still strong. I didn't want to hurt him, but I also didn't want him to get a chance to throw a lucky punch. I pushed him in the chest as hard as I could, and he went flying back into the table and fell to the floor. It was enough to convince him that he didn't want to try again. He got to his feet slowly.

"All right," I said. "Let's talk. Talk to me clearly and I'll leave. But any more bullshit, and I'll rip up every stamp in this room."

Light sat down on the armchair again. He was humiliated, and yet he knew there was nothing he could do about it. It was a terrible defeat for him, but I felt no pity.

"Tell me what it is," he said, "and I'll give you a straight answer."

"I want to know what you had on Chapman. I want to know what it was you thought could destroy him."

He was stunned. It hadn't occurred to him that I didn't know. His whole strategy had been based on the assumption that I had been privy to Chapman's secret, and now he realized that he had been wrong, that he had outtricked himself. It was an exquisite moment, and I savored it. More than a minute went by before Light spoke again.

"Chapman was involved with mobsters," he said, looking me in the eye, as if to prove it wasn't costing him anything to tell me.

"You mean Victor Contini?"

"That's right. Contini."

"Involved in what way?"

"Chapman owed him a great deal of money. Gambling debts which he refused to pay."

"And when Contini saw that he wasn't going to get it, he arranged Chapman's accident."

"You seem to know as much about it as I do."

"Not quite. There are things I still don't understand. The gambling, for example. Chapman didn't strike me as the kind of man who would go in for that sort of thing."

"It wasn't gambling in the usual sense. Chapman met Contini somehow, probably through the son, and got to know him fairly well."

"How did you find out about this friendship? It certainly wasn't common knowledge."

"I keep a close check on my players. It's a way of avoiding embarrassing situations before they get out of hand. Ball players become bored on the road, and they tend to run into trouble, especially with women."

"So what you're saying is that you hire spies to follow around the men who work for you."

"I don't think of it as spying. It's protection. We have to maintain the image of the team. Baseball players are easy targets for the press. For more than half the year, every move they make on and off the field is reported in the daily papers. These are just ordinary kids, and yet they're watched as closely as the President. A great actor or opera singer gets reviewed only on the opening night of a performance, but a baseball team gets reviewed one hundred sixty-two times a season. And not just in one city, but all around the country, and on television and radio as well as in magazines. The first hint of something unusual in a player's behavior, and it quickly becomes a major scandal. Baseball is the great American game, a symbol of all this country stands for, and I'll be damned if I'll let any player try to destroy it."

It calmed Light down to talk about how he controlled the private lives of his players. It reminded him of his own importance and reestablished a certain equilibrium in the struggle that had been going on between us. I didn't want to allow the conversation to meander and broke in on him before he could say anything else.

"Getting back to Chapman. What kind of gambling do you mean?"

"Chapman signed a pact with the devil."

"That might be your opinion of what he did, but you'll have to be more specific than that."

"I'm telling you, Chapman signed a pact with the devil. He gambled on himself. Before each game he would predict his performance—a certain number of hits, a certain number of runs batted in, a home run, two home runs, and so on—and then wager on the prediction with Contini. They played for high stakes. I believe he was nearly five hundred thousand dollars in the hole by the time the season was over."

I had been expecting something else—an unintentional mistake that Chapman wanted to cover up, a momentary lapse, a stupid blunder—anything but this. This was genuine madness, a pure and deliberate attempt to destroy himself. Chapman had tried to take control of his talent by pushing it so far that no matter what happened it was bound to fail him. He had had one of the most extraordinary seasons a baseball player could have, and yet it had all come to nothing. But in this way Chapman had gained ascendancy over the monster. It didn't matter that he would ruin himself in the process. Nothing mattered but coming into possession of himself, if only for an instant. It had been like walking through fire. The pain had made him real.

Light was grinning at me. It pleased him to witness my confusion, to know that he had been holding the trump card after all. It was a small victory, perhaps, but it made him momentarily forget that he had lost the war.

"I see that you're surprised, Mr. Klein," he gloated. "And small wonder. It's rather meaty stuff. You can see what it would have done to a man running for office. It would have finished him."

"Why didn't he pay Contini what he owed him? Given the insanity of the situation in the first place, you'd still think he would have paid up."

"I can't tell you that," Light said, not very interested in this point. "Perhaps he didn't have the money. Or perhaps he did it only as a game to amuse himself and never had any intention of paying. Chapman had one of the most inflated egos of any man I have ever met. He thought he was invulnerable."

"An inflated ego, but not nearly as big as yours."

"Perhaps." Light grinned at me again. He was enjoying himself now, and he seemed almost eager to prolong the conversation. I changed the subject abruptly, hoping to catch him off balance.

"What do you know about Bruno Pignato?"

The grin on Light's face vanished. He looked at me and frowned. "I never heard of him."

"It was in your interest to keep the facts about Chapman's accident quiet until the election campaign started. Pignato worked for Contini, and he was the driver of the truck that Chapman's car crashed into. I went to see Pignato on Wednesday, something I'm sure you were aware of. On Thursday he turned up dead, murdered in his own house. I want you to tell me about it."

"I still don't know what you're talking about. Why in God's name would I want to harm someone I didn't even know?"

"Because Pignato was a very unstable type. He was obsessed by guilt, felt responsible for ending Chapman's career, and seemed ready to talk about it to the first person who asked him. There was a good chance he would let the whole thing out before you wanted it out."

"You're wrong, Klein. I know nothing about any of this."

I didn't press the point. Chapman had been Light's sole obsession—he hadn't even bothered to consider the other man in the accident.

"There's just one more thing," I said. "I assume you got your information about Chapman's contact with Contini from your team spy. But all the rest—the details of the gambling, the fact that the accident was arranged—was given to you by someone else, wasn't it? A man by the name of Wallace Smart, an operative from the Dampler Agency."

"A very disagreeable little man."

"How much did you pay him? I'm curious to know how much the information was worth to you, just for the record."

"Twenty thousand dollars."

"He must have driven a hard bargain."

"He thought he was. But I was actually prepared to spend a great deal more. A man of his sort is always satisfied with too little. It worked out well for both of us."

"Until yesterday, that is."

Light shrugged. "That's one way of looking at it, I suppose. But I don't regret losing the money. It was all in a good cause."

"If destroying a man can ever be considered a good cause."

"For me it was."

I looked at Light with disgust. "It's too bad that people with money are always sons of bitches like you."

"Perhaps," Light said with a smile. "But at least I get a chance to enjoy life. You have no idea how wonderful it is to be me. Being Charles Light is the most exhilarating sensation in the whole world."

"In Charles Light's world, maybe. For the rest of us it looks about as appealing as a case of lung cancer. I know some lepers who wouldn't want to trade places with you, and they're not even alive anymore. Go on enjoying yourself, Mr. Light. Maybe you'll slip on the dance floor one day and break your neck."

I told him not to trouble himself about seeing me to the door. I knew the way out.

17

IT WAS WELL PAST midnight when I got back home. Walking into the lobby of the building, I felt like someone returning from a long stay in a foreign country. It had made me uncomfortable to be in Light's house, and I was glad to be back. I was a citizen of life on the ground, and in spite of the car exhaust, the overflowing garbage cans, and the smoke from greasy spoons, I was able to breathe there. To have lived in the upper reaches of the atmosphere as Light did would have meant wearing an oxygen mask, and that didn't interest me. Oxygen masks make you look like an insect.

It had been a long day, and I was dead tired. My body had been pushed as far as it could go, and more than anything I just wanted to sleep. I was a little less discouraged than I had been when the day started. The form of the case was taking shape in my mind, and I could see now that I wasn't going to get lost again. It was simply a matter of doing the work. I was on my way, but I still didn't know how far I'd have to travel before I came to the end.

I started to open the door of my apartment and saw that there was a light on somewhere inside. I knew I had turned out all the lights before leaving in the morning, and my body suddenly went taut with apprehension. I wasn't in the mood for another fight, and I didn't feel like getting shot at again. But it was too late to turn around and leave. Whoever was waiting for me in the apartment had heard me fumbling with my keys and had seen the door open. I decided to take my chances.

Judy Chapman looked up and smiled when she saw me enter. She was curled up on the sofa with her shoes off, reading a copy of John Donne's *Devotions* that she had taken from the bookcase. She was wearing green velour pants and a gray turtleneck sweater, and she looked beautiful.

"Hello, Max."

"How the hell did you get in here?" I asked. My voice came out sounding harsh and angry.

She gave me a devilish smile and said, "Your superintendent is a great romantic. I told him we had a lovers' quarrel and that I wanted to surprise you by being here when you got back. He liked the idea and opened the apartment for me. He even tried to give me some advice."

"You nearly scared me to death. It's lucky I didn't have my gun. I might have come in here shooting."

She was very different now than she had been during the afternoon. The nervous anxiety of twelve hours ago had given way to a kind of giddiness—and I wondered if this was the prelude to an even deeper anxiety, or if she was beginning to internalize the pressure, learning to live with it. There was a standing lamp behind the couch, and its light filtered through her hair with the strange glow of an obscured candle, creating an almost ethereal nimbus around her face, like something from a Renaissance portrait. She seemed incredibly fragile to me at that moment, as if the slightest stirring of air would go right through her and turn her into a cloud of vapor.

"Aren't you going to ask me why I came?"

I looked at her coyly and said, "I thought you just told me."

She was amused by that and smiled at me again. Then her face became serious. "Actually, I did come to apologize. I'm sorry about the way I acted this afternoon. That's not like me, really."

"It was one of those things," I said. "Everyone's been under a lot of pressure, and tempers flared for a moment."

"It's just that I wasn't expecting Bill to turn up. And when I saw the two of you going at each other . . ." She shook her head, leaving the rest of the sentence unfinished.

"Briles and I don't seem to get along very well. It must be some kind of astrological intolerance." I paused. "About the only thing we have in common is that we both like you."

It was a heavy remark, and it embarrassed us both into an awkward silence, the kind of silence that goes on just long enough to make you realize that your shoes are too tight. I was having trouble getting my bearings with the situation. It was unclear to me why she had come, and I was too tired to apply myself to the problem. The best thing I could do, I decided, was to play the scene out.

"Now that you're here," I said, "you might as well get a chance to taste some of the treasures of my wine cellar. I have a bottle of Bordeaux and a bottle of Bordeaux. Which would you like?"

"The Bordeaux, of course," she said without hesitating. "It sounds considerably better than the Bordeaux." We smiled at each other, and things were back on an even keel.

I retreated to the kitchen for the wine and a pair of glasses. When I returned to the living room she was standing by the table, smoking a cigarette and looking around.

"I like your apartment better than your office," she said. "It shows another side of you, and I think I like this side more than the other."

"It's just your average bachelor digs. Underfurnished, a bit ratty, and generally a mess. But this is elegance compared to when I first started living alone again. It used to be the New York version of the San Francisco earthquake."

We sat down at the table and started drinking the wine. It was a good bottle, and I was glad I had saved it.

After a few minutes of inconsequential talk, Judy said, "I didn't know you had been married."

"I guess we all have our little secrets from the past. There's a nine-year-old boy in my life too."

She seemed very interested by this, as if it somehow made me more tangible to her. Until now I had been a rather enigmatic figure, a mysterious investigator who did mysterious things, a man without a life. Suddenly I was a real person. It was a little like a school kid running into his science teacher at the movies on a Saturday night. It comes as a jolt to discover that he's just like anyone else, that he has a wife, a couple of kids, and that he enjoys eating popcorn. We get so used to seeing only parts of people, the parts we come in contact with, that it's almost as if they cease to exist as soon as they're out of sight.

She asked me about my marriage, and I told her about Cathy and how things between us had gradually fallen apart. She said that Cathy sounded like a good person, and I said that she was, that the divorce had been basically my fault. Then she wanted to know about Richie, and I talked about him for a while and explained how I tried to see him at least once a week. Judy seemed happy listening to me go on about these things, and I sensed it put us on a new footing. She had been attracted to me the first time we met, but now she was beginning to like me. It was an important distinction. The clever sexual jousting of our first few conversations had been replaced by something more straightforward and honest. We were getting to know each other.

I realized that she hadn't come to my apartment for anything more than a little company. She wanted to forget the things she had been through in the past two days, but she couldn't really turn to anyone else without having to talk about it. I was the one person who knew enough about her situation not to have to ask questions. She had probably come to my place in order to sleep with me, expecting nothing more than a kind of oblivion, a release from all her troubles. But it turned out to be one of those heart-to-heart conversations that create a deeper intimacy than blind physical contact does. Real talk is a kind of embracing of another person, and from the moment the first word was spoken I had the feeling that we had already begun to make love.

We moved on to the second bottle of Bordeaux. Judy kept asking me questions about myself, and I went on answering them. It puzzled her why I had given up being a lawyer to go into investigative work. She didn't know anyone who had deliberately thrown away a safe career, and I tried to explain it to her.

"I ran up against the old conflict between law and justice," I said.

"I don't understand."

"The conflict between doing what someone tells you to do and doing what's right. When I was a young kid and decided to become a lawyer, I thought I was being an idealist. I was going to help people in trouble and put a lot of bad men in jail and in the end the world would be a better place. But then I learned that being a lawyer has nothing to do with solving real problems and treating people as human beings. It's a game, with its own set of rules and procedures, and the only thing that matters is winning. I finally realized that I was wasting my time, throwing away my life."

"You're just not the type to play along. Most men would be lost without a system to fit into. But you want to take risks. It makes you a kind of outsider."

"I suppose so. But I like to think it gives me a better chance to get close to the people I deal with. I move in and out of other people's lives a lot, and I usually have to move quickly. If I don't have much now, it's because I don't want to have anything to lose. It frees me to commit myself to the people I work for."

"You have your life to lose. Why put yourself on the line for people you hardly even know?"

"Because they need me. Because they have problems they can't solve by themselves."

Judy paused for a moment and looked away. "You mean people like me, don't you?"

"Yes. People like you."

"But what do you get out of it? How does it help you?"

"I'm not sure. Maybe just that I'm able to live with myself. And maybe knowing that gives me a reason to get out of bed in the morning."

"It's more than a job for you, isn't it?" she said softly. "You really believe in it." She turned away again, as if suddenly embarrassed. "I think I could start falling in love with you, Max."

I lit a cigarette, paused for a few moments, and then smiled at her. "That's just the wine talking. It's going to your head and blurring your vision."

"No, it's me talking. I feel safe with you. You're the first man I've met who doesn't want to use me."

"But I am using you. I'm using you to stay on the case. And once it's over we'll probably never see each other again."

"Only if you want it to be that way, Max. But if you let me walk in, I'm not going to walk out unless I'm asked."

"The door was opened the first time we met," I said. "I suppose it's too late to do anything about it now. You're already in."

TIME WENT BY, and the thing that had been trying to happen for the past three days finally happened. We had both been through the ritual before, but this time neither one of us acted from memory. Shuddering in the darkness of each other's bodies, we reached a point where everything became new again, and even as it was happening we sensed that it had to be savored beyond measure. We had left ourselves behind.

It was after four o'clock. Judy and I were sitting up in bed smoking cigarettes. We weren't saying anything, were just letting ourselves be close, letting our exhausted bodies relax before floating off to sleep.

"There's something I've got to tell you," I said. "I might never get another chance, and I want you to hear it from me."

It took her a while to answer. I felt that she was reluctant to break the mood of our silence, unwilling to clutter the room with words. She put out her cigarette and then lay down with her head on my chest.

"Don't talk that way, Max. It frightens me."

"It doesn't have anything to do with us. It's about five years ago. I finally found out what really happened."

And then I told her about Chapman and what he had done to provoke Contini into arranging the accident. Judy was surprisingly unresponsive when I explained it to her. I couldn't tell if she had reached the point where nothing could shock her anymore, or if Chapman had come to mean so little to her that in the end she didn't care. One way or the other, I hadn't expected her to be indifferent.

"Let's not talk about these things anymore," she said after I was finished. "The only thing I want to talk about is tonight, about you and me. George is dead, and it doesn't matter anymore what he did when he was alive. What matters is what we do, that we go on loving each other."

After a long silence I said, "In spite of everything, it's hard to believe that George's death doesn't touch you. You don't have to hide your feelings from me, Judy. I'll listen if you want to talk about it."

"It does touch me. But in my own way, and for my own reasons. I can't pretend to grieve for a man who took my life away from me for ten years. I know it sounds horrible, but I think I'm actually glad George is dead. It's liberated me. I'm going to be able to start all over again."

"The irony is that even in death George is still calling the shots."

"I know. But that's only for the time being. I feel confident now. I think everything is going to work out. I know it is."

"I do too."

"And when it's all over, I'm going to love you so hard, Max, that it will make up for all the years we wasted by not knowing each other. I'm going to cook for you and sew for you and have babies with you and make love to you whenever you look at me."

She was so serious, so ardent, that I couldn't help laughing a little. "That hardly sounds like the life of a liberated woman."

"But it is. Only a liberated woman can make choices. You have to be free before you can know what you want. I can't help it if you're what I want. I've made my choice. I want you to be my man."

"I'll be your man," I said, "if you'll be my woman. And you don't have to do my laundry either. We can send it to Mr. Wei around the corner. He needs the business."

Ten minutes later we were asleep. Our arms and legs were knotted together, and my last thought before drifting off was that we were trying to become one body, that for this one night we wanted to believe we could no longer exist as separate beings. Somewhere in the distance a clock struck five. The cow jumped over the moon.

18

IT WAS NINE-THIRTY when I woke up. By the time I remembered where I was and what had happened during the night, I realized that Judy was gone. She had decided to spare us the morning after. It was too soon to confront each other again, and she needed time to be alone with her feelings, to assimilate the emotions we had lived through only a few hours before. For a moment I was disappointed not to find her there beside me, but then I understood that it was better this way. I needed time too.

I felt remarkably refreshed after so little sleep. For the past few days I had been running on a nearly empty tank, and sooner or later it was bound to go dry. I wondered how much longer my body would accept the demands I made on it, how many more beatings and sleepless nights it could take before it gave out on me. I was thirty-three, and most of the time I felt the same as I had at twenty. But I knew that one day in the not too distant future I would wake up in the morning and discover I had entered middle age. It wasn't that I was afraid of it; I just wanted to be prepared.

I took a shower, climbed into a pair of blue jeans and a sweater, and then made myself a big breakfast of juice, scrambled eggs, toast, the whole works. At ten-fifteen I was on my second cup of coffee, sitting at the living room table and reading the book of Donne's *Devotions* that Judy had taken down from the shelf the night before. I had not looked at it for more than ten years, and the power of it unsettled me. One passage struck me in particular: "We have a winding-sheet in our mother's womb which grows with us from our conception, and we come into the world wound up in that winding-sheet, for we come to seek a grave." I took it to mean that we live under the eyes of death and that no matter what we do, there is no escape. We do not meet our deaths, as the saying goes, but death is within us from the very beginning and goes with us wherever we go. It made sense to me to think of it this way. There is no escape. I understood that.

I was brooding over this when the door buzzer rang. I pushed the intercom button and asked who it was. Chip Contini's voice answered me. The intercom hardly worked anymore, and I had trouble understanding what he said. His voice sounded as though it was coming from a thousand miles away, wailing on some lonely heath in the middle of a storm like something from an ancient recording of *King Lear.* The only thing I could be sure of was that he urgently wanted to see me.

I walked around the living room, waiting for him to ride the elevator up to the ninth floor and ring my bell. I assumed he wanted to talk to me either about the case or about my conversation with his father yesterday. Probably his father, I decided, which meant that he really wanted to talk about himself. It seemed that I had triggered off some kind of crisis for Chip by forcing him to bring his father into the Chapman business. He was too old to be going through an adolescent trauma. But like an adult who unexpectedly comes down with a childhood disease, he was being hit hard by it.

He knocked—quickly, impatiently—and I opened the door. There was no time even to say hello. He burst through in a rage, pushed me in the chest with both hands, and sent me reeling back into the living room.

"You bastard," he said. "You goddamn filthy bastard, I could kill you with my bare hands."

He made a move to come at me again, and I backed away. "Sit the hell down and cool off, Chip. I'm not going to fight with you no matter how much you want to. Just sit down and tell me what it is."

This stopped his momentum a bit, but it did nothing to squelch his anger. I had never seen him act violently before, and it was clear that he didn't know how to deal with the hurricane that had broken loose inside him. He was contending with raw, untempered emotion for the first time in his life, and it had turned him into someone I hardly recognized.

"It's my father," he said, his face boiling with fury. "My father's dying. And you did it, Max—you're the one who killed him."

"I have no idea what you're talking about. Sit down and start from the beginning. I'm not going to listen to you unless you try to make some sense."

"I swear, Max, if he dies, I'm going to come back here and kill you with my own two hands. I don't care what happens to me. I'll kill you, I swear I will."

It was getting to be a little too much, and I ran out of patience. I shouted at him the way a drunken farmer shouts at his dog. I pointed to a chair, and I told him to sit. The loudness of my voice stunned him, and he just stood there staring at me. I shouted at him again, and he sat.

I went off to the kitchen and poured three or four ounces of Cutty Sark into a glass. I came back to the living room and found him sitting in exactly the same position, as if he had gone into a catatonic trance.

"Here, drink this first," I said, handing the glass to him. "Then we'll talk."

He drank down the Scotch as though it was water, and it hardly affected him at all. He was somehow outside himself, and he was no longer reacting normally to things. His body was wound up as tightly as a watch, and his mind was off somewhere else, burrowing into the anguish that surrounded him like a visible aura. I realized that he was exhausted. He was wearing the same clothes I had seen him in yesterday, and he needed a shave. I doubted if he had had any sleep in the past twenty-four hours.

"Now tell me about it," I said. "When I left your father yesterday he was fine."

"Well, he's not fine now," Chip mumbled, full of self-pity. "He's in an oxygen tent in the intensive care unit at Lenox Hill Hospital, and he's dying."

"Cut the melodrama, Chip," I said sharply. "I know he's dying—you told me that before. Just tell me what happened."

"It's what happened after you left. My father and I had an argument, a horrible argument. It was the worst thing I've ever been through. Screaming, shouting, terrible insults on both sides. At some point things calmed down a little, and we decided to leave the office and take an early train out to Westport. He had a heart attack right in the elevator." Chip stopped and looked up at me, on the verge of tears. There was such defeat in his eyes that I had to turn away. "It's all your fault, Max. You never should have asked me to arrange that meeting."

"What was the argument about?"

"I wanted to know the truth. I wanted to know why my father had lied to me."

"Did you find out?"

"Part of it. The rest I was able to figure out for myself."

Now that he was beginning to talk about it, I could feel him relaxing into a kind of grim fatalism. Describing what had happened out loud to someone else had the effect of putting the events into the past. They were placed out of reach and were made unalterable. They had to be accepted because they could no longer be changed.

I said, "It was you who introduced Chapman to your father, wasn't it?"

Chip nodded. "I didn't want to. But George kept insisting. He seemed so curious about my father. George was fascinated by all forms of power, and he wanted to get as close to it as he could. Eventually I gave in and had them both out to Westport for dinner."

"Was Judy Chapman there too?"

"No. She and George were in one of their bad periods. They hardly ever went out together."

"You knew about Briles back then?"

"I knew about Briles, and I knew about the others too. George would tell me. He liked to confide in me about his personal life."

"How did he feel about Judy? Did he try to make it work with her, or was he satisfied with a marriage of convenience?"

"No, he hated her. He hated her so much that sometimes I thought he would kill her. George was my good friend, but I never felt I understood him. He didn't have the same kinds of emotions as other people. There was something hard in him, as if he was all burned out inside. He used to hire detectives to follow her around and find out who she was sleeping with. You could understand it if he was planning to divorce her, but he never had any intention of doing that. He used to say that he was just collecting evidence. I never knew exactly what he meant."

"What's your opinion of Judy Chapman?"

"I think she's a good person. A little weak, but then she had to put up with an awful lot. I don't know how she took it for so long."

"Do you think she was capable of killing Chapman?"

"No. She's innocent. She never could have done anything like that."

I held out my cigarettes to him, but he shook his head. I lit up and asked, "Did Chapman and your father talk about gambling that night at your house?"

"No. It was a proper social occasion. There was nothing but small talk." He paused and looked at me with a puzzled expression. "Why would they have talked about gambling?"

"Didn't your father tell you yesterday?"

"Tell me what?"

I missed a beat, realizing that Chip's father had held back as many details as he could. "Obviously he didn't," I said.

And so I told him the story, the same story I had told Judy last night. Chip took it much harder. His mouth literally dropped open when I explained the arrangement Chapman had made with his father. After I finished, he got up from his chair and walked around the room several times in silence. Whatever else he was, Chip was also a decent man, and nothing in his life had prepared him to contend with the revulsion he now felt. It was as if I had just given him his first glimpse of hell.

"My father told me it was business," he said quietly. "But I didn't know what kind of business." He sat down on the couch, took off his glasses, and buried his face in his hands. "I can't believe such evil," he said over and over again, "I can't believe such evil."

"And then, when Chapman refused to pay up," I said, "your father invited him to the house in Millbrook for a conference. But of course, Chapman never made it. It was attempted murder. Although Chapman managed to survive, the effect was almost the same as if it had worked. He was finished. And your father, being the sporting gentleman that he is, decided to let the matter drop there. After all, he hadn't lost anything."

It had finally become too much for Chip. His big, bulky body started to quake with sobs, and the apartment filled with the noise of his misery. I didn't try to console him. He was mourning his father, mourning the loss of his own innocence, and nothing I said would have mattered. He had to let it out. There could be no more lies, no more escapes. The tears he wept were bitter, but they were necessary. They lay between him and his manhood.

When the onslaught was over I led him to the bathroom, gave him a towel, and told him to wash up. I went into the kitchen and did the breakfast dishes. Fifteen minutes later Chip appeared in the doorway and gave me a feeble smile. He was still red around the eyes, but he looked a little better. I noticed that he had used my razor to shave with and that he had cut himself on the chin. A blood-soaked patch of tissue paper stanched the wound.

"Come on," I said. "I'll walk you back to the hospital."

We went east on Seventy-second Street toward Central Park. It was another good day; somewhat chillier, the air clear, and the streets filled with a light that made strong, clean shadows. Until we reached the park, neither one of us said anything. It had been humiliating for Chip to break down in front of me, and he couldn't be sure if I wasn't secretly laughing at him for his show of weakness. I wasn't. But I had no intention of telling him that. He would have to figure it out for himself.

When we crossed to the other side of the stone wall that separated the park from the street, he began to talk. It was as though he found the grass and trees a more congenial audience for his thoughts. Lumbering along in his stolid cordovan shoes and wrinkled business suit, he looked like a displaced person in this land of cyclists, ball players, and joggers. But it hardly mattered where he was. He was oblivious to everything around him.

He talked about his father. His memories came at random, and he skipped back and forth across the years as the past came rushing over him. He went from his first day at college at Dartmouth to a Labrador retriever given to him when he was eight and then forward again to the birth of his youngest daughter. In each instance, his father had been present. There was nothing I hadn't heard before. In some sense, everyone's memories are the same. The events that give rise to them might differ, but the qualities we invest them with are the same. They are our lives, and we treat them with a respect accorded only to the most sacred things. Chip spoke of his father's generosity, his sense of humor, his love for his children. It was as though he was delivering the eulogy over his father's grave, and he said nothing that might have revealed the brutal reality of the man. The truth hovered like an avenging angel in each of his words, but for now he chose not to acknowledge its presence. He would have the rest of his life to wrestle with that angel. This was his farewell to the father he had pretended to have, and he said good-bye gently, with infinite kindness, in the way one dismantles a dollhouse.

When we reached the front door of Lenox Hill Hospital, I said, "Maybe he'll surprise you and pull through it."

"Sure," Chip said. "And maybe tomorrow is Christmas."

"You never know. He's a pretty tough old guy."

"You don't have to try to be nice, Max. It really doesn't matter anymore. I almost hope he's dead when I walk up there now. It would make things much simpler."

"Death is never simple."

"I know." He looked away from me and stared through the glass door. "It's just that I don't ever want to talk to him again."

As it turned out, he never did.

19

RICHIE WAS WAITING for me in the lobby of the East Eighty-third Street building. It was a little after one o'clock, and he had been waiting a long time. Dressed in his blue baseball cap with the famous NY logo, a yellow tee-shirt that had his name printed on the front, blue jeans, and a pair of white and green track shoes, he was sitting in an armchair large enough to hold five of him and quietly pounding his right fist into his baseball glove. A Pan Am flight bag lay at his feet, with a folded copy of *The Sporting News* on top of it. His skinny body was so hunched up as he concentrated on the pocket of his glove that it seemed to have taken on the form of a question mark.

"Boy," he said when he looked up and saw me, "are you late. The game's probably in the third inning already."

"No, we still have almost an hour. We'll get there in time if we step on it. Do you have a sweater?"

"In my bag."

"Okay, let's go."

I knew that I probably shouldn't be going off for an afternoon at the ball park when I was still in the middle of a case. But I needed some time to think, to step back a little from the whole business and look at it with fresh eyes. I also felt that nothing was as important as spending these few hours with Richie. I wanted to give him a good day, a day he would remember.

Cathy had sent him down to wait in the lobby, which was her way of saying that she didn't want to see me. I assumed this meant she had made her decision. I assumed she would be moving to New Hampshire.

*

WALKING INTO A major-league stadium is an experience like no other in the world. You've been in the subway, crowded into narrow spaces, surrounded by metal and machinery, and then you've gotten out to find yourself in yet another landscape of bricks, stones, and urban blight. You've circled the stadium with a few thousand other people looking for the right gate, given your ticket to a guy in a uniform, gone through the turnstile, and entered the gloom of bare concrete tunnels, echoing voices, and jostling bodies. It makes you feel you've come all this way just to become part of a dream sequence in a Fellini movie.

But then you walk up the ramp, and there it is. It's almost impossible to take it all in at once. The sudden sense of space is so powerful that for the first few moments you don't know where you are. Everything has become so vast, so green, so perfectly ordered, it's as if you've stepped into the formal garden of a giant's castle.

Little by little you begin to adjust. You notice the lesser details, the tiny things that help to create the overall effect. You admire the pristine whiteness of the bases, the symmetry of the pitcher's mound, the impeccably tended dirt of the infield. You see the enormous electric words and numbers on the scoreboard and slowly take in the crowd, starting with the strangers around you and then going off into the distance where the people are just a blur of colors and noise. For the next two or three hours the geometry of the field in front of you will hold your attention completely. In the middle of the city you will find yourself enveloped in a pastoral universe watching a white ball fly around in space and dictate the actions of eighteen grown men. Nothing will matter to you more than that ball. It will hold you so completely that when you at last file out and return to the normal world, it will stay with you like the afterglow of a flashbulb that's gone off in your eyes.

Our seats were between home plate and first base on ground level about halfway back, and we got to them just as the managers were walking out to consult with the umpires and exchange lineups. I was glad we hadn't missed any of the game. Until now the only baseball Richie had seen was on television, and the crazy, foreshortened perspectives of the camera have never done the game justice. It was important for him to understand that baseball is not a constant stream of words from the mouth of a play-by-play announcer punctuated by between-innings beer commercials. I wanted him to see the whole thing with his own eyes.

For the first few moments he was out of his skin. He had always been a rather secretive kid, not given to displaying his emotions, but this time he reacted the way any nine-year-old would have. He gawked, looked in every direction at once, and had trouble staying in his seat. What seemed to impress him most was the fact that the American players were not two-dimensional black-and-white shadows, but flesh and blood human beings. It overwhelmed him to realize that his heroes actually existed.

As the Americans took the field and everyone stood for the national anthem, Richie tugged at my sleeve and said, "When can we come back again, Dad?"

"The game hasn't even started yet. Why worry about next time?"

"Because I don't want to think that if I have to go to the bathroom or something I'll never get another chance. What if I miss a home run? I'd never forgive myself."

"Does that mean you have to go to the bathroom now?"

He was embarrassed and looked down at his feet, afraid to meet my eyes. "Yeah, I guess so."

"Come on, then. Nobody's going to hit a home run."

We left our seat at "twilight's last gleaming" and went off to the urinals. The men's room was crowded, and Richie seemed a little intimidated by the commotion and cigar smoke. I stood next to him as he waited his turn. Every time a noise erupted from the stands, he wanted to know if I thought it was a home run. I said no, probably only a good pitch or a nice play in the field, but he didn't believe me. By his count, five home runs were hit in our absence.

When we returned to our seats Detroit had two outs and a runner on first. It was still the top half of the first inning. There were no hits or errors on the scoreboard, so I told Richie the man had reached base on a walk. His look told me he had already figured it out for himself. Marston was on the mound for the Americans, a big mustachioed right-hander who had won eighteen games last season. He struck out the Detroit cleanup hitter with a very sleek breaking pitch low and away, and Richie concluded seriously that he had "good stuff."

He was right. Marston was sharp, and so was Amado, the Detroit pitcher, a veteran left-hander who had won over two hundred games in his career. The game quickly settled into one of those classic pitchers' duels, the kind of game that gets decided by a broken-bat single, an error, or a bases-loaded walk. After three innings there was no score; Detroit had one hit and New York none.

Cathy had packed the flight bag with sandwiches, instructing Richie not to let me buy any hot dogs until all the sandwiches were gone. I didn't want to be held responsible for giving him a stomach ache, so I made him stick to the bargain. He seemed satisfied to be indulged with a bag of peanuts and a couple of Cokes. Ten minutes after each soda we made another trip to the men's room.

I was impressed by the way Richie concentrated on the game. Sitting in one place for more than an hour can tax a nine-year-old's patience, but Richie was too absorbed to get restless. About the only thing that distracted him were the foul balls that came our way every now and then. At anything hit even remotely near us, he would stand up, pound his glove, and shout, "Here I am!" Once or twice he became so interested in seeing who finally got the ball that he lost track of what was happening in the game. But the rest of the time he was right there.

In the fifth inning the Detroit shortstop led off with a double, a clean shot into the right-field corner. Marston stomped angrily around the mound, picked up the resin bag, and threw it down in a cloud of white dust. Then he bore down and got the next two batters on pop flies to the infield. That brought up Hillman, the young Detroit third baseman, who was leading the league in both home runs and strikeouts. Without any fanfare, he calmly stroked Marston's first pitch into left center for a single, and Detroit was on the board. It stayed one to nothing for the next three innings. Amado's strange, twirling delivery, which resembled the motions of a mechanical toy, continually had the New York hitters off stride. Everything was working for him. His fastball was humming, his curveball was dipping, and the Americans couldn't touch him. The only difficult moment for him came when Webster, the Americans' right fielder, hit a bullet to the deepest part of right center field that looked like it would fall for a sure triple. But Green, the swift center fielder for Detroit, ran at least thirty yards to make a diving, acrobatic catch in the cinders of the warning track. After eight innings New York had managed only two base runners, both on walks. Amado was breezing along on his way to a no-hitter.

In the top of the ninth Detroit came up with a single, a sacrifice bunt, a groundout that advanced the runner to third, and then a scratch hit to take a two-to-nothing lead. Marston had pitched admirably, giving up only five hits, but apparently it wasn't going to be enough. When Amado took the mound in the bottom of the ninth, there probably wasn't a single person in the stadium who didn't think he would get the no-hitter. After the first batter struck out on three pitches, Richie shook his head morosely and said it was in the bag. But then the second baseman Royce came up—a good singles hitter but never much of a power threat—and everything suddenly changed. Trying to protect the plate, he stuck out his bat at a tough one-and-two fastball down and away. The ball blooped off the wood toward right field and just kept carrying, making it into the first row down the foul line for the shortest possible home run in the park. As Royce trotted around the bases there was bedlam in the house, a wild roar that went on so long that he had to come out of the dugout to tip his hat to the crowd. I liked the way Amado reacted. He simply held up his glove, got another ball from the umpire, and started rubbing it down in the same way he had rubbed down every ball he had ever held. Slowly, methodically, a bored expression on his face. It was all in a day's work.

Webster, the next batter, singled to center, and the tone of the game changed. Not only had Amado lost the no-hitter, but now he was in danger of losing the game as well. When Turner followed with a hit that was misplayed by the right fielder into a double, putting runners on second and third, Amado was gone. Wilton, the lanky Detroit relief pitcher, trotted in from the bullpen to face Costello, New York's hottest hitter at the moment. Richie was on his feet, screaming along with forty thousand other people as if his very life was at stake.

What happened was totally unexpected. I had seen the play only once before, fifteen years ago when I was playing for my high school team, and we lost an important game when the other team pulled it on us. The key is to have your best runners on second and third, and when it works it's fast as lightning. The moment Wilton went into his delivery to throw the first pitch, you could see it happening. Webster and Turner took off like a pair of gerbils on the basepaths, and Costello squared around to bunt. It was the suicide squeeze, and when it's executed properly there's no way to stop it. Costello laid down a good bunt to the right of the pitcher's mound. By the time Wilton picked up the ball, Webster was crossing the plate with the tying run. Wilton's only choice was to throw to first to get Costello out, and he made a leisurely toss that beat him by three or four steps. What he didn't realize, however, was that Turner had never stopped, and by the time the first baseman saw Turner flying around third on his way home, it was too late. There was a throw, there was a slide, there was a cloud of dust. But Turner was safe, and the game was over. A double suicide squeeze. Three–two Americans, and kiss it good-bye. They would be talking about that play for the rest of the season.

THE SUBWAY BACK to Manhattan was too crowded for anything but holding your breath and hoping you wouldn't get stepped on. I managed to find Richie the narrowest of seats, and he immersed himself in the Americans' yearbook I had bought for him at the game, poring over the statistics and pictures with the unbroken concentration of a medieval scholar in the Princeton library. I stood in the middle of a pack of sweating, beer-breathed fans, not bothering to reach for a pole, since there was no way I could possibly fall with so much flesh padded up around me. We rode that way for three-quarters of an hour.

It was on that subway car that everything finally became clear to me. An odd scrap of memory lodged in my mind, a few loose stones fell out of the wall I had been staring at for the past four days, and suddenly I was looking at the daylight on the other side. I had come to it so obliquely that at first I wasn't even aware of it. I had gone all around the world, and now that I was back I saw that my starting place had been my destination all along. I had ventured out looking for pious truths and all-encompassing answers, and I had discovered that the only things that really mattered were of no apparent consequence—the remarks of a ridiculous cabdriver and a piece of unorthodox strategy in a baseball game. Everything I had struggled to find out, all the supposedly important information I had fought for and risked my neck for, turned out to be mere details. The lessons I needed to learn had been given to me free of charge. J. Daniels had proved to me that things are sometimes only what they seem to be, and the double suicide squeeze play had demonstrated how the bunt can sometimes be as powerful as the home run. It had taken me a while to decipher these messages, to read them correctly as metaphors of the case. I had wanted facts, nothing but cold, hard reality, and now I had understood the most important fact of all—that reality doesn't exist without the imagination to see it. I didn't have to go any further. It would all be over by the time I turned in for the night.

The game had been played in a little over two hours, and it was only ten past five when I got Richie back home. Cathy asked me in for a drink, but I told her I would have to pass. I knew she wanted to talk, I knew what she was going to say, and I knew I could change her mind if I wanted to. She had made her decision, but I could tell from the look in her eyes that she was begging me to talk her out of it. This was my last chance, and for a fleeting instant I was tempted to walk through the door and tell her I was moving in. Richie stood there between us, looking back and forth at our faces, realizing that something important was happening but not quite understanding what it was. It flashed through my mind that this was the one moment he would remember from our day together. When Cathy invited me in again and I turned her down a second time, I saw something fall apart inside her. Her mouth tightened, her eyes became hard, and she stared at me as if I had just slapped her across the face. We were right back to where we had been five years ago.

"That was a cruel thing you did Wednesday night, Max," she said. "I'll never forgive you for it."

"I'm not asking for forgiveness, Cathy. I'm only asking that you do what you have to do."

We looked each other in the eyes, and then she collapsed into angry, devastated tears. She swore at me in a voice that was out of control, raging at me incomprehensibly in a stampede of bitterness. A second later she slammed the door shut. I stood there for a full minute, listening to the sounds of her moaning inside the apartment and to Richie shrieking at her in his high-pitched voice, asking her what was wrong. I didn't knock again.

As I walked toward the elevator, I started thinking about my gun. Losing it had been a stupid mistake, and I cursed myself for it. It was the one thing I needed to have with me now.

20

BRILES LIVED IN A cooperative apartment building on the corner of 116th Street and Morningside Drive. Nearly everyone who lived there was connected with Columbia in some way, and the block stood as a kind of fortress on the Heights, dividing the university community from the world below it. On the other side of the street was Morningside Park, an abrupt cliff of weeds and granite outcroppings that descended into the flatlands of Harlem and down through the endless neighborhoods of the poor. If you didn't know what was out there, you could stand on Morningside Drive, take in the panorama, and admire it all as scenery. But everyone knew what was there. It wasn't a neighborhood that attracted many sightseers.

As I was walking up the steps toward the entranceway, I saw an old man with a cane inching his way out of the building. He opened the door from the inside, and I rushed in to hold it for him. I had been hoping to enter the building without ringing the buzzer to Briles' apartment, and I took it as a good omen. The old man smiled up at me benevolently and said hello. It was Edward Bigelow, an economics professor who had been my teacher in the first semester of my freshman year. He must have been at least eighty now, and I found it hard to believe that he had recognized me. My face had been just one of thousands belonging to students of his over the years, and I remembered distinctly that I had never once uttered a word in his class. The apparent recognition in his eyes had been nothing more than a reasonable guess. There were even odds that anyone under fifty he encountered in this neighborhood had once been a student of his. If they were at all like me, not one of them knew a thing about economics.

Briles lived on the fourth floor, and I decided to take the stairs up. The bell in the green door of his apartment made a dull *ping-pong* noise when I pushed it. A few moments later the peephole slid open and an eye stared out at me. Another few moments passed before the eye spoke.

"What are you doing here?" Briles said from behind the door.

"I've come to apologize."

"For what?" His voice was still hostile. It sounded as if the chip on his shoulder had grown into a two-by-four.

"For the flare-up we had yesterday. I don't want there to be any hard feelings."

"All right. No hard feelings."

The peephole slid shut, and I heard him walk away from the door. I put my finger on the bell and punched it in and out for the next thirty seconds. At last the peephole opened again.

"Why don't you go away, Klein?" Briles said. "I'm trying to work, and you're beginning to be a nuisance."

"This is important. I've come up with information that might be enough to get Judy Chapman off the hook. But I need your help. If we get together on this thing, I think we can crack it. I know you don't want to see her go down the tubes, Briles. She means too much to you. Just let me in so we can talk about it."

The peephole slid shut once again, there was a long pause, and then the door opened. Briles was dressed in brown corduroys, a green-and-white-striped soccer shirt, and the kind of work boots that have become fashionable in intellectual circles. He held a book in his left hand, marking the place with his index finger. It was true that he had been working. His face, however, looked haggard, weary under the eyes, and he was showing his age. Briles was at the point in life where his looks depended on the amount of sleep he had had and the degree of tension he was under. On his good days it was possible for him to look like a young man. But this wasn't one of his good days.

He led me into a living room that featured a set of French windows which opened onto a small balcony and a view of the outlying areas below. It was a comfortable room, furnished in modest good taste. This was where Briles did his entertaining, and there were no books or papers in the room, nothing connected with his work. Briles sat down in an upholstered tweed armchair on one side of the windows. A large liquor cabinet made of lacquered bamboo stood against the wall to his left. I took a seat on the blue sofa on the other side of the windows. We studied each other across the early twilight that lay between us.

"You mentioned information," he said tightly. "I'd like to know what it is."

"It concerns a whole range of things." I didn't want to commit myself with too much too soon. "Most of it I've learned since our conversation in your office on Wednesday. I see now that it was a mistake to try to pressure you then. I suspected you were hiding something from me, but I didn't know it was something you weren't free to talk about."

"I assume you're referring to my relationship with Judy."

"That's right, with Judy. But also with George. I came in talking about him, and naturally he was the last person in the world you wanted to discuss. You thought I knew about your affair with Judy and that somehow I was planning to make use of it for my own purposes."

Briles tried to wave me off with his hand. "All right, so we were both wrong about each other that first day. But that's not important anymore. Everyone knows about my involvement with Judy now. It's one of the things they're using to slander her with." He leaned back in his chair and closed his eyes. "My God. I still can't believe she's been accused of murder. It's absolutely incredible."

"You still love her, don't you?" I asked.

His head was tilted back, looking up at the ceiling, and his eyes were still closed. I could barely hear him when he spoke. "Yes, I still love her. I still love her very much."

I fought back my disgust, trying to keep my emotions under control. I didn't want to repeat the scene we had played in Judy's apartment yesterday. No matter how much I despised him, it was important for me to stay calm. "I wouldn't worry about the murder charge against her," I went on. "I have enough to know that she didn't do it. With a little more, I think I can prove it. The case will never even go to court."

Briles opened his eyes and looked at me with a half-formed expression, as though wavering somewhere between hope and suspicion. He wanted to believe me, and yet he wasn't sure if I was leading him into a trap.

"Are you certain?" he asked. "What have you found?"

"George Chapman wasn't murdered by his wife. In fact, he wasn't murdered by anyone. He committed suicide."

It took a moment for my words to register with Briles. He had been so afraid of what I was going to say that at first it seemed he hadn't even heard me. Then his face lost its color; he let out a deep breath and slumped back in his chair. "He was insane," he said to himself. "He was even more insane than I thought."

"Knowing it was suicide is one thing, but proving it is another. This is where it all starts getting complicated. To get Judy off without a trial, the burden of proof falls on me."

"You must have some ideas. You couldn't have come this far without a fairly clear picture of the situation."

"I have a hundred ideas, and they all branch out in different directions. What I have to do is gather them all together in a tidy little package to put on Grimes' desk. Otherwise, he's not going to want to talk to me. As far as he's concerned, the case is already over."

"That doesn't sound very encouraging."

"Until yesterday it looked almost hopeless," I said. "Every time I thought I was getting close to an answer, something strange would happen. A letter would be missing from my safe, or a man would be murdered in New Jersey, or I would get a threatening phone call, or someone would try to gun me down—odd little things like that. It was enough to make me want to pack in the whole business and become a claims adjuster for an insurance company. But then I got some help from an unexpected source."

Briles looked at me curiously, still wanting to play along, but somehow knowing that I wasn't going to let him. "What source was that?"

"A very interesting one. Yesterday afternoon I went into a bookstore and bought several excellent works that gave me some fresh insights into the criminal mind. You're a very good writer, Professor Briles. I admire the precision of your style. It shows a remarkably clear intelligence."

"I'm flattered that you think so highly of my work," he said, standing up from his chair and walking over to the liquor cabinet. "But this kind of praise always tends to make me embarrassed. And when I'm embarrassed I seem to get thirsty." He gave me a falsely ingratiating smile. "Would you care to join me in a drink?"

"No, thanks," I said. "I'm still in training for my next fight."

Briles opened the double door of the cabinet and crouched down among the bottles and glasses. When he stood up again he wasn't holding anything to drink. There was a gun in his hand, and he was pointing it at my stomach. It was a forty-five, probably the same gun that had been used to kill Pignato. Briles grinned at me stupidly. He looked very nervous, as if the gun in his hand was a small and vicious animal he wasn't sure he could control.

"Please tell me more, Klein. It was just beginning to get interesting."

"You're not thinking clearly anymore, Muffle Mouth," I said. "By putting a bullet in me, you'll cancel out any chance Judy has of getting off. I'm the only hope she's got."

"Don't worry about that. Everything is going to work out just fine. Just go on with your story. I want to hear exactly how much you know before I get down to the other business I'm planning to take care of."

I decided to talk. My voice was the only thing that could keep me alive, and the longer I went on, the better my chances would be of walking out of there when it was over. I thought of Scheherazade, the woman who distracted the king with stories in order to delay the moment of her execution. She had been able to keep it going for a thousand and one nights. I didn't feel so optimistic. I was hoping for just a few more minutes.

"It was all in your books," I said. "*The Gangster in the Gray Flannel Suit,* for example. There was an interview in it with an unnamed party, a big shot who cooperated with you because—as he put it—he wanted to set the record straight and make people understand that the underworld had changed. No more Al Capone stuff, he said, he was just a businessman. Seeing that I've met the man myself and know some of his pet phrases, it wasn't too difficult for me to figure out his identity. Victor Contini is unmistakably himself, even on the printed page. The link between you and Contini was all I needed to get you into the picture. And then there was the matter of how the safe was broken into. If you had just forgotten about that idiotic letter you sent to Chapman, chances are nothing would have come of it. Grimes wasn't interested in it, and it never figured in the case he was building against Judy. But then the letter disappeared. It was such a clean job: no forcing, no tools, just a textbook lesson in how to crack a safe combination. I knew that no professional was even remotely involved in this business for himself, which meant that he had been hired by someone to retrieve the letter. I knew it had to be you. You wrote a whole goddamn book about a safecracker."

Briles couldn't help grinning at the thought. It amused him to realize how clever he had been. "Willie Shaw," he said, "the very best in the business. After the book came out, he said that I'd turned him into a star. The man worships me. When I called him the other day and asked him to do that little favor for me, he considered it a great honor."

"You're a curious man, Briles. On the one hand, you live a very safe and comfortable life. You're a distinguished professor at a famous university, and you spend your time writing books and teaching classes. But at the same time you're almost mesmerized by your obsession with dirt, with evil, with the freaks from the sewers of society. You remind me of those proper Victorian gentlemen who would indulge their passion for sin on a regular basis and then return smiling to their proper families. Everything went along fine for all these years. You managed to turn your obsession into a respectable career, to fit all the parts of yourself into neat compartments that never overlapped. You got your thrills by being close to the lawlessness that fascinated you, but you were still on the other side, a Peeping Tom looking in through the window. But then you got involved with a woman who was too much for you to handle, didn't you? Judy Chapman is a wicked little tramp with a perverse mind, and you grovel at her feet. You can't get enough of her."

"Don't talk that way about Judy. It's not true, and you know it. I won't let you say those things."

"Come off it, Briles. She's a slut, a cheap tart with a pretty face and nice-looking clothes, and she sucked you all the way down into the slime. She'll crawl into bed with anything in pants, and it drives you crazy, doesn't it? She'd fuck a dog without batting an eyelash. There's not an easier goddamn lay in this whole town. Why don't you call her up and ask her where she spent last night?"

"I know where she spent last night, you foul-mouthed bastard," Briles shouted. "Now just shut up. Shut that mouth of yours or I'll kill you."

"It all got to be too much for you, didn't it, Briles? You wanted her all for yourself, and when Chapman refused to give her a divorce, you knew that you had to do something to get him out of the way. Getting to know Contini gave you your chance. You found out about Chapman's gambling, and when Contini told you what he was planning to do about it, you said nothing to warn George off. It made you a part of the whole conspiracy."

Briles stared at me with wild eyes. It was agony for him to hear me talking about the things he had kept secret within himself for so long. But at the same time, he couldn't stop listening. It brought it all back again, and he stood in a kind of innocent wonder over the things he had done. At that moment I probably could have taken the gun from him without a struggle, but I didn't realize it until later, until it was too late. The scene was too charged with sudden shifts of emotion for me to make a move. Briles was going to crumble, but I didn't know how long it would take.

"And then George gradually recovered," I said, going on with the story. "Almost unbelievably, things returned to the way they had been before. And then they got worse. Judy began to lose interest in you. You had reached your peak with her the night Chapman's car went skidding into Pignato's truck, and it was all downhill after that, the tedium of an affair that had run itself out. Six months ago she finally dumped you. And that was the thing that undid you, Briles. You came apart at the seams."

"It wasn't fair. After all I had done for her, all the risks I had taken, it just wasn't fair. She owed me some loyalty."

"But you didn't give up. Her rejecting you only made you

more determined to win her back. It was still George who stood in your way. So for the second time you went about trying to destroy him, and this time you were much more thorough. You weren't content to sit back passively and watch it happen—you concocted the whole scheme yourself. It all started with the security check the Democrats ran on Chapman. Wallace Smart came to talk to you, and suddenly you saw a way to get the machinery rolling without even dirtying your hands. You gave Smart the story behind the accident and told him to go with it to Light. Smart was happy. He was able to retire on his profits from the transaction. Light was happy. Now he had what he needed to destroy Chapman. And you were happy—at least for a while. The trouble was that Light was sitting on the information, biding his time until the campaign, and you began to get impatient. So you wrote the letter to Chapman. You wanted to confuse him, to start putting the pressure on him by letting him know the secret was out. But George outsmarted you. No matter how crazy he might have been, he was also a man with guts. He realized that if the secret became public, his career in politics would be over just as it was starting, and he would be ruined. Nothing was more important to him than his reputation, not even his life. He went out like a Roman statesman in order to protect the secret. I think he knew all along that the crisis was bound to come. It was just a matter of doing as much with his life as he could until then, and when the moment finally came he was prepared. He mapped out his strategy very shrewdly, turning your letter to his own advantage. That's the reason I was hired. He wanted to establish the fact that someone was planning to murder him, and I was his witness. Now that he knew he was going to die, he was planning to take Judy down with him. He arranged his suicide to make it look like he had been murdered by her. He allowed himself to die a nightmare death just for revenge—he hated her that much. And he was so sure of himself that he didn't even feel he had to be around to see if his plan would work. He knew it would. And it did—to perfection. He died with his reputation intact, and his wife was accused of murder."

"George was a madman," Briles said. "If I hadn't sent that letter, he would have wound up killing Judy. You can see that for yourself. I did it to protect her from him. I wanted to save Judy."

"But there was no need for you to kill Pignato. He was just an innocent bystander. If you were so eager to hide your role in the accident five years ago, why didn't you go after the big man, Contini himself?"

"Because Contini never would have talked. But Pignato talked to you. I saw it with my own eyes. I followed you to New Jersey and saw you in that bar with him. He had to die. I didn't want him to be in a position to tell anyone else what he knew. I couldn't let my name get mixed up in it. It would send the police straight to Judy, and she wouldn't have a chance. They'd send her to prison for the rest of her life."

"As it is, she's probably going to prison anyway."

"No, she's not. You're going to get her off."

"I can't very well do that after you've killed me with that gun."

Briles looked down at the gun in his hand as if he had forgotten all about it. He was drained, paralyzed from exhaustion. He sat down in the chair across from me and said, "I'm not going to kill you, Klein. I tried to kill you yesterday, but that was only because I was angry at you. I don't want to kill you anymore. You're the one person who can help Judy, and I want you to do that."

His mood had slowly diminished into an almost wistful regret. It was as though time had backed up on him and he had become very young again, a little boy who realized he wasn't strong enough to go on playing adult games.

"What are you going to do now?" I asked.

"I don't know. I think I'll just sit here for a while." He was staring down at the floor between his feet.

"Don't you think you should give me the gun? You don't want it to go off accidentally."

He looked at the gun again, turning it around in his hand in the same way an infant examines a new object. "I don't want to give you the gun, Klein. This gun has been a good friend to me. I want to keep it."

Before I had a chance to say another word, Briles raised the gun and studied it at eye level. For a moment his face was blank. And then his eyes opened wide, as wide as the universe. There was nothing left in him but fear. He had suddenly found himself staring straight ahead at an onrushing truck, and there was no more time for him to get out of the way. He put the barrel of the gun into his mouth and squeezed the trigger.

21

GRIMES CAME. The Smiths came. The lab men came. And then Briles' body was carried out in a plastic bag. It took me almost an hour before I could talk to anyone. I had seen men die, and I had even killed a man myself. But Briles' death had been the worst. There was no way it was ever going to leave me.

From Morningside Drive we went downtown to the police station. Grimes led me into his office, switched on the tape recorder that sat on his desk, and told me to talk. I went on for about forty minutes, and when I was finished Grimes had a sergeant come in with a sandwich and a cup of coffee for me. I took one bite from the sandwich and put it aside. I managed to drink down the coffee. Grimes then opened a drawer in his desk, took out a bottle of Jack Daniel's, and poured some of it into my Styrofoam cup. I drank that down too. Then Grimes told me to go through the whole thing again, and I talked for another hour. Grimes hardly reacted to what I said. He sat leaning back in his chair with his eyes half closed, and every once in a while he would nod his head or let out a little grunt. I felt like a primitive storyteller recounting an ancient myth to the tribal chieftain. Every detail of the story was familiar to us, and we both knew that none of it could ever change. But it wasn't so much the story that was important, it was the telling of it, the act of living through it again that mattered. None of it made Grimes very happy, but I could see that he accepted it. He really didn't have much of a choice. He knew the case was over.

When I finished for the second time, he said, "Contini's dead, you know. He died in the hospital this afternoon." I didn't have anything to say about it, so I kept quiet. Grimes leaned forward with his arms flat on the desk and scowled at me impatiently. "It seems nearly everyone you've met this week has managed to make a quick departure from the stage, Klein. You must have some kind of magic touch. Everything you get close to just rolls over and dies." Again I said nothing. It was a thought that had occurred to me several times in the past few hours, and I didn't see any way to make the facts more palatable. Circumstances had turned me into a bringer of death, and now I was surrounded by the ghosts I had created. "They're all gone now," Grimes went on. "Chapman, Pignato, Contini, and Briles. I don't care if the story you've told me is true. There's no one left to talk about it anymore. It's going to be almost impossible to prove."

"You don't have to prove it," I said. "The only thing you have to do is convince the D.A. to drop the charges against Judy Chapman."

"You're thinking about the D.A.'s office you used to work in. This new guy Simmons is different. He's committed himself too far on this Chapman thing already. He'd rather see it through to the end than admit he made a mistake."

"He'll be a lot more embarrassed in court when Burleson starts making his case look like a leaky rowboat," I said. "The whole story will come out, and Chapman will wind up looking so bad that no jury would ever convict her. Simmons might be an ass, but he's smart enough not to risk making himself look like one in public. He's out on a limb because you put him there, Lieutenant, and he can back off gracefully by claiming new evidence has been discovered. Since you're the one who discovered it, he'll shake your hand for saving the people's money and cleaning up this complex and disturbing affair before it ever had to go to trial. You'll both come out looking good. The public will mourn George Chapman and his tragic suicide, and everyone will walk out of the theater wiping away the tears with a handkerchief."

"And what about you, Klein? You just get up on your horse and ride into the sunset?"

"That's right. With some sad harmonica music playing in the background."

THE NECESSARY CALLS were made. Grimes got in touch with his chief, who told him to handle it himself, and then Simmons was contacted at his apartment. The district attorney had gone to bed early with a cold and was none too pleased to be woken up by Grimes' rasping voice at eleven o'clock. But he would come. As soon as he learned what it was about, he said he would be there in an hour. I called Burleson at his house in Westchester and gave him the news. It would take him under an hour and a half to get to the city. After that I tried to reach Dave McBell, but he wasn't in. I made a mental note to invite him to lunch some day next week.

Simmons and Burleson both arrived in business suits. In spite of the late hour, they had come to work, and neither one of them would have felt comfortable out of uniform. I was still wearing the same blue jeans I had put on at the beginning of the day and felt a little like a ditchdigger who had been invited to a haberdasher's convention by mistake. But Grimes didn't look much better. The knot of his tie had wandered around the collar of his wash-and-wear shirt, and his jacket was showing as many wrinkles as a piece of crushed aluminum foil. The four of us made an unlikely combination. But we managed to do what needed to be done.

I let Grimes do most of the talking. I wanted it to be his show, and as he went back over the events that had led to Chapman's suicide, Simmons listened carefully with a grim face, gradually realizing that he was never going to get a chance to go up against Burleson in court. It took nearly three hours to work out the details, but in the end I got what I wanted. The charges against Judy Chapman would be dropped.

As we were walking out of the station, Burleson stopped me on the steps to shake my hand and congratulate me for the job I had done. But I was beyond caring anymore. Too many things had been destroyed for me to feel any satisfaction. I just wanted to get away from there.

"Why don't you call her," I said to Burleson, "and give her the good news."

"I will," he answered. "First thing in the morning."

"I mean now. She's not asleep anyway. If you told her she's off the hook, maybe she'd be able to get some rest. It's been a pretty ugly stretch of days for her."

Burleson was reluctant to call anyone at three o'clock in the morning, but I insisted, and he finally agreed to do it. We reentered the building and he made the call from one of the pay phones in the lobby. I told him not to let her know I was with him and then went outside to wait for him. He came through the door ten minutes later with a smile on his face.

"You were right," he said. "She wasn't sleeping."

"How did she react when you told her?"

"With enormous relief. She couldn't believe that it was over."

"Did you mention Briles?"

"Only after I had given her the good news first."

"What did she say?"

"She didn't say anything. It was probably too much for her to take in all at once."

"Did she ask to speak to me?"

"Of course. But I told her I didn't know where you were."

Burleson pointed to a light-blue Cadillac parked on the other side of the street and asked if he could drop me anywhere. I told him not to bother, I felt like walking. Once again we shook hands, and once again he thanked me for all I had done. I stood there watching him as he crossed the street, climbed into the big car, and started the engine. When he drove off I found myself glad to be alone. But that feeling lasted only a moment. By the time I couldn't hear his car anymore, I was back inside the desolation of my own thoughts.

I went through the next few hours in a blur. Instead of going back home to get some sleep, I tried to fight off my numbness by walking. I prowled the empty streets, keeping company with the sound of my own steps. I didn't see anyone except a few people straggling home drunkenly after a big Saturday night and one solitary bum poking his head into a garbage can. It was the one moment when things stop moving in New York. No longer night and not yet morning. Limbo. I felt that I belonged there.

Just after sunrise I went into an all-night Village restaurant for breakfast. Someone was reading the Sunday *Times* at the counter, and I saw that there was an article about Victor Contini's death on the front page. It occupied the same space that had been devoted to Chapman's accident five years earlier. Now they were both dead, and it was as if they had canceled each other out. I wondered if Chapman's reputation would survive after the real story of his death broke on Monday. Not that it could have mattered to him. Wherever he was now, he could go on dreaming his big dreams. He and Briles and Contini, they could all go on dreaming for the rest of time.

At a certain point during my meal in that restaurant I decided that I should get rid of the money Chapman had given me on

Wednesday. I realized that I didn't want his check to be feeding me and buying me cigarettes for the next few weeks. It would make me feel I was still connected to him, that I somehow still owed him something. He had used me as a pawn in his strategy to do away with himself, and I wanted to undo my part in it. Maybe Richie could use the money to buy a fleet of sleds for his new life in New Hampshire. He would never have to know where it came from. I paid for the breakfast and then started out on the long walk down to my office to get the check. I was glad to know what I was doing again, glad to be walking with a purpose. The early-morning sun climbed up over the buildings like the enormous, bleeding eye of a Cyclops.

JUDY CHAPMAN WAS sitting in my office when I got there. She was dressed in a pair of white slacks and a turquoise print blouse and was absently flicking her cigarette lighter on and off as she stared into the soot of the blank windows. Each time I had seen her this week she had been wearing a different outfit, and everything had looked good on her. It was impossible for her to look bad.

She turned around when she heard me enter and gave me one of those smiles that make you feel it will never rain again for the rest of your life. This was the morning-after we had missed out on yesterday. I smiled back at her and sat down in the chair behind the desk. I was so worn out I hardly knew I was there. Even as it was happening, I felt that I was living through a scene from the past, that it had all taken place before.

"It's all over now," I said. "No more police, no more lawyers. It's finished."

"I know," she said. "Burleson called me a few hours ago. I tried to reach you at your apartment, and when you weren't there, I thought I might be able to find you here. I couldn't wait to see you again."

"Briles is dead."

"I know. Burleson told me."

"He shot himself while I was sitting no more than three feet away from him."

She shuddered. "I had no idea you were there." The thought of seeing the suicide seemed to horrify her more than the act itself.

"I was there. And before it happened Briles and I had a long talk. He was still in love with you, you know. Desperately in love with you."

"It wasn't anything I wanted. You know that."

"You were wrong when you told me he wasn't capable of jealousy. He was mad with jealousy, and he turned himself into a murderer and a criminal because he thought it would win you back."

"Let's not talk about it, Max. It's too awful. I don't want to have to think about it anymore."

"But I want to talk about it," I said. "It's important that we go over it one last time."

She looked at me in a kind of panic. It wasn't going as she had thought it would, and she couldn't understand why I was pushing so hard. I was wounding her just when she was recovering from other wounds, and I could read the hurt in her face.

"Please, Max," she said. "I'd rather not. I want to make plans with you, go off somewhere away from the city, just the two of us. I have to recuperate from this . . . this ordeal."

"There are a few things I'd like to clear up first. I have this funny notion, you see, that Briles didn't quite tell me everything, and before we go anywhere together, I have to be sure of what I'm getting into. I mean, isn't it a little odd that all the men in your life seem to wind up committing suicide?"

She stared at me for a long moment, not wanting to believe what I had said. And then she started crying, silent tears that brimmed out from her eyes and washed down her cheeks, creating a network of tiny prisms that gleamed in the light of the room.

"How can you be so cruel, Max? Don't you think I have any feelings?"

"You have feelings, all right," I said, "but they're all for yourself."

"But what about Friday night? Doesn't that mean anything to you?"

"That's dead history. It means about as much as what the dinosaurs were thinking when they sank into the tar pits."

My bitterness shocked her into another silence, and then she began to cry more violently, as if she finally realized she had nothing to hide from me anymore. "I could have loved you so much, Max," she said. "I would have made you so happy. And now you've ruined everything."

"You were in on the scheme from the beginning, weren't you?" I said. "You used Briles to get rid of George for you. And you knew that even if Briles got caught, he would never tell about your part in it. You could count on that, couldn't you? He was so crazy about you, all you had to do was say jump and he would jump. He killed himself less than twelve hours ago to protect you, and your only reaction is to say you don't want to talk about it. Well, I do want to talk about it, and you're going to listen. You were the one who told Briles to send Smart to Charles Light, and you were the one who persuaded him to send George the letter when things didn't happen fast enough. You promised Briles that you would go back to him, and he believed you. But of course he was expendable. The only thing that really mattered was to get George out of your life, once and for all. You even let George know what you were up to. In fact, that was the essence of your plan. You worked at it so hard that in the end he had only two choices: either kill you or kill himself. If it had been me, I probably would have strangled you with my own hands. But George was too much of a gentleman, and you knew it. Whatever he did, he realized he was finished. It was quite a battle of nerves, wasn't it? You kept telling him how you were going to expose him and how he should hurry up and kill you before it was too late. And then Briles sent the letter, and George knew the time had come. He told you what he was going to do, how he was going to kill himself in a way that would make it look as though you had done it, and you dared him to do that too, didn't you? You sat there in the kitchen and watched him drink down the poison, and then you walked out calmly into the Lexington Avenue sun and did some shopping. There were some rough days after that, but now it's all over and you're in the clear. George is dead, Briles is dead, and you can do whatever you damn please. Just tell me what it was like watching George drink down the poison. I want to know what you felt, what was going through your mind at that moment."

As I spoke, she kept shaking her head back and forth, sobbing uncontrollably. It was as if part of her wanted to deny the anger of my accusation and another part of her was weeping because she knew that was impossible. She was drowning in her own wretchedness, swallowing down the thing she had done to her life, and she was learning that it tasted of venom. She would go on tasting it for as long as she lived. I kept my eyes fixed on her, unable to look at anything else. This was the face of death that had been stalking me from the very start, and it was beautiful beyond all imagining. No matter what happened to her, she would always be beautiful.

"You don't understand," she said when I had finished. "You don't understand, Max. It was horrible. I couldn't stand to see him do it. I had to run away from it all. It was a nightmare."

She covered her face with her hands and went on crying for a long time. When the siege was over, she gradually composed herself, took a handkerchief from her purse, and dried her face.

"I don't suppose you want to hear my side of it, do you?" she asked quietly.

"No. I don't want to hear another word about it."

"It doesn't matter to you that you're wrong, that you've made a terrible mistake?"

"No. It doesn't matter."

She stood up from her chair and said in a subdued, businesslike voice, "Just send me a bill for your services, Mr. Klein. I'll mail you a check."

"You don't owe me a penny," I said. "We're even up."

She looked at me with hard, determined eyes, searching my face for an opening, a sign of encouragement. I didn't give it to her.

"If you ever want to know the truth," she said, "just let me know. I'll be happy to tell you."

And then she walked out. For several minutes I just sat there looking at the door, not daring to move from my seat, not daring to breathe. Then I glanced down at my desk and saw that she had left her cigarette lighter behind. It was as if she was telling me that part of her was still there, that I could still keep the flame burning if I wanted to. I picked up the lighter and turned it on. The little yellow fire gave off a pale glow in the early morning light of the room. I watched it for a long while, staring at it so hard that eventually I couldn't see it anymore. Then the metal began to heat up in my hand. When it became too hot for me to hold anymore, I let the lighter drop to the desk.

It was the last time I ever saw her.

(1978)